D1338119

AUTHOR UNKNOWN

AUTHOR UNKNOWN

The Power of Anonymity in Ancient Rome

TOM GEUE

Harvard University Press

Cambridge, Massachusetts, & London, England

2019

First printing

*Library of Congress Cataloging-in-Publication Data is available
from the Library of Congress.*

ISBN 9780674988200

To Francesca Bellei:
five coauthored years, and still the end snuck up on us, unknown.
Love always.

Contents

All literature tends toward a condition of anonymity, and that, so far as words are creative, a signature merely distracts us from their true significance.

—E. M. Forster, *Anonymity*

Some one heard the song and remembered it for it was later written down, beautifully, on parchment. Thus the singer had his audience, but the audience was so little interested in his name that he never thought to give it. Anon is sometimes man; sometimes woman. He is the common voice singing out of doors, He has no house.

—Virginia Woolf, *Anon*

If one thinks a poem is coming on . . . you do make a retreat, a withdrawal into some kind of silence that cuts out every-thing around you. What you're taking on is really not a renewal of your identity but actually a renewal of your anonymity.

—Derek Walcott, *Paris Review*

Do I contradict myself?
Very well then I contradict myself,
(I am large, I contain multitudes.)

—Walt Whitman, *Song of Myself*

AUTHOR UNKNOWN

Introduction

Literature Unmastered

Much was inscribed [here] by many, I alone inscribed nothing.
—Graffito on Domus Tiberiana, in Zadorojnyi 2011: 130

WHEN CREATIVE AUTHORS WRITE, and write about writing, they sometimes fantasize that it is not them, or that it is more than them, getting the words out.[1] Ever since a collection of people called Homer blamed the muse to obfuscate their part in the crime, authors have mystified the very concepts of agency, individuality, responsibility, and personhood that are often taken for granted elsewhere. Perhaps authors often do this because they know they have no choice. They actively participate in the willful act of self-erasure at the heart of textuality: a traumatic separation of the maker from the made, a sabbatical retreat of creator from creation. If you can't beat the ranks of the anonymous, join 'em.

Literary critics sometimes give them a hand. A powerful strand of early twentieth-century English modernism reacted petulantly to the "confessional" spirit of the previous generation by insisting that the poet was a depersonalized entity, losing themselves in the act of writing.[2] T. S. Eliot's swamping of the poet in tradition was taken up in warped form by the New Criticism of the mid-twentieth century:[3] the text, with nothing outside it, became a sacral and fetishized object, precisely because it had no origin. This modernist moment is just one particularly obvious tipping point in the history of literature and literary criticism, which tends to cycle dialectically

I

through ages of greater or lesser attachment to the figure of the historical author. To borrow from Andrew Bennett's grand claim, the history of literary theory runs in lockstep with the history of thought about what an author is and how much a part of her work she should be.[4]

The tug between the strong or weak "sense of the author" dovetails with another philosophical spiral wending its way through literary scholarship over the past hundred-odd years: the antiphonal duet between formalism and historicism. Still reeling from the backlash against the formalistic New Criticism, the literary scholarship of Anglophone universities is nowadays run through by the dominance of what Joseph North calls "the historicist-contextualist paradigm."[5] Literature is treated not so much as an aesthetic object as a way of gaining information about the culture, society, politics, and history that produced it. The spirits of formalism and historicism, of course, are never reincarnated in the same bodies.[6] The historicisms now in circulation are as different from, say, nineteenth-century German historicism as the resurgent formalisms are proving to or will be from their New Critical ancestors. But most of them have some stake in the figure of the author: from Greenblattian New Historicism[7] to Marxist criticism to the curious mix of old and new historicisms incubating in Classics.[8] And that's to say nothing of "folk" habits of reading beyond the academy, which are usually quite invested in the biographical source behind the page. While twentieth-century theory went a long way toward unsettling our deep-seated addiction to the unitary subjectivity, we are still asking the question, "who speaks?"[9] The thing changing is the answer.

If reading the history of literary theory as a series of disavowals or embraces of the author winds up looking a little too tendentious, a better way to think about it might be as a run of conflicts between various discursive master-categories, whose empires are always short-lived. In addition to the author, there would be "context." Some historicisms privilege this vague term[10] as a background that has more imprint on the formation of literary texts than do the hands of the author themselves. In literary studies beyond Classics, the tide on context seems to be turning, with critics such as Rita Felski and Joseph North building on their outlier predecessors (e.g., Eve Sedgwick) to take issue with the whole framework known as "the hermeneutics of suspicion"[11] and to break literature out of the joyless prison of compulsive contexting in which it has been institutionalized.[12] As yet, there are few rumblings of the sort in Classics, because context is perhaps even more deeply soldered into a discipline fundamentally defined by historical period and shouldering such a strong nineteenth-century inheritance. Add to this the fact that your average classicist sees something in the word "context" very different from the vision of your average new historicist: in my own field of imperial Latin literature, for example, "context" has often meant little more than churning up information about elite addressees or looking for the incumbent emperor in the text (cf. the Conclusion). Despite these local disciplinary quirks, the thrust of critics such as Felski and North can still move us forward. I would like this book to carry on this nascent questioning of the value of context at all costs.

Author Unknown is about texts without authors and without contexts—in other words, texts that resist the mainstream modes of historicism currently on duty. They may do this actively (through a concerted effort to mask the conditions of their making, such as Calpurnius Siculus), or they may do it passively (through loss of certain contextual or paratextual information making things unknown *for us*), or they may do it both ways. However they do it, I shall argue, we should be paying attention. My central criterion—anonymity—is not really a thematic principle of organization designed to take us on a chronological romp through a particular lens of seeing something "in ancient Rome." It is more an epistemological condition, or a reception condition, loosely connecting the motley crew of texts represented herein (which no one would perhaps think to glue with conventional adhesive like theme or genre or period). The condition is that of ignorance. For we have little idea, in some cases, of who wrote what when. In other cases, the attribution has been historically contested (often for good reasons). In some sense, this is almost the general, and defining, state of our relationship to antiquity. "Homer" to us is little more than a shorthand for an oral tradition; statues come down to us without heads but also minus any reliable information on their makers; inscriptions arrive unattached. The classical is a world carved with the contours of loss and uncertainty, hence Tim Whitmarsh's apt new moniker "Quantum Classics."[13] But the texts I am bringing together here are in a special league of their own insofar as they are directly galvanized by the poverty of their authorial and contextual frames. I want to argue that these texts aren't merely the neglected orphans of the literary tradition but that their circumstances of deprivation actually serve them, actually *add* to them, in many different ways. This claim could leave some readers with a bad taste. So let's give it some air.

Fixing authors and dates has been a prized duty of classical philology for a long time; indeed our obsessive author-centricity perhaps owes something to the habits of ancient scholars.[14] The act of questioning or confirming or reassigning an attribution, or migrating a text into a different context, is still one of the holy grails of "high-impact" research in our discipline. This makes sense in a unique field characterized by the relatively static state of its objects of study. We don't see the sands turn up a new text all that often. So the ways forward are relatively circumscribed: we can change the text itself (textual criticism); we can put it into different combinations with other pieces of evidence (texts, intertextuality style; or alternatives, new historicism style) or other frameworks ("theory" style); or we can simply move it and see how different it looks in a new light. Much of the scholarship on the texts in this book has been preoccupied with the latter. For this historicist (in the older sense) scholarship, anonymity is anathema. It is a problem that needs to be solved before any of the other work can begin.[15] The inertia of classical scholarship makes us apply frames invented for cases where they work better (e.g., where relatively precise coordinates can be known, e.g., the dates of a Ciceronian letter or the publication of the *Aeneid*) to cases where they aren't wanted or warranted. There is a sense that we need *some* author or context (Anything!) to help a given anonymous text qualify for full citizenship rights within the canon. This is by no means a universal condition or necessary connection. Think of the suite of anonymous canonical texts in other literatures outside Classics.[16] The fact that we could have easily had a genuinely anonymous foundation myth for classical literature in the *Iliad* and the *Odyssey* but have inherited a named author instead speaks volumes about the classical tradition's desperate need for a certified source. At another end of the critical spectrum, the alternative to this age-old historicist project of fixing authors has usually been a "purely" intertextualist one, which takes the form "who wrote this, and when, has no bearing on my argument." So the historicist approach tries to conquer anonymity; the intertextualist tries to leave it alone; either way, it is made to disappear.

This book will try to do something a little zanier. It will work with anonymity, not against it. I have no intention of lodging these texts securely in time or putting them in any particular mouth. It is my deep conviction that these forms of argument can too easily turn into discursive cul-de-sacs usually resting on speculative evidence. Don't get me wrong: I'm not dismissing two thousand years of brilliant scholarship with a cavalier swoosh. All I am trying to say is that in certain cases, the search for authors, dates, and contexts stuffs square pegs into round holes. Instead, I want to escape the loops by treating anonymity not as a paralyzing lack but as a constitutive effect of the text, an enabling force fundamental to the way it works. This will involve an extreme kind of charitable reading. By that, I mean to practice a thought experiment, a hypothetical, an as-if, like so: What if we were to treat texts as deliberately or, better, *autonomously* anonymous—not always in the strict sense that they were designed that way by their primary authors (though I shall often float that possibility) but that the coauthors of history, time, and accident have together licked them into a shape where the anonymity is a nonnegotiable *part* of them needing to be critically fondled like all the other aspects of the text? What if we made our operative context the fact that these texts have no, or many, contexts? What if we read them as full-fledged artifacts of no, or many, hands and not victims of a critical handicap? What if we take our *adespota* to be forces for freedom— literally, literature unmastered?

At this point, I catch myself skirting the question of intentionality, which literary studies has never really resolved. And I also catch myself resisting the temptation to deploy, but deploying nonetheless, the gymnastics often used to get around it: the *intentio operis;* the ascription of a "will" to the text, to anthropomorphize it into doing your bidding ("the text wants to be read so");[17] all forms of "attenuated intentionality,"[18] or intentionality by other means. This is also partly because the will to anthropomorphize the textual object is even more seductive when that object lacks a visible human source. In a sense, the text *has* to take on the subjectivity, because no one else will. And yet, that said, my line in this book will zigzag. Occasionally, I will offer a suggestion that a text could have been circulated anonymously from birth, because that would somehow do the text a service in line with its poetics or program. For example, I'll speculate that the *Octavia* could have always been the work of an *ignotus,* because an unsigned work of *damnatio memoriae* slides more sneakily into collective memory than the acknowledged work of an elite scribbler with an axe to grind. This claim to a kind of "ideological" anonymity will seem no less plausible than the claim that, say, *Octavia* hit the stage and/or the shelves in precisely 69 CE. Sometimes, I will hedge on the question of "original" anonymity and push more for an accidental effect that is no less potent for being accidental. But in each and every case, I want to show that anonymity does something real and interesting for the text (i.e., to us), apart from rob it of its mojo.

I have no satisfying answer to the question "do you think some of these texts were originally circulated anonymously?" other than "possibly." The point of this project is to embrace the "unknown" as a crucial part not just of the texts *themselves* (whatever that might mean) but of their effect on us—which, according to I. A. Richards, is what we always mean when we locate things in texts anyway.[19] As such, this book scuttles promiscuously between past and present, historicism and reception; between informed guesswork about anonymity's possible ancient function and what difference anonymity makes for us reading now. I'm trying to create a new, double-visioned "context" that generates and proliferates, rather than restricts: the context of the *Unknown*.

Why Would You?

As soon as I invoke the term "anonymity," the question on everyone's lips purses almost instantly: why would an ancient Roman author want to be anonymous?[20] How could they be anonymous? The whole system of recitation and circulation militated against it. Also, the way texts were curated and preserved was so deeply allergic to anonymity,[21] so invested in nominal authority, that a text without a name tag would have been the fast-track to the dustbin. And besides, what is the point of writing not to be known?

In the Bourdieu-inflected world of Roman studies (a late-capitalist one of exhausting "competition" at that), it is hard to stomach the idea that authors might do anything noninstrumentally: "strategy," "social performance," "self-fashioning," "competition" are the watchwords we take for granted.[22] But these assume a certain structure of authorial motives and imply a specific function of literature across the board. It may be true that personal fame or social capital or intellectual prestige were often the highest concerns. But modes of literary production are never completely uniform. If that is no longer thinkable, then we're in trouble.

To be fair, it isn't all our fault for assuming the worst. Latin literature is littered with authors who want their names out there into infinity. Poets such as Horace, Ovid, and Martial place a heavy signature on their texts and hitch their own immaterial "survival" to that of their poetry.[23] Pliny does it too.[24] A good exemplar of this "authorship-as-brand" model might be found in the least self-abasing of classical authors, Cicero. Toward the end of the *Pro Archia,* Cicero is flogging the value of his client (the poet Archias) as a transmitter not just of the fame of the nobles he accompanies but of Rome itself. At this point, he launches a general defense of ambition for fame. Cicero naturalizes the urge to claim a text with a name, even among those from whom we might expect the anonymity of modesty:

> Neque enim est hoc dissimulandum, quod obscurari non potest, sed prae nobis ferendum, trahimur omnes studio laudis et optimus quisque maxime gloria ducitur. Ipsi illi philosophi etiam illis libellis, quos de contemnenda gloria scribunt, nomen suum inscribunt: in eo ipso, in quo praedicationem nobilitatemque despiciunt, praedicari de se ac nominari volunt. (Cicero, *Pro Archia* 26–27)

> We shouldn't disguise the fact—it can't be hidden anyway—but should just admit it: we're all motivated by the pursuit of fame, and the more outstanding someone is, the more he is driven by glory. Those philosophers inscribe their names even in those books they write about scorning glory: they look to get themselves publicized and named in the very place where they reject publicity and stand-out status.

So much a given is authorship as brand that not even the philosophers can help themselves from scratching in their names. All authors name themselves. For of course they want to be named (*nominari*). Cicero helps make our big assumption stick, because it is framed as what everyone does.

Even when Roman authors forget to name themselves—perhaps tradition has inadvertently let them slide, or they wrote in a genre less given to the fiction of individual genius—they often *get named* at the reception end. A classic case of the ideology of fame digging names out of obscurity would be Seneca the Elder's project in the *Controversiae*. Seneca's self-appointed job here is to save the sayings of various declaimers that have sunk into the impersonal muck of tradition. He frames his mission as a kind of commemorative salvation, a way of saving these neglected men from the dumpster of history:

ipsis quoque multum praestaturus videor, quibus oblivio inminet nisi aliquid quo memoria eorum producatur posteris tradetur. Fere enim aut nulli commentarii maximorum declamatorum extant aut, quod peius est, falsi. Itaque ne aut ignoti sint aut aliter quam debent noti, summa cum fide suum cuique reddam. (Seneca, *Controversiae* 1.11)

I think I'll be of most help to these declaimers, who have the cloud of oblivion hanging over them unless some form of memory extension is handed on to posterity. There are basically no notebooks of the greatest declaimers in existence—or, worse still, there are forged versions. So to save them from being unknown, or being known in the wrong way, I'll return each of them his own with the utmost reliability.

What this amounts to in practice is a giant exercise in the distribution and attribution of rhetorical material by name. Seneca ends up collecting gobbets of various declaimers—and assigns them their true owners, their true names. The deep assumption powering this entire enterprise of memory management is that there is nothing worse than being *ignotus* and that writing is about raising the *ignotus* up to the *notus*. The elite system of fame seeking, then, seems to take it for granted that (1) of course authors want to have their names known and (2) if their names aren't known, then it's up to good literary custodians to right the record.

But there is an alternative foundation story beyond all this name-dropping. The exception to this rule is Homer, the most famous name in antiquity. Ancient thinkers were always careful to point out that this was a later development,[25] a contribution of others—not the fame-mongering of Homer himself.[26] Dio Chrysostom praises precisely this aspect of Homer's literary practice, which is rehoused as an ethical one.[27] The modesty of self-erasure sets him apart from the norm:

Οὐ μὴν ἀλλὰ καὶ τὸν βίον ἐπαινέσαι τις ἂν τοῦ ἀνδρὸς πολὺ μᾶλλον τῆς ποιήσεως. τὸ γὰρ ἐν πενίᾳ διαγενέσθαι καὶ ἀλώμενον καὶ τοσοῦτον ἀπὸ τῶν ποιημάτων πορίζοντα ὅσον ἀποζῆν θαυμαστῆς ἀνδρείας καὶ μεγαλοφροσύνης· ἔτι δὲ τὸ μηδαμοῦ γεγραφέναι τὸ αὐτοῦ ὄνομα, ἀλλὰ μηδὲ ἐν τῇ ποιήσει αὐτοῦ μνησθῆναι, καίτοι τῶν ἄλλων ἁπάντων, ὁπόσοι τινὰ ἔδοξαν ἔχειν δύναμιν ἢ περὶ ποίησιν ἢ καταλογάδην συγγράφοντες, καὶ πρῶτον καὶ τελευταῖον τὸ ἑαυτῶν ὄνομα γραφόντων, πολλῶν δὲ καὶ ἐν αὐτοῖς τοῖς λόγοις τε καὶ ποιήμασιν, ὥσπερ Ἑκαταῖός τε καὶ Ἡρόδοτος καὶ Θουκυδίδης, οὗτος μὲν οὖν οὐχ ἅπαξ μόνον ἐν ἀρχῇ τῆς ἱστορίας, ἀλλὰ πολλάκις διαμαρτυρόμενος καθ᾽ ἕκαστον χειμῶνα καὶ θέρος ὅτι ταῦτα ξυνέγραψε

Θουκυδίδης. ὁ δὲ οὕτως ἄρα ἐλευθέριος ἦν καὶ μεγαλόφρων ὥστε οὐδαμοῦ φανήσεται τῆς ποιήσεως αὐτοῦ μεμνημένος, ἀλλὰ τῷ ὄντι ὥσπερ οἱ προφῆται τῶν θεῶν ἐξ ἀφανοῦς καὶ ἀδύτου ποθὲν φθεγγόμενος. (Dio Chrysostom, *Orations* 53.9–10)

Nevertheless, one should praise Homer's life much more than his poetry. The fact that he lived in poverty, a vagrant, earning from his poems just enough to live off—that shows incredible virtue and high-mindedness: also, the fact that his name wasn't written anywhere, that he never even mentioned himself in his poetry, though all the other writers known to have some ability in writing poetry or prose write their names both at the beginning and the end, and many write it in the text itself (whether prose or verse). Take Hecataeus, Herodotus, and Thucydides—the last one solemnly swearing not just once at the beginning of his history but several times, in line with each winter and summer, that "Thucydides composed this." But Homer was such a free and high-minded man that self-reference won't be found anywhere in his poetry, but rather, like the prophets of the gods, he speaks from the invisible realm, from somewhere deep in the innermost sanctuary.

Gentlemanly modesty seems the surface motive for anonymity here.[28] Homer's nonsigning habits are clearly an extension of his humble (Dio C–style) philosopher's existence, and the pose is pitched as characteristically aristocratic, the privilege of a "free man" speaking (ἐλευθέριος). But there is something a little more interesting here, which gets to the heart of the claims I want to make in this book. Dio C understands Homer's anonymity as something related to his soul-stretching plenitude, his "greateartedness" (μεγαλόφρων), his ability to contain multitudes, in rousing Whitmanian parlance.[29] And this brings him into the company of the divine.[30] Like the prophets of the gods, he speaks from the realm of the unseen, from "somewhere" off limits (ἀδύτου ποθὲν). It is precisely Homer's suppression of an individual human subjectivity, via withholding his name, that makes his poetry take on a universal valence.[31] Not *knowing* where it comes from lifts it (for us) into the divine.

This, in a slightly more theological form than I would frame it, is the kind of anonymity I will be circling throughout this book. It is the anonymity of the void,[32] a darkness that makes us attribute special power to a text along the following lines: because it could come from anyone, it might actually come from everyone; it might voice something bigger, broader,

more powerful than the hands of an individual subjectivity could ever produce. I'm not saying that this is true. But I am saying it is an effect, as well
as an affect. The other point to come from this Dio passage is that this effect was felt by ancient readers too. More importantly, it was conceivable
that authors could aim for this effect *deliberately*. If Homer did it, why
couldn't contemporaries of Dio? Well, some did. Cephalion, the second-
century-CE historian, wrote out his name and origin explicitly on Homer's
example. And many scholars have thought Arrian was up to the same thing
in his refusal to self-name.[33] One could argue that Strabo's "scientific" anonymity was a subset of the same Homeric spirit.[34] Likewise Pausanias.[35]
While we will never really know whether these authors' first scrolls
undid all their good work of intratext anonymity in admitting a paratextual identification, the point is that they had a good precedent for all-out
namelessness—the greatest precedent of them all.

Dio's position vis-à-vis Homer—a literary artifact from the distant past—
is parallel to ours vis-à-vis the vagrant texts of ancient Rome. Of course
I can't claim the same cultural weight to these lesser creatures as Dio reserves
for Homer. The thick reception histories, the bulking of canonical muscle
over time—the situations are completely different. But I would say that Dio
puts his finger on a mystical effect of the unsourced, which is still available
to us. It is a sensation we should work with rather than banish.

And Why Else?

Before prodding the inner workings of this "universalizing" force a little
more, I want to go over two other forms of, or contexts for, anonymity in
Rome. The first is a kind of play, or an erotics: an anonymity where the
author teases us precisely so we desire her or him the more. The second is
a sort of cultural/political anonymity, where the author expunges the self
out of modesty, self-abasement before a higher order, or the threat of danger.
Both will rear their heads occasionally throughout this book, so it is worth
laying the table.

The idea of anonymity as a deliberate "strategy" engineered to generate
interest certainly blooms later in history.[36] But it is also something ancient
authors seem to assume and tickle in their readers. Pliny tells a story about
an (anonymous) historian who stops dead in the middle of the story only
to leave the audience gagging for more: "for information withheld only

sharpens men's curiosity to hear it."[37] We could see this kind of erotics of narrative applied to the source of the words in the famous opener to Apuleius' *Metamorphoses: "quis ille?"* The postprologue question stages the reader's need to know who speaks.[38] This is a poststructuralist rendition of reading and interpretation as acts of desire and *play.* Irene Peirano Garrison has written well on this already, catching Barthes in recantation from the crime of killing the author:[39]

> Reading, as Eco has argued, is eminently a process of conjecture, one in which meaning is created by constructing from the text an authoritative voice to whose intention such meaning is assigned. The author thus constructed is a figure of reading or understanding that is activated to some extent in all texts. One might say with Barthes in the quotation with which I opened, that desire for the author ("in the text . . . I desire the author") is an essential component of the wider structures of desire which animate the reading process. (Peirano 2013: 252–253)

Peirano Garrison's Barthesian jouissance gives us another framework in which to understand why anonymity. Much of the time, there is a game "at play."[40] And I shall be arguing something not very far from that when we come to the book's star pseudonym, Phaedrus. In a related sense, we could picture anonymizing as a strong subset of an umbrella trope of "omission," silence, or unspeaking.[41] As Larry Kim has teased out brilliantly for Dio Chrysostom, you can get vast rhetorical bang for your buck by strategic use of figures such as aposiopesis, paraleipsis, and huposiopesis[42] (to which I'll add *antonomasia*,[43] a watchword of *Author Unknown*). In general, however, this book will steer away from anonymity as rhetorical sport, partly because that function has been so brilliantly rinsed out by Peirano Garrison. But Peirano Garrison's big take-home—that we should understand anonymity proper as an effect on the reader—is something I wholeheartedly internalize.

Readerly desire and authorial tease are transcendent explanations for anonymity,[44] because they operate wherever and whenever there is a culture of strong authorship. But the second "reason" is more local to the specific historical constraints of the early Roman principate.[45] One branch of anonymous authorship we shall brush is political graffiti and political lampoon: both dangerously interventive kinds of text, which need to be stripped of authorial brand for safety's sake.[46] But I'm not just talking about this obvious case. During our period, there seems to be a new form of elite subjectivity taking shape, which is marked precisely by a discomfort with traditional modes of self-memorialization—a turn, that is, toward "anonymity" in the sense of shirking the old republican forms of monumental self-preservation. Again, this shift, or unsettling, of first-person subjectivity[47] is worth a brief pause.

The trend is faint, and there are certainly currents and countercurrents swirling around that a finer-grained cultural history would be better able to detect. Nevertheless, in the first century CE we do see some signs of retreat across the board of elite[48] self-memorializing media, in both material culture and texts. Gallus is perhaps the paradigmatic trauma here—the one who got done by Augustus for going overboard with the self-visibility.[49] But that anecdote is really just code for a new neurosis over the line markings of self-monumentalization under principate.[50] Pliny the Elder moans hard over the decline in elite self-portraiture, which his nephew tries to revive post-Domitian.[51] Alexei Zadorojnyi lines up Plutarch's scorn for tomb inscriptions with a general late first-century nosedive in practices of self-commemoration in Roman necropoleis, a synergy that Zadorojnyi reads as Plutarch mirroring "the mainstream shift in the ideology of upper class publicity."[52] The textual equivalent of this—namely, elite "autobiography"[53]— also seems to tailspin. Tacitus complains that—under the jealous eyes of Domitian—the old elite tradition of self-magnifying autobiography has been unthinkable. The form of the *Agricola,* readable as Tacitus' attempt to write the self by other means, bears out the point. I think we also see this inability to redeem the license to write the self in the very different shapes of republican and imperial satire: from Lucilius, the man who wrote himself whole, to the confessional mode of Horace's *Satires* 1, to the drowned first person of *Satires* 2[54] (almost mapping on the self the switch from republic to principate), to the muted first-person (or zero-person) speakers of Persius and Juvenal.[55] It is as if the experience of subjugation to a higher political power actually ends up shrinking the first-person subjectivity, insofar as it comes through its monumental surrogates.

This is a historical condition that makes the ground particularly ripe for the budding of anonymous texts, not only for "Romans" writing in Latin, who felt the clammy halitosis of an emperor and his minions on their neck, but also for "Greeks," some of whom undoubtedly experienced the Roman empire as a political overlord.[56] This is what is behind Lucian's anecdote about Sostratus, the architect of the lighthouse at Pharos, which ends his *How to Write History*. Lucian—himself a wheeler and dealer in the anonymous[57]—seals the work by telling us that good history comes from a deliberate transcendence, rising above the material constraints of the present and writing for the future[58] (cf. [Longinus] in Chapter 8). He illustrates with a beautiful example of artistic anonymity and its engineered obsolescence:[59]

Τὸ δ᾿ ὅλον ἐκείνου μοι μέμνησο—πολλάκις γὰρ τοῦτο ἐρῶ—καὶ μὴ πρὸς τὸ παρὸν μόνον ὁρῶν γράφε ὡς οἱ νῦν ἐπαινέσονταί σε καὶ τιμήσουσιν, ἀλλὰ τοῦ σύμπαντος αἰῶνος ἐστοχασμένος πρὸς τοὺς ἔπειτα μᾶλλον σύγγραφε καὶ παρ᾿ ἐκείνων ἀπαίτει τὸν μισθὸν τῆς γραφῆς, ὡς λέγηται περὶ σοῦ, "ἐκεῖνος μέντοι ἐλεύθερος ἀνὴρ ἦν καὶ παρρησίας μεστός, οὐδὲν οὔτε κολακευτικὸν οὔτε δουλοπρεπές ἀλλ᾿ ἀλήθεια ἐπὶ πᾶσι." τοῦτ᾿, εἰ σωφρονοίη τις, ὑπὲρ πάσας τὰς νῦν ἐλπίδας θεῖτο ἄν, οὕτως ὀλιγοχρονίους οὔσας.

Ὁρᾷς τὸν Κνίδιον ἐκεῖνον ἀρχιτέκτονα οἷον ἐποίησεν; οἰκοδομήσας γὰρ τὸν ἐπὶ τῇ Φάρῳ πύργον, μέγιστον καὶ κάλλιστον ἔργων ἁπάντων, ὡς πυρσεύοιτο ἀπ᾿ αὐτοῦ τοῖς ναυτιλλομένοις ἐπὶ πολὺ τῆς θαλάττης καὶ μὴ καταφέροιντο ἐς τὴν Παραιτονίαν, παγχάλεπον, ὥς φασιν, οὖσαν καὶ ἄφυκτον εἴ τις ἐμπέσοι ἐς τὰ ἕρματα. οἰκοδομήσας οὖν τὸ ἔργον ἔνδοθεν μὲν κατὰ τῶν λίθων τὸ αὐτοῦ ὄνομα ἐπέγραψεν, ἐπιχρίσας δὲ τιτάνῳ καὶ ἐπικαλύψας ἐπέγραψε τοὔνομα τοῦ τότε βασιλεύοντος, εἰδώς, ὅπερ καὶ ἐγένετο, πάνυ ὀλίγου χρόνου συνεκπεσούμενα μὲν τῷ χρίσματι τὰ γράμματα ἐκφανησόμενον δέ, "Σώστρατος Δεξιφάνους Κνίδιος θεοῖς σωτῆρσιν ὑπὲρ τῶν πλωϊζομένων." οὕτως οὐδ᾿ ἐκεῖνος ἐς τὸν τότε καιρὸν οὐδὲ τὸν αὐτοῦ βίον τὸν ὀλίγον ἑώρα, ἀλλ᾿ εἰς τὸν νῦν καὶ τὸν ἀεί, ἄχρι ἂν ἑστήκῃ ὁ πύργος καὶ μένῃ αὐτοῦ ἡ τέχνη.

Χρὴ τοίνυν καὶ τὴν ἱστορίαν οὕτω γράφεσθαι σὺν τῷ ἀληθεῖ μᾶλλον πρὸς τὴν μέλλουσαν ἐλπίδα ἥπερ σὺν κολακείᾳ πρὸς τὸ ἡδὺ τοῖς νῦν ἐπαινουμένοις. οὗτός σοι κανὼν καὶ στάθμη ἱστορίας δικαίας. καὶ εἰ μὲν σταθμήσονταί τινες αὐτῇ, εὖ ἂν ἔχοι καὶ εἰς δέον ἡμῖν γέγραπται· εἰ δὲ μή, κεκύλισται ὁ πίθος ἐν Κρανείῳ. (Lucian, *How to Write History* 62)

In general, remember this—I'll say it often—don't write only with an eye on the present, trying to get praise and esteem from your contemporaries, but shoot for the whole of eternity, and write instead for posterity, ask them for compensation for your content, so that people say about you: "This man was truly free, full of free-speaking, he had no flattery of slavishness about him, just truth in all contexts." If someone had sense, he would set this above all present-day hopes, short-lasting as they are.

You know what the Knidian architect did? He built the Pharos tower, the greatest and most beautiful of all buildings, so that a light would shine from it for the sailors, far out to sea, and so they wouldn't be carried off to Paraetonia, which was said to be an impossible and impassable coast if you struck the reefs. When he had built it, he wrote his name under the stonework inside, smeared it in gypsum and hid it, and wrote the name of the current king, knowing that (and so it turned out) in a very short while the letters would crumble off with the plaster, and there would emerge: "Sostratos the Knidian, Dexiphanes' son, to the savior gods, for the benefit of the sailors." So he didn't look to his immediate moment, nor his own paltry life span, but he looked to us now, and eternity, as long as the lighthouse stands and his art survives.

So you should write history like that: with full truth bent on future hopes rather than with flattery bent on the pleasure of contemporary praise. That's your rule and measuring standard for balanced history. If some work to this standard, excellent—I'll have written for a purpose: if not, I've rolled my rock up the mountain.

Again, as with Dio earlier, *present* anonymity crosses with the exercise of a noble "freedom." But this anonymity is a long game *onymity*. It is a short-term self-sacrifice enforced by the constraints of power (having to pay credit to the incumbent monarch), which will come good eventually, as the letters of political power's name crumble away to reveal the true, deep, enduring author below. Context fades away; authors are forever. Lucian's modest proposal is to compromise on present fame to win something more lasting in the end. But the force understood as imposing this condition of anonymity—however temporarily—is that main man and the habits of self-censorship he implants. As is becoming clearer, Lucian shares more with his imperial Latin buddies than we first thought.[60] If Tacitus had read this advice, he might have nodded along.

This form of anonymity—"present-proofing" one's work under political constraints so as to liberate it for the future, denaming as a means of "rising above"—brings us back to the place I wanted to end up. Anonymity is not only a claim to universality. It can also be a device of transcendence, a shortcut to immortality, but not quite in the way Lucian's Sostratus might have it. Sostratus' engineered obsolescence only ties namelessness to the *present,* but it marries the name itself to eternity, another version of Ovid's maneuver at the end of the *Metamorphoses*—there also, the material body falls apart while the name stands firm forever. But anonymity can be the express-lane wormhole to a future anticipated precisely as a state of loss and oblivion, a condition of naked contextlessness.[61] In talking of the delicate push and pull between the situated and the timeless that we understand as "literature," Michèle Lowrie mentions "disembedding devices," the equipment of a given literary text that allows it the privilege of time travel[62]—in other words, the oil that greases the future acts of reception. We have tended to think of an authorless text as something hampered on its future-quest, but counterintuitively, anonymity can serve as the ultimate *accelerant*—it "disembeds" a text so thoroughly that it becomes easier for future readers to bend it to their own ends.[63] It grants to texts the jolting New Critical fiction that they are nothing more than *the texts themselves,* primed for the intimate readerly encounter. Because we know little, or nothing, about these texts' origin in an individual subjectivity, making them our own feels all that more *direct.*

It is that supercharged immediacy that crouches behind so many moments in the reception history of anonymous texts, from the "non"- or "sub"-literary upward. Kristina Milnor has written brilliantly of how a "popular" anonymous form of authorship works in certain Pompeian graffiti,[64] especially the Basilica poems, whose unmarked medium serves their gnomic message.[65] But in a way, Milnor's hint that the anonymity of graffiti could have been a deliberate strategy is a reorientation into the literary sphere of a critical impulse that has been there for a very long time. I am talking about our tendency, shared explicitly by the earliest scholarship on this corpus, to take graffiti as an unmediated *vox populi,*[66] an utterance that gives us special access to the ancient world precisely because of its *lack* of situatedness, its status as a social butterfly of evidence. This purest form of writing seems to have a social pull and leverage that outstrips anything Virgil, for all his synecdochic national-poet credentials, could ever have written.

Graffiti might seem like a special case of the power of the anonymous because of its exceptionally public-facing nature. But I would reckon that similar reception logics are at play in the special privileges afforded to those quasi-literary beasts the next rung up the generic *scala naturae.* Low-life texts of uncertain authorship such as the *Satyrica* or the *Aesop Romance* have been charged with just as much social and historical purchase as Pompeian graffiti.[67] This may have something to do with a crypto-classist tendency of (mainly) posh classicists to identify "reality" with the representation of humble humans. But that is only half the story. Keith Hopkins' wonderful treatment of the *Aesop Romance* as a transcript of popular attitudes toward slavery would probably never have even occurred to him had the *Aesop Romance*'s authorship been singular and known. It was only because it was multiple and anonymous, a floating and unfixed textual artifact,[68] that he could take it as the voiced collective and convince that it could be part of the historian's proper ambit as "novel evidence."[69] Similar could be said of the *Satyrica*. The authorship conditions are different, but its fragmentary form, the result of manhandling by a contact sport of an excerpting and interpolating and generally "disrespectful" tradition, brings it closer to Romance than author-invested Latinists might want. The uncertainty over author and date has often bent the *Satyrica* much more toward a *sociological* value in scholarship.[70] That hidden author is not just smirking from behind[71] but also furnishing an impersonality that seems to kit the text out for use as something *trans*personal: a cultural/social document, an authoritative bearer of witness to something bigger than itself.[72] And while those styles of reading have fallen out of favor as naïve in the suspicious wing of "literary" Classics, their history still tells us something about the capacity of anonymity to create windows of invisible glass.

We are acculturated to thinking about authority as a property of names. But I want this book to show that there is an equally trenchant authority to namelessness. This authority is a function of reception. It works whether authors will it or not. But I am convinced that ancient imperial authors grasped this authority too and could be positively prescient about the future status of their texts as words universalized *because* stripped of their author. Not only this: anonymity could also make powerful ripples in the present. Though nothing much of it survives, this is the rationale behind the tradition of unsigned lampoons popping up in Suetonius.[73] Sometimes we catch a faint sign that these could get real political traction. Note how Domitian—an especially paranoid Roman reader but a Roman reader all the same—responds to an ominous piece of the anonymous:

> Quare pavidus semper atque anxius minimis etiam suspicionibus praeter modum commovebatur. Ut edicti de excidendis vineis propositi gratiam faceret, non alia magis re compulsus creditur, quam quod sparsi libelli cum his versibus erant:
>
> κἄν με φάγῃς ἐπὶ ῥίζαν, ὅμως ἔτι καρποφορήσω,
>   ὅσσον ἐπισπεῖσαι σοί, κάπρε, θυομένῳ. (Suetonius, *Domitian* 14)

So he was always jittery and anxious, excessively upset even by the tiniest suspicions. It's generally thought that what forced him to ignore his edict about cutting down the vineyards was nothing more than slips with these verses being passed around:

Chew on my root all you want, I'll still have more than enough juice to pour on you, my boar, when you're on the verge of slaughter.

Domitian's policy reversal is pricked by these *libelli* from who knows where. They menace precisely because they seem to index an opposition made to look like a tip of an iceberg. Whoever was doing the scattering, the effect is palpable. The tyrant feels compelled (*compulsus*).[74] If these pamphlets had been signed, "Yours Truly, Herennius Senecio" (*vel sim.*), they just wouldn't have packed the same punch.

That clincher anecdote may be an outlier. But I hope to have given you a taster of how the logic of anonymity could have worked, from ancient authors, on ancient readers, and how it has worked, how it *still* works on us. There is a profound migratory power to anonymous words that sets them off from the work of known individuals. Anonymity lubricates the processes of "transcendence" and universality that are at the heart of the literary.[75] It furnishes speculative fuel for the inquisitive reader. It makes sense as a tool of contextlessness, at the same time as it paradoxically makes particular sense in the cultural swamp of self-erasing elite subjectivity that was the early principate. For these reasons, perhaps the more pertinent question to ask is, *why wouldn't you?*

How Do You Say "Unknown" at Rome?

I have tried to give a taster of the power of anonymity. When I was struggling to miniaturize the point of this book in an earlier version of this very introduction, Yelena Baraz wired it in the perfect circuitry of computer science lingo: "anonymity is a feature, not a bug." But it wouldn't be a very stable mainframe with which to tinker if I didn't interrogate the categories I'm using here and set them against the conceptual motherboards of "contemporary" Rome. Through this, I hope to arrive at an even stronger formulation of the point I was building toward in the preceding section: the strange *authority* of the anonymous.

English is so used to thinking with the metaphor of "anonymity" and the "anonymous" that I need to remind myself that it's a relatively recent coinage.[76] Nowhere in Greek literature does the adjective ἀνώνυμος refer to unnamed literary works, nor does the presumed Latin equivalent *sine nomine:* the former can,[77] and the latter usually does, mean "not famous," "without glory."[78] Nor does ἀδέσποτος, the totem of this Introduction's subtitle ("Literature Unmastered"), turn into the category "adespota" till much later.[79] I spy only three relevant uses from antiquity: two referring to rumors (more on this later),[80] one of an unsigned letter.[81] In Latin, neither of these concepts of (negated) name or master have much purchase. Instead, the way Romans talk anonymous is through the absence or indeterminacy of the author figure: *sine auctore, nullus auctor, auctor incertus.* If we like to say "anonymous," they prefer "authorless."

This gets to the heart of why Rome—and, by long extension, we—have gotten so used to thinking of authorless texts as somehow deficient, somehow impoverished, somehow "going without." Texts weren't considered free-standing agents able to function in the world all by themselves. Their claims to value were lodged with the quasi-legal force of the *auctor*—the witness, the guarantor, the honorable and present person. Books needed backup. In an elite system of face-to-face responsibility, the worth of a text took a dive if an author wasn't forthcoming to stand surety for it. The three preceding formulations—*sine auctore, nullus auctor, auctor incertus*—are most often used to disqualify rumor or gossip that travels without a proper posh guarantor to confirm its truth.[82] So when they do strictly refer to authorless texts, that spirit of distrust often carries over: Trajan's rule against anonymous (*sine auctore*) *libelli* that were defamatory to Christians being allowed as evidence in court;[83] Augustus' rooting out of anonymous (*nullis . . . auctoribus*) Sibylline prophecies;[84] Suetonius' isolation of the genuine *commentarii* of Caesar from the spurious, whose author is unknown (*incertus auctor est*); the same scholar's judgment that one story about Gaius' birthplace be taken over the other, because one has a named letter as authority behind it, the other only *versus sine auctore*;[85] Tacitus' discounting of oral evidence because it's backed up by no solid author(ity) (*nullo auctore certo*);[86] or again, Suetonius' recommending some extra spicy details about Agrippina's death on the grounds that the sources are good for it and *known* for it (*nec incertis auctoribus,* Suet. *Nero* 34). Again and again, elite (and imperial) discourse[87] polices information according to legal standards: if no source can be found to vouch, the writing is written off.

But as usual with police work, the regulation is a way of acknowledging the power of the thing policed. As we saw with the Domitian anecdote earlier, unauthored verses can send an emperor into a nosedive. But it isn't just paranoid or sensitive emperors who feel the jolt. Look at how Seneca pays grudging respect to the outsize psychological effects of gossip *sine auctore*:

> Ita est, mi Lucili; cito accedimus opinioni. Non coarguimus illa, quae nos in metum adducunt, nec excutimus, sed trepidamus et sic vertimus terga, quemadmodum illi, quos pulvis motus fuga pecorum exuit castris, **aut quos aliqua fabula sine auctore sparsa conterruit. Nescio quomodo magis vana perturbant.** Vera enim modum suum habent; quicquid ex incerto venit, coniecturae et paventis animi licentiae traditur. (Seneca, *Ep.* 13.9)

> It's true, my Lucilius; we go along too readily with what people say. We don't subject to proof the things which make us afraid, we don't scrutinize them, but we tremble and turn our backs like those who have to leave the camp because of a dust disturbance caused by cattle, **or those whom the spread of some authorless tale has terrified. In some sense the groundless things get to us the most.** That's because truth has its own definite bounds; but whatever comes from uncertainty is made over to the speculation and creative license of a mind afraid.

Here we can see the *fabula sine auctore* working its black magic, getting a handle inside us through our overactive imaginations.[88] I can think of no better analysis of why many conjecture-happy scholars over the years have been alternately terrified and fascinated by the many *sine auctore* texts of this book. The anonymous breeds fear, paranoia, defensiveness, projection, and prolific imagination. The unknown fires our minds.

And that is precisely because authorless discourse had—still has—a power and *authority* all its own. Elite epistemologies have often tasked themselves with pushing it beyond the pale. This is a prejudice we have inherited. But occasionally, the authority is allowed up for air, not just as negative power to be feared but as an effect of a universalizing truth to be *used*. Quintilian plays on this in talking of how to deploy *auctoritas* in rhetoric, understood as another kind of external slam-dunk proof to employ in a case. This kind of authority doesn't stem from the individual but from the *collective*:

> Adhibebitur extrinsecus in causam et auctoritas. Haec secuti Graecos, a quibus κρίσεις dicuntur, iudicia aut iudicationes vocant, non de quibus ex causa dicta sententia est (nam ea quidem in exemplorum locum cedunt), sed si quid ita visum gentibus, populis, sapientibus viris, claris civibus,

inlustribus poetis referri potest. Ne haec quidem vulgo dicta et recepta persuasione populari sine usu fuerint. Testimonia sunt enim quodam modo, vel potentiora etiam quod non causis accommodata sunt, sed liberis odio et gratia mentibus ideo tantum dicta factaque quia aut honestissima aut verissima videbantur. (Quintilian, *IO* 5.11.36–38)

Authority is another sort of external proof that can be applied in a case. After the Greeks, who term these things *kriseis,* the Romans call them judgments or investigations—not meaning a verdict given in a case (those fall under "Examples") but the thoughts attributable to nations, peoples, sage men, famous citizens, great poets. Even run-of-the-mill sayings and popular wisdom have their uses. In some sense they're testimonies, even more powerful because they're not serving specific causes but spoken or created by minds free from resentment and favor—for the sole reason that they seemed the best or the truest things to say.

He gives a few general examples, then lands on expanding how these "common sayings" (*uulgo dicta*) function:

Ea quoque quae vulgo recepta sunt hoc ipso, **quod incertum auctorem habent,** velut omnium fiunt, quale est: "ubi amici, ibi opes," et "conscientia mille testes," et apud Ciceronem: "pares autem, ut est in vetere proverbio, cum paribus maxime congregantur;" neque enim durassent haec in aeternum nisi vera omnibus viderentur. (Quintilian, *IO* 5.11.41)

Those common sayings also become essentially everyone's property, **because they have no known author.** Things like this: "where there are friends, there's wealth"; "conscience is equal to a thousand witnesses"; and Cicero's "like forms flocks with like, as the old proverb goes." These sayings wouldn't have lasted for eternity if they didn't seem true to everyone.

These things become true, they count as common property, they have staying power down the generations *because their author is unknown.* Though Quintilian probably didn't know it, his point about *auctoritas* pitches the argument of this book perfectly. His comment shows that there is an inherent potency to the words of a mystery author. And if that potency can be channeled through the quotation of proverbs,[89] why couldn't a Roman author magnify it to the text as a whole? All I want this book to do is scale Quintilian's logic of *auctor incertus* up from the *dicta* of the odd sentence to the *dicta* of the literary work. So please, come leap with me into the . . .

[Author] Unknown

That void between the brackets looks a little something like this. The book is a series of close readings trained on eleven texts (ten Latin, one Greek) from the rough region of the first two centuries CE (possibly beyond). The close readings are mainly sequential, and I have chosen this form because it comes across less like an assured scholar confidently manipulating a text into an object of knowledge and more like an engaged reader open to the full range of bemusement and uncertainty.[90] Of course, that is a performative illusion—I have read, reread, thought over these texts endlessly. But this illusion feels more honest to the project of anonymity than the other possible illusions for which we might reach.

From a critical distance, the collection of texts covered in this book may seem a touch motley. Let me try to justify my ecumenical ways with a brief manifesto of the selection criteria. First, I am hustling for diversity of genre, form (verse *and* prose), likely date range, and subsets of anonymity (internal, external, universalizing, politicizing, the nameless as timeless). I want to show that these issues thread imperial Latin literature in and out, even where the stitching is subtlest. I wanted to avoid giving the impression that this phenomenon can be ring-fenced off in its cute little summer camp of "marginality," "triviality," "playfulness." True, the lion's share of *Author Unknown* is taken with the traditional miscellany crew, the "minors" of Roman literature: Phaedrus, Calpurnius Siculus, et al. But my mission is to spread the word of the anonymous beyond these, as well as beyond the *strictly* anonymous texts at the book's core (*Octavia, Laus Pisonis*), to some of the real heavy hitters that *are* blessed/burdened by authors: at the more certain end, Augustus' *Res Gestae*, Suetonius' *Augustus*, and Ovid's *Ibis*, as well as the less certain, Seneca's *Apocolocyntosis*, Petronius' *Satyrica*, and Tacitus' *Dialogus*. My hope is that the mainstream will then have fewer excuses to snub the "marginal"; and that it will realize that the hitherto-marginalized are actually galloping down front, at the very vanguard of the imperial literary system.

Second, disappointingly, the principle of diversity in form and canonical "status" made me shut out some likely suspects, which would have led to a richer book: certain texts in the *Appendix Vergiliana* (e.g., *Copa, Moretum, Culex, Aetna*), the *Pervigilium Veneris*, the *Elegiae in Maecenatem*, Sulpicia, a few disputed *Heroides*. In fact, I deliberately steered around these texts for two reasons. On the one hand, many have enjoyed the acute and thorough critical treatment of Peirano (2012), and any follow-up would be but whimpering coda;[91] on the other, I wanted to turn the study of the anonymous away from the recent critical paradigms of fakery and forgery. Anonymity is more than just a subset of, or condition related to, pseude-pigraphy. It is a galvanizing frame with a lot of wattage, and its effects can be felt across the grid of imperial Roman literature. I selected the texts to reflect the depth of the surge.

I have split the book into three thematic clusters, but there are respon-sions all the way through. Part I, "The Power of the Name," handles the politics of anonymity from various angles. Chapter 1 kicks us off with an unlikely candidate—the aggressively authored *Res Gestae* of Augustus— to show us how the fixing of discourse by author and date becomes an ob-session of nascent imperial power but also how the logic of anonymity can work for all the things that the emperor *doesn't* expressly sign under his subjectivity. The dual mania for authorship *and* anonymity seen in the *Res Gestae* is absorbed into Suetonius' *Augustus* but processed into slightly dif-ferent form over the course of the *Caesars,* as we see the cautious scholar Suetonius transition from attributed documents to anonymous evidence. Both these figures whom you would associate with an all-out feel for named subjectivity and definite attribution—the Scholar and the Caesar—turn out to reach for the power of anonymity too.

Chapter 1 prepares the ground, also, for another form of anonymity that will shoot up in the next two chapters: antonomasia, the suppression and substitution of proper names. Augustus famously nails this technique in his omission of enemy names in the *Res Gestae*. But the texts of Chapters 2 and 3 take the trope to gargantuan proportions. The first is Ovid's *Ibis*. This poem is deeply aware of the Roman literary name economy. Its prize swipe against its target is to deprive him of a name. I track the relation between this aspect and the poem's weaponry of anonymizing the figures of its quick-fire riddles, which is aimed, I argue, primarily at the *victims* rather than the perpetrators. Refusing a name saps the bearer of his or her strength. I also treat the *Ibis'* array of indefinites as ways of "universalizing" the poem be-yond the bounds of its crazed utterance. Chapter 3 moves on to an equally striking burst of antonomasia: the *Octavia*. Here, again, I chart the power patterns inherent in name use and denial, how deprivation of names allows for manipulation and control, *on/in one's own terms*. The lack of proper names also helps prepare character and play for a heightened form of exemplarity (i.e., lets them stay mobile across history). Here, for the first time, I posit a possible connection between internal and external forms of anonymity. I suggest that the play's membership in the corpus of author unknown may be no accident but a deliberate ploy to make the contingent blackening of Nero much more "obvious," much more widespread than it actually was. Just as the *Octavia* attempts to speak for the people in terms of its chorus, so it attempts to give them—"everyone"—a play that belongs to no one in particular.

That "nobody" is the star of Part II: "The Universal No-Name." Here I go full pelt exploring texts whose potential seems to depend precisely on us not knowing who wrote them. Chapter 4 takes Phaedrus' *Fables* and runs with the idea that they pose as a creation of an entirely fictional creature. The comedy stems partly from the attempts of Phaedrus to knock on the door of literary society and never gain admission. This is antiquity's greatest attempt at a wholesale invention of a sociological apparatus: author name, biography, patrons, political context—the whole thing conjured from thin air.

Chapter 5 takes us to a brief reading of a tinier poem that doesn't even grant us the luxury of a made-up name: instead, the *Laus Pisonis* rests its drama of the outsider neophyte of a poet on the fact that we—and the putative Piso—don't know him. Of Piso, the addressee, I say putative because I argue against the notion that this Piso has a historical referent, rather than channeling the essence of patronage in the abstract. Similarly, I go to town with the notion that the *Laus Pisonis* is experimenting with the paradox of writing multicontextual praise valid *for all times*. With author, addressee, and context all concealed, the joke falls on the obsessively historicizing scholar (us).

Chapter 6 switches to another text with a problematic name, which has often been bundled with the *Laus*: the *Eclogues* of Calpurnius Siculus. I argue that the perpetual disagreement among daters of the poem (first century/third century CE) responds to the unique contextlessness (or context-fullness) of the poems, which eschew the Virgilian technique of plugging remote Pastoral into real History by judicious use of real-life, named historical agents. I play with the poems as testaments to their own attribution problems and look at how they stow authority in a place that is ever receding, just over the horizon. If Corydon can't glimpse his Caesar,

nor can we. All of this helps the poems survive the vicissitudes of principate, as well as pitch that principate in a realm beyond time.

Part III, "Whence and When," rolls through four prose texts, two apiece
in Chapters 7 and 8. The first coupling deals with the problems of source
and context in two classic multiform texts that happen to have their own
authorship problems: the *Apocolocyntosis* and the *Satyrica*. I read the first
as an exercise in restoring knowledge according to the system of the proverb,
which offers the authority of being shared "by everyone" (cf. Quintilian
earlier) and which stops us asking the scholarly question, "from where?"
The *Apocolocyntosis* thus "proverbializes" Claudius into an obvious
monster—and the power of the *damnatio* stems from a cultural outburst
made to transcend the particular frustrations of its author (analogous to
Octavia). For that reason, I ask the unaskable question yet again: was this
really *Seneca's* sketch? I then skate on to the world of writing and inscription in the *Satyrica*. Through the *Cena Trimalchionis* and beyond, I spotlight
the many moments wherein writing becomes a misleading form of context
(or paratext) ill matching the reality it frames. I then speculate on whether
the dodgy *tituli* of the *Satyrica* might not be an extended exposition, even
ideological justification, of the text's own framelessness.

While Chapter 7 tries another way of binding two traditionally paired
(thinly compared) texts under the broad umbrella of anonymity, Chapter 8
does the same with two more: Tacitus' (?) *Dialogus* and [Longinus]' *On
the Sublime*. I parse how these texts spread discourse beyond the moment
of utterance, how they try to throw off the shackles of historical time, and
how they *might* make forms of anonymity work toward those goals. With
the *Dialogus,* I follow the work's striking (much-noted) absenting of the
author, as well as its problematic relationship to dates (both dramatic and
compositional). I square these effects with the *Dialogus'* concerted efforts
to slip the time of the one-off and to inhabit the often, the customary, the
usual, and the habitual—its move from moment to period. I then tease out
similar tricks of escaping time in that mystery treatise: [Longinus]' *On the
Sublime*. I try to place this text seriously between its brackets, as a piece of
literature actively working toward its own transcendence by anonymous
quotation—not only that but self-quotation too: the famous dialogue with
the philosopher at the end becomes [Longinus]' way of apotheosing himself into a timeless classic through citation and of lifting the text above the
drags of history.

After the calm of summary, the storm of apology. This is a risky book. I don't expect it to win over many readers. But I hope it will continue the important work of shepherding these texts more into the mainstream of a community, horizontal in space and vertical in time, that has often not known what to do with them apart from exercise a scholarly mastery over them and work to *put them in their place*. I think it's high time we embraced them more fully, if only by letting them go.

I

THE POWER OF THE NAME

Author Unknown takes its corpus from *imperial* Roman literature. That choice is important. Accordingly, that *imperial* is italicized for good reason, not just as a chronological designator, as it so often is ("Augustus and after"), but as a particular historical hinge that activates key issues of this book—anonymity, authorship, accountability, agency, naming rights—and sears them into sudden urgency. But why retrace the lines of an arbitrary periodization at which many contemporary historians now wince? Does the republic-principate boundary mark really still matter? For anonymity, I would have to say it does. I have moved to kick off with the *Res Gestae*—a good candidate for the principate's founding charter—precisely because it opens up new relations between authorship and authority. And these conditions must be in place for us to grasp how the anonymities of the *Ibis* and the *Octavia* play out. In fact, they could be considered further probings, appropriations, refractions, even *reductiones ad absurdum,* of a politics first trialed in the *Res Gestae*.

Republican naming practice had room for several experiments in anonymized fun. Cato's suppression of the names of Roman commanders in the *Origines* is a good prototype for the political antonomasia vibrating through the next three chapters.[1] According to Nepos, Cato rattled off the events of various wars down to the praetorship of Servius Galba in summary fashion and left out a fairly key ingredient—names:

> Atque horum bellorum duces non nominavit sed sine nominibus res notauit. (Nepos, *Cato* 3.4)

> And he failed to name the generals of these wars. Instead he marked the events without names.

This feature is mentioned, presumably, because it is so damn mentionable. To a Roman believer in fame and name, this is a jarring narrative innovation. Pliny the Elder also feels the need to remark on it, if only to snipe how perverse it is that Cato was able to name elephants in the *Origines* but not commanders.[2] The purpose behind this counterintuitive move is debatable. Perhaps it was designed to decouple the deep aristocratic pairing of particular agent and glorious/infamous action and put this load more onto "Rome" itself as trans-historical entity; perhaps it was a chip on Cato's shoulder as *homo novus* speaking, which led him to wipe out the whole system of competitive elite shuffling to claim deeds under names.[3] Whatever its political function, the shock running through its reception history suggests that it remained very much out of the ordinary, sticking out like a sore thumb within an ideological system that took the linkage of names and achievements for granted.[4]

Come the principate, there is a crucial remapping of the political terrain that leaves names and power jigging in slightly different relations. First, an antonomasia far more destructive than Cato's becomes a key political weapon. Depriving targets of names strips them of power and legibility within the discourse of fame. We shall see this flourish echoing throughout the politicized texts of this section: from Augustus' silent treatment of Antony to the screaming scratch-outs of the *Ibis* to the *Octavia*'s eerie effects of undoing the names of its nonagents. All of these fall under the umbrella of antonomasia as the literary wing of *damnatio memoriae*. Once Augustus gets the ball rolling on that front, it is only for our imperial authors to send it flying off apace.

So antonomasia is an Augustan technology. Better yet, it is a technology enabled by the particularly complex and pressing needs of memory management under the principate, wherein the power play of depriving names and assigning substitute definitions becomes bread and butter for cut-and-thrust politics. So far so good. The other kind of political anonymity I shall discuss is not quite as obvious but still derivative from the *Res Gestae* revolution. While the *Res Gestae* can deprive agents of names where it is ideologically useful, it is also invested in pinning names to actions: specifically, lumping all the golden credit for Rome's refoundation at the door of the first-person agent of the text, Augustus himself. This hogging of responsibility is also balanced with the assignment of responsibility to other named agents and authors, as we shall see in Suetonius' *Augustus:* under the new dispensation, it is imperative that texts (like actions) have names. But there is a strange counterstrand acting within this general imperial tendency to trace names to agents. Augustus also dallies with *concealing* his authorship. As he nobly refrains from inscribing his name on a temple in *Res Gestae* or gets saddled with quotation of anonymous verses in the *Augustus,* the written Augustus subtly shows us that anonymity can have as much power as marked authorship, because it spreads the sites of Augustus' subjectivity beyond those that are explicitly stamped with his name. Anonymity as a universalizing force: this too is an angle inaugurated by the *Res Gestae* (engineered as it may be as another form of credit claiming) but taken far beyond its logical conclusion in the *Ibis* and to an even greater extent in the *Octavia*. Whereas Augustus dabbles in anonymity as a megalomaniac move to bring everything and more under his name, a centripetal anonymity if you will, the *Ibis* and *Octavia* use a centrifugal anonymity to fling their words beyond individual subjectivity. The *Ibis* can be read as a dark distortion of the *Res Gestae*'s approach to name erasure as well as an attempt at a "universalizing" speech act; the *Octavia* can be read this way too, but, as I shall argue, it is a real working out in full of the power of concealed authorship. The monster-germs of authorial anonymity that Augustus cultured in the most "authored" text in Roman history eventually end up a full-fledged biohazard in the play plotted to take down the end of the Augustan line, namely, Nero. Anonymity sure can be used to prop up emperors. But the technology is flexible. It can also be used to bring them down.

In this cluster of chapters, I show off the political potential of anonymity in its specifically early imperial guise. If this seems a remnant of the sluggish historicism I have only just freshly disavowed in the Introduction, I beg to differ. What I offer here is not a wild goose chase after authors and dates but a laying out of why those things become a little more scrambled and a lot less visible under the principate. The remainder of the book will be less locked with this overtly political brand of anonymity, although it will erupt virally here and there (particularly in Calpurnius Siculus, the *Apocolocyntosis,* or the *Dialogus*). Moreover, the universalizing anonymity to which most of the texts of this book have recourse is always political in the wider sense (i.e., an ideological Gatling gun that wins a text more purchase for being from everywhere and nowhere). But the general point of this opener is that all these modes of anonymized authorship—the meat of this book—are set loose by the historical tensions of writing under principate. Unfortunately, we wouldn't have had so many authors unknown without that best-known author Augustus. But that doesn't mean we should give him credit for everything. Once he's gone, the floor is theirs.

Name Power

THIS IS A STORY OF WRITING that does not belong. But I have opted
to begin with two texts that do. At the beginning of the Roman principate lies a founding document so far from namelessness that you might
call it the antonym of anonymity: Augustus' *Res Gestae* (*RG*). Posted up
on Augustus' mausoleum soon after his death in 14 CE, transcribed into
copies, and thrown up in several public locations throughout the Roman
empire, this gigantic textual monument yells from the rafters all the things
the first princeps wants totted under his name: battles won, temples (re)
founded, honors endowed, the lot. The text's major project is to solidify
power precisely by tattooing first-person identity.[1] All of its many affirma-
tions of Augustan achievement are inscribed under the nominal umbrella
of the ultimate author.[2]

One-man rule likes to assign agency and responsibility to individuals,
so that actions can be traced. So empire is also invested in pinning names
to texts. Augustus models himself as he would like his authors to be: up
front about owning their words. Yet there is also a tempting power in different forms of anonymity, be that authorial self-erasure or the redaction
of names you would rather leave unmentioned. It is this dialectic that is
the background tune for this chapter (and section): namely, the transport
between the overdetermination of names that is state power and the resistant anonymity of literature, which often seeks to shirk the official record.
I want to show that naming and not-naming are both bound up with power

and that these political relationships are already being brokered within a foundational act of naming the new age, from a hand that would take responsibility, and later be given it, for everything to come.

The *RG* stakes a claim to a new kind of "imperial authorship," where utterance is signed and sealed with a clear time and date stamp. But it also contains the germs of a different discourse, whose lack of authorization leaves it free to roam.[3] The *RG* also floats Augustan experiments with a sublime anonymity, at the level of both the first-person agent and the third-person names that are left out. I shall argue that the second firmly housed text of this unrepresentative beginning—Suetonius' *Caesars* and specifically the *Augustus*—amplifies even further these two conflicting forces at work within paradigmatic power. Suetonius' third-person Augustus is just as obsessed with putting names to faces as his first-person version in the *RG*. Yet the Suetonian Augustus also represents a condition of anonymity keyed to the underworld of the *Caesars,* which always trades an anti-imperial knowledge via gossip, snippets, unsourced sound bites, verses *sine auctore*. Common sense would have us tag the Caesarean project of signed discourse as the polar opposite of the subversive energies sparking round the unsigned masses. The point of this chapter is to show how close they may come.

Res Gestae [Augusti]

The birth of the principate doubles as a primal act of naming. The advent of the "Augustan age" comes retrospectively through a kind of magical fiat/speech act: open sesame, suddenly we have an Augustus (27 BCE), not an Octavian. Although the *RG* falls much later than this initial hailing, it is still deeply engaged in an extended baptism of fire, a christening ceremony that performatively brings the principate into being. Indeed, this text, spoken so clearly in Augustus' "own words"[4] and posted up on various big screens around the empire, almost single-handedly does the work of trumpeting the absorption of the age under one name only. As Francesca Martelli has shown, part of the *RG*'s point is to launch a centripetal project attracting all of Augustus' many former names into the orbit of the most important one of all,[5] to prove that *Augustus,* himself, newest and most improved model, is (has been all along) the wizard pulling the strings.

Public inscription is a medium particularly prone to declaring its source in the boldest terms. Publicity and immortality for the author are part and parcel of the affordances of stone and bronze. But the *RG* truly cranks this up a notch.[6] In contrast to most of the texts in this book, the *RG* is neurotically insistent about where it comes from and when it was made. Regarding the "when," its definition of a writing present is so crystal clear that we almost catch Augustus' hand at work, smell the wake of his auratic cologne:

> Consul fueram terdeciens, cum scribebam haec, et eram septimum et tricensimum tribuniciae potestatis. (4)[7]

> At the moment I composed this, I have been consul thirteen times and am in year thirty-seven of my tribunician power.

> Princeps senatus fui usque ad eum diem quo scripseram haec per annos quadraginta. (7)

> All the way up to the day I wrote this, I have been the *princeps senatus* for forty years.

This strict, metric presentation of the text's date of birth[8] goes hand in hand with an overwhelming identification of its maker. Augustus' name is everywhere: it infuses the festival calendar in the form of the Augustalia (*RG* 11), labels physical space via the *Ara Pacis Augustae* (*RG* 12), and makes its presence felt through named philanthropy (donations made in Augustus' "own name," *RG* 15; games given likewise, *RG* 22) or offerings made to Apollo (*RG* 24). Though the Augustan name peppers the *RG* throughout, the text's momentum weights toward the naming ceremony itself as climactic sign-off. "I dub thee Augustus" is where we end up in section 34, the quid pro quo for returning the republic to SPQR:[9]

> In consulatu sexto et septimo, postquam bella civilia exstinxeram, per consensum universorum potens rerum omnium, rem publicam ex mea potestate in senatus populique Romani arbitrium transtuli. Quo pro merito meo senatus consulto Augustus appellatus sum et laureis postes aedium mearum vestiti publice coronaque civica super ianuam meam fixa est, et clupeus aureus in curia Iulia positus, quem mihi senatum populumque Romanum dare virtutis clementiaeque iustitiae et pietatis causa testatum est per eius clupei inscriptionem. (34)

> In consulships numbers 6 and 7, after I had snuffed out the civil wars and had gained power over everything by unanimous consent, I transplanted the republic from my own power to the dominion of senate and

the Roman people. For that contribution, I was dubbed "Augustus" by
senatorial decree, the doorposts of my house were officially decked with
laurels, the Civic Crown was lodged over my door, and the Golden Shield
was stowed in the Curia Iulia—and by this shield's inscription, it was established that the senate and Roman people gave it to me because of my
heroism, mercy, justice, and deep religion.

Note how Augustus gets his name just after he has asserted possession of
time.[10] Earlier in the work, he was careful to plug his *res gestae* into years
notched up politically correctly, annalistically, with consul names other than
himself (e.g., 8, 10, 6). But by the end, we settle on Augustus' name and
titles embedded *in his own time:*

> Tertium decimum consulatum cum gerebam, senatus et equester ordo
> populusque Romanus universus appellavit me patrem patriae, idque
> in vestibulo aedium mearum inscribendum et in curia Iulia et in foro
> Aug(usto) sub quadrigis, quae mihi ex s(enatus) c(onsulto) positae sunt
> censuit. Cum scripsi haec, annum agebam septuagensumum sextum. (35)

> As I was serving out consulship number 13, the senate, equestrians, and
> the united Roman people dubbed me father of the fatherland, moving that
> this should be inscribed on the vestibule of my house, in the Curia Iulia,
> and in the forum Augustum under the horse and chariots set up for me
> there by senate decree. At time of writing this, I am seventy-five years old.

This last shot of the extant *RG* is full of nominal, temporal, and spatial
markers, designed to *sign*.[11] It makes the text into a crisp certificate stamped
with the certainty of official discourse. We know exactly when Augustus
was granted his proudest name (note that this takes place in a Rome already inked by the Augustan name, i.e., the *forum Augustum*); we know
which bodies did the granting; we have another inscription built into this
inscription, and we know exactly where it was decreed to have gone;[12] and
we know when all of this was written. The final temporal marker is purely
biographical: time is no longer counted politically, by consuls, but instead
the man himself becomes the measure of the age.

The *RG* plots a mode of first-person authorship that oversupplies its
unique serial number. Its job is to make its origin visible to us, at every turn,
for its branded manufacture is the source of its authority. In that sense, it
is the strangest example with which to kick-start a book about anonymity.

But the *RG* does speak to the theme even more directly than it does qua antonym. It does so in two ways. The first is its regular motioning toward the moments when Augustus acts not in his own name but in someone else's.[13] The second takes the form of Augustus' suppression of other people's names—historical actors stricken from the record. This kind of anonymity, or antonomasia, will be important throughout Part I. Both of these methods complement and offset the overdetermined name games of the *RG*. Both of them unlock a different side of the power of anonymity.

As well as a giant gesture of taking personal responsibility (*meo nomine* is one of the *RG*'s pet phrases),[14] the *RG* also flaunts cases where Augustus conceals his own subjectivity and acts in the names of others.[15] I mentioned earlier that Augustus is "generous" with allowing other names to color calendrical time (e.g., 18), before the monopoly solidifies; he is similarly generous in farming out building credits. He lets the name Octavia stick to the portico at the Circus Flaminius, after the man who funded the original (19); of course, the name Octavius belongs to Augustus as an older stratum of his nominal geology anyway. Augustus' name extensions mainly keep within the family. He spreads his tentacles wide by building tall in the names of his sons (20) or his former son-in-law Marcellus (21), or donating in the name of the previous generation (his father, 15), or staging games in the names of the next generations (sons and grandsons, 22). But the truly bold experiments with this form of pseudepigraphic euergetism involve an explicit *withholding* of the Augustan name, in favor of something more counterintuitive:

> Capitolium et Pompeium theatrum utrumque opus impensa grandi refeci sine ulla inscriptione nominis mei. (20)

> I rebuilt the Capitolium and the theater of Pompey—both of them expensive operations—without inscribing my own name once.

Our savior lets the Pompeian theater retain its name, without even so much as a scratch hinting at the roots of the renovation.[16] Republican memory is buffed with a shiny paradox, both left alone and refreshed at the same time—subsumed into a controlled version. As we shall see, Augustus is a smooth operator of sublime anonymity. He knows when to leave himself out of it.

Of course, if we think of the *RG* as a kind of user's guide to the refurbished

Rome or a supplement that politically labels the topography, we might say this is not "genuine" anonymity at all. The *RG* acts as a key to the real agency behind such acts of apparent self-canceling.[17] It shows that Augustus is the true name pulling all the strings, even if those strings look like they were hung by someone else.[18] But this subtle anonymous act goes above and beyond. For it introduces a logic that is exportable to *all* the things Augustus *doesn't* mention in the work, all the named deeds that *don't* at first sight appear to be done on his watch. By this, I mean that Augustus assuming responsibility for an act that doesn't bear his name (*sine ulla inscriptione nominis mei*) makes us think that anything, everything else in the Roman ambit, could be his work also. The truest and most versatile marker of "Augustus was here" becomes the *absence* of his inscription. Labeling lays clear claim to possession and responsibility, but it is limited by how many words you can cram into a monumental inscription. For everything else, the logic of anonymity will do the job.

This is a significant part of the Augustan ideological sweatshop's genius. It correlates a widely declared authorship with a subtle claim to clandestine authorship, to make Augustus' agency truly all-encompassing. So *RG*-Augustus understands, and bends in his direction, one of the powers of anonymity so central to this book: universality. But he gives it his signature twist. Whereas many of the texts we shall treat make use of the idea that they could have come from anywhere, Augustus makes us think that everything could have come from him. This is the poisonous pathology of much scholarship on the Augustan period—the attribution to *personal* Augustan "stage-management" of everything that happens on the big man's watch—and we can and should resist it where possible.[19] But we still need to acknowledge that Augustus qua author worked very hard to make us think like that. The *RG* is the how-to manual that activates the possibility, the performative reality, of Augustan ubiquity.[20]

So anonymity is ironically crucial to the Augustan project of "taking responsibility." But it also exercises another mode of power and another leitmotif of the book: the power to snuff out the agents of history by massacring their names.[21] In a culture that prized the name so highly as a hook of fame, such a technique is devastating, violent. It has the ring of *abolitio* or the mark of the censor about it. The *RG*-Augustus has long been hailed as an expert player in this game. Early on, he calls his father's murderers (i.e., Brutus and Cassius) by that very name, only:

Qui parentem meum interfecerunt, eos in exilium expuli iudiciis legitimis ultus eorum facinus, et postea bellum inferentis rei publicae vici bis acie. (2)

The assassins of my father I drove into exile, avenging their crime through orthodox legal process, and after that, as they waged war on the republic, I subdued them in battle twice.

These people are nothing more than the grave crime they committed. Lepidus and Antony, his old triumviral colleagues turned mortal enemies, are similarly paved over with evasive relative clauses:[22]

Quod sacerdotium aliquot post annos, eo mortuo demum qui civilis tumultus occasione occupaverat, cuncta ex Italia ad comitia mea confluente multitudine, quanta Romae nunquam fertur ante id tempus fuisse, recepi, P(ublio) Sulpicio C(aio) Valgio consulibus. (10)

After some years I took up that priesthood—when he was finally dead, the one who had taken it by exploiting the opportunity of civil unrest—and a big crowd from all over Italy flooded in for my election during the consulships of Publius Sulpicius and Gaius Valgius—prior to that moment, Rome had reportedly never had such a big crowd.

In templis omnium civitatium provinciae Asiae victor ornamenta reposui quae spoliatis templis is cum quo bellum gesseram privatim possederat. (24)

As victor, I restored to the temples of all the townships of the province of Asia the trophies that This Man With Whom I Had Waged War had expropriated into his private collection, after plundering the temples.

What this denial of the name does is take away the general condition of personhood from the agents it blocks. Lepidus can no longer be Lepidus,[23] Antony no longer Antony. Instead, each antagonist is boiled down to the contextually relevant act. They become nothing more than the thing making them wrong in that particular moment. This is not solely about dismantling the infrastructure of fame. Anonymizing these men makes them into things they have *done,* things *done,* the implicit index of the self in the *RG.* But compared to Augustus, they have not done many things. And what they are allowed to have done is negative, negligible. They are relegated to history's dark relative clauses, while the first person runs the syntactical show.

In the end, the *RG* coordinates all these potent forces of nominal autonomy—claiming clearly with a name or making an active bid for the unnamed or denying historical actors a named subjectivity—to make the Augustan brand into a super-agency. The techniques reinforce each other, as we can see by zooming a little further out around the Antony passage:

> In templis omnium civitatium provinciae Asiae victor ornamenta reposui quae spoliatis templis is cum quo bellum gesseram privatim possederat. Statuae meae pedestres et equestres et in quadrigeis argenteae steterunt in urbe XXC circiter, quas ipse sustuli, exque ea pecunia dona aurea in aede Apollinis meo nomine et illorum qui mihi statuarum honorem habuerunt posui. (24)

> As victor, I restored to the temples of all the townships of the province of Asia the trophies that This Man With Whom I Had Waged War had expropriated into his private collection, after plundering the temples. Silver statues of me—on foot, on horse, in chariot—sprang up in the city (about eighty of them). I myself took them down, and from the proceeds I set up golden gifts in the temple of Apollo—both in my own name and in the name of those who gave me the honor of the statues.

Just as he performs a nominal *damnatio* on Antony, Augustus brings his own statues down.[24] From the proceeds, he makes some lavish offerings to Apollo, both for himself, in his own name, and crucially, in the names of the people who had set up the statues in the first place. As the universal, public man, Augustus can act both for himself and for or as his "constituents." He is a representative: a proxy authorized to act in the name of others. This is critical. Augustus becomes someone who can assert his own name, stake his claim to others, and erase yet more—all in the breath of a couple of sentences.

The *RG* will be a foundational text for us, though not as it is usually set up to be. I have tried to show that its universalizing idiom does two major things. On the one hand, it perfects the kind of first-person fingerprint authorship that many of our texts will grate against (and so proves generative for them); on the other, it also strays into strategies of anonymity—namely, acting without inscribing a name and effacing the names of others—that our corpus will stretch in different directions. I want now to skip across to the end of our anonymous first century,[25] to show how these tics of authorship are mimed in Roman biography, where Augustan anonymity starts to run deep.

Suetonius Augustus: Lie Down and Play Anonymous

Suetonius' *Augustus,* the paradigm and guidebook of the *Twelve Caesars,* hasn't always been paired willingly with the *RG.*[26] It is true that Suetonius tiptoes around much of the content of the document we feel it should respect more. But I shall argue that there is one major track in the *RG* that Suetonius takes up: none other than the riff of *Augustus as author,* with name and without.

Suetonius' *Caesars* are a series of biographies running the full gamut of "emperors," Julius Caesar to Domitian. They are forms of history written through lives and the work of someone likely to have been pretty close to the corridors of power. Suetonius seems to have beavered away for much of his career in the important role of court scribe/scholar/correspondence secretary under Hadrian. The *Caesars* are generally billed to have hit the shelves sometime around the early 120s CE—so wherefore this shocking temporal leap in the wake of *RG?* Here's why: I want to ply the *Caesars* for their help as revealing moments in the reception history of Augustus and Augustan anonymity. One hundred years on, this text shows just how deeply a politics of authorship had percolated into elite thought about emperors. This is not only about the ideology of clear authorship or fixing agents to products; it is also about how anonymity can mutate and migrate from the emperor's repertoire into a dark strategy of resistance, as well as how it can gain a truth-value more authoritative than conventional named authority.

Suetonius as scholar has an obvious investment in names and authorship.[27] In the *De Grammaticis,* part of his job is keen attributive thinking, such as distinguishing the various homonymous grammarians or declaring whose text belongs to whom. If he is trained in distinguishing hands and styles, he is also trained in aping them. As *ab epistulis,* one of the central tasks would probably have been to write letters in the emperor's voice, to *be* him in text.[28] These kinds of attributive and pseudepigraphic practices of course conditioned what Suetonius saw in his *Caesars.* And what he sees in Augustus is little short of a graphomaniac,[29] a man addicted to authoring his own words and making his own words look like the work of others.

In obvious ways, the Suetonian *Augustus* takes a solid leaf out of the *RG*-Augustus' book in plumping for a perfect overdetermined authorship.[30] One of the striking points of difference about the *Augustus* is the sheer volume of documentary matter that Suetonius furnishes. Most of this comes straight from the *hand* of Augustus himself.[31] This may well have something to do with the distinctiveness of Augustan handwriting, which Suetonius fetishizes:

> Notavi et in chirographo eius illa praecipue: non dividit verba nec ab extrema parte versuum abundantis litteras in alterum transfert sed ibidem statim subicit circumducitque.[32] (87)

> I've noted this quirk in his handwriting: he doesn't divide words, nor does he transfer overspilling letters from the end of one line down to the start of the next, but he crams the letters under the same word, and draws a circle round them.

That sort of quirk makes Augustus' writing instantly identifiable and so functions as a means of authentication. We might also compare his idiosyncratic orthography in the next section (88). So, at the same time as Suetonius buffs up his access to authoritative Augustan documents,[33] he also shows them off *as* authoritative. You can tell, just by looking at them.

The same project of fixity and authentication is behind the way in which Suetonius handles two other important landmarks of Augustan authorship: the name and the signature. On the first, Suetonius is much more forthcoming with the deep history of Augustus' name than the *RG*-author. Right from the off, Suetonius prizes the palimpsest of Augustus' historical names into their various layers[34]—but only to shore up the most recent, most definitive title as the telos:

> Infanti cognomen Thurino inditum est in memoriam maiorum originis vel quod regione Thurina recens eo nato pater Octavius adversus fugitivos rem prospere gesserat. Thurinum cognominatum satis certa probatione tradiderim nactus puerilem imagunculam eius aeream veterem ferreis et paene iam exolescentibus litteris hoc nomine inscriptam, quae dono a me principi data inter cubiculi Lares colitur. Sed et a M. Antonio in epistulis per contumeliam saepe Thurinus appellatur, et ipse nihil amplius quam mirari se rescribit pro obprobrio sibi prius nomen obici. Postea {Gai} Caesaris et deinde Augusti cognomen assumpsit, alterum testamento maioris avunculi, alterum Munati Planci sententia, cum quibusdam censentibus Romulum appellari oportere quasi et ipsum conditorem urbis, praevaluisset ut Augustus potius vocaretur non tantum novo sed etiam ampliore cognomine, quod loca quoque religiosa et in quibus augurato

quid consecratur augusta dicantur, ab auctu vel ab avium gestu gustuve,
sicut etiam Ennius docet scribens:

augusto augurio postquam incluta condita Roma est. (7)

As a kid he was given the cognomen Thurinus, to recall the origin of the
family line or because it was near Thurii that, soon after his birth, his
father, Octavius, had conducted a successful campaign against the run-
away slaves. I would relay the fact that his name was Thurinus with fairly
solid proof: I got hold of a little bronze statue of him as a boy, pretty old
from the look of the iron letters that were almost disappearing, and inscribed with this name; I gave it to the princeps as a gift, and it has pride
of place among the Lares of his bedroom. Also, he's often called Thurinus
by Mark Antony in his letters, as a term of abuse; to which he replies
nothing more than he finds it puzzling to have his first name thrown back
at him as an insult. Afterward, he adopted the name of Caesar and Augustus: the first through his great uncle's will; the second on the official
proposal of Munatius Plancus. When certain people were moving that
he should be called Romulus as if he too were the city's founder, the suggestion won out that he rather be called Augustus, because it was not only
a new name but also a more dignified one—sacred spaces, and whatever
is consecrated by augury, are called "august," either from the augmenta-
tion or the "gesture" or "digestion" of the birds, as Ennius also teaches
us. He writes:

After lustrous Rome had been founded by august augury.

As scholars have said before, this etymological game shows how many boxes
the name Augustus can tick[35] and almost goes so far as to tether it to the state
of being an *auctor* (stemming from *auctus*) per se.[36] The role of "Augustus"
as a nominal unifier embracing all of its predecessors into a retrospectively
settled subjectivity is clear from the way Suetonius *uses* it all the way through,
from the very beginning of Augustus' life.[37] Whereas modern scholarship
is quaintly committed to resisting Augustan teleology by preserving his
named stages (Octavian before twenty-seven, Augustus thereafter), Suetonius
folds all these former identities into the capacious super-title. A similar pro-
gression works behind Suetonius' comments on Augustus' seal.[38] We move
from a confusion—perfectly embodied in the form of the sphinx—to a "fore-
father" avatar to the unmistakable brand of Augustus himself: Thurinus—
Gaius Caesar—Augustus > Sphinx—Alexander the Great—Augustus.

In diplomatibus libellisque et epistulis signandis initio sphinge usus est, mox imagine Magni Alexandri, novissime sua Dioscuridis manu scalpta, qua signare insecuti quoque principes perseverarunt. Ad epistulas omnis horarum quoque momenta—nec diei modo sed et noctis—quibus datae significarentur addebat. (50)

In notes of recommendation, rescripts, and letters, he first used the sphinx as a seal, soon after an image of Alexander the Great, and most recently his own, carved by Dioscurides' hand. The next emperors also stuck with it as their seal. He added the precise hour to every letter—both the hour of the day and of the night—to mark their moment of composition.

As with the name, so with the seal. First-person Augustan identity is shored up in a tripartite scheme, such that the former forms are swallowed slickly into the instantly recognizable comfort (and superior definition)[39] of the latter. We also see Suetonius confirming the postmark precision of the RG and extending it to all Augustan "correspondence." Name, signature, date: the verifying gestures of imperial bureaucracy, au(c)to(r)cratic heart and soul.[40]

The Suetonian Augustus is not only a scholar's dream because the outlines of his written self are shapely and defined. He is also a scholarly wonder himself, a Suetonian boffin who pushes his program of traceability onto the written world around him. After the milestone of assuming the pontificate, Augustus' first act is to perform an editorial recension on the tattered corpus of Sibylline oracles,[41] a corpus of verse prophecies that carried a heavy cultural authority:

Postquam vero pontificatum maximum, quem numquam vivo Lepido auferre sustinuerat, mortuo demum suscepit, quidquid fatidicorum librorum Graeci Latinique generis nullis vel parum idoneis auctoribus vulgo ferebatur, supra duo milia contracta undique cremavit ac solos retinuit Sibyllinos—hos quoque dilectu habito—condiditque duobus forulis auratis sub Palatini Apollinis basi. (31)

After he finally took up the post of Pontifex Maximus on the death of Lepidus (he couldn't bring himself to strip him of it while he was alive), whatever books of prophecy, Greek or Latin, were doing the rounds, the ones with either no or low-brow authors, he gathered them up and completely incinerated more than two thousand of them. He kept only the Sibylline books—these also selectively—and stowed them in two golden chests under the base of the Palatine Apollo.

Augustus' intervention is here textbook antianonymity: the nameless and obscure prophecies are mercilessly culled, and only a selection of the named *Sibyllini* make the cut. Augustus clearly takes it upon himself to produce an authoritative edition of the future.[42] His approach to the imperial bugbear of the furtive lampoon stacks up on the same continuum.[43] The kind emperor Augustus grins and bears the usual squirreling of secret critique without persecuting the culprits.[44] All he does is legislate against the *future*:

> Etiam sparsos de se in curia famosos libellos nec expavit et magna cura redarguit ac ne requisitis quidem auctoribus id modo censuit, cognoscendum posthac de iis qui libellos aut carmina ad infamiam cuiuspiam sub alieno nomine edant. (55)

> He wasn't afraid of the notorious squibs about him that had been distributed in the senate house. He just rebutted them diligently, didn't even go after the authors, and merely proposed that from this point on the people who publish squibs or songs under another's name, aiming at ruining someone's reputation, should be investigated.

The targets of the proposal here are those who knock up defamatory pamphlets under someone else's name. Importantly, this is a ruling against *pseudonymity*,[45] against the socially disruptive, explosive force of writing against someone, *as* someone else.[46] Both the Sibylline and lampoon acts of Augustus, then, agitate against unclaimed, or wrongly attributed, discourse. What's more, this latter moment carefully packages the decree in the impersonal, anonymous envelope of the law. This is not about Augustus. It is about anyone, everyone (*ad infamiam cuiuspiam*).

Perhaps Augustus is so sensitive about the pseudonymous because he understands its spark and wants to harness it for himself, for the good of the social order. For Augustus himself engages in at least two forms of anonymity/pseudonymity, which serve as the mirror image of the Sibylline pretenders and mischievous lampooners. The first takes its cue from the *RG* and gets to the crux of the rhetoric of restoration that is also a powerful kind of anonymity ("this isn't me; it's someone else"). Shortly after Augustus' work on the prophecies, he renovates the building works of great republican leaders, leaving the original inscriptions intact:[47]

> Proximum a dis immortalibus honorem memoriae ducum praestitit qui imperium p. R. ex minimo maximum reddidissent. Itaque et opera cuiusque manentibus titulis restituit et statuas omnium triumphali effigie in

utraque fori sui porticu dedicavit, professus et edicto commentum id se
ut ad illorum velut ad exemplar et ipse dum viveret et insequentium aeta-
tium principes exigerentur a civibus. Pompei quoque statuam contra
theatri eius regiam marmoreo iano superposuit translatam e curia in qua
C. Caesar fuerat occisus. (31)

Next to the Gods, he gave honor to the memory of the generals who had
expanded the power of the Roman people from tiny to gargantuan. So
he restored the works of these men while keeping their inscriptions, and
dedicated statues of all of them in triumphal gear, in both porticos of his
forum. He declared in an edict: "I have arranged this so that both I (as
long as I live) and the *principes* to come will be held by our citizens to
the standards of these men, as it were." He also shifted the statue of
Pompey from the curia where Caesar had been killed and put it on a
marble arch, opposite the entrance to his theater.

That action of "preserving the original" (*manentibus titulis*) of course builds
on Augustus' generous anonymizing in the *RG*.[48] But it also forms the sun-
nier side of a practice he is trying to stamp out: doing something in
someone else's name. Augustan "restoration" is the gilt flip side of socially
corrosive lampooning.

In the *RG* and the *Augustus* both, then, Augustus expertly parasites on
the names of old, rather than exclusively acting in his own. But Suetonius
pushes his Augustus one better in the anonymity stakes. Right at the end
of the biography, we have an Augustus relaxing into his impending death.
In a telling exchange with the astrologer Thrasyllus, he jostles jollily with
the symbolic future and bests it in a philological exchange that proves his
scholarly chops. Observing the funeral of one of his favorite boys on Capri,
Augustus corrals the know-all Thrasyllus into a game of spot-the-poet:

Huius Masgabae ante annum defuncti tumulum cum e triclinio animad-
vertisset magna turba multisque luminibus frequentari, versum compos-
itum *ex tempore* clare pronuntiavit,

κτίστου δὲ τύμβον εἰσορῶ πυρούμενον,

conversusque ad Thrasyllum Tiberi comitem, contra accubantem et ig-
narum rei interrogavit cuiusnam poetae putaret esse. Quo haesitante
subiecit alium,

ὁρᾷς φάεσσι Μασγάβαν τιμώμενον;

ac de hoc quoque consuluit. Cum ille nihil aliud responderet quam cuiuscumque essent optimos esse, cachinnum sustulit atque in iocos effusus
est. (98)

When he had clocked from the dining room that this Masgaba's tomb
(he'd died the year before) was being thronged by a huge crowd with
many a torch, he said out loud the following verse that he had composed
on the spot:

I see the founder's tomb on fire.

He turned to Thrasyllus, Tiberius' companion, who was sitting opposite
him and had no idea what this was about. He asked him to which poet
he thought the verse belonged. As Thrasyllus balked, he flung another at
him:

Do you see Masgaba's respects paid with lights?

He asked him about this one also. When he offered nothing else by way
of reply other than that they were top work, whosever they were, he burst
into a chuckle and cracked some jokes.

So whose lines are these anyway? Thrasyllus can't quite pick the author of
the neat little trimeters but swears that they are fine stuff, whosever they
might be (*cuiuscumque essent*). The joke here is that the lines "belong to"
Augustus. They have been knocked up on the spot, *ex tempore*.[49] But they
are delivered *as if* quoted and so passed off as someone else's. The framing
throws Thrasyllus off.[50] The move from "founder" to "Masgaba" perhaps
also misdirects. Otherwise we might have been forgiven for thinking of the
κτίστης in front of us, Augustus himself. But the question of "whose verses"
is almost functionally irrelevant. Augustus has secured such power at this
point that there is only one bland response: they are the best, *optimos*,
purely because he says them, says so. Augustus has tipped into the most
sublime state of authorship possible, where no one can recognize that you
are the one making it up. Invention is mistaken for quotation. This is the
true coup of Augustan authorship: writing the script, even when it looks
like the work of another (anyone but you).

This bite-size, light-touch anecdote is actually one of Augustus' proudest
victories. It flings him into a role of cosmic responsibility that goes one step
beyond the *RG*'s committed flirtation with the anonymous. In the *RG*, Augustus was still "taking responsibility," marking the anonymous as *his*,

even if the wider ideological function was to seed the possibility that everything without his name could really have his name all over it. Come this attribution scene at the end of his Suetonian life, he no longer feels the need to sign off. He is content to let the words remain homeless. A retrospective Augustus, by now shored up securely in the second century, knows that whatever happens, the entire future of the principate will always be traced back to its author: *him*. Anonymous authorship leashes the world to the puppet master, via a cascade of invisible strings.

Off the Record

I have tried to show that the bureaucratic stranglehold of the first princeps is tightened through complementary strands in both the *RG* and Suetonius: first, an obsessive clamping of authorial identity; second, a release from that grip to project a "universal" responsibility. Augustus has both of these under his control. Yet this control cannot be communicated downstream.[51] As is well known, the *Caesars* tell a story of double-dip decline: two dynasties work from auspicious beginnings only to go spectacularly wrong. In this last section, I want to chart how this plays out through the flickering dialectic between fixed and floating authorship. In the process, I shall expand on a suggestion I have made elsewhere:[52] that the perceived tumble[53] in the quality of the *Caesars* may not be Suetonius' fault but rather a deliberately induced epistemological earthquake.[54] In any event, I want to suggest that the more chaotic (and chthonic) forces of anonymous authorship are unleashed over the course of the *Caesars*. The clue is in the handwriting.

I showed earlier that Augustus manipulates anonymity like a boss. But there is another current of the anonymous flowing throughout the *Caesars* that I have left unmentioned. These are the unhoused rounds of popular verse and oral gossip—important trademarks of the Suetonian program but also responsible for this author's often cavalier mishandling by scholarship.[55] If we think about Caesarean lives as jumping between two epistemological realms, roughly synchronized with different forms of authorship, we can skip the usual condescension. On the one hand, we have "official" knowledge, sanctioned by the instruments of emperor and court. This is the "documentary" mode of the earlier *Caesars* and the reason why books such as the *Augustus* seem fuller and better researched than the emaciated beasts toward the end. On the other hand, we have the unofficial sound bites of "vulgate" knowledge, *sine auctore* and beyond the court.[56] The pull of the *Caesars* seems to move us from the former to the latter. I would venture that this has a lot to do with the death, or at least discrediting, of the emperor as author.

The relationship between these competing forms of authorship and episteme is billed as one of *hierarchy* in the *Augustus*. There is a brilliant example deep in the thick of the life, (i.e., within the "private" section, from 61 onwards) purportedly allowing us a glimpse of the man off duty. In sections 69–70, Suetonius admits all sorts of gossip about Augustus' moral peccadilloes, sourced from all over the shop.[57] On top of the letters of Antony (obvious sourcebooks for the anti-Augustan tradition), we have the famous cryptic verses about Augustus' banquet of the twelve gods or graffiti jokes about his Corinthian bronze habits scrawled on his statue or the epigram about his dice addiction. All of these are framed as rumor bubbling from the dark depths of the anonymous: *sine auctore notissimi versus* (70).[58] The knowledge arrives in the passive, trafficked impersonally:

Cena quoque eius secretior in fabulis fuit, quae **vulgo** δωδεκάθεος **vocabatur;** . . . auxit cenae rumorem summa tunc in civitate penuria ac fames, **adclamatumque** est postridie . . . **notatus est** et ut pretiosae supellectilis Corinthiorumque praecupidus et aleae indulgens. Nam et proscriptionis tempore ad statuam eius **ascriptum est** . . . cum **existimaretur** quosdam propter vasa Corinthia inter proscriptos curasse referendos, et deinde bello Siciliensi epigramma **vulgatum est:** (70)

There was also gossip about a secret dinner of his, which **was dubbed in common parlance** the "twelve gods": . . . what fanned the rumor of this dinner were the dearth and famine in the state, at that time at their height, and the next day **there was a public outcry** . . . **he was also censured** for wanting the finest furniture and Corinthian bronzes, and for being fond of gambling. Even during the period of the proscriptions his statue **was inscribed** . . . since **it was thought** he made sure to include some men on the list because of their Corinthian vases, and then during the Sicilian war this epigram **went into circulation:**

These unassigned energies are released into the air, certainly. And it might be argued that the very act of airing them is at least a little disruptive to the staid court history. But in the next section, Augustus himself is given back center stage and breezily refutes (*refutavit,* 71) most of these charges through countering anecdotes. Alternatively—and this is the key point—he renders them obsolete by trumping them with *better* evidence straight from the horse's hand.[59] On the topic of gambling, for example, Suetonius undergirds Augustan openness and indifference with an autographed letter:[60]

> Aleae rumorem nullo modo expavit lusitque simpliciter et palam oblecta-menti causa etiam senex ac praeterquam Decembri mense aliis quoque festis et profestis diebus. Nec id dubium est. Autographa quadam epistula, "Cenavi," ait, "mi Tiberi, cum isdem, accesserunt convivae Vinicius et Silius pater. Inter cenam lusimus geronticos et heri et hodie. Talis enim iactatis, ut quisque canem aut senionem miserat, in singulos talos singulos denarios in medium conferebat quos tollebat universos qui Venerem iecerat." (71)

> He wasn't at all bothered about his gambling reputation and played straightforwardly and openly for pleasure, even as an old man—in the month of December but also on other holidays, workdays too. This is beyond doubt. A letter in his own handwriting says, "I dined, my good Tiberius, with the same people; Vinicius and Silius the elder came along as guests. At dinner we gambled old-man style, both yesterday and today. When the dice were thrown, whoever got a dog or a six contributed one denarius to the pot per number of dice; whoever threw a Venus took the lot."

That handwritten letter (*autographa quaedam epistula*) is the gold standard of documentary evidence for Augustus' life.[61] Augustus is the first and best author of *Augustus*. Suetonius allows himself to quote two more such juicy epistles, in section 71 alone. No matter how much unattributed gossip is still doing the rounds, Suetonius can shoo it away with the ultimate author's final word. That characteristically overwritten first-person authorship pioneered in the *RG* authenticates this Caesar, and the information mined to write him, through and through.

As I said earlier, the existence of trustworthy documents, drawn up in distinctive Augustan handwriting, is crucial to the "official" knowledge system behind the *Augustus*. But the order is upset as we make our way through the *Caesars*. The later lives become altogether more reliant on those same anonymous fragments that were clearly subordinated in the schema of the *Augustus*. In other words, the quality of the life, and the quality of the source material, varies directly with the quality of the *principal* hand-writing at its base. Let us slide to a couple of examples from the other end of the imperial spectrum.

I quoted the passage about Augustan handwriting earlier to make a point about distinctiveness. But what makes this script, understood as extension of self, particularly striking is the *neatness* of it all. Words and letters are grouped in a tight order; that is, the metaphysics of the Augustan cosmos is mapped onto the page. Like a literary general, Augustus *subicit circum-ducitque* his letters: "subjects" them to his will, "draws around them," as if he were yanking his army around. This is a closed, decided universe under Augustan control. By contrast, Nero's handwriting is a shambolic mess of indecision, a confounding window onto a mind not made but in the making:

> Itaque ad poeticam pronus carmina libenter ac sine labore composuit nec, ut quidam putant, aliena pro suis edidit. Venere in manus meas pugillares libellique cum quibusdam notissimis versibus ipsius chirographo scriptis, ut facile appareret non tralatos aut dictante aliquo exceptos sed plane quasi a cogitante atque generante exaratos: ita multa et deleta et inducta et superscripta inerant. (*Nero* 52)

> Moving on to poetry, he wrote verse fluently and easily; and he didn't (as some moot) publish others' as his own. Some diaries and booklets fell into my hands with some famous verses of his, written up in his script, so that it was perfectly obvious they weren't copied or taken from someone dictating but scratched down just as someone ruminating or composing does it: there were so many parts deleted and blacked out and written above.

Interestingly, the gossip around Nero's literary activity is that he plagiarized (and we could picture plagiarism as the darker side of the Augustan ex-periments with anonymity). Suetonius dispels the charge using the same sort of handwriting-as-authentication strategy: no, the verses are real; I've seen the drafts. This focus on Nero's hand as work-in-progress is obviously meant to play off Augustus' obsessively neat penmanship. The statesman writes clearly and intelligibly; the monster writes up a deviant palimpsest. But even though Suetonius is talking about Nero's off-record poetic handi-craft here, I think this comment functions at a higher level than mere unfa-vorable comparison with the imperial father. For this blotted page gets to the heart of what it is to write about such a disputed reign as Nero's. That is especially the case from Suetonius' vantage point, by which time the records of Nero's stint have suffered from several waves of fiddle, erasure, rewriting, overwriting. Nero is difficult to write authoritatively about, because he is a moving target.[62] His handwriting splits his mind schizophrenically, and the tradition murmurs different kinds of noise. It is hard to get to the bottom of him.

If Nero's handwriting is impossible to get a handle on, it is, at least, recognizably Neronian. Suetonius avers he has seen it in the flesh (*chirographo*). Once we get to the Flavians, however, access to firsthand imperial truth is muddied even further. This last book of the *Caesars* has come in for the most criticism for shriveling without excuse, at least according to Andrew Wallace-Hadrill.[63] But I would argue that there is method in the atrophy, because, by this point in the *Caesars,* the value of the handwritten document has been ransacked. Take Golden Boy Titus' flexible script:

> E pluribus comperi notis quoque excipere velocissime solitum, cum amanuensibus suis per ludum iocumque certantem, imitarique chirographa quaecumque vidisset ac saepe profiteri maximum falsarium esse potuisse. (*Titus* 3)

> I've gathered from many sources that he was also given to writing express shorthand, that he would vie with his scribes for fun and a laugh, and that he would imitate whatever handwriting he had laid eyes on and often proclaimed that he could have taken the title "world's best forger."

Unlike Augustus' distinct and consistent style or Nero's unmistakable goings-over, Titus has no essential written identity.[64] He can fake whatever *chirographa* he has seen.[65] But note how this also sets off ripples in the epistemological plane, the means by which Suetonius can actually garner such a factoid. He no longer gets it from the imperial pen (no letters of the Flavians are quoted, as they are for Augustus)[66] but from general, anonymized sources: *e pluribus comperi*. The evidence is as motley and fluid as the hand with which it deals.

The Flavians in general suffer from a surplus of forged official documents, which obstructs Suetonius' and our ability to get to "know" them firsthand. The *Domitian* brings this out in Technicolor detail. Confusion about authenticity reigns under this horror-emperor. Domitian suspects that his brother doctored their father Vespasian's will (2). Not even the writing of this dynasty's golden Augustus figure has full fidelity. Our last and worst emperor, Domitian himself, actively cooks the books too, perverting the Augustan legacy of writing as and for others:

> Pari arrogantia, cum procuratorum suorum nomine formalem dictaret epistulam, sic coepit, "Dominus et deus noster hoc fieri iubet", unde institutum posthac ut ne scripto quidem ac sermone cuiusquam appellaretur aliter. (*Domitian* 13)

> With the same conceit, dictating a form letter in the name of his procurators, he began like this: "Our master and god orders this be done." So after that, it was established that he had to be addressed in no other way, not even in writing or casual conversation.

So Domitian scripts for his underlings. But he also has others write for him. Suetonius deducts points for his failing to put in the hard yards to develop a good literary style and for leaning on "others' talents" (*alieno . . . ingenio,* 20) to craft his letters, speeches, and edicts.[67] Domitian lacks a strong first-person signature. But again, the interesting point is how this weakened imperial script is correlated with an overall rise in the intensity of "anonymous" information now flooding into the work. Unauthorizing constructions, such as passive forms of *ferre* or *vulgare,* start to supply unverified knowledge. Suetonius can only give out a rumor about a handwritten letter of Domitian at several levels' remove; he can no longer claim to have seen it himself. Unnamed background murmurs come out of the woodwork to cast their slanted gossip, which Suetonius is forced to retail, by the paucity of the firsthand: *nec defuerunt qui affirmarent, corruptum Domitianum et a Nerva successore mox suo.* (cf. *nec defuit qui ostentum sic interpretaretur,* 33). What's more, the anonymous knowledge not only has an effect on how this kind of biographical history is written. It affects the history itself. As we saw in the introduction, Domitian is moved by the gossip:

> Ut edicti de excidendis vineis propositi gratiam faceret non alia magis re compulsus creditur quam quod sparsi libelli cum his versibus erant:

> κἄν με φάγῃς ἐπὶ ῥίζαν, ὅμως ἔτι καρποφορήσω,
>   ὅσσον ἐπισπεῖσαί σοί, κάπρε, θυομένῳ. (14)

> It's generally thought that what forced him to ignore his edict about cutting down the vineyards was nothing more than slips with these verses being passed around:

Chew on my root all you want, I'll still have more than enough juice to pour on you, my boar, when you're on the verge of slaughter.

Again, an anonymous source (*creditur*) frames a statement about the relationship between power and anonymity. But this time, we are in deep. This is not just hidden transcript material that the emperor rises above or tries to root out. It actually has a direct impact on him. It sets the policy. The emperor no longer controls the anonymous; the anonymous controls him. And Suetonius is rendered the plaything of exactly the same forces.

By the end of the *Caesars,* then, the ordered hierarchy of named, official discourse over the dark realm *sine auctore* is flipped on its head. Emperors do not write like they used to. They write as, or are written by, willy-nilly. This has a huge, underappreciated corollary for the Suetonian method. The *Caesars* become unraveled and shriveled, since the guarantee of the first-hand is ripped out from underneath them. The overdetermined author of the *RG,* who had tickled anonymity only to bolster a megalomaniac and centripetal universalism, crumbles under the pressure of a history without imperial signature. Suetonius steps into the ruins, staking his claim to become one of the great authors of the anonymous.

2

Tongue Ties

Ovid's Ibis

For Peacock's first readers, reading meant putting in the
names—and wondering about the most important name:
the author's.

—John Mullan (2007: 244–245)

IN THE EARLY DAYS of Chapter 1, we spotlighted the Augustan penchant for antonomasia as a way of unmemorializing one's enemies, a
way of cattle branding them with one's own negative imprint forevermore.
Our next target, Ovid's *Ibis,* is an outsized, deformed monster of that in-
cipient tradition snapping hard in its wake. This poem—Ovid's last, if conventional dating/authorship can be bought, written in the dying days of
exile before his death around 17 CE—is a loud and unruly curse against
an unnamed enemy made back at the Roman ranch: the eponymous un-
sung villain, Ibis. It is a work of two parts. First is an "introduction" composed of proem-style saber rattling over Ibis's crimes (1–66), prayers to the
gods to make it rain revenge on him (67–126), the extralong afterlife of
Ibis's punishments (127–208), Ibis's early days, and Ovid's divinely sanctioned mission to destroy him (209–250). Second is the bulk: a long, winding,
and quick-fire litany of couplet-curses taken from all over Greco-Roman
mythology and history, designed to grind Ibis down by a succession of
analogies to cases of grisly death and suffering. As a blow of cathartic or

performative hatred and anger, it is one of the ancient world's most remarkable artifacts, a spray of vented spleen gone horribly right.

The *Ibis* is also a heavily redacted poem. Anonymity, pseudonymity, and
antonomasia froth at its core. Anonymous on the inside, for a while it also
looked bad for its outside. It was long left to hover on the margins of the
genuinely Ovidian (taking up space as a genuine fake); nowadays it is
treated as a fully-fledged limb of the corpus.[1] That particular possibility of
the *Ibis* springing from a non-Ovidian pen is something I intend to raise
here only to repress. May it smolder in the backs of your minds.[2] Far be it
from this chapter to resurrect that dead horse for another round of flogging. Rather, I want to map out a rough nominal politics for *Ibis,* which is
one of antiquity's greatest experiments with the power of the name. I shall
look specifically at the logic of depriving and assigning names;[3] how this
might knot with the text's voodoo aspirations of rage and harm, obsession
and control; and how the subtraction of names can bring with it an alarming
power of universality, as well as the specter of annihilation.

The *Ibis* plugs nicely into the real-world tradition of curse tablets (*defixiones*).[4] But one of the caveats stopping scholars short of forging an all-
out equivalence is the curious fact that Ovid does not name his victim.[5]
The whole point of the *defixio* was to fix the target beyond doubt.[6] The
surviving tablets often name their sucker to the nth degree, resorting to *prae-
nomina, nomina, cognomina,* places of origin, all to make sure the curse
gets to exactly the right place. This *defixio* in elegy, however, runs to the
other corner. Instead of pinning an exact dummy, it gives us a pseudonym
modeled on the identical made-up name of Ibis v. 1.0 (in that sense, *Ibis*
doubles as both pseudonym and homonym) and revels in the nebula that
ensues.[7] Ovid makes vague promises to give Ibis' "true name" at some later
point, but this is an obvious tease for a payoff that will never come. So what
is the point of a curse poem that dare not speak its bogey's name?[8]

On one level, we could proffer a swift and painless literary answer to
the puzzle: this is a poem luxuriating in the Hellenistic allusivity of the
doctus poeta, which consistently makes use of name substitution as a cognitive challenge thrown down to the reader for the sake of riddle.[9] And so
this would apply to the macro-level of the anonymized target (Ibis) as much
as to the micro-level of the largely anonymized couplets themselves. But
Hellenistic aesthetics don't quite finish the explanatory job here (if they ever

can). The formal resemblance to *defixiones* whets our expectations for a named target, even if the context of the *doctus poeta* might send us back down the antonomastic rabbit hole into a world of colorful question marks. The tension springs from this strange combination of writing traditions, one of which is happy with anonymity, the other of which is not. That tension makes the *Ibis'* multiform commitment to anonymity all the more striking.

The problem, I think, is that there is another pressuring discourse operating in the wings. Ancient poetry has its own internal logic of the name, which requires working with, not grating against. In the Ovidian system particularly (but holding basically for most ancient poetry), the name is the currency of fame.[10] Every time you use a proper name, you single out the bearer to enjoy another round of proliferating immortality. Ovid's regular self-naming (of which *Ibis* partakes) is a way of seeding the selfish genes of poetry so they pass down the line,[11] *possessions* for all time: as the end of the *Metamorphoses* heralds, *nomenque erit indelebile nostrum* (15.876).[12] Of course, naming as faming applies to names beyond oneself too. The name in verse is a form of magical pickling and radical empowerment. To have a name is to have power, and to lose one is to lose *it*.

That is the main operative discourse behind the *Ibis:* poet and poetry have the ability to grant and withhold power, precisely by giving or confiscating the name.[13] From the beginning, this is the central asymmetry between Ovid and Ibis, a granularity that cannot be resolved in the recent deconstructive readings of the poem seeking to make the twain into dark twins.[14] Ovid identifies both by finger-pointing at himself but does so also via Ibis' publicity efforts.[15] Our poet signs on as Naso in line 4; the author of the dreaded *Ars* in 6; and the target of Ibis' open-air defamation in 13–14:

> vulneraque inmitis requiem quaerentia vexat,
> iactat et in toto nomina nostra foro, (13–14)[16]

> He harshly irritates the wounds that are desperate for rest, and loudmouths my name over the whole forum,

Although Ovid makes it there to shout "Naso" before Ibis gets a chance to do the same, we feel there isn't such a strong objection to the image of it being bandied about the forum by his sworn enemy. All publicity is good publicity. Ovid takes revenge by reversal. Before Ibis is called Ibis even, he is shrouded in indefinites and silence:[17]

> quisquis is est, nam nomen adhuc utcumque tacebo,
>   cogit inassuetas sumere tela manus. (9–10)

> Whoever he is (I'll still keep his name quiet in any way I can), he makes my untried hands pick up heavy artillery.

Ovid's weapon-wielding technique will be very much scattershot, more nail bomb than precision archery:

> sic ego te nondum ferro iaculabor acuto,
>   protinus invisum nec petet hasta caput,
> et neque nomen in hoc nec dicam facta libello,
>   teque brevi qui sis dissimulare sinam. (47–50)

> So I won't quite yet hurl at you with sharp steel, nor will my spear seek your hated head right this minute, and I'll utter neither your name nor your deeds in this book, and I'll let you disguise who you are for another short while.

At this point, the hated/unseen (*invisum*) dome will have no name or biography to individuate it.[18] When the moniker "Ibis" does arrive in the next passage, Ovid lets us know it is nothing more than a placeholder shroud, a solution that works well enough to forge the Callimachean poetics of obscurity[19] for which he is limbering up (*Illius ambages imitatus in Ibide dicar* 59–60). As I pointed out earlier, this is no mere pseudonym: it is a used-up pseudonym, something a much more famous predecessor has already rinsed out.[20] In that sense, it is another version, or a continuation of, the "no-name" with which the enemy is originally saddled. Withholding the real name and doubling up on the pseudonym are a two-pronged attack. They are both ways of scrubbing "Ibis," whoever he is, from anything remotely resembling agent or actor. Anonymizing, pseudonymizing, and homonymizing Ibis leaves him uniquely exposed to the purposive yanking from context to context that we see so extensively rolled out across the *Ibis* as a whole (more on this later).

If Ibis is branded the nothing, the nobody,[21] the nonentity of blinding obscurity, Ovid is the named individual working from the light. That central, unbridgeable gulf between Ovid and nemesis extends well beyond the opening. Take the brilliant prophecy scene at Ibis' unholy birth. The Eumenides nurse the little nipper with dogs' milk, swaddle him in dark colors, and squeeze out the tears by sticking a smoky torch in his face. Suddenly, one of the "three sisters" pipes up:

> flebat, ut est fumis infans contactus amaris:
>> de tribus est cum sic una locuta soror:
> "tempus in inmensum lacrimas tibi movimus istas,
>> quae semper causa sufficiente cadent." (237–240)

The baby was weeping, infected with the strong smoke, when one of the three sisters spoke so: "we've stirred those tears of yours right up into the infinite future; with a rich supply of causes, they'll fall forever."

Because the prophecy revolves around Ibis, its terms of introduction are suitably vague: we don't know which one of the euphemized Eumenides speaks, and we don't even know the "three sisters" could actually refer to another divine sorority (i.e., the Fates)[22] until we get there in the next lines.[23] Spot the difference in the way the prophecy of Naso is handled immediately after:

> dixerat: at Clotho iussit promissa valere,
>> nevit et infesta stamina pulla manu;
> et, ne longa suo praesagia diceret ore,
>> "fata canet vates qui tua," dixit, "erit."
> ille ego sum vates: ex me tua vulnera disces,
>> dent modo di vires in mea verba suas. (241–246)

She finished speaking: but Clotho fixed it so her promises made good, and with inimical hands spun out dark threads; so that she wouldn't issue lengthy prophecies from her own mouth, she said, "There'll be a bard to sing your fates." *I am that bard:* you'll learn your wounds from me, if the gods would only lend my words their force.

The named Clotho is allowed to speak the other half of the prophecy. And Ovid offers himself up as the fulfillment of it immediately, with none other than the classic formula of authorial identification, *ille ego*.[24] So while Ibis is kept in the dark by an untitled sister, the solution to the authorized Clotho's prophetic riddle steps out and identifies himself the very next instant. Even if Ovid doesn't explicitly self-name here, he bucks the obscure trend of the entire poem by giving a simple declarative identification: *ille ego sum vates.* As Ovid joins the team of definition, Ibis, like most of his sorry company of nameless analogies to come, is put out to rot with the indefinites.

The system of the poem (such as there is one) is crafted around this structural weigh-off between names as vehicles of power and their elimination as method of control. The "norm" of the litany of bad examples that bulks out the *Ibis* is to withhold the victims' names. This is no iron law (more on the exceptions later), but it is a rule of thumb so strong that Housman even daggered a particular couplet as spurious pretty much solely because it directly named the victim on which it focused.[25] Name suppression is obviously part and parcel of the riddling form of the poem. But this has been taken as obscurity for the sake of "game" and "puzzle" for far too long. I shall argue in the next section that this practice is not just a bit of sport with the reader but a technique fundamental to the politics of naming. If part of the power of an established name lies in its "independence"—the idea that it is something preexisting, borrowed, someone else's, not yours—stripping the name is a way of redefining the bearer on one's own terms, controlling the bearer through the language of substitution chosen by *you,* not him or her. Failing to name, then, is not just about wrapping the voodoo doll in a dark cloak; it is about dressing it and pinning it in a very specific way indeed.

Hell's Christening

If we defined epic as a medium of kleos, designed to preserve and pump the names of its all-star heroic cast, we would have to call *Ibis* epic's dark opposite. This is a poem that covers an incredibly vast swathe of Greco-Roman history and mythology in breathless, bite-size couplets. But it imprisons most of its bloodied victims in the same periphrastic prison that also houses its antagonist. Many big names of the canonical corpus (e.g., Odysseus) are muscled out in a masterful program of nominal shepherding. Not naming is far more common than naming. Of the minority that are gifted proper names, many are gods or other "powerful" beings (more on this later). In the case of the silent majority, Ovid has a suite of techniques up his sleeve to say without saying. Substitutions such as patronymics, clues based on places of origin, family relationships, and relative pronouns deck out the text. There are myriad ways of keeping us in the dark and trilling the cognitive thrill of the riddle.

These methods don't just work on us, however. They also work on their victims. An interesting example of the way a name alternative can "discipline" a bearer, and sort out a power relationship with one efficient stroke, is the patronymic. In a general sense, the patronymic is always a title that onomastically reroutes power away from the bearer, toward the paternal "source" holding claim over it. In the father-focused cultures of the ancient world, it cannot but serve an innate ideological function, to lodge power with the male center of gravity, to root it in the past. Sometimes it can denote efficient social reproduction: "look, I am as good as my father!" Other times, irony creeps in: "I'm not worthy to bear his name!" In the *Ibis,* Ovid trots the patronymic out in a very pointed way. Its role is to rob its bearer of power and to show who is the boss.

All of the modes of substitution with which Ovid deals out nameless-ness involve some form of subordination, both political and grammatical: defining figures in relation to father, mother, wife, husband, sister, aunty, uncle, child takes away the independence of the simple proper name.[26] Relative clauses also define in relation to something else and stow the figure out of the way, in the secondary part of the sentence. But patronymics can play subordinators extremely well in certain cases where the father (as so often happens in the repressive nuclear units of Greco-Roman myth) is the perpetrator. In those cases, he becomes the one who both names and *looms* over the victim. In the section where Ovid goes through the list of blinded greats, there are two examples where the relationship is clear. The first is Phoenix, or should I say Amyntorides:

> id quod Amyntorides videas trepidumque ministro
>   praetemptes baculo luminis orbus iter. (257–258)

May you see what Amyntor's son saw, and may you suss out a tentative path without any light, by the help of a stick.

Amyntorides is no "neutral" patronymic here but a way of signaling that Amyntor was actually *responsible* for the blinding of his son (he reputedly punished Phoenix for shacking up with his concubine).[27] The man with the power gets the name. He fills the visual field of the poor blind Phoenix, writes him out, and takes his place. Something similar happens a few lines later with the sons of Phineus, who took out his sons' eyes on very similar grounds to the Amyntor-Phoenix affair (stealing daddy's precious concubine, again):

> ut duo Phinidae, quibus idem lumen ademit
>   qui dedit: (269–270)

> Like the two sons of Phineus–the very same man who gave them light, also stripped them of it:

As with Phoenix, so with these lost souls:[28] their father's domination is entailed in the very use of the patronymic (and his crime is explicitly flagged in the second half of the line).[29] We could dole out similar situations with the *-ides* or *-ide* termination name in the cases of Hippomeneide (333), Tantalides (432), Tereus/Tereides (432), all of which point to a looming, name-assigning-cum-depriving father. Compare the other form of the patronymic, which can slip in a similar point:

> aut ut Abantiades, aut ut Cycneius heros,
>   clausus in aequoreas praecipiteris aquas. (461–462)

> Or like the son of Abas, or the Cycnean hero, be flung, incarcerated, into the waters of the sea.

Referring to Tenes by his daddy's name (after Cycnus, king of Colonae) bites him with the same hand that fed him and threw him into the sea. This hero is "imprisoned" (*clausus*) by his father,[30] but he is also linguistically trapped by the stamp of the father's name claiming ownership over him. In the *Ibis,* patronymics serve alongside the central pseudonym/homonym of the antagonist himself: they allow naming, without naming, even as they make our reading process into a kind of naming (cursing, defaming).

Not all patronymics in the poem function in that neat double-edged fashion. Some, as Aeacides in a second, lend spark to the perpetrator, rather than maul the victim. Again, the rule guides, rather than legislates. The poem regularly keeps the agent of death or pain behind any given couplet as hidden as the one suffering (although more often than not, the perpetrator has naming rights). But another technology of namelessness throws up the guiding principle quite nicely. I mentioned earlier that the relative clause is one of Ovid's favorite methods of throwing us off the scent and filling up the couplet while he's at it. But at one point, the obfuscating power of the relative is multiplied tenfold by the switch to a focus on *collective* victims. These are important because they actually remove any semblance of a name, *even if "decoded."* There is no nameable single "referent" beneath the cloudy periphrasis. We can reconstruct the dramatic situation, but the victims shall remain nameless by virtue of being lumped into plurals. What's more, the power difference can be upped by naming the agent who lords it over the masses. Achilles is instantly recognizable under the famous patronymic Aeacides, though his victims are merely fodder piled high on the pyre:[31]

> ut quorum Aeacides misit violentus in altum
> corpora cum senis altera sena rogum, (373–374)

> Like: those whose bodies, six plus six, the raging son of Aeacus sent to the towering pyre,

Ovid's precursor in riddling ruin, the Sphinx, ironically looks clear as daylight alongside his heaped victims, *quos . . . victos:*

> ut quos obscuri victos ambagibus oris
> legimus infandae Sphinga dedisse neci, (375–376)

> Like: those conquered by the riddles of the Sphinx's dark mouth, whom (we read) she gave over to unspeakable death,

Only death and the names of the victims are truly unspeakable. The Sphinx itself easily picks up a direct mention. Then there are Scylla and Charybdis, who also preside over an anonymous slew:

> ut quos Scylla vorax Scyllaeque adversa Charybdis
> Dulichiae pavidos eripuere rati, (383–384)

> Like: the men whom ravenous Scylla and Charybdis (facing Scylla) snatched, jittering, from the Dulichian skiff,

In fact, Scylla is named not only once but *twice* in the same line. To the victor go the names.

The plural form of the relative pronoun, dark as the mask of a hanged criminal, thus offsets nicely against the terrifying brilliance of the identified offender. But there is another, even crisper way to trace this pattern of power play. So broad is Ovid's coverage of past exempla in the *Ibis*, he forces himself to double up on personnel. Let's take three good men/monsters who rear their heads more than once: Polyphemus, Antaeus, and Hercules. This will give us an opportunity to run a sort of scientific trial or control experiment to mark out named perpetrator from unnamed victim. In their incarnations as victims, all of these figures peep out of the poem as referential cripples (i.e., periphrastically):

> **pastor** ut **Aetnaeus,** cui casus ante futuros
>   Telemus Eurymides vaticinatus erat, (267–268)

Like: **Aetna's shepherd,** to whom Telemus son of Eurymus foretold his fate in advance,

> mens quoque sic furiis vecors agitetur, ut illi
>   unum qui toto corpore vulnus habet,
> utque Dryantiadae Rhodopeia regna tenenti,
>   in gemino dispar cui pede cultus erat,
> ut fuit **Oetaeo** quondam generoque draconum
>   Tisamenique patri Callirhoesque viro. (341–346)

May your mind also be driven mad in the same way as the one who has just one wound in his whole body, or as the son of Dryas had, who kept the land of Rhodope, dressed in ill-matched gear on both feet, or as **the Oetean** once had or the serpents' son-in-law or Tisamenus' father or Callirhoe's husband.

> ut iacet Aonio **luctator** ab hospite fusus,
>   qui, mirum, victor, cum cecidisset, erat, (391–392)

Like: **the wrestler** lying there, vanquished by the Aonian guest, whose fall (remarkably) made him win,

In all three examples, we can see how naming saps the strength of these heavy hitters at their moment of embarrassing truth. First, Polyphemus is cut right down to size as *pastor . . . Aetnaeus,* just another shepherd roaming the slopes of Etna (and note how the fullest name is reserved for Telemus Eurymides,[32] the prophet figure aligned, through nominal clarity, with Naso and Clotho). Hercules, in a flurry of precedents for heroes sent bonkers, is gifted nothing more than the topographical adjective marking the place of his death (*Oetaeus,* from Mt. Oeta).[33] Finally, Antaeus becomes nothing more than a run-of-the-mill wrestler (*luctator*).[34] Qua victims, these big guns are cut down to size by the deflationary surrogates made to stand in for them.

Yet observe how these same figures are attracted into their true, glory-heavy names as soon as they get the upper hand. For Polyphemus and Hercules:

> ut quos demisit vastam **Polyphemus** in alvum:
>> ut Laestrygonias qui subiere manus, (385–386)

> Like: the men whom **Polyphemus** sent right down into his huge stomach; or like those who met Laestrygonian force,

> aut, ut Erechthides magno ter ab **Hercule** victus,
>> caesus in inmensum proiciare fretum. (291–292)

> Or like: Erechthides, three times loser to the great **Hercules**, may you be struck down and tossed into vast waters.

Lording it right over a nameless collective or an unidentified Erechthides[35] (beaten three times over), Polyphemus and Hercules can safely reclaim themselves. But the dynamic is even more obvious with Antaeus, who is flipped from periphrastic dunce to full naming rights within the pressure cooker of two contiguous couplets:

> ut iacet Aonio **luctator** ab hospite fusus
>> qui, mirum, victor, cum cecidisset, erat,
> ut quos **Antaei** fortes pressere lacerti
>> quosque ferae morti Lemnia turba dedit, (391–394)

> Like: the wrestler lying there, vanquished by the Aonian guest, whose fall (remarkably) made him win, or like: the men whom the powerful arms of Antaeus crushed, and whom the Lemnian crowd gave over to savage death,

The process of recuperation even begins in the pentameter of defeat (392), where we see Antaeus' collapse as a mere harbinger of his recharge; and sure enough, from *luctator* to *victor*, he becomes *Antaeus* in 393.[36] The re-fitting of the name signals the restoration of power and self-possession.

This rough association between namelessness and weakness, name and power, has big implications for the way we retrospectively attack the poem's beginning. For it isn't just Ibis whom Ovid rubs out. Immediately after the couplet on Ibis' bandying of Ovid's name around the forum (see earlier), there is a kind of complementary moratorium on the names of wife and husband, which becomes an index of Ovid's exilic deprivation:

> vulneraque inmitis requiem quaerentia vexat,
>   iactat et in toto nomina nostra foro,
> perpetuoque mihi sociatam foedere lecti
>   non patitur miseri funera flere viri. (13–16)

> He harshly irritates the wounds that are desperate for rest, and loud-mouths my name over the whole forum, and doesn't let the lady bonded to me under the everlasting writ of the marriage bed mourn the death of her poor husband.

In a perverse way, Ibis is granted the familiarity (and power) of naming rights over Ovid. His wife, and he, can only be approached through periphrases or substitutions. Although we saw that *Nasonis* of line 4 as an attempt to wrest back control of the name, there is also a kind of abjection visited on him and his wife, a "pathetic" redaction of identity, a distancing between "wife" and "husband."[37] Indeed the distance is so overwhelming that Ovid doesn't even use the term *uxor* or equivalent, going instead for the color-less participle *sociatam* as a placeholder. Less pathetic, more aggressive is the operation Ovid performs on Augustus soon after.[38] The main man is called a god. But this "god" is carefully anonymized as an afterthought, unworthy of real invocation:

> di melius, quorum longe mihi maximus ille est,
>   qui nostras inopes noluit esse vias.
> huic igitur meritas grates, ubicumque licebit,
>   pro tam mansueto pectore semper agam.
> audiet hoc Pontus. faciet quoque forsitan idem
>   terra sit ut propior testificanda mihi. (23–28)

> Gods forbid! The greatest of whom, by far, is the man who didn't want my trip to be completely third class. So to him I'll give much-earned thanks for his soft heart, forever, and wherever possible. Pontus will hear this. Maybe that same man will fix it so I can call a nearer land to witness.

These are thanks but no thanks. In this largely nameless poem, Ovid does not struggle to name powerful divinities regularly. The decision to snub Augustus here will only become clear as the poem's broad naming patterns settle into relief: the implication is that even Augustus is de-named into willed victimhood. Ovid also marks Augustus' uselessness as "god" by shifting the responsibility of response onto a personified Pontus straight-away: this entity, so named, will listen more receptively than *maximus ille.* The other authority figures whom Ovid empties out in this opening section belong to the iambic family tree. Archilochus goes completely unmentioned, while the mention of Lycambes' blood perhaps gives Ibis a taste of what it might mean to be a named victim (cf. later). Callimachus is kept under wraps with a little more subtlety. His patronymic Battiades carries a subtle dose of the same slight we have seen in other patronymics thus far:

postmodo, si perges, in te mihi liber iambus
    tincta Lycambeo sanguine tela dabit.
nunc, quo Battiades inimicum devovet Ibin,
    hoc ego devoveo teque tuosque modo. (51–54)

Afterward, if you keep going, my loose iambic will fling projectiles at you, and they'll be tinged with the blood of Lycambes. Now, in the same way that Battus' son curses his enemy Ibis, I'll curse you and yours.

Battiades is Ovid's standard go-to for Callimachus,[39] but in the specific terms of the *Ibis,* we might catch a faint whiff of condescension. The poet still under the thumb of Battus can only manage an attack on his singular enemy, the individual Ibis—but Ovid will go one better with the scatter-shot tactics, broadening out the onslaught to embrace the individual *and* his nearest/dearest (*teque tuosque*). Perhaps that is all too faint. Nevertheless, we can definitely note the same suppression of names (via substitution, relative clause, patronymic) budding here already, only to blossom with insane fecundity in the rest of the poem.

So far, we have fixed fairly squarely on the "system" tying names to power. I said earlier that this is more tendency than ironclad law. There are a host of exceptions, especially in the realm of directly named victims. While the poem certainly bends toward the mass-assemblage anonymizing of those who die or suffer, in order to bring them into a production line with the unnamed target, there are also many cases where the victim's simple title pokes through. I would like to run over a selection of these now, to see if we can't help them fall into rank with the nominational phenomena we have already attempted to assemble.

Name Your Victim

Of all the *Ibis'* myriad victims who are paid, in their final moments, the brief compliment of a "straight" name, most can boast extenuating circumstances. Some straddle precariously the line between victim and victor; others are both, as active participants in their own demise (incest, suicide, self-harm); for yet others, the name does not do anything for the bearer, because it is too obscure to recognize or too confusing to resist conjecturing a textual alternative; or again, homonymy messes with the identification.[40] In all of these cases, there is a politics of naming that complements rather than crosses the trend above. The victim's attrition and attenuation can be guaranteed, that is, not only by depriving them of a name, but also by using their name against them.

Sisyphus is a good example of a character cutting across roles—and arguably, the fact that he wins a direct name says as much. When Ovid projects Ibis onto the various racks of the underworld, Sisyphus opens the catalog of the usual suspects, and he is, strangely, the only one roll called without fuss:

> Sisyphus est illic saxum volvensque petensque,
> quique agitur rapidae vinctus ab orbe rotae,
> quaeque gerunt umeris perituras Belides undas,
> exulis Aegypti, turba cruenta, nurus;
> poma pater Pelopis praesentia quaerit et idem
> semper eget liquidis semper abundat aquis.
> iugeribusque novem summus qui distat ab imo,
> visceraque assiduae debita praebet avi. (173–180)

Sisyphus is there, rolling and chasing his rock, and the one who is turned, pinned fast, by the circle of the hurried wheel, and the daughters of Belus, shouldering the water even as they lose it, the daughters-in-law of Aegyptus the exile, a bloody mob; Pelops' father makes for the fruit that is just there, permanently short and flush with running water. And the one who measures nine acres top to bottom offers his gut debt to the thorough bird.

Why should Sisyphus be the exception here? It might just be that Ovid is grooming him to be relieved of his duties, by the named (hence powerful) Aeacus:

noxia mille modis lacerabitur umbra, tuasque
   Aeacus in poenas ingeniosus erit.
in te transcribet veterum tormenta virorum:
   omnibus antiquis causa quietis eris.
Sisyphe, cui tradas revolubile pondus, habebis:
   versabunt celeres nunc nova membra rotae.
hic et erit, ramos frustra qui captet et undas:
   hic inconsumpto viscere pascet avis. (185–192)

Your offensive shade will be ripped up in a thousand ways, and Aeacus
will be inventive in making up your punishments. He'll transfer to you
the torture instruments of olden men: you'll be responsible for the peace
of all the old timers. Sisyphus, you'll have someone to whom you can
hand on your revolving burden: the quick wheels will now turn new
limbs. It'll be this man to grope for branches and waters in vain; this one
will feed the birds without ever running out of innards.

Sisyphus is singled out to stand in for the sinners liberated, and so he gets
the direct apostrophe. After Aeacus' "transfer,"[41] Ibis takes the place of all
these various underworld jailbirds and is anonymized appropriately (*cui . . .
hic . . . qui . . . hic*). Sisyphus' suffering is not long for that world. The rock
will "roll back" to a different porter. Revolution is in the air; hence, the
victim *can* be named.[42]

   Sometimes the victim is granted special status or has a duplicitous mythological identity bridging between victor and victim, which Ovid flags in
the naming. When Ovid piles up the body count for deaths by boar, Idmon
stands out from the rest by his name and epithet:

quique Lycurgiden letavit et arbore natum
   Idmonaque audacem, te quoque rumpat aper. (501–502)

The boar who finished Lycurgus' son, and the one born of the tree, and
daring Idmon, let it burst you as well.

Audax might tell us that Idmon didn't go down without a fight or, as Carol
Gordon notes, might mark his peculiar bravery as a seer who got on board
the *Argo* knowing full well he wouldn't come back.[43] At any rate, again it
is the prophet figure who gets full naming privileges. A few lines earlier,
Ovid had granted them to Cacus, a very different kind of victim:

> tamque cadas domitus, quam quisquis ad arma vocantem
>   iuvit inhumanum Thiodamanta Dryops,
> quam ferus ipse suo periit mactatus in antro
>   proditus inclusae Cacus ab ore bovis, (485–488)

> May you fall as absolutely beaten as whichever Dryopian it was who
> helped the barbarous Thiodamas when he gave the call to arms, and as
> ferocious Cacus himself died, massacred in his own cave, betrayed by
> the cry of a captured cow,

Again, the adjective, here combined with the added weight of *ipse,* seems
to bulk out Cacus as an especially worthy victim, an especially hard-fighting
loser. He was also a good figure turned bad: the Etruscan version of the
myth had him pegged as the hero of the story, the one from whom the
cows were stolen, until the Greek version massaged him into villain
status.[44] Both Cacus and Idmon, then, are lodged in their own special victims unit.

There is another exceptional category of named loser, which occupies
the winner space at the same time: and that is the people who do it to themselves. This particular blend of victim and perpetrator takes many forms in
the *Ibis.* There are suicides such as Sardanapallus (310), Haemon (559),
and Macareus (560), all assigned their names; pride-before-the-fall, don't-
know-your-own-strength figures such as Milo (323) or incautious souls
such as Elpenor (483), who end up killing themselves unwittingly; self-
harmers such as Attis (453), who end up actively emasculating themselves.
In at least two cases, the named self-harmers are explicitly chalked up as
their own worst enemies:

> muneribusque tuis laedaris, ut Icarus, in quem
>   intulit armatas ebria turba manus. (609–610)

> May you get harmed by your own gifts—as Icarus, on whom a drunk
> crowd laid armed hands.

> utve soror Pelopis, saxo dureris oborto,
>   ut laesus lingua Battus ab ipse sua. (583–584)

> Or like: Pelops' sister, may you stiffen with a sprung stone, or like: Battus
> himself, injured by his very own tongue.

Even though there are strictly other agents behind the downfall of the victims in both of these myths, Ovid puts it down to the victims *themselves*. This puts a slightly different (more worrying?) complexion on Ovid's own self-naming at the beginning, which also introduced a self-reflexive damage (*Nec quemquam nostri nisi me laesere libelli,/Artificis periit cum caput Arte sua*, 5–6).[45] Analogous to this kind of self-harm is incest, in which the victims and perpetrators often slide into one another. The "crime" can often seem like it comes from one's self, or an extended version of oneself, merely by virtue of falling so firmly within the family (e.g., father and daughter). As expected, the incest section has one of the heaviest densities of named "victims" in the poem:

> Byblidos et Canaces, sicut facit, ardeat igne,
>   nec nisi per crimen sit tibi fida soror.
> filia si fuerit, sit quod Pelopea Thyestae,
>   Myrrha suo patri Nyctimeneque suo.
> neve magis pia sit capitique parentis amica
>   quam sua vel Pterelae, vel tibi, Nise, fuit, (355–360)

May your sister burn, as she does, with the flame of Byblis and Canace, nor let her be trusted without committing a crime. If you have a daughter, let her be like Pelopea to Thyestes, or Myrrha to her father, or Nyctimene to hers. Don't let her be more goodly or tendering to her father's head than Pterelas' daughter was to him, or yours was to you, Nisus;

Byblis, Canace, Pelopea, Thyestes, Myrrha, Nyctimene, Pterelas, Nisus: this swarm of eight unvarnished names in as many lines is unprecedented in the *Ibis*. The heavy dose of reflexives (*suo . . . suo . . . sua*) tells us why: whether we put the daughter or father on the receiving end, these "crimes" of incest are a mode of self-harm, a species of "doing it" to oneself.[46] As such, they are allowed the power of the direct name.

By far the most common form of victim naming and shaming, however, is that which gets us no closer to the target it is supposed to finger. I mentioned earlier that the *Ibis'* systemic suppression of names perhaps qualifies it as an inverse of epic, insofar as it captures fates within couplets and tends not to pay its most famous heroes (such as Odysseus) even the most cursory of courtesies. But this extends to the flip side of such a project: Ovid not only tends to avoid famous names but actively pushes the most obscure ones into the harsh light of day. We have very little idea who the hell the following figures are: Aleuas (321), Milo (323), Adimantus (325), Theudotus (464), Macelo (473), Thasus (476), Brotea (515), Mamertas (546), Lycurgus (605). Often these figures are prime candidates for aggressive textual manhandling, and the context doesn't tend to help the sleuth work. If we were sure the following couplet were about Hipponax the iambic poet,[47] for example, we would be a little more confident in the conjecture *Athenin* (one of Hipponax's known targets) for the manuscript's *Athenas:*

> utque parum stabili qui carmine laesit Athenas [Athenin],
>   invisus pereas deficiente cibo. (521–522)

> Like: the one who assaulted Athens with off-kilter song, may you die, hated, from lack of food.

And even if we did settle on *Athenin,* we could still note that Ovid opts to clue Hipponax with his less famous target (Athenis, not Bupalus).[48] Something similar plays out as Ovid goes over the ground of death-by-dragging, where we have a relatively unknown duo of Eurydamas and Thrasyllus given pride of place over one of epic's biggest names (here, of course, suppressed):

> utque vel Eurydamas ter circum busta Thrasylli
>   est Larisaeis raptus ab hoste rotis,
> vel qui quae fuerat tutatus moenia saepe
>   corpore lustravit non diuturna suo, (329–332)

> And like: Eurydamas yanked three times around Thrasyllus' tomb by his enemy on Larissean wheels, or the man who ritually purified the walls (not long for this world) with his body, the walls he had often protected,

In the Ibidian scheme, "Eurydamas" trumps Hector![49] Then there are cases where we think we know who we are dealing with, only for Ovid to throw us out with a sneaky curveball:

> ut Sinis et Sciron et cum Polypemone natus
>   quique homo parte sui parte iuvencus erat, (405–406)

> Like: Sinis and Sciron and Polypemon plus son, and the figure who was half man, half bull,

The kicker here is that both Sinis and Sciron are alternatively identified in various traditions as "the son of Polypemon."[50] So, does that make us second-guess ourselves as to the "real" referents of both Sinis and Sciron, make us think that both designate different people of the same name? To this merry band of uncertain/unknown/multireferential names, we could add figures such as Pyrrhus (301), Glaucus (553–554), and Eupolis (528),[51] all of whom get doubles or triples, whether explicit or not. The point of all this is that Ovid is much freer with names that he knows will fail to designate, and hence to boost, their bearer. None of them are really cut out to perform their presumptive job of reference. Again, this could all quite easily be written off as Hellenistic fireworks, a Callimachean game of elevating the obscure and obscuring the elevated (cf. earlier in the introduction to this chapter). But game is not all it is. There is a lot more at stake in this poem's politics of naming, because of the project of social shaming humming ever away in the background. Ovid puts on show that even if a victim is named, it won't necessarily redound to the victim's glory—especially if the victim is otherwise unknown. Ibis, heads up: eventual revelation could be just another form of erasure.

I have tried to explain away most of the poem's named victims as special cases in different categories of limbo. But to end this section, I would like to focus on a place in the poem where victim naming seems to become more rule than exception: the end. At some point—and it is hard to nail it down exactly, because the poem runs on fluid and fuzzy logic—the system of naming seems to budge a little. Instead of wiping victim names left, right, and center, the intensity of the poem almost starts curdling into a more bitter *fixation*, something that will end up in the promise (if not delivery) of Ibis' true name (*nomen . . . verum*, 641) right at the end. Midway through the poem, Ovid signals clearly that the game of name suppression has something to do with killing Ibis' fame:

> aut eques in medii mergare voragine caeni,
>   dum modo sint fati nomina nulla tui. (441–442)

Or may you be a horseman mired midmud, so long as no name goes to your fate.

That is a key paradox of this anonymizing poem: Ovid wants Ibis to suffer but not at the expense of gaining notoriety from the fall. And yet a little later, he seems resigned to giving Ibis a certain infamy, and true *nomina* arrive with the declaration:

utque vel Evenus, torrenti flumine mersus
   nomina des rapidae, vel Tiberinus, aquae. (511–512)

Or like: Evenus, drowned in the rapids, or Tiberinus, may you give your
name to fast-flowing water.

So a nominal possession for all time might be admissible, as long as the
memory is painful. In like fashion, the poet Cinna crops up, a figure ruined
by his name (although he is left to stew anonymously here, like most of the
poem's poets):[52]

conditor ut tardae, laesus cognomine, Myrrhae,
   urbis in innumeris inveniare locis. (537–538)[53]

Like: the author of Myrrha the late, tripped up by his surname, may you
be turned up in a thousand city sites.

While these two moments are over in a flash (what moments in the *Ibis*
aren't?), I suspect that they quietly announce a breaking of the seal: the
signal that certain kinds of name can be *destructive* as well as empowering.[54]
And so, while this section harbors many candidates who bring up the problems of referentiality discussed earlier, we nevertheless have a string of *directly named* victims grating against the poem's previous direction of travel:
Evenus, Tiberinus, Broteas, Athenis, Orestes, Lycophron, Thyestes, Mamertas, the Glauci, Haemon, Macareus, Anaxarchus, Damasichthon, Battus,
Palinurus, Orpheus, Pentelides Lycurgus, Milo, Icarus, Aethalos. The run
culminates in an assonant barrage of victims beginning *R*—all of them famous, all of them named:

nec tu quam Rhesus somno meliore quiescas,
   quam comites Rhesi tum necis, ante viae,
quam quos cum Rutulo morti Rhamnete dederunt
   impiger Hyrtacides Hyrtacidaeque comes.
Cliniadaeve modo circumdatus ignibus atris
   membra feras Stygiae semicremata neci.
utque Remo muros auso transire recentes,
   noxia sint capiti rustica tela tuo. (627–634)

Nor may you sleep a sleep better than Rhesus, nor better than the companions (on the road, then in death) of Rhesus; nor better than those
whom the son of Hyrtacus and his comrade gave away to death, along

with the Rutulian Rhamnes. Or in the fashion of Clinias' son, engulfed
by pitch-black flames, may you cart your half-burned limbs to a death-
on-the-Styx. And as they were to Remus who ventured to jump the newly
built walls, may country weapons harm your head.

Rhesus wins two mentions in as many lines. Remus, the paradigmatic
Roman loser, gets his comeuppance without any beating about the nominal
bush.[55] But the new system is reflected best, I think, in the couplet about
Ramnes. Now it is the victim who occupies pride of place in the heroic
hexameter. And the assailants, Nisus and Euryalus, are boxed in the pentameter with a patronymic and a relational substitute made from the same
thing. This layout of *named* victim alongside *unnamed* perpetrators is extremely rare in the poem, and I would say it marks a new relationship, ac-
tivated, or at least highlighted, by the named company in the neighbor-
hood. Ovid is doing nothing less than giving Ibis a taste of what is to come
in the next poem:

> postmodo plura leges et nomen habentia verum,
> et pede quo debent acria bella geri. (641–642)

You'll read more later, material that bears your real name and composed
in the meter in which grim wars should be waged.

A taste of what it is like to be named, truly—all in a meter that cannot,
after all that, quite be named.

In this sense, the *Ibis* manages to play and win two serious games at the
same time. It deprives the vast majority of its injured, dead, or dying of the
consolation of their name, performing a sociological murder on them all
over again, a twist every bit as painful as the knife itself. It shows Ibis
what it is like to be unnamed and dangles the names of the powerful and
the obscure in front of him, showing him that he will never have this. On the
other hand, the poem also manages to give a hint, amped up toward the
close, of what it would be like to have that eternal *shame* hanging over you,
to be known forever as the loser in the pair, the Remus of the couple. The
cake is not just eaten and had. It is shoved down the unseen enemy's throat.
Gulp. Enjoy.

Indefinitely Maybe

We have plotted the implication of names and power: how the assignment or erasure of a name can give or take, depending on the context. In this last section, I want to explore briefly another side effect of anonymizing, which gives the poem a kind of magical reach beyond itself and then some: universality and replicability, through time and space.[56] Ovid leaves blanks not only as aggressive punctures but as holes of openness, "generative absences,"[57] to sprawl out the poem's reach and span.

The first 250 lines of the poem are mostly occupied with a bloated curse on Ibis, a prayer to every capable god in the area, and a quasi-ceremonial vow that Ovid will keep on hounding Ibis beyond life, into the afterlife, and beyond that too. This part of the poem is tailor-made to spread the word as far and wide and loud as possible, and one of the major ways of ensuring the scattergun dissemination is the heavy-duty use of indefinites. We have already glimpsed this as a technique of erasure when it comes to Ibis' name. Note how Ovid also rechannels the destructive energy of his earlier poetry, which (he claims) explicitly avoided targeting "just anyone":

nec **quemquam** nostri, nisi me, laesere libelli, (5)

Nor have my books harmed anyone (but me)

quisquis is est, nam nomen adhuc utcumque tacebo, (9)

Whoever he is (I'll still keep his name quiet in any way I can)

Ibis, *quisquis,*[58] becomes the very unspecified target Ovid has been avoiding up till now. But these indefinites tend to infect all the discourse around Ibis, not just his name.[59] The nameless invocation of Augustus folds out into the "always" and "everywhere":

huic igitur meritas grates, **ubicumque licebit,**
    pro tam mansueto pectore **semper** agam. (25–26)

So to him I'll give much-earned thanks for his soft heart, **forever, and wherever possible.**

Compare that with Ovid's pledge to keep hostile to Ibis, wherever possible:

at tibi, calcasti qui me, violente, iacentem,
    qua licet ei misero! debitus hostis ero. (29–30)[60]

But to you who kicked me while I was down, you maniac, **wherever I may**—you wretch—I'll be your dedicated enemy.

While these might be taken more as limiting caveats, setting Ovid within the manageable expectations of exile ("as much as I can, given my situation"), this section is also about wriggling out of that straitjacket through dedicated evasion of specifics. For example, Ovid envisages a nameless general reader who will pass all this on to Ibis, twice a year:

haec tibi natali facito Ianique kalendis
　non mentituro **quilibet** ore legat. (63–64)

Make this what you get on your birthday and Janus' Kalends, **whoever** reads with truth-talking lips.

This kind of vagueness is typical of rituals in poetry,[61] and Ovid will up the indefinites with his general instructions very shortly. For now, I merely want to note the basic point that Ovid wants to gift the *Ibis* a power of spatio-temporal locomotion, to make it travel, that is, beyond himself, beyond now—and the anonymous *quilibet* multiplies the places it might go.

Ovid makes sure to be equally exhaustive with the gods he summons.[62] Line 67 and the verses following list the lot, spatially (earth, sea, heaven) but also, weirdly enough, temporally:

denique ab antiquo divi veteresque novique
　in nostrum cuncti tempus adeste Chao, (81–82)

Lastly, gods—old and new, from ancient chaos right down to our own times, all of you—be here,

Ovid wants in on the job every divinity that is or was: old and new, from the beginning to now. He asks them *all* to fulfill everything he asks—but not just everything, more than everything, even the things he omits:

annuite optatis omnes ex ordine nostris,
　et sit pars voti nulla caduca mei.
quaeque precor fiant, ut non mea dicta, sed illa
　Pasiphaës generi verba fuisse putet.
quasque ego transiero poenas, patiatur et illas:
　plenius ingenio sit miser ille meo. (85–90)

All of you, one by one, favor my hopes; let no part of my prayer fall away. Whatever I pray for, make it happen, so he thinks them not my own pronouncements but the words of Pasiphae's son-in-law. Whatever punishments I skip, let him endure those as well: let him be fuller with horror than my talent can muster.

The indefinites *quaeque* and *quasque* are fitted to give a sense of the vastness of the litany itself but also the gaping black hole beyond the surface words of the poem. Indeed, there is a rhetoric of the unnameable here, bouncing off the eerie wish that the poem go beyond Ovid's authorship, that it be almost mistaken for the words of (the unnamed) Theseus. These indefinites help the megalomaniac project glide along no end. Among other things, this section is a prayer for a poem that is more than the author's words and more than its own words.

This push for the "beyond," to make the poem generally replicable and "multicontextual" outside the particular parameters of a one-off speech act, is part of the point of these lengthy preliminaries. Ibis' first and finest pseudonym, *quisquis,* actually comes back in full force a few lines later. Ovid slips back into the old clothes of the *Fasti,* the poem of festivals in which he had often played a ritual emcee,[63] and starts directing the virtual ritual back in Rome, telling everyone what to do without specifying who is to do the doing:

nulla mora est in me: peragam rata vota sacerdos.
　　quisquis ades sacris, ore favete, meis.
quisquis ades sacris, lugubria dicite verba,
　　et fletu madidis Ibin adite genis:
ominibusque malis pedibusque occurrite laevis,
　　et nigrae vestes corpora vestra tegant.
tu quoque, quid dubitas ferales sumere vittas?
　　iam stat, ut ipse vides, funeris ara tui.
pompa parata tibi est: votis mora tristibus absit:
　　da iugulum cultris hostia dira meis. (95–104)

No more dithering for me: I'll discharge the planned prayers, playing the priest. **Whoever** you are at these rites of mine, say it right. **Whoever** you are at the rites, speak the words of the dead, approach Ibis with your weepy wet cheeks: meet him with terrible omens, left feet first, and let black robes cover up your bodies. And as for you, why do you shrink from putting on some death-bands? Your funeral altar is already there, as you can see. Your procession is ready: no more delay for these grim prayers: offer up your throat to my knife, my monstrous sacrificial lamb.

Just as *quisquis ades sacris* is multiplied across the verses,[64] so we move from singular to plural (*dicite, adite, occurite, pedibusque . . . laevis, corpora vestra*):[65] Ovid's creative vision sees double, triple, more, turning the "whoever" into "everyone who" will partake of the rite across time. I read the indefinite as a kind of placeholder vacancy for a vast temporal spray and an open-rank position for any given occupier of the ritual repetition, because there is so much surrounding fuss about the timelessness of curse and hatred. *Semper* keeps rebounding,[66] reaching highest pitch in the curse of the fates/furies at 239–240 (cf. *semper* 26, highlighted earlier):

> "**tempus in inmensum** lacrimas tibi movimus istas,
>   quae **semper** causa sufficiente cadent." (239–240)

> "we've stirred those tears of yours right up **into the infinite future**; with a rich supply of causes, they'll fall **forever**."

This is a bid for the ritual time of unstoppable repetition, which transcends context. The fates/furies have removed the usual limits. And so we need as many candidates for *quisquis* as possible to do the job over those endless years.

So far we have seen how Ovid brings a flexible "whoever" onstage to do his bidding at distance of space and time. But he also makes use of an even broader "whatever," to make sure Ibis understands the completely conditionless nature of the rage, burning bright on the bottomless fuel of "no matter what." Ovid pledges a hot pursuit of Ibis even after his own death. He glories in the many forms that could take, indulging in every single eventuality (we will see the *sive* taken to another nth degree in the *Laus Pisonis*).[67] But he ends up as something so indefinite that "he" becomes a kind of "it":

> sive ego, quod nolim, longis consumptus ab annis,
>   sive manu facta morte solutus ero,
> sive per inmensas iactabor naufragus undas,
>   nostraque longinquus viscera piscis edet,
> sive peregrinae carpent mea membra volucres,

    sive meo tinguent sanguine rostra lupi,
  sive aliquis dignatus erit supponere terrae
    et dare plebeio corpus inane rogo:
quidquid ero, Stygiis erumpere nitar ab oris,
    et tendam gelidas ultor in ora manus. (143–152)

Whether I get eaten up by the long years (and hopefully not), or I get released by death of my own making, or get tossed as a shipwreck over endless seas, and a far-flung fish eats my innards, whether foreign birds pick at my limbs, or wolves color their mouths with my blood, or someone thinks it worthwhile to put me six feet under or give my useless body to a lowly pyre: **whatever I'm to be**, I'll press to burst out from the shores of the Styx, and I'll stretch chill hands to your face—your worst nightmare.

Again, the indefinite flings the poem beyond the Ovidian self, to an "after-life" of limitless possibles. The Ovidian soul colonizes territory beyond the strict limits of the *quisquis* or *quilibet* identity hitherto reserved for Ibis,[68] the reader, and the proxy practitioner of the sacrifice. Ovid could quite literally be *anything* after death, not just *anyone*.[69] When the same indefinite springs back a couple of lines later, it has a similar totalizing effect but with a key difference:

denique **quidquid ages**, ante os oculosque volabo
    et querar, et nulla sede quietus eris. (155–156)

At last, **whatever you do**, I'll fly before your face and eyes and wail, and you'll have nowhere to rest.

Ovid will be there whatever Ibis *does*. But the ordinary-sounding *quidquid ages* binds Ibis within the sphere of normal action. Ovid the whatever won't just *do* whatever it takes; he will *be* whatever it takes. Liberated from the bonds of the body while his foe pads along on workaday terrestrial toes, this Ovid can do it all—even fly.[70]

    These indefinites bring a slightly different brand of anonymity to the *Ibis*. Instead of scrubbing the antagonist and his covictims of all their precious social identity and controlling them with straitening buckles of substitute language, this anonymity takes the poem outside itself. It makes Ibis into anyone; lets the poem slip into any given reader; calls on every possible god; builds an endless imaginary iceberg of curse beneath the visible tip; invites whoever to perform the rite, forevermore; promises that no matter what Ibis does, Ovid will meet it by being whatever it takes.[71] While the traditional curse tablet is drawn with fairly bold contextual lines,[72] Ovid wants none of that. The point of this rage and fire is to flare beyond reasonable bounds of space and time.[73] In that sense, the praenomen of Ibis, *quisquis,* makes him into an everyman, as well as a nobody. The more targets you set up, the more chance you have of hitting them. Anonymizing doesn't just inflict damage; it multiplies it into collateral.

3

A Play without Names

Octavia

It is rather the cry of the whole human race than mine.

—Alfred, Lord Tennyson (in Knowles 1893)

Authorship, to put it glibly, authorizes certain lines of
interpretation. Anonymity sets criticism adrift.

—Sander Goldberg (2003: 26)

As we watched ibis writhe under the rack in Chapter 2, we saw
two connected forms of anonymity working side by side. The first was
a heavy antonomasia, a committed redaction of names designed to bury
the victims all over again and to inflict an equally grisly predeath fate of
social erasure on the bogeyman himself. The second was a kind of sprawl
tool: by making Ibis everyone and spreading the love (hate) across a wide
desert of indefinites, Ovid fans the poem's reach right out to its widest setting. These two possibilities of anonymity, let's call them destructive and
amplificatory, were resident already within the *Res Gestae*. But now it's time
for the *Octavia*. Cue those anonymities, stage left, stage right, truly about
to spark to life.

The *Octavia* can be thought of as the death knell on the Julio-Claudian
principate, just as the *Res Gestae* holds the position of birth certificate. This

is a play contracted to bury the last Julio-Claudian emperor, Nero, under the inchoate myth of his own monstrosity. And what a job it does. The play stages Nero's divorce of his first wife, Octavia, and subsequent marriage to his next target, Poppaea, over three solid days (before wedding, wedding, after wedding). Throughout, Nero plays the perfect tyrant, while Octavia, Seneca, and the Roman people vie for the martyr/hero(ine) position. While the ins and outs of the play's political message can be bunted around, one thing seems clear: this is a project of destroying Nero root and branch. The emperor gets his *damnatio* comeuppance. And it is partly with the help of those good imperial weapons of anonymity that the killer blow arrives.

The plot goes something like this. Octavia opens with a lament for her fate and solemnly swears her hatred of Nero to her trusty nurse. A chorus of brave Roman citizens then sings a nostalgic ode about early Romans kicking out tyrants—and speaking of tyrants, look what Nero did to his mother, Agrippina. The play launches regular flashbacks to the house traumas of the previous Julio-Claudian generation: Agrippina's death at the hands of Nero but also Claudius' death at the hands of Agrippina, Britannicus' (Claudius' son and Octavia's sister) assassination by Nero, and Messalina's (Octavia's mother and Claudius' first wife) fall to Claudius. Like a particularly dramatic mob soap opera, everyone in the family is killing everyone. Seneca next bursts onstage with a soliloquy on moral decline; Nero waltzes on as the climax to the story, orders some executions, and doesn't listen to a jot of Seneca's protreptic to clemency. Agrippina's ghost shivers into the next scene, predicting, of course, bad things on the horizon for Nero. Following that, Octavia leaves the palace. The chorus comes back, vowing in another ode to fight Poppaea's marriage with violence. Time to introduce Poppaea, who recounts a pretty gloomy dream to her nurse. The nurse palms it off with a positive spin. Another chorus—or perhaps the same one at war with itself (see note 84 in this chapter)—odes to Poppaea's mythical beauty. Messenger comes on to report a project of popular assault on statues of Poppaea, plus a looming attack on the palace. The second chorus then sings a reassuring ode: don't worry, revolutionaries can't beat Cupid. Nero froths himself into a rage to crush the revolt. Chorus (-es?) returns to point out that the support of the people can actually be harmful. Finally, there is a lyric exchange between Octavia—now poised for the boat to exile—and the chorus. The heroine's destruction is tied to Rome's historical trauma of repeatedly stabbing itself in the back. Curtain, applause, boos for Nero (hopefully).

Octavia can seem a simpleton of a play. Its language is more translucent than the Senecan norm, and it has always come in for criticism for being too repetitive, too symmetrical, too heavy-handed. But for a supposedly simple play, it has a very complex name problem. Over its long and checkered history, both title and author, the usual double act framing a given ancient text for responsible handling,[1] have both been in dispute. The play traveled down to us on the Senecan bandwagon, as part of the philosopher-tragedian's literary luggage, but it has since been definitively thrown off.[2] It is now pretty well agreed that what we have are the words of a clever *ignotus*[3] scribbled out at some point in the post-Neronian crush (though just how far "post" is still a tough bone of contention).[4] The "Octavia" part of *Octavia* has also caused problems. The misdirection of the name Octavia might have something to do with the disappointment so many readers have felt in embracing our one and only *praetexta* tragedy.[5] "Octavia" makes us think the spotlight will well and truly fall on the eponymous woman as tragic heroine, but in practice, the play's multiple and distributed focal points create a kind of centrifugal force at odds with that very centripetal title. This play, then, has labeling issues. We can't quite settle on a clean, art-exhibition-style paratext to stick next to it, to clear up those big questions of whom it's by and what it's about (not to mention when).

Instead of fretting over the various historicist traps of "securing" author, date, and context,[6] this chapter will attempt to show how important it is that we have no good answers to these questions. In other words, the *Octavia* makes something of its anonymity. The first way in which it does this is formal and "internal." This is a play that stands out in the crowd of ancient drama for the remarkable degree of its eschewal of proper names. Like the *Ibis,* it is a text that salivates over periphrasis. It defines its characters, and has its characters define themselves, through relationships and substitutes rather than names, all the while building a tight nexus of naming and power. The denial of names in the *Octavia* again helps to lubricate a form of universality or "timelessness."[7] Mythological and historical exempla are encouraged to crash into each other, because agents are reduced to replicable roles and shrunken into recurrent epithets.[8] But the *Octavia* also goes one better than the *Ibis* in combining the "internal" effects of anonymity with a spectacular—dare I say *deliberate*—"external" flourish. As we shall see, the fact that the *Octavia* shakes loose of author, date, and context actually lends it an eerie authority. It becomes a particularly effective piece of elite propaganda and a particularly convincing (if suspicious) claim to be a repository of "cultural memory,"[9] precisely because it could have been written by anyone. It is a piece of literary graffiti deriving its universalism from an implied collective of authorial possibilities. If it did belong to Seneca, it wouldn't have worked as well.[10]

The Nameless Heroine

The Octavia of the *Octavia* is a curiously name-starved figure. "Eponymous" would be putting it strongly. In contrast to her Senecan cousins (i.e., the protagonists of their respective plays) she seems to lack a key ingredient of identity performance. She never self-names in the way that a Medea might (*Medea nunc sum,* Sen. *Med.* 910).[11] In fact no one in this play does.[12] The *Octavia* is short on (bare of) characters who can name and assert themselves in the larger-than-life modality of Senecan tragedy. The name Octavia only pops up twice (both discussed later, in the section "Disambiguating"), and we have to wait most of the play for the first occurrence. What's more, this accords with the practice at large. The default of the *Octavia* is to prevaricate around naming the human figures of which it speaks. The odd name, again, glints only as exception to the rule.

The pattern starts from the top. Octavia's opening lament sets the action in the historical relief of family tragedy. She talks of her mother, Messalina, as *genetrix* (10); her stepmother, Agrippina, as *noverca* (21, then *illa, illa,* 23); her father, Claudius, as *pater* (25, 31); Agrippina again as her father's wife (*coniugis,* 31); and finally Nero as tyrant (*tyranno,* 33) in a strangely distant way,[13] as if the dramatis personae of her life were picked from a lineup in an anonymized declamation.[14] To be fair, it may not strike us as immediately out of the ordinary that Octavia would talk via relationships rather than proper names, especially of her nearest and dearest. But the strangest thing is that this opening monologue seems to set the tone for other characters whose speech we wouldn't expect to be so peppered with family connections. The nurse is the next to speak, and her style is just as vague:[15]

fulgore primo captus et fragili bono
fallacis aulae quisquis attonitus stupet,
subito latentis ecce Fortunae impetu
modo praepotentem cernat eversam domum
stirpemque Claudi, cuius imperio fuit
subiectus orbis, paruit liber diu
Oceanus et recepit invitus rates.
en qui Britannis primus imposuit iugum,
ignota tantis classibus texit freta,
interque gentes barbaras tutus fuit
et saeva maria, coniugis scelere occidit;
mox illa nati: cuius extinctus iacet
frater venenis, maeret infelix soror
eademque coniunx nec graves luctus valet
ira coacta tegere crudelis viri.
secreta repetit semper, atque odio pari
ardent mariti, mutua flagrant face.
animum dolentis nostra solatur fides
pietasque frustra: vincit immitis dolor
consilia nostra nec regi mentis potest
generosus ardor, sed malis vires capit.
heu quam nefandum prospicit noster timor
scelus, quod utinam numen avertat deum.[16] (*Octavia* 34–56)

Whoever is captive to the first thunderbolt, dumbstruck, stupefied by the brittle boon of a deceptive court—they should look to what the sudden assault of hidden fortune has done, the overturning of a house that was just now right up there, Claudius', his offspring too. The whole world was subject to his power; Ocean, free for so long up to then, obeyed him, and grudgingly received his ships. The man who first forced the yoke on the Britons, decked unknown straits with such fleets—he was safe among distant peoples and savage seas—died through his wife's crime; then she through her son's. His brother lies there, dead, poisoned; his unlucky sister-wife mourns and struggles to bury her deep grief, although forced to do it by her cruel husband's anger. She always makes for the inner rooms; both wife and husband burn with equal hatred, blaze with shared fire. My faith and devotion bring her grieving mind solace, but in vain; her sharp pain trumps my advice, and the highborn outrage of her mind is ungovernable—it even gets strength from the trouble. My fear is looking out for some big, unspeakable crime; may the gods' power turn it away.

We know this is a plague on Claudius' house, but otherwise the story is stripped of specifics. All the stars are there—Claudius (*en qui* . . .), Agrippina (*coniugis, illa*), Nero (*nati, viri, mariti*), Britannicus (*frater*), Octavia (*soror/eademque coniunx*),[17] half of the *mariti*[18]—but they are characterized first and foremost by relative positions rather than free-floating names. There is something particularly "in the family" about this incestuous tragedy, something particularly "unspeakable" (*nefandum,* one of the play's favorite Senecan concepts),[19] which attracts the agents into a world that dare not speak their names.

The *Octavia*'s quirk of name suppression has been noticed before and explained in various ways. For example, one scholar takes it as a sign of performance: the argument runs that speaker identities must have been clearly marked through visual cues (masks etc.) to make up for the gaping textual deficit.[20] But that line doesn't account for the many *offstage* agents who are left hanging in periphrastic no-man's-land. Nor does it explain the thematics of namelessness that crop up consistently. A brilliant example is the very next passage, where Octavia famously laminates herself with an obvious overlay of quotation:

Octavia: O mea nullis aequanda malis
       fortuna, licet
    repetam luctus, Electra, tuos!
    tibi maerenti
    caesum licuit flere parentem,
    scelus ulcisci vindice fratre,
    tua quem pietas hosti rapuit
       texitque fides:
    me crudeli sorte parentes
    raptos prohibet lugere timor
    fratrisque necem deflere vetat,
    in quo fuerat spes una mihi
    totque malorum breve solamen.
    nunc in luctus servata meos
    magni resto nominis umbra. (57–71)

Octavia: My fate can't be matched by any struggles—even if I bring up
    your trials, Electra! As you grieved, you were allowed to weep
    for your father's death, and to avenge the crime, with your
    brother playing avenger; your devotion and faith wrenched

> him from the enemy and hid him away. But my fear stops me
> mourning my parents, wrenched off in harsh fate, and forbids
> me to mourn my brother's death—he was my one hope, the
> short-lived balm for all my troubles. Now I'm left behind, a
> museum piece of grief, a penumbra of a mighty name.

Again we have family relations anonymized (*parentem, fratre, parentes, fratris*), but in this case the antonomasia beautifully solves the problem of repetition with a difference that the paradigm of Electra sets up.[21] Octavia is connected to Electra by the recurring relational terms of parent and brother, but they also show up just how much worse it is for her: both parents, Claudius and Messalina, lost (not just her father, as in the case of Agamemnon-Electra); her brother Britannicus murdered, rather than coming to her aid like another Orestes. The difference, I think, is also inscribed in the name use. Electra is allowed to stand on her own nominal feet, but Octavia is reduced to nothing more than the label on Lucan's Pompey (*stat magni nominis umbra* [Lucan *BC* 1.135] becomes *magni resto nominis umbra*).[22] At that point in Lucan, right at the beginning of the Pompey-Caesar civil war, Pompey was a great name and nothing more, and that was encoded in the punning onomastics of the tag ("the great," *magnus*). But Octavia is truly less than that, a shadow not of her own name, or her own making, but of *someone else's*—a name that isn't even *there*. She is more shadow, more remnant, more leftover (*stat > resto*) than her distant ancestor of "imperial victim," who at least had an identifier and laurels to lean back on. And so, fittingly, this heroine shall remain nameless proper. In a sense, this *is* Octavia's triumphant Senecan self-hailing moment:[23] but instead of a name, we get a shadow of (n)one.

So Octavia can't grant herself a name in the first person. But she is also mercilessly denied one in the second. No character addresses her by the name Octavia. The best she gets is something of this ilk:

> *Octavia:* Excipe nostras lacrimas, **nutrix,**
>　　　　　 testis nostri fida doloris.
> *Nutrix:*　Quis te tantis solvet curis,
>　　　　　 **miseranda,** dies? (75–78)

> *Octavia:* **Nurse,** take on my tears, be a trusty witness to my pain.
> *Nurse:* **Poor girl,** what day will set you free from such terrible woes?

The epithet *miseranda* keeps coming round on a conveyer belt, connecting Octavia to other sad cases of pity incarnate across the play (used of Claudius at 25, 340; Lucretia at 301; Cornelia at 881).[24] But as we saw in the *Ibis,* this kind of substitution saps the puppet through a constraining definition in a certain direction over others, although it also, in the *Octavia,* slicks comparisons *between* exempla: in this case, *miserand-* epithetically tethers Octavia to her father, Claudius, and seals the generational continuity. (More on this later.)

Much of the *Octavia*'s dialogue is taken up with a struggle for the right term. Because the play defies the proper name with such commitment, spaces are opened up for tendentious rollouts of ersatz titles. Octavia, it turns out, is expert at this. When the nurse, the optimist by trade, tries to plug her back into Nero with the term "husband" (*uirum*), Octavia immediately responds with a devastating linguistic divorce:

> *Nvtrix:* Dabit afflictae meliora deus
>   tempora mitis;
>   tu modo blando uince obsequio
>   placata **virum.**
> *Octavia:* Vincam saeuos ante leones
>   tigresque truces
>   fera quam saeui corda **tyranni!** (83–87)

> *Nurse:* A nice god will give better times to the stricken; you just play
>   placid, and win over your **husband** with sugared flattery.
> *Octavia:* I'll beat rabid lions and brute tigers sooner than the fierce
>   heart of this wild **tyrant.**

No more "husband." "Tyrant" is the name with which Octavia rechristens Nero, and she will stick to that term (as will we, by force of sympathy) for the rest of the play.[25] Note how she also manipulates Agrippina through a suite of relational names that the ghost herself will pick up and shuffle later on:

> *Octavia:* odit genitos sanguine claro,
>   spernit superos hominesque simul,
>   nec fortunam capit ipse suam,
>   quam dedit illi per scelus ingens
>   infanda parens.

> licet ingratum dirae pudeat
> >munere matris
> hoc imperium cepisse, licet
> tantum munus morte rependat,
> feret hunc titulum post fata tamen
> femina longo semper in aevo. (88–97)

Octavia: He hates people of noble blood, despises gods and humans
both; he can't take his own fortune, which his unspeakable
parent gave him, through an enormous crime. Although he
was ungrateful, nay ashamed, to have got this imperial power
as the gift of his terrible mother, although he repaid such a
service with death, this woman will nevertheless carry this
posthumous title forever, far into the future.

The *infanda parens* Agrippina (again, *infandus* marks namelessness as well
as "unspeakability")[26] becomes the *mater* whom Nero repays with death.
And the title she takes for committing that crime to give him everything is
nothing much more than *femina* (cf. *feminae,* 158; and Nero's *mulier,* 868),
the final insult. Octavia knows how to pick the generic shoe to fit, depending
on what aspect of these monsters she wants to bring out.

These early exchanges between nurse and Octavia are packed to the rafters with unnamed agents, making the situation (despite its familiarity) a
tough act to follow. The cognitive challenges are sometimes marked by the
litmus adjective *infandus/nefandus,* which, as earlier, becomes a key index
of the play's unmentionables: *auctor infandae necis* (i.e., Nero, 114), *iuvenis
infandi ingeni* (again Nero, 152), *spes nefandas feminae* (Agrippina again,
158). But usually, the barrage of roles and relations doesn't even allow us
the pause of a self-reflexive adjective. Often, the unspoken is just that: unspoken. Look at the way the *antilabe* between Octavia and nurse barrels
through almost every possible relationship in a few breathless lines:

Nutrix: Vince obsequendo potius immitem virum.
Octavia: Vt fratrem ademptum scelere restituat mihi?
Nutrix: Incolumis ut sis ipsa, labentem ut domum
>genitoris olim subole restituas tua.
Octavia: Expectat aliam principis subolem domus;
>me dira miseri fata germani trahunt.
Nutrix: Confirmet animum ciuium tantus favor.
Octavia: Solatur iste nostra, non relevat mala.

Nutrix: Vis magna populi est.
Octavia: Principis maior tamen.
Nutrix: Respiciet ipse coniugem.
Octavia: Paelex vetat.
Nutrix: Invisa cunctis nempe.
Octavia: Sed cara est viro.
Nutrix: Nondum uxor est.
Octavia: Iam fiet, et genetrix simul. (177–188)

Nurse: You should rather win over your resistant husband by cooing.
Octavia: Will that get him to replace the brother of whom he illegitimately robbed me?
Nurse: It will make you safe and allow you to restore the collapsing house of your father one day, with your very own children.
Octavia: The princeps' house is expecting someone else's children; the terrible fate of my poor brother drags me down with it.
Nurse: Let the full backing of the citizens reinforce your mind.
Octavia: It soothes my troubles—it doesn't reduce them.
Nurse: The people have a lot of power.
Octavia: The princeps has more.
Nurse: The man himself will look out for his wife.
Octavia: His mistress outlaws it.
Nurse: But everyone hates her, it's obvious.
Octavia: Her husband loves her.
Nurse: She's no wife just yet.
Octavia: Soon enough she will be—and a mother to boot.

Again, Octavia and nurse rub each other up the wrong way, starting with friction over biological versus marital allegiance: nurse tries to claim Octavia for the marriage via *virum,* but Octavia prefers to keep with her true brother, Britannicus.[27] Nurse responds to the biological with an appeal to Octavia's father; Octavia fires back with some more fraternal fatalism. Nurse changes tack to the people; Octavia trumps it with emperor. Nurse picks the emperor up, trying to bind him to Octavia as "wife" (*coniugem*); Octavia reminds her that there is a mistress in the way. Nurse wipes out mistress and writes Poppaea up as *invisa cunctis;* Octavia hits back with a preemptive linguistic marriage, promoting Nero to husband—of Poppaea, that is. Nurse corrects this future disguised as fait accompli, denying Poppaea the status of *uxor;* Octavia says she will be soon, as well as a *genetrix* (the very role that Octavia, in her plot-generating barrenness, will never be able to play). This is a dizzying miniature of a cycle through the full gamut of familial (and political) positions that sum to make up this dark drama. It is a special challenge to follow because the roles can contain a referential double-up (*frater* is Britannicus but also, in a prophetic sense, Nero, husband *and* brother? *Viro* is "Poppaea's husband" but also "mine," Octavia's?). But for us, the main point is that these eddies of headache are stirred by a studied observance of anonymity. It allows both characters to manhandle the agents in question, in just the way they want.

The dual between the nurse and Octavia buzzes on. Nurse tries convincing Octavia that this too shall pass with an anecdote about Nero's (unnamed) mistress Acte,[28] now flung from her pedestal in Nero's affections, plus a wee story about Juno weathering Jupiter's faddish love interests. She closes the sale with yet another appeal to certain family bonds, addressing Octavia with the words she wants her to be: a second Juno, the sister of Augustus, and a wife (219–221). Again, Octavia rejects the *terms* of the offer: she will stay focused on her dead brother (*fratris extincti,* 226) over her monster husband (*scelesti coniugis,* 225), making sure, by punning on *iungere* (*iungentur,* 222), that we understand *coniugis* here in the ironic sense. In case we felt that term carried too much intimacy, Octavia straightaway rectifies it: *nefandi principis* she calls him in 227, whereby Nero becomes the "unspeakable," unspoken princeps. She hauls him over the coals of *saevi ducis* (235) and *dux impius* (237) a few lines later. These terms flat out refuse to admit any familial or marital bond into Octavia's relationship with Nero. They stow the emperor far off where Octavia's hostility wants him, in the "political" (over the domestic) realm. But Octavia's devastating rejoinder to the nurse's conclusion plays the name game even more supremely:

> *Octavia:* utinam suorum facinorum poenas luat
> Nero insitivus, Domitio genitus patre,
> orbis tyrannus, quem premit turpi iugo
> morumque vitiis nomen Augustum inquinat! (248–251)

> *Octavia:* If only this Nero-wannabe paid the price for his crimes—the true son of Domitius, a tyrant of the globe, which he squashes beneath a disgraceful yoke, dirtying the name Augustus with his low-life behavior.

For the first time in the play, Nero is named—but only to show the name is a sham. This "Nero" is really a Domitius, a global tyrant (*tyrannus* again).[29] Far from the nurse latching onto Octavia as a *soror Augusti,* Nero can't even call himself Augustus. He devalues the very name. To the nurse's attempt at social glue, Octavia responds with a spray of the most caustic solvent: she is none of those things, because Nero cannot live up to any of his official names. Octavia makes sure to give him true ones.[30]

The nurse tries one last time to appeal to Octavia's nonexistent feeling for her "husband" (*mariti,* 255), or at least her fear of his anger. Octavia replies with yet another realignment of unnamed relations: she connects herself to the story of her mother, Messalina, where the imperial marital trouble all began (Claudius had got rid of her after she got hitched to Gaius Silius, while still married to Claudius). Relations/positions again, not proper names—all the better to slide Octavia into the drama one branch up the family tree (cf. *coniugis,* 261; *principis,* 266; *parens,* 266; *coniugem,* 268; not to mention a *caedem . . . nefandam,* 266). Nurse makes a last-ditch plea to Octavia not to bring up this Messalina comparison, not to stir up her mother's shade (271). And when the floor goes to the chorus for their first ode immediately after, they take a new tack, playing up Octavia's paternal rather than maternal line. Our heroine gets a brand-new name to match:

> *Chorus:* nec nova coniunx nostri thalamos
> principis intret, teneatque suos
> nupta penates Claudia proles.
> edat partu pignora pacis,
> qua tranquillus gaudeat orbis
> servetque decus Roma aeternum.
> Fratris thalamos sortita tenet
>   maxima Iuno,
> soror Augusti sociata toris
> cur a patria pellitur aula? (276–285)

> *Chorus:* Let no new wife enter our princeps' inner sanctum; let
> Claudius' child hold onto her hearth and home, her marriage.
> May she produce pledges of peace via childbirth, through
> which our tranquil world can smile, and Rome keep her
> everlasting glory. Juno the great keeps her brother's bed-
> chamber, that's her role; so why is the sister and marriage
> companion of Augustus being thrust from her father's house?

Octavia is here dubbed Claudia, because it is the daddy-daughter bond that the chorus wants to jack up.[31] As Claudius loyalists, this gang takes up the nurse's Juno analogy, and refits Octavia with the *soror Augusti* moniker, but makes sure to add that the palace still belongs to the father, Claudius. The chorus' thinking in this section is deeply paternal. It tries to rev itself up with an appeal to hereditary examples of ancient Roman manhood in action (*vera priorum/virtus quondam Romana fuit/verumque genus Martis in illis/sanguisque viris*, 291–294). The stories of Verginia and Lucretia are built in anonymously, for maximum convergence with the Octavia strand at hand (note especially *miseranda*, 301; and *tyranni*, 303). Both these heroines are classic republican victims used to dig out Octavia's moral high ground: Verginia, who is killed by her father, reportedly as a way of preserving her from the dastardly designs of Appius Claudius the Decemvir; Lucretia, who killed herself after suffering a horrific rape by the tyrannical last king of Rome, Tarquin the Proud. For both of these figures, the father-daughter relationship comes across strongly (*parentis*, 296; *nata Lucreti*, 302), which is bulked out even further when we do have a rare case of straight naming in the next exemplum: Tullia the *coniunx* of Tarquin gets an honorable mention for running over her father's (*parentis*, 306) body as a daughter (*violenta ... nata*, 308; incidentally, yet another *infandi sceleris*, 304). Although the parallels slip and slide a little, the main point to note is that the chorus is trying to restore paternal authority over Octavia, make Claudia subject to Claudius, like the possessive Pops of Verginia and Lucretia (with Tullia as the terrifying antitype). Again, a combination of antonomasia with the right familial relationships does the job of oiling the comparisons.

The masterpiece of this choral ode—the story of Agrippina's death—likewise musters ideological strength from its refusal to lend the main actors their names. The chorus masterfully papers over the gaping crack between Tullia and Nero by calling them *nata* (308) and *nati* (309) from one verse to the other. But the other terms brought on for the beginning of this Nero show are not exactly innocent:

> *Chorus:* "haec quoque nati videre nefas
>   saecula magnum,
>   cum Tyrrhenum rate ferali
>   princeps captam fraude parentem
>   misit in aequor." (309–313)

> *Chorus:* "These times too have witnessed a son's enormous crime—
> when the princeps took his mother by trickery and sent her
> out upon the Tyrrhenian sea in a deadly craft."

That pattern again: *nefas* with an unnamed agent, *nati*. But *princeps* and *parentem* tell us almost everything we need to know about how the chorus will color this story, before it has even told it. *Princeps,* the political, isolated term, in conjunction with the familial *parentem,* means that Nero rejects the parental claim on him implied by *nati* and *parentem*. *Princeps* distances him from his mother, in the same way that Octavia had used *princeps* to distance Nero from her. We can sense a kind of "synergy" between the chorus and Octavia already here. But the nominal practice of the rest of the Ode brings it home. Agrippina becomes *Augusta* in 328, the rightful possession and patron spirit of patrilineal principate, in the same way that Octavia was wrenched into the paternal orbit with *Claudia*. When Agrippina speaks, she riffs on Octavia's point about Nero failing to live up to the Augustan name:

> *Chorus:* "hac sum, fateor, digna carina,
> quae te genui, quae tibi lucem
> atque imperium nomenque dedi
> Caesaris amens." (334–337)

> *Chorus:* "I've earned this ship, I own it—because I gave birth to you,
> because I gave you the light, imperial power, and even (how
> crazy!) the name of Caesar."

But we notice the demotion: Agrippina keeps Augusta for herself and only gives Nero a Caesar (which she claims as hers to give).[32] She also hugs close to Claudius as Octavia has been doing, and the chorus with her:

> *Chorus:* "exere vultus Acheronte tuos
> poenisque meis pascere, coniunx:
> ego causa tuae, miserande, necis
> natoque tuo funeris auctor
> en, ut merui,
> ferar ad manes inhumata tuos,
> obruta saevis aequoris undis." (338–344)

> *Chorus:* "Pull your eyes up from Acheron and feast them on my
> punishment, my husband: I, the driving force behind your

> murder, poor man, the source of your son's death—look, I've
> earned it, I'm brought to your shades without a grave, buried
> only in the rough waters of the sea."

Miserande reprises Octavia's own epithet for her father in her opening speech (line 25), and, as mentioned earlier, the adjective will stick to Octavia herself on several occasions. The similar *miserae* cleaves to *parentis* for Agrippina again in 364 (cf. *matrem*, 362; and *nefas*, 363), to ham up the perversity of son finishing off his maker. And when Agrippina invites the last straw, she builds on Octavia's good abusive work by calling Nero *monstrum* (371—making *tyrannus* pale in comparison). We can see, then, how these networks of moral clarity play out so effectively *because* the characters are never named. Agrippina and Octavia are bonded together, through a mutual connection to husband and father, Claudius. Quarantined on the side of pure evil is Nero the bad husband, bad son, nasty princeps, and outright *monstrum*. The terms do all the relational tunneling, forming wormholes in the fabric of the play. In other words, anonymizing makes for a formidable system of intratextual networking, forming clear linguistic alliances, drawing bold lines in the sand.[33]

We have so far seen some related dynamics play out under the umbrella of dedicated anonymity: characters either trying to forge or break allegiances according to the terms they pick; "roles," rather than names, easing the blend of characters and generations; and a new form of anti-Senecan protagonist, who willfully withdraws into the penumbra of namelessness. From these patterns among women and chorus, I want now to kick onto the men. We shall see that the name takes on yet more weight and measure when Seneca and Nero enter stage left.

Power Names

Up to now, I have tried to show that this play's default mode is essentially an anonymous one. Characters avoid names like the plague, in order to swing their usual bearers in particular directions. When Seneca hits our screens, his long-winded set piece on moral decline doesn't seem much of a departure from the status quo. This soliloquy is a repackaging of the myth of races, from gold to iron, past to present, and it sticks firmly to a very general plane—until the specific culmination of Nero comes on right at the moment when vice has reached its zenith. Seneca's tendency to speak in philosophical abstracts[34] here almost removes the space for historical agents completely. We are now operating in a higher, less human sphere. And the modulation is ticked in the transfer of the key term *parens* (385) to "mother nature," whom the iron race of humankind has butchered in exactly the same way as Nero lovingly finished off his own mother.[35] Seneca tends to speak in terms of broad-brush generations (*aetas*, 417) or vague divine presences (*virgo Astraea*, 424) or moral forces (*luxuria*, 427, 433)[36]—but nothing much in the way of concrete, named entities.

We are in for a shock, then, when suddenly a character gets the call-up with the play's first unproblematic case of straight naming:

Seneca: Sed ecce, gressu fertur attonito **Nero**
trucique vultu. quid ferat mente horreo. (435–436)

Seneca: But look: **Nero** is coming, his gait upset, his face fierce. What he has in his mind, I can't bear to think.

It is hard to capture quite how radical, how explosive this moment is. After 434 lines of committed mincing,[37] wham! Nero arrives, and *Nero* he is called.[38] But that is not the monster's only privilege. As soon as he is announced, he himself is given free rein over the naming of others:

Nero: Perage imperata: mitte, qui **Plauti** mihi
Sullaeque caesi referat abscisum caput. (437–438)

Nero: Carry out these orders: send someone to kill **Plautus** and **Sulla**. Chop off their heads. Bring them to me.

Plautus and Sulla, off with their heads![39] Within four brief lines, we are treated to a veritable explosion of names—and all of them, no coincidence, cluster around the tyrannical cloud of Nero himself: the named, the namer.

The stichomythic mirror piece that follows between Seneca and Nero flashes us the monster in the flesh, and we see how he really is everything Octavia and the chorus painted him to be, and more—quite literally, in fact. Nero's self-naming as *princeps* (456) and *Caesar* (457) tell us he conforms perfectly to the prefab caricatures of Octavia and Agrippina, for these are *their* terms. In fact, when Nero isn't devastating his aristocratic male targets with the cold steel of direct naming (*Plautum atque Sullam*, again at 465), he proves himself a canny recycler of other people's substitute terms.

When time comes to mention Octavia herself, the intratextual effects are boosted, again, by the namelessness:

> *Nero:* tollantur hostes ense suspecti mihi,
> invisa coniunx pereat et carum sibi
> fratrem sequatur. quidquid excelsum est cadat! (469–471)

> *Nero:* Anyone under suspicion of being my enemy should be removed
> by sword; my hated wife must die, must follow her beloved
> brother. Whatever towers high must fall.

Octavia called herself "hated by husband" (*coniugi invisa,* 104). Nero deftly transfers the entire linguistic unit to her and yanks *invisa* back from its assignment to Poppaea (Nurse: *Invisa cunctis nempe,* 187), reverses Seneca's charge (*invisum . . .* , 455), all the while changing the recipient of *carus* from Poppaea to Octavia's beloved brother (Octavia: *Sed cara est viro,* 187 becomes Nero: *carum sibi/fratrem,* 470–471). As well as being able to deploy names with unparalleled precision, Nero is expert at picking these substitutes up and flinging them right back.[40] He is, in a sense, a master manipulator of the controlling verbal echo.

It is precisely to this sensitivity for naming as power that Seneca plays in his rejoinder to Nero, the good mirror of the prince discourse lopped from the *De Clementia*.[41] As many readers have noted, Seneca is the nurse of this scene, attempting to play moderator and brake on his advisee's overzealousness.[42] Like his earlier counterpart did with Octavia, he attempts to redefine Nero through choice language. Nurse had wanted Octavia to stick to her guns as *coniunx*. Seneca, on the other hand, wants Nero to become the nurturing *parens* of his moralizing, not to mention the "true Augustus" whose name Octavia quarantined from Nero:[43]

> *Seneca:* haec summa virtus, petitur hac caelum via.
> sic ille patriae primus Augustus parens
> complexus astra est, colitur et templis deus. (476–478)

> *Seneca:* This is virtue supreme; one makes for heaven by that route. This
> way, that first father of the fatherland, the original Augustus,
> clasped the stars, and is worshipped in temples—as a god!

And just as the chorus made of Octavia a daddy's little girl for its own ideological ends, so Seneca here tries to turn Nero into a *father* pure and simple:

> *Seneca:* tu pacis auctor, generis humani arbiter, (488)
>   patriae parens: quod nomen ut serves petit
>   suosque cives Roma commendat tibi. (490–491)

> *Seneca:* You are the guarantor of peace, the umpire of humankind,
>   father of the fatherland: Rome asks you to keep to that name
>   and charges you with her citizens.

These titles, themselves granted by fathers (*iudicio patrum* 487), run in ascending order: *patriae parens* is the climax, the true *nomen* that Seneca tries to nudge Nero into satisfying. But Nero has very different ideas about what *nomina* can do:

> *Nero:* servare cives principi et patriae graves,
>   claro tumentes genere, quae dementia est,
>   cum liceat una voce suspectos sibi
>   mori iubere? **Brutus** in caedem ducis,
>   a quo salutem tulerat, armavit manus;
>   invictus acie, gentium domitor, Iovi
>   aequatus altos saepe per honorum gradus,
>   Caesar nefando civium scelere occidit. (495–502)

> *Nero:* Protecting citizens who are a nuisance to princeps and country
>   both, swollen with pride in their noble lineage—what kind of
>   madness is that, when it's in my power to sentence suspects to
>   death with one single word?! **Brutus** armed himself to kill the
>   leader who saved him; no defeats in battle, conqueror of
>   peoples everywhere, matched with Jupiter through a constant
>   string of high offices, Caesar died by an unspeakable crime at
>   the hands of *citizens*.

What is that single word, *una vox*, the word of death? I would wager it is nothing more or less than the victim's *name*—a chilling truth that Nero mimes in his immediate revenge reference to Brutus, plain and simple. Nero in fact takes back the power of "Augustus" and identifies it with a logic of *proscriptive*,[44] rather than protreptic, naming:

> *Nero:* Quantum cruoris Roma tunc vidit sui,
>   lacerata totiens! ille qui meruit pia
>   virtute caelum, divus Augustus, viros
>   quot interemit nobiles, iuvenes senes,

　　　sparsos per orbem, cum suos mortis metu
　　　fugerent penates et trium ferrum ducum,
　　　tabula notante deditos tristi neci! (503–509)

Nero:　Then Rome saw a huge amount of her own blood flow—she
　　　was gashed so often! He who earned his position in heaven by
　　　"dutiful virtue," "divine Augustus"—how many nobles did *he*
　　　kill, both young and old! They were flushed all over the world
　　　as they fled their homes and the steel of the triumvirate out of
　　　fear for their lives; a billboard listed those marked for a
　　　horrific death!

The sinister *tabula* registers and performs the deaths of these menacing *nob-iles* precisely by naming them. We now see, perhaps, why the play gave us Plautus and Sulla[45] as (almost) the tyrant's very first words. Nor is *Augustus* the only word Nero flips to his own devices.[46] He also laughs in the face of Seneca's attempt to make him a father, by glorying in the grim spectacle shoved in the *patres'* line of sight:

Nero:　exposita rostris capita caesorum patres
　　　videre maesti, flere nec licuit suos,
　　　non gemere dira tabe polluto foro,
　　　stillante sanie per putres vultus gravi. (510–513)

Nero:　Fathers in mourning saw the heads of the assassinated
　　　displayed on the rostra; they couldn't even weep for their
　　　own, nor lament in the forum, tainted as it was with disgusting
　　　gore, chunks of pus dripping down their rotten faces.

The *patres* are chewed up and spat out as the *putres* (*vultus*) they are forced to feast their eyes on. Nero can pun,[47] as well as name, his sparring partner into the ground.

　　After a brief nod to Augustus' victory in the civil wars (incidentally, Nero collaborates nicely with the unnaming strategies of *RG*, passing over Antony periphrastically),[48] the two settle back to a familiar dynamic. Seneca scrubs Octavia up as Claudius' daughter, and a Juno analogue (534–535), tying himself yet again to the arguments of nurse and chorus. Nero strikes back with a line of unrelating:

　　Incesta genetrix detrahit generi fidem,
　　animusque numquam coniugis iunctus mihi. (536–537)

The impure mother makes the family line unreliable, and my wife's mind has never been truly "married" to mine.

Once more the riff is on Octavia's words and concerns the term *coniunx:* as Octavia had done with *iungere,* so here Nero affects a *disjoining* of his spouse via an even more intense version of the pun (*coniugis iunctus*). And so it continues. Seneca's verbal acts of marriage in response—his words, namely, pushing the role and relation of the ideal wife (*coniugis,* 547)— are brushed off by Nero. The conflict then moves up a few notches into a debate about the definition of love, Cupid/Amor, which Nero terms (tell-ingly) a *tyrannus* like himself (555). Seneca thus tries both father and wife as ways into the impenetrable Neronian armor—and although it becomes fairly clear he won't budge, that doesn't stop Seneca from making one more downtrodden appeal to both:

> *Seneca:* facile opprimetur. merita te divi *patris*
> aetasque frangat *coniugis,* probitas pudor. (586–587)

> *Seneca:* It will be crushed, no problem. Your debts to your deified
> father, your wife's youth, unimpeachability, modesty—let them
> bend you.

Bearing in mind the politics of naming in this section, Nero's dismissive re-sponse couldn't be more damning:

> *Nero:* Desiste tandem, iam gravis nimium mihi,
> instare! liceat facere quod Seneca improbat. (588–589)

> *Nero:* Stop insisting, enough already. This is already too much for me.
> I can do what Seneca vetoes.

What that "Seneca" does is not only reject the natural bonds of second-person address (distancing the interlocutor and ringing a composition with Seneca's scene-opening declaration *Nero*) but tell us, in no uncertain terms, that *Seneca* will be next. It also explains why Nero evades naming Poppaea in the subsequent lines, shepherding the future mother of his child with soft billowy antonomasia.[49] Seneca isn't so lucky. This tyrant, we remember, has the proscriptive gift. One word, and you are as good as Plautus and Sulla (. . . dead).

Nero proves more than a match for Seneca (and Octavia) in his quick-fire manipulation of name fillers. But he is also the first character in the play to have the terrifying red button of direct naming squarely under his thumbs. It will take the ghost of his mother to clue us into his weak spot—and give us yet another window onto the *Octavia*'s breathtaking nominal gymnastics.

Damnatio Neronis

Nero has the last word in the scene with Seneca, and the tyrant ends up where he was going all along: the point of Poppaea is motherhood, Neronian reproduction, the generation of a little *"partem mei"* (591). The *Octavia*'s scene transitions tend to "grow" or "generate" using the very nodes of familial relationships we have been tracking thus far. This transition is one of the tightest. For no sooner does Nero talk of motherhood, the *uterus* of Poppaea (591), than the echo backfires, and on marches the very *uterus* (recall *utero,* 370) that produced him (and died by him): yes, finally, the ghost of Agrippina herself.

Agrippina's ghost speech heralds the new dawn of Nero and Poppaea's wedding day—but ushers it in with a prophetic curse, rather than a blessing. The ghost comes straight from the underworld to rain down fire-and-brimstone pledges of revenge on Nero. Hell hath no fury like a mother killed. Her speech picks up on the mother-son relationship straightaway. While Poppaea gets a rare name (so far the only other occurrence has come from the mouth of Nero; is this another signal of her meteoric rise?), Nero is hemmed in to the generic evil son role (*nato,* 596; marked by *natique crudelis nefas,* 603; cf. *nefas,* 605). But the only thing Agrippina is nursing nowadays is her hatred in the underworld, and once again the choice term *tyrannus* (610, 620) for Nero puts her squarely with the Octavia-chorus axis. But there is also a hint of a new application for anonymity here:

> *Umbra Agrippinae:* sanguine extinxi meo
> nec odia nati: saevit in nomen ferus
> matris tyrannus, obrui meritum cupit,
> simulacra, titulos destruit memores mei
> totum per orbem, quem dedit poenam in meam
> puero regendum noster infelix amor. (608–613)

> *Agrippina's ghost:* But my blood didn't get rid of my son's hate: the
> rabid tyrant goes wild against his mother's name,
> wants my contributions eliminated, destroys the

>statues and inscriptions, vehicles of my memory all
>over the world—that world that my cursed love
>gave him to govern as a boy, ultimately, to my own
>cost.

Agrippina picks up on Nero's campaign of *abolitio:* the job to chisel his mother out of Rome's material record. But Agrippina importantly phrases this as a crime against her *name.* Nero is deleting her inscribed name, all over the world. As payment in kind from the spooky vantage point of death, she does him the favor of deleting *Nero,* and replacing with *tyrannus.*[50]

The link between these two strands—let's say, material memory sanctions and the refusal to name in a dramatic speech—might seem too subtle to entertain.[51] But as Boyle rightly spotlights, Agrippina's name is wiped from the play (as is Messalina's—a historical object of official memory sanctions).[52] It is precisely this traffic between dramatic antonomasia and *damnatio memoriae* that Agrippina plays on at the end of her prophecy, the famous counterfactual excursion into child mortality:

Umbra Agrippinae: utinam, antequam te parvulum in lucem edidi
aluique, saevae nostra lacerassent ferae
viscera: sine ullo scelere, sine sensu innocens
meus occidisses; iunctus atque haerens mihi
semper quieta cerneres sede inferum
proavos patremque, **nominis magni** viros—
quos nunc pudor luctusque perpetuus manet
ex te, **nefande,** meque quae talem tuli. (636–643)

Agrippina's ghost: If only—before I'd even brought you into the light
as a little one and nurtured you—wild beasts had
ripped up my womb: you would have died an
innocent child of mine, minus crime and awareness;
joined, even clinging to me in a quiet patch of the
world below, you would be watching your ancestors
and father forever, men **of great name**—now infinite
shame and grief awaits them, because of you, **my
unspeakable,** and me, who bore such a thing.

Agrippina's brief fantasy restores the same paternal relations that Seneca had daydreamed about in his exchange with Nero. But it also doles out that familiar tag *nominis magni*,[53] to show how far Nero falls beneath the great-name fathers he would be forced to sit down and watch, an abortive Ascanius playing an Aeneas in the underworld of *Aeneid* 6 (forever).[54] Agrippina's parting shot—*nefande*—is an address that reflexively deprives Nero of the great name these proper *viri* possess. It is a brilliant nod to the ineffability of this monster. What Agrippina is doing here, I think, is something like performatively turning Nero into the very nameless nonentity into which Nero would like to see *her* ground down. This is Agrippina's instant revenge, brokered well before the sword even hits the throat.

Agrippina clues us into a broader function for the heavy anonymizing ways of the *Octavia*. A lot has been propped lately on the subject of the play as a form of *abolitio* in itself: we can read the *Octavia* against the curtain coming down on Nero, indeed read it as a key intervention into the tradition-in-the-making of casting Nero as monster.[55] This is certainly true, and we shall make space later to discuss how the play's "external" anonymity, as well as its claim to voice the position of the chorus, makes it an especially cutting and cunning piece of elite propaganda. But the play also, on cue with Agrippina's prophecy, performs an internal erasure of Nero's name that mimics the scrubbing of reviled figures from the material record. So many times when the playwright could have said *Nero,* he opted for something like *tyrannus* instead. Such striking out and overwriting is a *damning* two-pronged attack.

Disambiguating

When time comes (and it comes soon) for Octavia to face the music of her divorce and *substitution* (yet another way to conceptualize the namelessness of this play about replacing one with another), she gives Nero a brief ironic send-off with *saevi . . . coniugis* (654–655) and *diri . . . viri* (661). She dispatches the mistress Acte—or could it actually be Poppaea?!—with the dismissive *famulae* (657).[56] But she also plays around with her own self-address, upholding the tradition of *miseranda,* while performing another divorce speech act, a card we shall see Nero play shortly: *soror Augusti, non uxor ero* (652; cf. Nero's *sororis,* 861). Next up, the chorus gives itself a pep talk to take some destructive action and again gives Octavia her pet name *Claudia*.[57] It also picks up *diri* for Nero, but interestingly, at this moment of truth, the happy couple are allowed to sign the register, not once:

Chorus: cessit thalamis
Claudia diri pulsa **Neronis,**
quos iam victrix **Poppaea** tenet, (671–672)

Chorus: Claudius' daughter is on her way, driven from **Nero's** marriage chambers, which **Poppaea** the Conqueror now keeps,

But twice:

Chorus: gravis en oculis undique nostris
iam **Poppaeae** fulget imago,
iuncta **Neroni!** (683–684)

Chorus: All over the place, hard in our eyes—look around!—**Poppaea's** image flashes, married to **Nero's.**

As we are seeing more and more, the seething power play of the scenario is written through the names.[58] Nero and Poppaea are in fact the most heavily named characters of this largely nameless play (Nero winning seven mentions, Poppaea six), and that roughly maps onto their power/favor/fortune in the dramatic instant of the play. But these two sets of married names also tell us something about the people who speak them, the chorus. Clear naming is nigh on a miracle in the *Octavia*. The only other time we got two in a row like this was when Nero plucked Plautus and Sulla out of thin air (437–438; then again at 465). Importantly, the chorus is given almost equivalent naming rights. And it is, right this moment, pumping up to give Nero his worst headaches of revolt in the course of the plot. The ominous—and easy—identification of man and wife here undergirds the suspicions we were starting to have anyway: that the only figure in the play who can hope to match Neronian violence, however temporarily, is this bursting collective in revolt.

The nominal climax of the play pivots about another exceptional case of clear naming, and this time it is the other mirror scene of the opener: Poppaea and her nurse. This scene features a brilliant exchange involving Poppaea's dream of an unhappy end for a husband and the nurse's creative misreading of what it all might mean. Poppaea—feeling all comforted in her bedchamber by the named Nero's (*Neronis,* 716) affectionate spooning—suddenly falls headlong into a nightmare of mourning matrons, with a zoom on Agrippina wielding a bloody torch amid the racket. The rest of the dream (like most ancient dreams) is wreathed in nebulous language but through that very obscurity curtly condenses some of the play's problems with family ties, incest, self-destruction:

> *Poppaea:* quam dum sequor coacta praesenti metu,
> diducta subito patuit ingenti mihi
> tellus hiatu; lata quo praeceps toros
> cerno iugales pariter et miror meos,
> in quis resedi fessa. venientem intuor
> comitante turba coniugem quondam meum
> natumque. properat petere complexus meos
> Crispinus, intermissa libare oscula,
> irrupit intra tecta cum trepidus mea
> ensemque iugulo condidit saevum Nero. (724–733)

> *Poppaea:* While following her, forced on by pressing fear, suddenly the
> earth split into a huge crack; sucked in headlong, I am
> stunned to see my marriage bed, on which I recline, tired out.
> I then see my ex-husband and son approaching, with a crowd
> in tow. Crispinus makes straight to embrace me and starts
> showering me with kisses again. At that point Nero burst
> into my house, agitated, and buried a cruel sword in a throat.

Even though two solid names (Crispinus and Nero) poke out of the muck here, it doesn't actually help us work out the agents.[59] Both Poppaea's former husband and son are called Rufrius Crispinus,[60] so glossing Crispinus makes no headway on identification; similarly, one of the *cruces* of the play is about whose throat (Nero's or Crispinus') Nero is stabbing here, left provocatively unclear despite the assassin's name crowning the verse (*Nero*, 734). We are still deliberately in the dark when Octavia talks of the *cruorem coniugis* (739) to cap her speech—a husband's blood, but which husband?

The stage is set for the nurse's spectacular disambiguation. But she won't disambiguate what we think she will:

> *Nutrix:* coniugem thalamos toros
> vidisse te miraris amplexu novi
> haerens mariti? sed movent laeto die
> pulsata palmis pectora et fusae comae?
> **Octaviae** discidia planxerunt sacros
> intra penates fratris et patrium larem.
> fax illa, quam secuta es, Augustae manu

praelata **clarum nomen** invidia tibi
partum ominatur; inferum sedes toros
stabiles futuros spondet aeternae domus.
iugulo quod ensem condidit princeps tuus,
bella haud movebit, pace sed ferrum teget. (742–753)

Nurse: You're surprised you saw your husband, marriage chamber, and bed, while you were embedded in the arms of a new husband?! But the sight of beaten breasts and loosed hair on a happy day upsets you? They were thumping in mourning for *Octavia's* divorce, inside her brother's sacred hearth, her father's house. The torch you followed, held up high in the Augusta's hand, presages **fame and name** for you, born out of envy; the underworld address assures you there'll be stable marriage beds in an everlasting home. Your princeps buried a sword in a throat—that means he won't cause wars but will sheathe the sword in peace.

Just as that *Nero* of Seneca's sent shockwaves coursing through us after reams of antonomastic verse, so now, after 745 lines, we are stunned to find our heroine finally gifted her true name (albeit in a context where the name behind *fratris* retreats into the woodwork).[61] *Clarum nomen*[62] in close proximity makes an occasion out of it; it becomes a way of bolding the play's biggest moment of direct naming. But it is telling that one of only two times Octavia comes up (see the next paragraph for the second, on line 786), it is in a context of deft manipulation of the brand. Nurse is doing everything she can to make the disturbing elements of this dream *not* about Poppaea but about *Octavia*. She *needs* to be named. As for *our* key confusion—namely, whose throat—the nurse gets us no closer to enlightenment: *iugulo*. But whose *iugulum?*[63] She hedges with the throat.[64] But about the "target" of the dream's ominous vulture-circling, she makes sure there is no mistake.

The only other time Octavia's name comes up is in another context of "clarification." After the people's revolt breaks out offstage, the messenger runs on in a huff to report the situation to the chorus leader. When he asks the source of the chaos, the *nuntius* has to give it to him straight:

Chorus: Quis iste mentes agitat attonitus furor?
Nuntius: Octaviae furore percussa agmina
et efferata per nefas ingens ruunt. (785–787)[65]

> *Chorus:* What is this thunderbolt of rage stirring their minds?
> *Messenger:* Rage for Octavia—the crowd are crazed with it, wildly
> hell-bent on some great outrage.

Note again the ironic proximity of *nefas*. But it is clear again from the subsequent return to the natural linguistic order of Octavia—namely, the suppression of the name Octavia—that this is another one-off, for the *nuntius* wheels out *Claudia* again, twice, in a jiffy:

> *Nuntius:* reddere penates Claudiae divi parant
> torosque fratris, debitam partem imperi. (789–790)
> *Messenger:* They're preparing to restore Claudius' daughter her divine
> father's home, the marriage to her brother, and her deserved share of imperial power.

> *Nuntius:* saepire flammis principis sedem parant,
> populi nisi irae coniugem reddat novam,
> reddat penates Claudiae victus suos. (801–803)
> *Messenger:* They're preparing to surround the princeps' house with
> fire, unless he returns his new wife to the angry mob, gives
> up, and returns her rightful home to Claudius' daughter.

Both of these uses polemically focalize the people's viewpoint by calling her Claudia,[66] a name cut to link its bearer to those domestic, paternal *penates*. No sooner is Octavia *Octavia* than she is returned to *Claudia* once more.

What both of these moments of necessary disambiguation throw up is this: Octavia is never allowed to float free, to be named as herself, *called* independently to function as an agent in her own right. The first time her name pops us, she is nothing more than an interpretative pin; the second time, nothing more than an explanatory tool. Both times she is in the objective genitive, rolled on merely as qualifier for the more important noun. For the brief moments she is allowed to stand with a modicum of nominal independence, she is still the relative of something, someone else.

The Making of a Sister / Woman / Enemy / Citizen

We have seen how Octavia—bar a few explicable slips—serves as the play's talisman of anonymity. She is the paradigmatic victim—and paradigmatic paradigm—because she carries so many substitute names, each of which seeks to make her into the thing she is called (*miseranda, coniunx, soror*) or blend her into something else (Claudia, Juno, etc.). The next phase in this saga of manipulations comes from Nero himself. His tête-à-tête with the prefect, as with Seneca before, borders on the magisterial. While before we saw him strut his ability to name, his second and final scene shows us just how deeply he has mastered the power of anonymity.

Nero explains his decision to junk Octavia with the same pair of epithets she used of herself earlier:

> Nero: et **illa,** cui me civium subicit furor,
>   suspecta **coniunx** et **soror** semper mihi,
>   tandem dolori spiritum reddat meo
>   iramque nostram sanguine extinguat suo. (827–830)

> Nero: And **that woman,** to whom citizen rage would have me
>   beholden, that **wife** and **sister,** ever suspect to me, must at
>   last give her life to my anguish and put out my anger's fire
>   with her blood.

Importantly, she is *illa . . . coniunx et soror, that* wife (and sister), the other wife. The true, singular, present *coniunx* is of course Poppaea (*coniugis,* 841). Nero is an incredible user and abuser of name substitutes as forms of guaranteeing a deathly loyalty,[67] or conversely propping up alienation, and we see it so clearly in his announcement of the prefect's entry a few lines later:

> Nero: Sed adesse cerno rara quem pietas virum
>   fidesque castris nota praeposuit meis. (844–845)

> Nero: But I see on his way the man whom rare duty and remarkable reliability have appointed to govern my camp.

Our monster doesn't say a plain-old "here comes <insert name>," the usual practice with entry announcements with *adesse* in Senecan tragedy.[68] Nor does he say the more neutral, "here comes the prefect." He says, effectively, "here comes the man whose loyalty to me is absolute."[69] Saying makes it so. Definitions (backed up by legions) are power. It is no surprise, then, that this section performs a stunning nominal butchery on Octavia herself:

> Nero: Iram expiabit prima quae meruit meam.
> Praefectus: Quam poscat ede, nostra ne parcat manus.
> Nero: Caedem sororis poscit et dirum caput. (859–861)

> *Nero:* The one who first earned my anger will pay it off.
> *Prefect:* Say whom it demands; my hand won't spare her.
> *Nero:* It demands my sister's death and her monstrous head.

Nero answers the prefect's request for identification with a bold shrinking of Octavia's roles and another linguistic divorce (the final cut): she was set up as *coniunx et soror* but is now simply, plainly, *soror.* And of course, that epithet *dirus*—given to Nero earlier—is repurposed to fit that sister's head, a flash-forward to the decapitation on the horizon.[70] But Nero is a long way from being finished with her, nominally speaking:

> *Praefectus:* Cur meam damnas fidem?
> *Nero:* Quod parcis hosti.
> *Praefectus:* Femina hoc nomen capit?
> *Nero:* Si scelera cepit.
> *Praefectus:* Estne qui sontem arguat?
> *Nero:* Populi furor.
> *Praefectus:* Quis regere dementes valet?
> *Nero:* Qui concitare potuit.
> *Praefectus:* Haud quemquam reor—
> *Nero:* Mulier, dedit natura cui pronum malo
> animum, ad nocendum pectus instruxit dolis. (863–869)

> *Prefect:* Why question my loyalty?
> *Nero:* Because you want to spare my enemy.
> *Prefect:* A woman, with that name?!
> *Nero:* With those crimes, yes!
> *Prefect:* Is there anyone to charge her with guilt?
> *Nero:* The people's rage.
> *Prefect:* Who can control *their* madness?
> *Nero:* The one who could cause it.
> *Prefect:* I don't think anyone could . . .
> *Nero:* A *woman* could! Nature has given her a predisposition to
> evil, equipped her heart with guile for harm.

Notch by notch, Nero dials up the distance between himself and Octavia: she is now an enemy,[71] despite the prefect's pushback at the idea of a woman taking that name. And she is, perhaps worst of all in the tyrant's misogynistic logic, a *woman*. Indeed the distance becomes physical as well as nominal in Nero's final command to see the back of her, once and for all:

> *Nero:* ut ne inexpugnabilis
> esset, sed aegras frangeret vires timor
> vel poena; quae iam sera damnatam premet
> diu nocentem. tolle consilium ac preces
> et imperata perage: devectam rate
> procul in remotum litus interimi iube,
> tandem ut residat pectoris nostri tumor. (870–876)

> *Nero:* So she wouldn't be invincible, but fear or punishment would
> shatter her reduced strength; punishment, already long due,
> will crush this condemned party, this long-standing criminal.
> Enough counsel, enough requests. Execute your orders: have
> her taken by ship to some distant, far-flung shore, and kill her
> there, so my swollen heart can finally return to size.

Nero packs her up into a couple of accusatory participles (*damnatam, nocentem*) and ships her off (*devectam*) into the exile that was always on its way. In the tyrant's final linguistic massacre—the culmination of a gradual process of linguistic and physical *distancing*—the once queen and wife, then just sister, now enemy and woman, does not even get a proper substantive to herself.[72]

This becomes, more or less, Octavia's fate for the rest of the play: adjectival, supplementary, passive.[73] The chorus starts citing instances of people brought down by popular support. The nameless kindred spirit Cornelia comes up, whose only descriptor is *miseranda* (882). Octavia is truncated right down to the pitiable weeping maiden in the very same chorus speech (*flentem miseram*, 895). But *miseranda* is all Octavia can muster for herself, twice, in her next flat lament:

> *Octavia:* fratris cerno **miseranda** ratem.
> hac est cuius vecta carina
> quondam genetrix;
> nunc et thalamis expulsa soror
> **miseranda** vehar. (907–910)

> *Octavia:* I see my brother's boat. **Have pity on me!** This is the very
> ship on which his mother was once borne. Now his sister,
> driven from the marriage chamber, will be the cargo; have
> **pity on me!**

Curving in the same direction as the pose of being yanked and carried
(*vexitque,* 879; *trahi,* 894; *quo me trahitis,* 899; *vecta,* 908; *vehar,* 910),
Octavia, the self-diagnosed *soror* (cf. her self-describing *soror . . . non
uxor* at 658), can now only muster that bland gerundive as identifying
badge. She can only stroke herself into a passive object of pity to be bunted
along by the *tyrannus* and his *regina* (note Poppaea's promotion, plus
iubet, 900). Nero had squashed Octavia into adjectival boxes. Now she
finishes the job herself.

Before Octavia's final whimpers, the chorus tries to steel her with a
litany of previous examples, all imperial women, all victims. Most of these
women, like Octavia, are stripped of their names and broken down into
the roles that broke them. Agrippina the elder is officially another *nomen
clarum,* but here we see no name, only a string of positions relative to the
men in her life:[74]

> *Chorus:* tu mihi primum
> tot natorum memoranda parens,
> nata Agrippae,
> nurus Augusti, Caesaris uxor,
> cuius nomen clarum toto
> fulsit in orbe—(932–935)

> *Chorus:* You need the first mention, mother of so many children,
> daughter of Agrippa, Augustus' daughter-in-law, Caesar's
> wife, your bright name gleamed worldwide—

That triangle of *nata Agrippae, nurus Augusti,* and *Caesaris uxor* intensively
boils down the yawning difference between the imperial men and women of
the *Octavia.* The former are named and in possession; the latter are nameless,
owned, retreaded into *roles.* Similar fates awaited Messalina and Agrippina the younger (the latter of whom has already given herself the trifecta
noverca coniunx mater, 645), both here left without names:

> *Chorus:* quid non potuit quondam genetrix
> tua quae rexit principis aulam
> cara marito partuque potens?

> eadem famulo subiecta suo
> cecidit diri militis ense.
> quid cui licuit regnum et caelum
> sperare, parens tanta Neronis?
> non funesta violata manu
> remigis ante,
> mox et ferro lacerata diu
> saevi iacuit victima nati? (947–957)

Chorus: What was your mother not capable of, once upon a time—she
ruled the princeps' palace, dear to her husband, powerful
through childbearing? She too went under the thumb of her
slave and fell to a cruel soldier's sword. What about her, the
one who could legitimately hope for kingdom and heaven,
Nero's great mother? First defiled by the death-dealing hands
of the sailor, then sliced up slowly by the sword, did she not
fall as sacrificial victim to her monstrous son?

Both women are also shriveled into victimhood despite and because of their
motherhood: Messalina from *genetrix . . . potens* to *famulo subiecta suo;*
Agrippina from *parens tanta Neronis* to a woman *violata, lacerata,* and finally, like Iphigenia coming up, a pure *victima.* No matter how *clarum*
their *nomen* may have once been, these women now form an unnamed sorority with which Octavia is made to go quietly.

Octavia has few fighting words left in her. By this point resigned to her
fate, she trots out a halfhearted parting curse, and the chorus[75] picks up
where it left off with one more comparison, the most famous female *victima* of all:

Chorus: Lenes aurae zephyrique leves,
tectam quondam nube aetheria
qui vexistis raptam saevae
virginis aris Iphigeniam, (972–975)

Chorus: Cool breezes, gentle zephyrs, you once carried a girl, hidden in
heaven's clouds, whisked from a cruel virgin's
altars—Iphigenia,

Iphigenia is lucky enough to get a name at least. Octavia, not so much:

Chorus: hanc quoque tristi procul a poena
portate, precor, templa ad Triviae.

> urbe est nostra mitior Aulis
> et Taurorum barbara tellus:
> hospitis illic caede litatur
> numen superum;
> civis gaudet Roma cruore. (976–982)

Chorus: Take this one too, we beg you—take her far from grim punishment, to Trivia's temple. Aulis is nicer than our city, the "bar-
barian" land of the Tauri too. There the powers above are paid
off with the death of a foreigner. Rome celebrates citizen blood.

Octavia becomes little more than a pronoun now: *hanc quoque,* an ap-
pendage to, and a repetition of, the Iphigenia myth.[76] And lest we think
there is redemption in that final *civis,* a kind of symbolic reinstatement into
the community of Roman citizens from which the tyrant has sliced her away
(remember *hostis*), the gnomic form complicates our desire. We have no idea
whether *civis* means "a citizen in general" or "the citizen, Octavia."[77] Perhaps it doesn't matter, and perhaps that's the nub. The woman who has
been swept up from day one in other people's definitions of her, hauled from
miseranda, to *coniunx,* to *soror,* to *hostis,* to *mulier,* to assorted adjectives,
and the mediocre *haec,* is chained to a final cause, the civil cause. This
shadow of a great name, who has no name herself, is always turned into a
symbol, an example, of something more and less than herself. She never
gets to be what the title promises: Octavia.

The Play of Anon

In this chapter, as in Chapter 2, we have chased a primarily *internal* anonymity. We have followed the *Octavia*'s flickering strobes of name suppression and name use and tried to show how this both reflects and manipulates the power play, as well as fueling its impressive pistons of
intratextuality and exemplarity. To end this mammoth chapter, I would like
to briefly shimmy to the world of anonymity "outside" (while relying on
"internal" hooks all the same). I would like to propose that the anonymity
of this play (whether *ignotus* wanted to be *ignotus* or not) actually sparks
important knock-ons for *Octavia*'s social and cultural power—and not, as
you might be thinking, in a negative sense.

Whenever we date the *Octavia* post-Nero,[78] it is relatively uncontroversial that the play tackles enthusiastically the project of hacking away at

Nero's political memory.[79] This was partly a job that needed doing because Nero was a problem who refused to go away. The "monster" still had plenty of pockets of loyalty causing headaches long after his death (hence the phenomenon of the Nero *redivivus*).[80] Our sources tell us that he continued to poll much higher with the rank-and-file "people" than with the elite.[81] It follows that one of the most pressing tasks for a certain ideological wing of the Roman ruling class was to ruin Nero's reputation with those boiling masses. This is what the *Octavia* takes as its solemn commitment: to pull Nero's pants down, as the most tyrannical of tyrants, in front of the people who had no burning reason to think he was all that bad.[82]

As many scholars have recognized, the *Octavia* fights this ideological battle not merely by blackening Nero but by inhabiting the "people" it seeks to speak for, by voicing the collective. The chorus is a raging body of citizens in this play, much more bolshy, much more "activist," much more verbal *and* plot motivating than in most other (especially Senecan) tragedy.[83] Well, at least one half of the chorus: the jury is still out on whether the chorus that marches round rioting is the same as the one that goes with the wind and supports Poppaea.[84] In any case, those who are behind Octavia, as I said earlier, are the closest thing to Nero's counterforce that the play can stage. And we see it reflected in the patterns of direct naming. This is a revolting mass that Nero must actively crush, consciously pursue. While they wear Octavia as their brand (pushing her around with the same nominal manhandling she gets from everyone), they, rather than Octavia, are the entity of which Nero is most terrified. While their protest wins them nothing but violent reprisals in the end, they surely come nearest to the heroic vertex in a condescending triangle,[85] whose other points are Nero-villain and Octavia-damsel in distress.

So *Octavia* speaks for and as the people, and it does that through its chorus. Now imagine for a second that this play was known to be the work of Seneca or Pomponius Secundus[86] or X or Y or whatever other paid-up employee of the Roman elite. Its staunch anti-Neronian perspective would be fobbed off, among the "people" that is, as so much ruling-class chatter—of course, Seneca *would* write that. But its energy and reach as propaganda become that much more impressive when it becomes the work of *anonymous*—in other words, when it becomes not just a voicing of the collective but a genuine part of it, when it speaks as everyone, because it could belong to any and all of them. The *Octavia*'s punch comes from the fiction that it works chorally, without the blinkers of an individual author. This is also why, I would venture, the play seems to form such a good mining target for "cultural memory"[87]—its lack of author donates it instead to the culture from which it seems to spring spontaneously.

Anonymity spreads *Octavia* not just horizontally, across audience and readership, but vertically too, over time. For the other major effect of having an unknown author is that it intensifies the play's already stunning tricks of temporality. As in this chapter and in other scholarship, *Octavia* slips its titular character in and out of a huge index of female roles culled from history and mythology. Such bending and bracing of exemplarity makes this most historical of plays up its game, right deep into the realms of the time-less and the universal.[88] The anonymity helps with this.[89] Just as the un-named Octavia is constantly reformatted into her precedents and doubles, and vice versa, so the play is set free to occupy multiple contexts, multiple temporalities. Timeless on the outside, timeless on the inside: a true play of the Unknown.

II

THE UNIVERSAL NO-NAME

Part I was tasked with finding a politics of the anonymous that would hold for many early (and later) imperial texts. We saw the strands of experimentation with antonomasia and anonymous authorship in the *Res Gestae* feed back into Suetonius' *Caesars*. We then blitzed through two heavily political texts—the *Ibis*, the *Octavia*—to show how these relations of naming and power could be played out in the literature written under the (lengthening) shadow of Augustan authorship. While we did end up on a case of genuine "external" anonymity with the *Octavia* (a positioning calculated to grade us gently into this next section), in the sense that the lack of an author behind that text is more or less secure, the lion's share of the "anonymity" on display to date has been internal: theme and variation around the problem of antonomasia, anonymity *in* more than *of*.

Now for the real thing. Part II will rifle through three texts traditionally pegged to the ranks of the minor or the miscellaneous: Phaedrus' *Fables*, *Laus Pisonis*, and Calpurnius Siculus' *Eclogues*. The common thread through all of these is manifold. First, these texts are all cases where we have nonexistent or minimal external information about their authors. Thus they are essentially anonymous, in my most catholic sense of the term: authors, that is, who leave very weak historical footprints. Phaedrus is anonymous through pseudonym; *Laus Pisonis*, through full-fledged lack of an author; and Calpurnius Siculus through an extremely untrustworthy manuscript tag combined with lack of attestation in the world around. Second, they are all texts bent on teasing out the dramatic repercussions of writing *as* unknown authors. And finally, they all (though the *Laus Pisonis* and Calpurnius more than Phaedrus) unleash hell on our habitual expectations over temporality and context. These texts lack absolutely nothing. Their status as the work of no-names merely requires a criticism sensitive to the props of unknowing on which they are built.

4

Phaedrus by Name

erit ille notus quem per te cognoueris (The only man you
know is the one you know *personally*)

—Phaedrus, *Fables* 3.10.58

It would be a ragged truism these days to assert that all classical authors are invented in some sense, whether by themselves or by the tradition nagging after them. By "invented," I mean nothing much more than the common, garden concept of a fictionalized persona. We know, we can see, how the conventions of literary representation rule the seasons of a varying authorial self. "Horace" looks different, is different, depending on the genre in which you catch him being "himself."[1] But even in this suspicious age, which takes the "purely literary" quality of authorial self-representation for granted[2] and likes to quarantine anything a Latin author writes about themselves from an unrecoverable "outside" that wrote it, there are certain nonnegotiable axes of overlap between inside and outside—and these perhaps root scholarship more than we like to admit. However much we distrust the cheek with which they're delivered, the factoids of the *vita* bear loads for the work: Catullus *did* have a relationship with Lesbia; Horace *was* the son of a freedman and smuggled himself into Maecenas' patronage; Ovid *was* exiled.[3] Such nuggets form a limiting barrier protecting us lost literary critics from *absolute* abdication to the persona, from the full-pelt postmodern irony of the quotation marks in "Horace." In many cases, they make us understand the persona as a magnified, reduced, distorted, or contorted version of the "real" author's face it is made to mask.

From another angle, there often seems to us a very real connection between historical author and authorial persona, in the sense that the former
often declares *ownership* over the latter. For far the lion's share of Latin
authors, we assume, and find, an active stake in the claiming of the text:
this is my poem, *mine;* the historical Naso lies behind the poetic Naso, hustling for the cultural capital of authorship, raking it up for both now and
the future.[4] That assumption/finding in fact lies at the core of much of our
work on ancient Roman authors, and it is a transferred form of how we
think about individuals in a capitalist economy: they must act primarily
from self-interest; they are always trying to get something out of it, their
"self-representation" not much more than a serial jockeying for position.
This chapter will aim to show that some authors do not necessarily write
for "themselves," to push themselves up the ranks of their contemporaries
or to inject themselves into the bloodstream of posterity. And this is because
they do not necessarily write *as* (buffed up versions of) themselves.

This chapter will take you for a ride through the highlights and low-
lights of Phaedrus' *Fables,* with the intention of convincing you that there
was such a thing in antiquity as the trialing of a thoroughly made-up no-
name of a persona. These five books of fable come down to us in a bit of a
hot textual mess. But we do know, more or less, that they are versified versions of classic Aesopic animal fables, with more than a pinch of contemporary Roman politics worked in for good measure. Despite solid rumblings of praise and attention, Phaedrus has not caused much of a murmur
in literary history.[5] For a while, perhaps, scholars took him at his word to
be a mere "versifier" of Aesop: a repackager of raw materials, a decorator
at the end of the supply chain.[6] But I want this chapter to restore, or perhaps even capture for the first time, the shock of this new kind of poet.
I shall argue that Phaedrus bucks the trend of Latin literature, or takes it
to its logical conclusion, to become the most "invented" (self-created) author
in its register. By this I mean that these five books of fable are an exercise
in creating a literary self that has *no knowable relation* to the hand holding
the pen. Name, "patrons,"[7] biographical episodes, growth up the "career"
ladder: Phaedrus is the most brilliant wisecrack surviving from antiquity
to have made good at inventing them *all*.[8]

There are, of course, scores of cases of pseudepigrapha, "fakes" that pur-
port to be the work of a big name.[9] As Irene Peirano Garrison has shown

so well, Roman rhetorical culture was an education in thinking and speaking as famous historical figures, and pseudepigraphic poetic ventures were an easy outgrowth therefrom.[10] Writing as (= to become) early Virgil is one thing. Writing as a no-name, and not just a no-name but a full-fledged character of a no-name, is quite another. I shall put it to you that Phaedrus the unheard-of is the dark underside of the Latin tradition of fame-seeking, name-shrieking poets. He is the author who tries to write himself into the world of contemporary notice and hijack its ripples into immortality like a good Horace or Ovid (or even Martial) but ends up bombing out before he gets anywhere close.[11] This is the tale of the one who got away—and it relies on us having no idea who, beyond the fabulous version, that might have been.[12] Now for the story of the no-name, for whom anonymity is everything.

Inventing a No-Name

The fable, like its "romance" cousin, was among the most despicable forms of literary lowlife in antiquity.[13] And that status was tuned to accord with its shrugging indifference to authorship. If high literature was characterized by a bard with special backdoor access to the music of divinity, and each line became a sealed and sacred possession of said bard, fable, like anecdote (or *chreia*),[14] seems to be packed anonymously for smooth and painless migration all over the shop, mouth to mouth, text to text, genre to genre. It is "folk"-owned material (i.e., it belongs to no one).[15] Fables are also designed for broadest applicability across the board. They do not name names but truck in the "timeless" antics of the animal kingdom.[16]

To turn this motley crew into a proper genre based on the usual story of Greek founder passing into Latin emulator, Phaedrus has to give it a name. And the obvious candidate surfaces straightaway:

> Aesopus auctor quam materiam repperit,
> hanc ego polivi versibus senariis.
> duplex libelli dos est: quod risum movet,
> et quod prudenti vitam consilio monet.
> calumniari si quis autem voluerit,
> quod arbores loquantur, non tantum ferae,
> fictis iocari nos meminerit fabulis. (*Fables* I Prol.)[17]

Aesop is my source. The material he made up, I buffed into senarii. This book is a two-for-one: it cracks you up, and it puts your life on track by sensible advice. If anyone opts to slander it—trees speak, not just animals—they should remember I'm joshing with made-up tales.

The division of labor at this gingerly beginning is pretty clear. Aesop is the ur-author, the "discoverer" of the literary cont(in)ent. Phaedrus is the spit-and-polisher, merely the technical support setting it to verse. That *nos* is not just a pretty face of a poetic plural, for this is a genuine "collaboration," Aesop and Phaedrus, with the latter playing very much the junior partner. Even at this earliest point, we might sniff where this is going: the classic "humble-brag" approach of self-promotion via self-effacement, no? No Latin poet worth their salt mentions their Greek predecessor in a breath of humility without at the same time launching their bid for all-out *emulation*.[18] But book 1 certainly pushes a sense of a minor, modest pitch on the poet's part, inviting us to read these pieces as both Aesop *and* Phaedrus (at best). Take the explicit attribution in 1.10:

Quicumque turpi fraude semel innotuit,
etiam si verum dicit, amittit fidem.
hoc adtestatur brevis Aesopi fabula.
lupus arguebat vulpem furti crimine;
negabat illa se esse culpae proximam.
tunc iudex inter illos sedit simius.
uterque causam cum perorassent suam,
dixisse fertur simius sententiam:
"tu non videris perdidisse quod petis;
te credo subripuisse quod pulchre negas." (1.10)

Those people who've got a reputation for ugly deceit once—even when they're telling the truth, no one believes them. A short Aesop fable supports this. A wolf was trying to prosecute a fox for theft. The fox pled not-guilty. A monkey took up the chair to judge between them. When both had done their wrap-up speech, the monkey is said to have offered the following verdict: "You—you don't seem to have lost what you're trying to gain; and you—I'll bet you pilfered the very thing you cutely deny."

Phaedrus is keen to deflect charges of literary theft in a fable about *furtum*. Hence the name *Aesopus* making sure the deniability is secured. And yet suddenly our authors seem to morph into the animals of which they write: Aesop becomes the wolf suing foxy Phaedrus for the theft he tried to mask with the name Aesop. The ape[19] concludes, paradoxically, that both parties are wrong; this is both theft and not-theft. Phaedrus is taking from Aesop, while Aesop isn't losing anything, for fable both is and is not fable, and "ownership" both does and doesn't exist.

As many scholars have teased out already, the story of Phaedrus is largely a story of growing out of Aesop.[20] The point less traveled, perhaps, is that this liberation from the paternal shadow of the predecessor is a rite of passage through which every teenage Latin poet must go.[21] By prologue 2, Phaedrus is well and truly on his way. Aesop appears in the first line again but only in a restrictive way: *Exemplis continetur Aesopi genus;* "That which is Aesopic in kind is confined to instructive examples" (2 Prol. 1). Phaedrus wants the work to be judged on its own terms, regardless of its source. He doesn't want it judged, that is, by the name of the author (*non auctoris nomine,* 2 Prol. 7). He asks the dear reader to be indulgent with his addition of new material (*aliquid interponere,* 9) for the sake of variety and toots his own horn as a great example of *brevitas* (12). By the epilogue to book 2, Aesop becomes his own exemplum for Phaedrus' all-out glory bid. We have accelerated hard and fast. Full self-monumentalizing is now in his sights:

> Aesopi ingenio statuam posuere Attici,
> servumque collocarunt aeterna in basi,
> patere honoris scirent ut cuncti viam
> nec generi tribui sed virtuti gloriam.
> quoniam occuparat alter ut primus foret,
> ne solus esset, studui, quod superfuit.
> nec haec invidia, verum est aemulatio.
> quodsi labori faverit Latium meo,
> plures habebit quos opponat Graeciae.
> si Livor obtrectare curam voluerit,
> non tamen eripiet laudis conscientiam. (2 Epil. 1–11)

The Athenians set up a statue for the talented Mr. Aesop and put a slave on the pedestal of forever, so that everyone would know that the honorable way is open and that glory is parceled out based on merit over birth. Since someone else has pipped me from first place, I made sure he wouldn't be the only one (that was all I could do). It's not envy, just rivalry. But if

Latium looks kindly on my work, it will have more authors to match against Greece. If Envy wants to underrate my efforts, she won't take away the feeling that I've earned the praise.

The *Aesopi genus* now becomes the *Aesopi ingenio*. A different type of genus is devalued over pure *virtus* (*nec generi tribui sed virtuti gloriam*). This section holds out big words reserved for ambitious poets: *virtus, studere, invidia, aemulatio, labor, Livor, laus*. Phaedrus claims an active rivalry with his statue-based trailblazer, a rivalry so big it can be mapped onto the cultural Olympics of Greece versus Rome. He even goes so far as to dictate an appreciative readership and then to envisage another crew of rabble-rousers (*rabulae*) who couldn't tell a good fable from a bad one if it bit them on the bum. It is, arguably, in the *negative* reception that Phaedrus' career is truly written into getting going. For no one notices a nonentity enough to bother to carp at him. But this is more than a couple of bad reviews:

> fatale exilium corde durato feram,
> donec Fortunam criminis pudeat sui. (2 Epil. 18–19)

> I'll take my deadly exile with a fortified heart—till Fortune feels ashamed of her charge.

Just as the cash-out for Phaedrus' success is fame and glory, so the cost of a bad wrap is . . . *exile?!* This is "just" a metaphor here, of course. But its deployment suddenly takes us into a world of Ovid-sized aspiration,[22] where stakes are much higher than a literary carpenter sitting in his workshop polishing up some Aesopic wood. *Exilium, crimen*: the prospect of a poet sent down into social death on a trumped-up charge. Phaedrus' autopoetics are kneading the corpus into something that can make a real splash.

It's not until the prologue to book 3—where this *exilium* is written into existence, out of thin air, in the story about Phaedrus' falling out with Tiberius' second-in-command, Sejanus—that we wise up to what Phaedrus is doing here. The moment the epilogue to one book foreshadows perfectly the traumatic "biographical" rupture that inaugurates the next, we have a sense of something strange in the air. Certain Latin poets had done expert jobs of fashioning neat career structures using crafty joinery at certain hinge points of book and work. Virgil, for example, had lit the way forward from *Eclogues* to *Georgics,* and from *Georgics* to *Aeneid,* with an uncanny kind of prophesizing (less charitably, he only had a limited repertoire of thematic obsessions).[23] But some big life "events" can't be planned—Ovidian exile,[24] for instance: the paradigmatic bolt from the blue. What Phaedrus does with the bridge over books 2 and 3 is mingle these various forms of the poet's biographical time. He makes the signpost to the next subject direction (the "thematic" future, usually dressed to look "known") bleed into the lament for an unforeseen event (the "traumatic" future, by definition "unknown"). He tells us, in other words, that he is making it all up as he goes along, alchemizing a text into a "life," and not the other way round.

One of the dead giveaways to betray the "fictiveness" of this schtick is the way Phaedrus interleaves the famous autobiographical scripts of Latin literature.[25] In Ovid/Horace,[26] these are drawn up at different points of the career, but now, in Phaedrus' hands, they collapse into a comical simultaneity. First the prologue to book 3 gives us the poet at the height of his powers, soaring high on the fumes of success:

Phaedri libellos legere si desideras,
vaces oportet, Eutyche, a negotiis,
ut liber animus sentiat vim carminis. (3 Prol. 1–3)

If you're feeling the urge to read the books of Phaedrus, you have to take a vacation, Eutychus, so your mind is free to grasp the full force of the verse.

Suddenly we have a real, embedded, "sociology" of Phaedrian poetry. The author gives us his name for the first and only time—*first word*—and also flings his verse at a very particular target, Eutychus,[27] supposedly a busy and important man.[28] That first line looks something like the confident signature[29] marking the start of Ovid's very first work (retrospectively, from the point of revision):

Qui modo Nasonis fueramus quinque libelli,
    tres sumus; hoc illi praetulit auctor opus. (Epigram to Ovid, *Amores* 1)

Once we were five books of Naso, now we're three; the author preferred this work to the last one.

And, as we have seen, this brand of self-naming is a catch-cry of Ovidian exile. Naso lurks near the beginning of many an *epistula ex Ponto*.[30] The new voice is just as loud as the name. Phaedrus positively orders his patron to down tools and start reading and lectures him on his priorities much more than a Horace delicately testing the occupied ears of a busy Caesar ever would.[31] All these touches signal to us readers that we are at peak fabulist.[32]

And we are. Phaedrus transforms himself into an author worthy of a full-on foundation biopic:

> ego, quem Pierio mater enixa est iugo,
> in quo Tonanti sancta Mnemosyne Iovi,
> fecunda novies, artium peperit chorum,
> quamvis in ipsa paene natus sim schola,
> curamque habendi penitus corde eraserim,
> nec Pallade hanc invita in vitam incubuerim,
> fastidiose tamen in coetum recipior.
> quid credis illi accidere qui magnas opes
> exaggerare quaerit omni vigilia,
> docto labori dulce praeponens lucrum?
> sed iam, "quodcumque fuerit," ut dixit Sinon
> ad regem cum Dardaniae perductus foret,
> librum exarabo tertium Aesopi stilo,
> honori et meritis dedicans illum tuis.
> quem si leges, laetabor; sin autem minus,
> habebunt certe quo se oblectent posteri. (3 Prol. 17–32)

And *me?* My mother produced me on the Pierian ridges, where sacred Mnemosyne, a nine-times child-bearer, delivered the Chorus of the Arts to Jupiter the Thunderer. Even though I was almost born in the school itself, even though I expunged all concern for owning property from the depths of my heart, even though I settled on this life with Pallas Athena's blessing—*still* I'm taken into the artsy circles only grudgingly. What do you think happens to someone who's looking to heap up piles of wealth, every waking moment, preferring sweet cash to good honest scholarship? But now "whatever happens," as Sinon said when he was brought to the king of Dardania, I'll scratch out a third book with Aesop's pen, and I'll dedicate it in the name of your Honor and Loyal Service. If you read it, I'll be thrilled; if you don't, posterity will have a little something with which they can enjoy themselves.

This is a far cry from the usual lowlands of fable: machinery of the Muses, Athena's support, attributed literary quotation—prestige material.[33] Crucially, that material no longer belongs to Aesop. Only the instrument is his, the *stilus* used to till the fertile literary earth. Aesop is no longer the most important name, for the "dedication" goes to this most honorable patron. But Phaedrus even manages to waft up a bit of insouciance, not caring either way, for *posteri* are now yet *another* target audience. Indeed Eutychus is no sooner flattered than rendered small fry next to the stomping reader who soon comes a-knocking:

> ego illius pro semita feci viam,
> et cogitavi plura quam reliquerat,
> in calamitatem deligens quaedam meam.
> quodsi accusator alius Seiano foret,
> si testis alius, iudex alius denique,
> dignum faterer esse me tantis malis,
> nec his dolorem delenirem remediis. (3 Prol. 38–44)

> I upgraded Aesop's footpath to a highway; I've dreamed up more than he left behind, going for some things that ended in my own disaster. But if there were an accuser other than Sejanus, if there were another witness, and yes, another judge, I'd confess I deserved such trouble; but I wouldn't be calming my pain with these balms.

Sejanus the simultaneous *accusator, iudex,* and *testis* lobs us into another register of notice at Rome. Yet another box of big-splash poetry is ticked off: political offense, legal trouble, just as if this were Horace's *Satires* 2.1 looking back on the "Too much? Too soon?" of book 1.[34] Nothing screams important poet like a fallout with the powers on high. Shortly after, an elevated poetic genealogy also gets a look-in: Aesop the Phrygian, Anacharsis the Scythian get everlasting fame (*aeternam* again, 3 Prol. 53) by their outstanding talent, so why not Phaedrus the Thracian—closer to Greece than these and from the same line of godlike authors (*auctores*—no more "Aesopus auctor!" business) as Apollo-born Linus and Muse-born Orpheus (54–59). This is all addictively, deliciously over the top, and Phaedrus marks it as such with the wry sign-off:

> Induxi te ad legendum? sincerum mihi
> candore noto reddas iudicium peto. (3 Prol. 62–63)

> Have I got you to read? I'm looking for your real opinion; give it to me straight, you're famous for it.

So he has merely been writing for the patron,[35] giving the Man what he wants to suck him into the vortex of page-turning. All the glossy presentation of high readership (*posteri*, Sejanus) and divine predecessors has been handcrafted to get this unknown patron (us?) with the "famous critical acumen" reading for the plot, at pace.

Scholarship has already pored over this at some length.[36] What I want to bring out here is the strange effect of the *immediate* climb-down from the heights of Helicon, which scrambles the scripts behind the "great poet" character acts of Latin literature. Because straightaway, while the triumphant trumpets are still ringing in our ears, the next fable, 3.1, takes us down a peg:

> Anus iacere vidit epotam amphoram,
> adhuc Falerna faece e testa nobili
> odorem quae iucundum late spargeret.
> hunc postquam totis avida traxit naribus:
> "O suavis anima, quale in te dicam bonum
> antehac fuisse, tales cum sint reliquiae!"
> hoc quo pertineat dicet qui me noverit. (3.1)

> Old woman sees an emptied wine jar lying there, but from the dregs of Falernian in its brand-name shell, it was exuding all about a lovely aroma. After she'd greedily drunk it in with both nostrils flared: "O sweet fume, how good I'll have to say you were before, if your leftovers are like this!" The reader who knows me will say what this is all about.

Like all good Roman poets, Phaedrus makes sure to create the conditions of eavesdropping, the two-track readership. The reader in the know who "gets it," the outsider who doesn't.[37] The problem is that the cryptic message doesn't seem that tough to get. Phaedrus is telling us that he was better in the past, no? All we need to make that leap of detective work is the knowledge that he has written two books before this. So all of a sudden we move from the poet on top of the world to the middle-age third-album syndrome, the poet in decline (fully worked out in book 5). Of course, the political fallout with Sejanus will do that, as Ovid's with Augustus had done to his sense of his own droning abilities.[38] Political trouble or "exile" necessitates a dip in quality. But the comic sparks here fly through the suddenness of the deceleration. It was all going so well, for about the length of a prologue. We *just* missed him at his peak!

There is, however, another way to read this crucial turning-point fable. We took those *reliquiae* as temporal or biographical (a clue retrospectively left by *aliquae reliquiae*, used of 'life remains' in 3. Epil. 15)—what remains of Phaedrus' writing life, once all the juicy stuff of youth has been poured out. But we could also read those pleasant vapors as *textual* remnants: written leftovers, hints not only of walnut and raspberry but of the author who is no longer there—"trace elements." To start with, *Falernea faex* is already a form of trace element left over from Horace (same collocation at *Sat.* 2.4.55)—leaving us with the dregs of the very dregs. But the real missing person here is Phaedrus. The sense of lagging behind and chasing the author at one remove is something *Hoc quo pertineat dicet qui me noverit* helps thrust in our face: the difference between knowing Phaedrus and knowing *Phaedrus*. The only way in which we can meaningfully get to know him is textual—through the hack biographical one-man-shows and the odd tidbit from time to time.[39] It is this complete erasure of the extra-textual "sense of an author" that enables Phaedrus to run. "He" is nothing but the afterthought, the lingering smell in the room (even if that smell is of high-class booze), the ruffles and dimples left in the bed. His mission is to exist purely in and as text, to become a kind of cavity holding only the memories of full presence. The name also tells us as much: this Phaedrus is an author who is a Platonic text about writing—*Phaedrus*.[40]

For all Phaedrus' fame talk in prologue 3, we get the sense that the author is a secondary product, a self-written man rather than a genuine celebrity—and whatever fame is happening is essentially aspirational. The moment he meets one of his idols, Socrates, is telling:

> vulgare amici nomen sed rara est fides.
> cum parvas aedes sibi fundasset Socrates
> (cuius non fugio mortem si famam adsequar,
> et cedo invidiae dummodo absolvar cinis),
> ex populo sic nescioquis, ut fieri solet:
> "quaeso, tam angustam talis vir ponis domum?"
> "utinam" inquit "veris hanc amicis impleam!" (3.9)

The name of "friend" is a dime a dozen—loyalty is the precious thing. When Socrates had laid the groundwork for a small house (by the way, I don't shun his death if only I can win his fame, and I concede to envy if I'm vindicated as ash), one of the people (as tends to happen) said: "You're really building such a tiny house for such a quality man?" He came back: "If only I could fill it with real friends!"

The aside brackets a conditional of a fabulist still hungry for fame, but one who also still has a long way to go. Phaedrus talks the talk with ambition, but the walking of the walk is still very much lacking: he has all the textual trappings of a famous-ish poet, without the real public "presence" to back it up yet. We clock, retrospectively, that all that fame talk of prologue 3 was very much a down payment for a future far from guaranteed.

The other point of that fable is again, I think, the notion that we can only know Phaedrus *qua* his remains: he will have fame when he's disappeared into ash (*cinis*). As the story with the Falernian dregs went, so here: we are constantly chasing Phaedrus by the tail/tale of his traces. The author will never appear. A similar message is wired across in 3.13, a trickier fable dedicated more explicitly to authorship. This feature piece on the bees and the drones seems to be about hacks plagiarizing Phaedrus' work (yet another marker of the big poet, like the Sejanus episode—for no one would plagiarize a no-name, right?).[41] The drones claim the bees' beautiful honeycomb work as their own. A wasp is wheeled out as judge and proposes that the two groups have a kind of buzz-off to determine the true creators:

"sed, ne religio peccet inprudens mea,
alvos accipite et ceris opus infundite,
ut ex sapore mellis et forma favi,
de quis nunc agitur, auctor horum appareat."
fuci recusant, apibus condicio placet,
tunc illa talem rettulit sententiam:
"apertum est quis non possit et quis fecerit.
quapropter apibus fructum restituo suum."
hanc praeterissem fabulam silentio,
si pactam fuci non recusassent fidem. (3.13)

"But—so my scruples don't fail through lack of knowledge—take the hives, melt the sculpture into wax cells, so I can tell from the taste of the honey and the structure of the comb—the subject of the dispute—the true author." The drones excuse themselves, but the stipulation pleased the bees. Then the wasp gave the following verdict: "It's clear who couldn't make this and who did. Therefore, I restore to the bees their rightful property." I would have skipped this fable in silence, if the drones hadn't defaulted on our agreement.

The promise of the wasp's authentication method is that the author will appear (*auctor horum appareat*). But we never actually get that degree of incontrovertible proof. Instead, the drones back down, and the wasp, like Phaedrus, fixes the interpretation of that retreat: it means that it is completely obvious (*apertum est*) who produced the thing. But the wasp exercising his inferential powers is not quite the same thing as the author coming forward, doing it on the spot, right in front of our eyes, in the flesh. Again, this is the same dynamic that reaches across prologue 3 to 3.1. It may feel like we have enough of "Phaedrus," a name, a biography, what have you. But this is not quite enough to know him, to know who is really behind all this. At the last ditch, the author is withheld.

This telltale move of dangle and retraction, of flash and tease, becomes ever more classic Phaedrus at the end of the book 3 road. The epilogue to this book spends a lot of precious energy trying to convince someone—presumably Eutychus, the patron of prologue 3, now retreated into a nameless retirement—to make good on the promise and give this jobbing writer some dosh, while he's still young. Even though the dramatic situation and social embedding of this paratextual bookmark are retained from prologue 3, in that they both situate author asking for patron's attention, the claims and (no-)names are completely different. Epilogue 3 has a kind of dark interchangeability about it at so many levels. From the one-and-only Phaedrus of prologue 3, Proper Author Extraordinaire, now *anyone* seems to be able to write fable. It can be left to others because the material is so abundant:

> Supersunt mihi quae scribam, sed parco sciens:
> primum, esse videar ne tibi molestior,
> distringit quem multarum rerum varietas;
> dein, si quis eadem forte conari velit,
> habere ut possit aliquid operis residui;
> quamvis materiae tanta abundet copia,
> labori faber ut desit, non fabro labor. (3 Epil. 1–7)

I have plenty more where that came from to write up, but I deliberately hold back: first, so I don't seem too annoying to you, because a pile of different things pulls you every which way; second, if anyone wanted to have a go at the same things, they could have something left to do. Yet the amount of material is so overflowing, the work might not have a craftsman, but the craftsman certainly won't lack work.

This doesn't look much like the high-lit *labor* of the divine *auctores* of prologue 3. *Materia* and *faber* put us back in the realm of the spit-and-polish,
menial labor of prologue 1. Phaedrus seems to pass on the task to any old
craftsman out there willing to pick up the work. But he also seems to be
scrolling through patrons as if their identity were equally unimportant, for
after his various invoices for payment have been lodged with "you," he
pretty much tells us he is moving on:

> tuae sunt partes; fuerunt aliorum prius;
> dein simili gyro venient aliorum vices. (3 Epil. 24–25)

> It's your case now; before, it was others' responsibility; soon others will
> have their turn, with the same twist.

This emphasis on the wheel of fortune, the statement that there have been
and will be others in "your" place, accords more with the lowlife ethics of
fable, which tend to show how the little guys get the same raw deal no
matter the master's name.[42] Indeed just as 3.1 knocked us down from the
scaled heights of prologue 3, so this epilogue seems to shatter the insane
driving ambition of that prologue at the level of book-frame. Spot the difference, now we're crashing back to earth:

> excedit animus quem proposui terminum,
> sed difficulter continetur spiritus,
> integritatis qui sincerae conscius
> a noxiorum premitur insolentiis.
> qui sint, requiris? apparebunt tempore.
> ego, quondam legi quam puer sententiam
> "Palam muttire plebeio piaculum est,"
> dum sanitas constabit, pulchre meminero. (3 Epil. 28–34)

> My mind took me far past the end I appointed, but the spirit is only held
> back with difficulty, when it's aware of unimpeachable integrity and is
> crushed by the abuse of the people looking to harm. Who are these people?
> you ask. They'll come out of the woodwork in time. For me, I once read
> this saying as a boy—"It's a sin for the lowly to grumble in public"—and
> I'll do well to remember it, as long as my good sense survives.

The same pose of an offended public obtains. But whereas we had the important names named in prologue 3, here the anonymous patron's freedom-of-
information request is fobbed off with the bathetic, slightly sinister *appare-*

bunt tempore (cf. *appareat* earlier). The only ways people "appear" in this book is in the unfulfilled subjunctive (*appareat*) or the distant future (*apparebunt*)—both disappointing deferrals. What's more, the confident attributed quotation of Sinon back in prologue 3 (*quodcumque fuerit*) is peeled back to the anonymized verse circulations of childhood education[43]—a line that tells the plebs to shut up and stay within their station. Phaedrus' "ego"— once shouted so loud from the rafters of famed-name biographical discourse—crawls back into its shell, the chastened little critter sent packing back to timid childhood. In this send-off to mid-career, there are no names. For our poet has regressed to his native state, the no-name.

Particulo Poetics

At this point, let's take stock. The main takeaway message might be something like this: the story of Phaedrus is no straightforward Hollywood arc of rags to riches, obscurity to success, dependence on Aesop to confidently shaking off the maker. Rather, it is a bumpier track along which our fabulist makes comedy of the failure of it all. His attempts to create a world-famous poet merely by the drop of a speech-act fiat are shown as the empty (albeit energetic) gestures they are. The fun of Phaedrus runs on the fact that none of us (now or then) have ever heard of this fast up-and-coming(-and-going) wordsmith.[44] We will never "know" him in the sense that famous authors are known quantities celebrated as subjects of their own recognition anecdotes—Tacitus and Pliny, Simonides, Menander[45]—and that is because Phaedrus exists only in the vanishing vapors of text and fiction. Thin air.

Hope springs eternal, however, and so it does in the prologue to book 4. The author who had decided to hang up his pen is now back at it and better than ever:

> Cum destinassem terminum operi statuere,
> in hoc ut aliis esset materiae satis,
> consilium tacito corde damnavi <meum>.
> nam si quis etiam talis est tituli <appetens>,
> quo pacto divinabit quidnam omiserim,
> ut illud ipse incipiat famae tradere,
> sua cuique cum sit animi cogitatio
> colorque proprius? ergo non levitas mihi,
> sed certa ratio causam scribendi dedit. (4 Prol. 1–9)

When I'd decided to bring my work to an end, to leave enough material for others to chase up, I then wrote this plan off in an interior monologue. For if anyone is after such a title, how is he going to guess what I left out, so he can start to hand that on to fame, since everyone has their own mode of thought and their own special brand? You see then: it's not my frippery but pure logic that has given me reason to write.

Indeed suddenly we are slung from the slightly downtrodden "someone else will do it" of the last epilogue back to the one-and-only author situation. Phaedrus again creates a sense of flesh-and-blood beyond the text: whatever he set down on paper, he immediately thought in his "silent mind" to be a stupid idea. The change of direction isn't mere flip-flopping (*levitas*) but based in solid reason. No one will pick up where Phaedrus has left off, because each author is absolutely singular and no one would be able to even if they tried. In case you were unconvinced, the other *ratio* chases it up:

> quare, Particulo, quoniam caperis fabulis,
> (quas Aesopias, non Aesopi, nomino,
> quia paucas ille ostendit, ego plures sero,
> usus vetusto genere sed rebus novis)
> quartum libellum cum vacaris perleges. (4 Prol. 10–14)

> So, Particulo, since you're into fables (I call them Aesopic rather than "Aesop's," because he put out a few, but I plant more, making use of the old style, but new subjects), you'll read my fourth book start to finish. When you're ready.

Now there is a new patron on the scene—something the turnstile of people on the case had prepared us for back in epilogue 3, just as the generic exile of epilogue 2 primed us for the Sejanus bust of prologue 3. A newfound pluckiness follows: Phaedrus rebrands the fables with the vague adjectival spirit of Aesop, without the ur-author's ownership—Aesopish, not Aesop's. Phaedrus' debt again lies in the kind (*genus*), the form, rather than the content. The approach to patron is also a little more straight shooting. With Eutychus, we had entertaining sidesteps of roundabout request.[46] Now we have the blunt imperative of a full read-through: *quartum libellum cum vacaris perleges*—not only that but an assertion that the inimitable Phaedrus will be copied and recopied into the mainstream of elite lit:

hunc obtrectare si volet malignitas,
imitari dum non possit, obtrectet licet.
mihi parta laus est quod tu, quod similes tui
vestras in chartas verba transfertis mea,
dignumque longa iudicatis memoria.
inlitteratum plausum nec desidero. (4 Prol. 15–20)

If ill will wanted to knock it—as long as they can't imitate me, let them knock it. I've already got the glory because you and others like you copy my words into your books, and you deem me worth conserving. I have no interest in the approval of illiterates.

Phaedrus presents his *laus* as already guaranteed, precisely because, precisely *for the fact that* the patron class is making their words his.[47] Just as the fabulized plagiarism of 3.13 implied Phaedrus to be an author worth plagiarizing, so here with the transcription into personal pages: he can't be imitated, but copying is the highest form of flattery. Phaedrus deserves some memory and has already earned some.

And yet later in the book,[48] he seems to put the backpedal to the meddle, faced with only the lightest critical pressure. This latest feeble of Phaedrus deals with the Aesop relationship from the perspective of the carping naysayer Livor and tends to bend to Livor's terms:

Quid iudicare cogitas, Livor, modo?
licet dissimulet, pulchre tamen intellego.
quicquid putabit esse dignum memoria,
Aesopi dicet; si quid minus adriserit,
a me contendet fictum quovis pignore.
quem volo refelli iam nunc responso meo:
sive hoc ineptum sive laudandum est opus,
invenit ille, nostra perfecit manus.
sed exsequamur coepti propositum ordinem. (4.22)

What judgment are you now plotting, Envy? Though he hides it, I apprehend it well enough. Whatever he deems worth preserving, he'll say it's Aesop's; if he finds something less amusing, he'll bet on any money that it was my addition. I want to rebut him with this here response: whether this work is bad or whether it's commendable, *he* thought it up; my hand just plied the finishing touches. But let's see this through according to the original plan.

That crucial genitive of possession, *Aesopi,* of Aesop, was banished in prologue 4; now it's back in full force as a brand only for the Phaedrian matter
that Livor likes. Phaedrus throws it back at him: no, actually, everything
I write is strictly "of Aesop." That forces Livor into a logical corner, but it
is a kind of battle-war situation. In asserting that everything is Aesop's,
Phaedrus can escape the exigencies of the local crisis but ends up folding
beneath the bigger issue, the idea he has been battling on and off for
books—that all this is just Aesop! *Invenit ille, nostra perfecit manus* pretty
much takes us right back to where we started (*Aesopus auctor quam ma-
teriam repperit,/hanc ego polivi versibus senariis*).[49] Aesop matter, Phaedrus
finishing touches—a division of labor fairly distant from the upbeat
"Aesopish" relationship of prologue 4.

Of course, you have to be a famous poet for Livor to love and hate you in
the first place. The line between puff piece and flatulence is always wafer
thin in Phaedrus. For the next run of fables beam us back up to the realms
of fame and recognition—albeit for another poet, the great Simonides. These
in fact build a miniature suite that straddles the book 4–book 5 division as
it stands and perhaps speaks to the idea that it shouldn't.[50] In any case, all
these poems are crushed together by the theme of poetic fame and recognition. But even these, if put in sequence, tell a story of slightly diminishing
returns. The first Simonides fable features a mercenary poet, grown rich off
his patrons' generosity (Particulo take note), taking a boat trip. He cares so
little for possessions that he travels light, taking along just himself (*"Mecum"
inquit "mea sunt cuncta,"* 4.23.14), while all his shipmates pack very heavy.
When the inevitable shipwreck happens, some of the encumbered comrades
die at sea. Others lose their effects via onshore robbery. Simonides, however,
is taken care of and then some—and only because he is known (*cognitum*):

> hic litterarum quidam studio deditus,
> Simonidis qui saepe versus legerat,
> eratque absentis admirator maximus,
> sermone ab ipso cognitum cupidissime
> ad se recepit; veste, nummis, familia
> hominem exornavit. ceteri tabulam suam
> portant, rogantes victum. quos casu obvios
> Simonides ut vidit, "dixi" inquit "mea
> mecum esse cuncta; vos quod rapuistis perit." (4.23.19–27)

Here a certain someone, a devotee of things literary, who had often read
Simonides' poetry and was a huge fan from a distance, recognized him
from his speech, and received him into his home enthusiastically; he kitted
him out with clothes, money, and slaves. The others ported their little
paintings about, begging for food. When Simonides ran into them by
chance, he said: "I told you, all my things were with me; what you
snatched up, you lost."

Simonides has a fan in this random rich man who knows him from his
voice. Clothes, money, and a suite of slaves are all his, aligning his good
financial returns from patronage (*mercede accepta,* 5) earlier in the poem.
As fables often do,[51] this one seems to grate against, or unveil another underside of, its promythium that *Homo doctus in se semper divitias habet*
(1)—for Simonides' fame brings him wealth, is directly convertible into material possessions, not just "wealth within."

The next Simonides fable makes a similar point, but it backtracks in at
least one respect: the famous poet is no longer getting paid. Phaedrus starts
out implying that doesn't matter, for the rewards this time will be celestial.
The poem signals it will be moving upward in response:

Quantum valerent inter homines litterae
dixi superius; quantus nunc illis honos
a superis sit tributus tradam memoriae. (4.26.1–3)

How much letters are worth among men, I said above; now I'll tell posterity how much honor they're given among the gods.

Again Phaedrus moves into famous poet mode (*tradam memoriae*), in order
to write about the famous poet.[52] The situation: Simonides is charged with
the banal piecework of turning a boxer into high poetry. He starts off de-
pressed by the material constraints but manages to transcend:

Simonides idem ille de quo rettuli,
victori laudem cuidam pyctae ut scriberet
certo conductus pretio, secretum petit,
exigua cum frenaret materia impetum,
usus poetae more est et licentia
atque interposuit gemina Ledae sidera,
auctoritatem similis referens gloriae. (4.26.4–10)

That very Simonides I mentioned above was contracted for a certain amount to write some panegyric for some victorious boxer. He withdrew into private. Since the material gave slim pickings and put the brake on his momentum, he employed the usual poetic license and inserted the twin stars of Leda, claiming them as precedents for equivalent glory.

Like Phaedrus adding bits to Aesop or adding Aesop to his bits (see *interposuero* 5 Prol. 1; and cf. *interponere* 2 Prol. 9), Simonides exercises some poetic license and inserts (*interposuit*) some elevated exempla to lift the tone a little. The stingy patron only offers him a third of the agreed sum, in proportion to his own presence in the poem. But he feels a little shame for the snub and so invites Simonides to dinner as recompense:

> "Illi" inquit "reddent quorum sunt laudis duae.
> verum, ut ne irate te dimissum sentiant,
> ad cenam mihi promitte; *cognatos* volo
> hodie invitare, quorum es in numero mihi." (4.26.13–16)

He put it: "Let those two pay you; they're two parts of the praise. But so people don't think you've been abandoned by my anger, please have an invite to dinner; I'm going to ask my relatives today, and I count you among them."

Cognatos is crucial to the smarting pain of demotion here: from being the star of 4.23, rewarded handsomely for the recognition (*cognitum*), Simonides plunges down to just another member of the circle of patron's *cognati* (kinsmen). The poet grudgingly agrees and is rewarded for it, sort of. Two young men call him out of the dinner party just as the roof of the dining room falls in and squashes everyone else inside. Phaedrus gives us the consensus moral in case we missed it:

> ut est vulgatus ordo narratae rei
> omnes scierunt numinum praesentiam
> vati dedisse vitam mercedis loco. (4.26.31–33)

When the course of the story, as I've told it, was made known, everyone knew that a divine presence had given the poet his life instead of his pay.

You could say that *vitam mercedis loco* is a good deal. But if we think back to what Simonides got from pure recognition in 4.23—clothes, money, even slaves—the payment of life here doesn't look so crash hot. Simonides escapes with a stroke of divine favor, but that is only because the breakdown of patronage put him in a position of humiliating danger in the first place.

All this hoo-ha seems to move us from the wishful, magical thinking of a recognized poet rewarded handsomely to the "realistic" pessimism of a poet who doesn't even get the promised dinner from the deal, indeed is lucky to escape with his life. And this must have something to do with the following epilogue, which invokes patron Particulo yet again:

Adhuc supersunt multa quae possim loqui,
et copiosa abundat rerum varietas;
sed temperatae suaves sunt argutiae,
immodicae offendunt. quare, vir sanctissime,
Particulo, chartis nomen victurum meis,
Latinis dum manebit pretium litteris,
si non ingenium, certe brevitatem adproba;
quae commendari tanto debet iustius,
quanto cantores sunt molesti validius. (4 Epil.)

There are still a thousand things to talk about, and the huge array of available subjects is overflowing; but jokes are only sweet in moderation— and anything more, downright offensive. So, my honorable Particulo, since your name is due to survive in my pages, as long as Latin literature fetches a price, you'll certainly appreciate my brevity, if not my literary skill. My brevity should get as much due praise, as the extreme annoyance caused by poetasters.

Phaedrus promises to immortalize Particulo's name "if and only if Latin literature stays valuable" (i.e., fetches a *pretium*). The stipulation and haggling of all this seems to tell us that Particulo, like the tightfisted boxer of the previous poem, still hasn't come through with the goods (and that even after Phaedrus has resorted to fabled death threats). The move to the next book confirms Particulo's thanks but no thanks, for Phaedrus is all of a sudden reduced to the most bargain-basement form of artistic quackery:

Aesopi nomen sicubi interposuero,
cui reddidi iam pridem quicquid debui,
auctoritatis esse scito gratia;
ut quidam artifices nostro faciunt saeculo,
qui pretium operibus maius inveniunt novis
si marmori adscripserunt Praxitelen suo,

detrito Myn argento, tabulae Zeuxidem.
adeo fucatae plus vetustati favet
Invidia mordax quam bonis praesentibus.
sed iam ad fabellam talis exempli feror. (5 Prol.)

Just know that wherever I introduced the name "Aesop" (to whom I repaid whatever I owed a while ago), it was for the sake of authority, just
as certain craftsmen of our generation do, those who fetch a better price
for new works if they scribble "Praxiteles" onto their own marble or
"Mys" onto their polished silver or "Zeuxis" on their paintings. So much
more does snapping envy go in for browned old-age than for brand-
spanking-new goods. But now it's time for a story to illustrate such an
instance.

The insertion of the *Aesopi nomen* (in a statement about its many inser-
tions) effectively picks up where the *nomen victurum* of Particulo left off.
The patron of book 4, like the patron of book 3 (and all the other attempted
"friends" of epilogue 3), has passed. When everything's said and done, good
old Aesop is the only one left standing—and Phaedrus has spent much of
his career paying *him* (*reddidi*)! Some critics have taken this as Phaedrus'
most confident declaration of independence to date,[53] but I have no idea
how it can look like that. His analogues are no longer the real godlike *auctores* of prologue 3 but *artifices* (more like *fabri?*) who trade in cheap
knockoffs. The only thing they can "create" (*inveniunt;* cf. the *invenit* of
Aesop in 4.22) is a price tag for their fakes.[54] Now stripped of a patron to
make himself look pretty for, Phaedrus drops the act and picks up a new
one: an Aesop imitator who signs the master's name only to get a few more
bucks on the open market. No more pretense of genteel gift exchange between poet and patron, for that just didn't work. Time for no-holds-barred
commerce.[55] With the latest Particulo gone, Phaedrus is truly bankrupt.
    The fable promised to bear out this message does deliver, in a sense. It
is, yet again, a recognition scene involving a famous poet. But this time,
the recognition needs some help. And the poet is seen at a much greater
distance from the power he is supposed to be playing profitable footsies
with, in serving up praise for hire. King Demetrius (of Phalerum, but min-
gled with tones of namesake Poliorcetes)[56] was receiving his daily adula-
tion from pretty much every Athenian citizen, even the ones in retirement
or outside politics—for fear of the consequences of not showing up (*ne de-*

fuisse noceat, 5.1.8). Menander comes in train with these. The famous poet is forced to trot along in the worst kind of conga-line obeisance. Demetrius admires him but doesn't recognize him at first. All he sees is another *cinaedus.* Once his aids fill him in, he changes his tune:

> in quis Menander, nobilis comoediis,
> quas ipsum ignorans legerat Demetrius
> et admiratus fuerat ingenium viri,
> unguento delibutus, vestitu fluens,
> veniebat gressu delicato et languido.
> hunc ubi tyrannus vidit extremo agmine:
> "Quisnam cinaedus ille in conspectu meo
> audet cevere?" responderunt proximi
> "Hic est Menander scriptor." mutatus statim
> "Homo" inquit "fieri non potest formosior." (5.1.9–18)

Menander was among them, a star through his comedies, which Demetrius had read; even though he didn't know him personally, he was a fan of the man's talents. Menander came along oozing perfume, his garments flowing, his gait dainty and dandyish. When the tyrant saw him at the end of the crowd: "Who's that fag who dares to shake his arse in my line of sight?" Those around him replied: "That's him, that's Menander the playwright!" He changed tack immediately: "there could be no finer specimen!"

The point here does gel with the previous epilogue: a famous name has a lot of power and can change the evaluation straightaway. But I think this fable is also asking us to measure the distance traveled from the halcyon days (wishful thinking) of the old Simonides. There, patronage functioned beautifully, so that the poet had stuff thrown at him, even from anonymous fans who could pick him by his voice. The *new* Simonides was kicked around and underpaid, but at least the gods still granted him his life. Now the powers that be are so distant from the poet that they can't even see him when he is marching up to say hello, staring them in the face. They have to be *told* to recognize.[57] This is very much a relation of reader to writer—mediated, ignorant of the person at the other end—rather than the face-to-face contact relationship of poet to patron. And the fact that Menander is called *scriptor,* not *auctor,* puts that aspect of distance front and center.[58] Textualizing that key relationship of "recognition" means that the poet figure is now nothing more than a name. He gets his just deserts to suit—

no more free stuff, no more life whisked from the jaws of death, merely a bland approving: *"Homo" inquit "fieri non potest formosior."*

It is that sort of "pure textuality" on which the whole phenomenon of Phaedrus—complete with all the real-world furnishings—has depended and with which our unknown fabulist will brilliantly end. Here comes the last installment in this long line of topping and tailing our down-and-out poet, the one where Phaedrus finally admits he's had it:

> Adversus omnes fortis et velox feras
> canis cum domino semper fecisset satis,
> languere coepit annis ingravantibus.
> aliquando obiectus hispidi pugnae suis,
> arripuit aurem; sed cariosis dentibus
> praedam dimisit rictus, venator dolens
> canem obiurgabat. cui senex contra Lacon:
> "Non te destituit animus, sed vires meae.
> quod fuimus lauda, si iam damnas quod sumus."
> hoc cur, Philete, **scripserim** pulchre vides. (5.10)

A certain dog, once robust and quick in facing any kind of beast, who had always done enough for his master, began to fade out as the years weighed. At one point, thrown into battle with a hairy boar, he plucked it by the ear, but because of his decaying teeth, his bite lost its prey, and the angry hunter hurled abuse at him. The old Spartan answered back: "My spirit hasn't abandoned me; my strength has. Praise what I was, if you have to damn what I am." You know full well why **I've written** this, Philetas.

Consistent with prologue 5, this fable loses the sugarcoating and sells Phaedrus for what he is: a beaten-up old model who can't quite cut it anymore. As with the wine scent of 3.1, so with this one: we are given an internal audience as a model of "getting it," and this is deeply connected to the fact that we are asked to know Phaedrus by *what is left*.[59] But even more than 3.1, "Philetus" (?) doesn't have to know anything to decode this fable except for the fact that it comes at the end of a long and rubbishy career. All it takes is to have read Phaedrus (and even a brief flick through would have done the job). That is why, I think, that last line is explicitly about *writing*. It fulfills Phaedrus' long project of boiling his existence down into a text that has no author beyond the myths that the author peddles about "himself." Phaedrus becomes the Platonic ideal of the Menandrian *scriptor* whom no one can recognize, because "he" is no one. He writes, therefore he is.

I have tried to show that the autobiography of Phaedrus is no smooth march up the ranks but a textual *vita* full of pushes and pulls, onslaughts made and retreats beaten. If your vision is blurry, the story can look like a big circle, bending in an arc from debut nerves to growing confidence to big fame to secure patronage to precarious zero-hours con artist to past it; but with granular detail, the geometry is more like a sine curve, up and down, up and down, the downs inevitably trumping the ups. The story flashes the successes but is always quick to turn them into comic failures.[60] Retrospectively, that story makes us doubt those successes as fictive thinking, empty words, all along. The play of Phaedrus features a no-name protagonist who stays that way, despite his best attempts to talk himself up by fiat from unknown to known. It is this full-pelt fictionality to which Martial responds in 3.20, the only remaining trace of ancient Phaedrian reception:

> Dic, Musa, quid agat Canius meus Rufus:
> utrumne chartis tradit ille victuris
> legenda temporum acta Claudianorum?
> an quae Neroni falsus astruit scriptor,
> an aemulatur improbi λόγους Phaedri? (Martial *Ep.* 3.20.1–5)

> Tell me, Muse, what my old Canius Rufus is up to: is he handing the events of the Claudian age on to everlasting paper, making them into reading material? Or is he trying to rival what a fake author ascribed to Nero or the fables of cheeky Phaedrus?

It is no coincidence that Martial chucks Phaedrus in with a lying *scriptor* who falsely attributes some writing. The "made-up" status of Phaedrus' name is marked in the very Phaedrian epithet *improbus*, "mischievous."[61] It takes a Martial, highly attuned to writing pseudonymously,[62] to sniff the fiction.

Phaedrus may not have had much take-up. All the same, he remains one of antiquity's great performances of authorial invention, because the entire biographical framework, designed to be at least a little "referential," is mixed and matched artificially from the high-culture poets this two-bit fabulist can never hope to match. The author loses all external reference in the process. Phaedrus is completely "Phaedrus"; there is no Phaedrus, just "Phaedrus." His precondition is absolute anonymity, textuality neat.[63] There will be no "real" fame, no "true" recognition, because there is no one home to get famous or be recognized. The immortality is reserved for the *character*. The comedy depends on that character never getting anywhere, on being more the perpetual harassing Boor of Horace's *Satires* 1.9 than the Lord High Poet Himself.[64] It depends on us not knowing the lead script-writer, the contents of the wine jar, the young dog we have lost forever, or the look of this cheeky *cinaedus*, even if we smelled it, even if he wiggled his bum in our face.

5

Poet Seeks Patron

An Open Letter from Me to You,
Or Numerosa Laus

PHAEDRUS GAVE US A TALE of a made-up poet buzzing the doorbell of grandee patrons who never bothered to answer (because their names were snatched, like Phaedrus', from the thinnest air). But he at least left a calling card of a sort, which would ensure that the tradition would know him by his character title. With our next piece, we have no such luck. The *Laus Pisonis* (*LP*) is the work of a genuine *ignotus*. Various cracks have been made at attributing this poem,[1] but they are little more than stabs in the dark. No one has convincingly brought this self-consciously obscure poet into the light he politely requests. In fact, even the identity we would hope most uncontroversial—that is, the Piso of the praise, the *laudandus* himself—has proved controversial.[2] Dating, too, has leaked straight through scholars' porous hands.[3] I shall contend in this chapter that this poem's mechanics rely on the unknown status of all these three key threads of historicist detective work—author, patron, date—to produce a curious freak of literary history: praise without occasion,[4] a poem for all occasions.

The *LP* is a puzzle of a praise poem. "Technically competent, conceptually bizarre,"[5] Edward Champlin dubbed it, not without good reason. The panegyric circles around strange topics that are usually, shall we say, not quite front and center in the ideal elite Roman bag of tricks. Piso's pedigree (2–24) and formidable eloquence in the courtroom get us off to a strong start; but then we are derailed onto lighter, more couch-style rhetorical pursuits such as declamation and literature (81–96) or stuck with nothing better to talk about than Piso's visage, bearing, and character (97–108) and his chummy relations with friends and clients (109–137). We then steer into eighty-odd lines on Piso's more frivolous pursuits (137–208): a rider justifying these frivolous activities; Piso's skill at composing poetry or playing the lyre and why that's okay (164–177); or Piso's aptitude for the noble arts of play fighting in arms (178–184), ball games (*lusus pilae,* 185–189), and, wait for it, board games (the *ludus latrunculorum,* 190–208). Following that stirring climax, our poet, tongue somewhere in cheek perhaps, concludes with an apology for not producing poetry worthier of Piso. That will only come if and when Piso starts paying him (209–261). So the slightly satiric, quasi-commercial logic of the poem can be seen even at this level of zoom. The poem's strangeness and mediocrity is banked as merely a first skeletal overture, to be fleshed out after the poet matures into Piso's money. In other words, the praise is predicated on Piso and poet having nothing to do with each other (yet).

The scholarship on the *LP* is a stunning example of the kind of historicist mania that this book is doing its best to offset, if not overhaul. One of the most recent influential articles on the poem—an attempt to pin down the addressee and to place the poem in a meaningful political "context"—transcribes the collective assumptions of this gang of Mr. Fix-Its, the time and date stamp-ede: "In order to do any sort of justice to the poem, it needs to be contextualized, and this has proved to be the essential stumbling block."[6] This is perhaps one of the great abiding principles of Latin literary studies nowadays. But across the board, it doesn't quite hold up. First, the narrow (and normative) understanding of "contextualization" as placement within a context of elite power relations can throttle texts as much as do them justice.[7] Justice can be done with other forms of context (for the *Laus,* e.g., the poem's place in the history of praise or its underappreciated role in constructing the general paradigm "patron"). Second, political-context-ing can work beautifully where that context is easily recovered. But in cases such as the *LP,* completely unhoused and unhinged, the conjectural labor required for this "contextualization" gets us nowhere fast. More than that, it can also blind us to the stunning effects of a text's active resistance to these kinds of context-fixing landgrabs. Constant mourning for the "loss" of contextual information and obsessive combing to win it back may actually stop us from facing the more confronting prospect: that the "loss" may be part of the fun. So there may be no such "loss" after all.

I want to show in this chapter that the *LP* exploits the creative possibilities of an unknown and unknowable context to form a strange creature of praise poetry, which seeks to stay valid for all time, to transcend the specificity of the limiting "moment."[8] We shall also see that the poem's effects depend on poet and patron not knowing each other. They lean on anonymity to make the drama work. Any detective work designed to fling this dark young poet into the light should at least start with the acknowledgment that the darkness is a key part of the performance. For true redistributive justice to be done to the *LP*, we'll just have to work with ignorance. That is our bargain with the no-name.

Pisones: Patrons Plural

For one of *the* leading lights of the imperial aristocracy, the Pisones are often tough prosopographical nuts to crack. No one can claim complete confidence with the gingerly consensus that the Piso of the *LP* is the famous Neronian conspirator;[9] but that is perhaps because he comes from a line of genetic question marks. Let's take Horace's *Ars Poetica* as a kind of precursor of a "Piso-addressed" envelope (not to mention the fact that the *Ars Poetica* exerts an undersold sway on the *LP*).[10] In the case of the *Ars Poetica*, the addressees—a three-pronged attack of Pisones, father and two sons—are limited to two options: the branch of Piso the Pontifex (consul 15 BCE) and the branch of Gnaeus Calpurnius Piso (consul 23 BCE). Scholarly consensus has settled on Piso the Pontifex because the family had more ties to poetry. But that move requires the astounding doublethink of blocking out the fact that this Piso has no attested sons, and the other Piso has two sons more or less fitting the bill.[11] The problem of Piso the Pontifex's phantom sons also haunts the *LP*. Since Champlin, the orthodoxy is pretty much that the *LP* addresses Piso the famous Neronian conspirator, at a to-be-determined point in his career (Champlin goes for 39/40, under Caligula; recently Steven Green and Gottfried Mader have pushed much later, around the time of the conspiracy itself).[12] And this conspirator is thought to be the grandson of the pontifex (i.e., a son of one of his unattested sons[13]—evidence for whom can be supplied on request—just ask the *Ars Poetica!*). So a particularly privileged branch of the Pisones is getting all the poems. Lucky them.

The jewel in the crown of this Piso identification is Tacitus' character sketch of the conspirator at *Annals* 15.48. Champlin nicely showed how

each of his traits—popularity, eloquence, good looks, etc.—has its counterpart in the *LP*.[14] Now that in itself could go another way: it could show
us that Tacitus took the *LP* to be addressed to the conspirator, recycled the
qualities, and hence the *LP* could be allowed—shock and / or horror—a
more influential place in The Tradition. It could also show, however, that
these are inherently Calpurnian / Pisonian characteristics, traveling with the
blood and the name. The features themselves are particularly difficult to
make out: indeed, they are more like nonfeatures. Piso is pleasing to
everyone, has a *decora facies,* etc. Big deal. Even for Champlin, he is a "man
without qualities."[15] Tacitus nods to the twin issues of the slippery catch-
all nature of Piso, as well as the difficulty of performing a conclusive genetic test to establish identity, when he says,

> Is Calpurnio genere ortus ac **multas insignisque familias paterna nobili-
> tate complexus,** claro apud vulgum rumore erat per virtutem aut species
> virtutibus similes. (Tac. *Ann.* 15.48)

> Piso, offspring of the Calpurnian clan, **embodied many illustrious fami-
> lies through his father's nobility**; he had a famous reputation for virtue
> among the common people, or at least for showy qualities that looked
> like virtues.

That is, every Piso is an amalgam of Pisones, which makes them impossible to identify whenever they come up in literature. By the time of Martial and Juvenal, they are a shorthand for aristocratic patron, like
"Maecenas"[16]—couldn't they have been by the time of the *LP* too?[17] The
poem is actually ultra self-aware about the process whereby a brand name
loses its referential specificity and becomes synonymous with a type, the
product itself, Kleenex into tissue, Maecenas into patron: the poet promises Piso he will be sung "as a Maecenas" toward the end (248). Not only
this, but all "historicizable" strings to Piso's bow are left pointedly slack.
His own praise oration for the emperor—highly commended at 68–71—is
left uncredited, a floating *Caesareum numen.* Piso is addressed as *iuvenis*
(which word's flexibility always creates headaches for Latin poem daters)[18]
or *decus*—and in fact this latter word gets to the heart of the poem's compelling *Ars Poetica*–inflected poetics of decorum (more on which later).
That's to say that the *LP* makes its lead character into everything, fitting
every single context.

The Piso of the *LP* is the extreme of "Piso's" traditional plurality; he becomes less a person than a prolifically branching idea, a paradoxical essence of variability. True, the rhetoric of abundance is a stock-in-trade of praise poetry,[19] and we're inoculated enough to take the following in our stride, label it as mediocrity to be drowned under a thousand parallels:

> Unde prius coepti surgat mihi carminis ordo
> quosve canam titulos, dubius feror.[20] (*LP* 1–2)

> Where should the order of the poem first begin? Which titles should I hymn? I'm torn in doubt.

> nec si cuncta velim breviter decurrere possim;
> et prius aethereae moles circumvaga flammae
> annua bissenis revocabit mensibus astra,
> quam mihi priscorum titulos operosaque bella
> contigerit memorare. (18–22)

> I couldn't run over everything in brief, even if I wanted; the huge cycling mass of ethereal flame will recall its yearly stars in its twelve-month period, before I could recall the titles and laborious wars of the older guard.

But as the poem hits its rhythm, we find that Piso is truly unsummarizable because he embodies within him "excellence" in basically every field of contemporary elite striving, to the point where he is always caught doing at least both things, usually many things, at once. The first aspect of Piso's multitalents to get the spotlight is his rhetoric in the law courts. He can run the full gamut of emotions, taking the judge with him wherever he wants.[21] He speaks all weathers, rain, hail, or lightning, and piles the merits of Odysseus, Menelaus, and Nestor,[22] the golden trifecta, all in one:

> nam tu, sive libet pariter cum grandine nimbos
> densaque vibrata iaculari fulmina lingua,
> seu iuvat adstrictas in nodum cogere voces
> et dare subtili vivacia verba catenae,
> vim Laertiadae, brevitatem vincis Atridae;
> dulcia seu mavis liquidoque fluentia cursu
> verba nec incluso sed aperto pingere flore,
> inclita Nestorei cedit tibi gratia mellis. (57–64)

You, whether you want to toss rain, as well as hail, and frequent bolts of thunder, tonguing in double time, or whether you like to force dense expressions into a unit and lend live words to your intricate series, you outdo Odysseus' force and Menelaus' concision; or whether you prefer to paint up words as they flow on their limpid watercourse, not with cramped but open flourishes, the world-famous beauty of honeyed Nestor trails behind you.

So he can modulate his style wherever, however, at will, all out there in the open (contrast Piso's Technicolor light show of a word painting with our poet's pointed *obscurity* below, on verses 253–258).[23] But he also floats the boat of whoever is in the audience, be it citizens, senate, or even emperor:

> nec te, Piso, tamen populo sub iudice sola
> mirantur fora; sed numerosa laude senatus
> excipit et meritas reddit tibi curia voces.
> quis digne referat, qualis tibi luce sub illa
> gloria contigerit, qua tu, reticente senatu,
> cum tua bissenos numeraret purpura fasces,
> Caesareum grato cecinisti pectore numen? (65–71)

It's not just the courts beneath a popular jury who love you, Piso: the senate embraces you with multiform praise, and the curia gives you well-earned cheers. Who could properly recount the type of glory that you received on that day when you—the senate all hushed, your purple totting up its twelve fasces—sang Caesar's divinity with a grateful heart?

The senate claps with equal heart; note the "multifaceted" (*numerosa*) praise, a form of *laus* that captures the voluminous methods of the *LP* (*numerosus* and *numerare* are all over the poem).[24] And as hinted earlier, that *Caesareum numen* is left without license and registration for a reason: Piso's praise skill is so flexible, so multicontextual, that it goes beyond the particulars of any one Caesar.[25] Piso pleases, no matter who, what, when.

Next, poet opens up the doors to reveal a domestic Piso doing his declamatory exercises. The material to work with here is just as plural, just as abundant (*plura supersunt*). The youth from all over Rome flock to hear him at it. What they hear is perfect Greek from Roman lips, full language studded with tropes, and a veritable smorgasbord to pander to all palates:

magna quidem virtus erat, et si sola fuisset,
eloquio sanctum modo permulcere senatum,
exonerare pios modo, nunc onerare nocentes (97–99)

It was a big virtue (even were it the only one), now to fondle the sacred senate with his smooth speaking, now to unburden the innocent, now to burden the guilty:

Piso's *uirtus* is put under a multiplier (*magna . . . et si sola fuisset*) until it eventually becomes *numerosa* too (*virtus numerosa,* 137).[26] With a *virtus* that big, his style works for the senate or for the contexts of prosecution and/or defense equally well. Our little poet applies his own virtuoso *variatio* (e.g., changing up adverb and relative position from *modo* to *nunc*).[27] The numerous style *is* the appearance, for Piso's noble setup gives him the look for every occasion:

sed super ista movet plenus gravitate serena
vultus et insigni praestringit imagine visus.
talis inest habitus, qualem nec dicere maestum
nec fluidum, laeta sed tetricitate decorum
possumus: ingenitae stat nobilitatis in illo
pulcher honos et digna suis natalibus ora. (100–105)

But even more than those things, his expression, packed with tranquil dignity, has a big impact, and his look transfixes with its impressive image. He has such an appearance as we could call neither weighty nor lax but perfectly moderate in its charming seriousness. A handsome honor of inborn nobility resides in him; the face he presents measures up to his birth.

His physical qualities[28]—such as they can be described as being in any true sense "described"—are summed in that key word *decorum*:[29] not too happy, not too sad, the golden mean, just right. In other words, the essence of Piso is to bend with the wind. He is a blank slate inscribable according to the demands of *kairos*.[30]

Piso's home patronage practice is likewise a broad church. The poet tells us this open house is there for all and sundry and doesn't discriminate by class or birth: *unus amicitiae summos tenor ambit et imos* (117). Piso's tastes in his rent-a-crowd, no surprise, are just as wide ranging as his other remarkably varied skills:

cuncta domus varia cultorum personat arte,
cuncta movet studium; nec enim tibi dura clientum
turba rudisve placet, misero quae freta labore
nil nisi summoto novit praecedere vulgo;
sed virtus numerosa iuvat. (133–137)

The entire house buzzes with the diverse skills of its salon: enthusiasm gets everything going; for an uncouth or rough-around-the-edges mob of clients does nothing for you, a mob relying on lowly work, which knows nothing apart from how to walk ahead once the common throng have been swept away. By contrast, a many-sided virtue is more your style.

Piso hates a one-trick pony of a crowd only qualified to do just one thing (*nil nisi*), walk in front. He likes a multifaceted (*numerosa*) character, to go with the "diverse" (*varia*) skill set of the housebound masses. And that catholic taste in people goes well with Piso's feel for every sort of pursuit, from low to high:

tu pronus in omne
pectora ducis opus, seu te graviora vocarunt
seu leviora iuvant. nec enim facundia semper
adducta cum fronte placet: nec semper in armis
bellica turba manet, . . . (137–141)

You readily rope your spirit into every kind of work, whether more serious things are calling or whether you're leaning more to the light. For eloquence, with its furrowed brow, isn't always the ticket: nor does a war mob always stay in its arms, . . .

For the next twenty lines, the changes are rung on that same topos of changeability. As the seasons change, so does Piso. The moveable feast that is this unique everyman of a patron of course also extends into poetry:

si carmina forte
nectere ludenti iuvit fluitantia versu,
Aonium facilis deducit pagina carmen;
sive chelyn digitis et eburno verbere pulsas,
dulcis Apollinea sequitur testudine cantus,
et te credibile est Phoebo didicisse magistro.
ne pudeat pepulisse lyram, cum pace serena
publica securis exultent otia terris,
ne pudeat: Phoebea chelys sic creditur illis
pulsari manibus, quibus et contenditur arcus; (163–172)

If you maybe liked to weave something easy-listening through playful verse, the page collaborates, spinning down an Aonian song; or if you pluck your lyre with your fingers and an ivory rod, a sweet song trails from the Apolline shell, and it's plausible you learned the trade from Phoebus' class. Don't be shy to strike the lyre; with peace and tranquility, let official holidays rejoice in a world without care; don't be shy. In that very way—so we think—Apollo's lyre is twanged by the very same hands that stretch the bow;

Of course, Piso's poetic output is multigeneric, flitting effortlessly between Hesiodic Muse-based tunes and Apollonian lyric. And like Apollo himself, Piso's hands can move smoothly from plucking string to drawing bow. Peace or war, poetry or practice, he's got it covered.

When poet moves from poetry to the gym, it's clear that the same principles of full coverage obtain—indeed even more so, as the acrobatics of this all-in-one miracle of a man start looking more and more improbable. If Piso is play fighting, it looks as if he can pull off basically every move under the sun, essentially at the same time:

arma tuis etiam si forte rotare lacertis
inque gradum clausis libuit consistere membris
et vitare **simul, simul** et captare petentem,
mobilitate pedum celeres super orbibus orbes
plectis et obliquis fugientem cursibus urges:
et **nunc** vivaci scrutaris pectora dextra,
nunc latus adversum necopino percutis ictu. (178–184)

If you've maybe felt the need to whizz weapons with your arms and take the position, your limbs on lockdown, and **at the very same time** both swerve clear of and hit your opponent, with fancy footwork you leaf in circle on circle and press your enemy in flight, chasing him from the side; and **now** you make for his chest with your agile right hand, **now** you strike his exposed side with a blow out of nowhere.

Poet piles *simul* upon *simul* and *nunc* upon *nunc* to paint a portrait of a Piso in motion, a patron able to pull it all off at once. Indeed *simul* geminates across the caesura as if there were no pause, and each action overlapped in the blink of an eye. We race with fully dactylic agility through the verse on *mobilitas*.[31] Piso's *mobilitas* with the ball turns out just as nippy and impressive. In fact Piso's Harlem Globetrotter–style maneuvers are so slick that they seem almost to defy the laws of gravity:

> nec tibi mobilitas minor est, si forte volantem
> aut geminare pilam iuvat aut revocare cadentem
> et non sperato fugientem reddere gestu. (185–187)

> Your agility is just as special, should you want to turn back the ball in flight, or save it as it's falling, and by a shock move keep it in play.

Piso's actions in the infinitives are so quick and decisive that they can even anticipate the ball's participial movements (*volantem . . . geminare* becomes *revocare cadentem*). He is at one with the game. But this kind of quick-fire, miracle dexterity reaches peak virtuoso in Piso's style of *ludus latrunculorum,* "The Brigands' Game."[32] Our miracle man is also an outstanding player of this chess-like Roman board game. Piso starts playing commander with his troops on the board. Liberated from the bounds of one body, he is split into many agents performing different actions at the same time:

> te si forte iuvat studiorum pondere fessum
> non languere tamen lususque movere per artem,
> callidiore modo tabula variatur aperta
> calculus et vitreo peraguntur milite bella,
> ut niveus nigros, nunc et niger alliget albos. (190–194)

> When you're tired out from an intense study session, if you're nevertheless happy not to go off duty, but to play board games, then you manipulate a piece on an open board with high craft, and you polish off the wars with glass soldiers such that the white checks the black, and now the black the white.

The rules of this game are difficult to reconstruct, but whatever the precise ins and outs, the point seems to be that multiple moves are happening *at once.* The calculus is moved this way and that (*variatur* again); the glass army does its thing; white pieces hem in black, black white. It seems that on Piso's watch, every strategic permutation can play itself out:

> mille modis acies tua dimicat: ille petentem,
> dum fugit, ipse rapit; longo venit ille recessu,
> qui stetit in speculis; hic se committere rixae
> audet et in praedam venientem decipit hostem;
> ancipites subit ille moras similisque ligato

obligat ipse duos; hic ad maiora movetur,
ut citus ecfracta prorumpat in agmina mandra
clausaque deiecto populetur moenia vallo. (197–204)

Your formation sparkles in a thousand ways: one piece takes its pursuer
even as it's pursued; another comes on from the bench, standing on the
lookout; this one dives into battle and tricks the enemy as it comes for
its booty; this one dallies dangerously and checks two pieces while it's
looking checked; this one goes for the big payoff, to break the enemy's
defenses by surprise, burst out against his forces, demolish the rampart,
and ransack the walls.

The variation (*mille modis*) and simultaneity is exhausting.[33] One piece
turns hunted into hunter; another converts checked into checker. Piso's
pieces are masters of the brisk reversal, almost to the point of playing two
roles at the same time. By the end of this section, we can see why he wins
with his phalanx intact (*plena . . . phalange,* 206), and *both hands* echo, resound (*resonat,* 208), with the crowd of pieces the master has managed to
capture. Piso is the ultimate multitasker. He can get away with doing two
things at once, keeping both hands full.

As poet moves to his stirring peroration, he has one more card of Pisonian versatility[34] left to play. He follows up the promise for more and better
poetry, plus a plea for committed patronage, with a long tract on Maecenas,
the Pisonian patron par excellence. Scrolling through the history of Mae-
cenetan aid, poet shows the multigeneric generosity of the old minister of
culture. First Virgil comes up—epic Virgil, but if it weren't for Maecenas,
he could have been stuck in the obscurity of the pastoral hinterland forever (230–237). Horace the lyric genius of course wins a mention too (242).
But given the poem's heavy focus on the Pisonian versatility through *varius*
and *variare,* the standout of the Maecenatan poetic trio could well be
Varius:[35]

qui tamen haut uni patefecit limina vati
nec sua Vergilio permisit numina soli:
Maecenas tragico quatientem pulpita gestu
euexit Varium, Maecenas alta tonantis
eruit et populis ostendit nomina Graiis. (236–240)[36]

He didn't throw open his doors to one bard and one only, nor did he invest
his divinity in Virgil alone: Maecenas brought out Varius, who rattled

the stage with his tragic moves; Maecenas dug out the deepest notes of
the thundering poet and unveiled names to the Greek people.

Not just one poet (Virgil) but many, and the first of which is many poets in
one (Varius). Perhaps that is even the gist of the weirdly obscure line *et
populis ostendit nomina Graiis:*[37] Maecenas was so good that he managed to
make many poets (*nomina*) out of the same one (i.e., Varius the epic and
elegiac author in addition to the tragic?).[38] Indeed just as Maecenas' varied
tastes back Varius but also Virgil and Horace all at once, so we spy a kind of
logic collapsing Piso and Maecenas, allowing Piso to be Maecenas (and vice
versa). Poet addresses Maecenas (ostensibly) with the very term, and rhetoric
of the interminable, that he has been applying to Piso thus far:

> o decus, in totum merito venerabilis aevum, (243)

> Grace itself, ripe for and deserving of eternal worship!

It is as if he is addressing Piso through Maecenas,[39] as if both patrons are
so capacious, so multitalented, that each can be the other—which is exactly
what happens more explicitly in a jiffy:

> quod si quis nostris precibus locus, et mea vota
> si mentem subiere tuam, memorabilis olim
> tu mihi Maecenas tereti cantabere versu. (246–248)

> But if there's any room for my requests, and my prayers have stolen into
> your heart, you'll one day be the star of your own polished verse, remem-
> bered forever, my Maecenas.

The versatility of Maecenas becomes the versatility of Piso: "you my Maecenas" becomes "you as my Maecenas." Indeed the fungibility of these two
characters seems to point, right at the end, to what Piso has been all along:
no piece of context meat, no hook of political reality, but a *byword* for the
ideal patron, a capacious proverb for everything an obscure young poet
could want—and more.

Ancient praise is packed with the rhetoric of exhaustiveness that the *LP*
pushes to its logical conclusion.[40] But the *LP* is particularly fecund and particularly exhausting. The poem runs on a bottomless fuel of alternatives,
simultaneities, and potentials. The poet piles up all the items in Piso's astounding bag of tricks via various ways and means: *si forte* (178, 185, 190)
turns us onto another sphere of activity,[41] another thing he could be doing;

hinc . . . hinc (2/5, 94/95), *nunc . . . nunc* (183/184), *modo . . . modo*
(51/52, 98/99) distribute his talents beautifully; *sive . . . seu . . . seu* (41/43,
57/59/62, 138/139) spread Piso's wings; *simul* (180, twice), *mille modis*
(197), *ille . . . hic* (197/198/199/201/202), and *forsan/forsitan* (216/33)
work similar magic to make Piso into a moving target. At times, when he
doesn't feel quite up to the job of combing through all the permutations,
poet resorts to the old rhetorical-question shortcut to gesture toward the
wilderness of untreated abundance, whose surface we won't even come
close to scratching:

> quis digne referat, qualis tibi luce sub illa
> gloria contigerit, qua tu, reticente senatu,
> cum tua bissenos numeraret purpura fasces,
> Caesareum grato cecinisti pectore numen? (68–71)

Who could properly recount the type of glory that you received on that
day when you—the senate all hushed, your purple totting up its twelve
fasces—sang Caesar's divinity with a grateful heart?

> quis tua cultorum, iuvenis facunde, tuorum
> limina pauper adit, quem non animosa beatum
> excipit et subito iuvat indulgentia censu? (109–111)

Who among your clients, silver-tongued young man, makes for your
house in poverty whom your hearty generosity *doesn't* welcome and make
rich, *doesn't* boost with a sudden donation?

All of these strategies are of course forms of comprehensiveness to build
Piso's résumé.[42] But I want to argue in the next section that they also carry
a more literal justification or stem from a dramatic scenario set up by the
poet. For those speculations (*si forte . . .*) and questions are also necessary
to the whole framework of ignorance on which the poem is based. By that
I mean this: our poet dresses as a creative at the start of his career, on the
outside, without any direct personal knowledge of Piso. So *of course* this
letter of introduction must speculate on, and ask questions about, its addressee. The poet has no idea about the specifics of this "Piso," only a litany
of possibilities drawn up after the kinds of things an elite patron might get
up to, as well as the "man without qualities" openness of the Pisonian name.
The poet doesn't know this particular patron very well. And he is not a
particular patron. But this is also predicated on the fact that the poet

himself is "unknown." As we shall see in the next section, he wallows in a liberating obscurity of his own making, to help knock up a praise poem of and for all time(s).

Signed, X (Poet)

For a poem plagued by interminable squabbles over its authorial source, the *LP*'s opening word almost doubles as a lightning conductor of scholarly frustration: *unde*—where does this thing come from?![43] But the black hole of anonymity is not necessarily a gutting effect of loss wrought by time and transmission. Again, switching the lights off is a key part of the show. As I sketched earlier, the speaking voice of the *LP* is positioned on the outside, in full obscurity. It does its best to play that up to maximum pitch, such that the combination of no one poet and everyman patron creates an absolute firecracker of a "timeless" poem, valid across the board.

Protests of inadequacy to the task are basic stuff of praise poetry. But they usually carry more than a little faux modesty, especially when they come from established poets. The creator of the *LP*, by contrast, makes sure we know how small he really is compared to the glaring giant of Piso. These are very much juvenile efforts:

> quodsi iam validae mihi robur mentis inesset
> et solidus primos impleret spiritus annos,
> auderem voces per carmina nostra referre,
> Piso, tuas: (72–75)

> But if I had a solid base of intelligence in me, and a stout spirit were bolstering these first years of mine, I'd be bold enough to capture your speech in my song, Piso:

Our boy is just getting his career off the ground, and feels as self-conscious as a swallow trying to sing a swan's song or a grasshopper next to nightingales (77–80).[44] Poet knows he can get a whole lot better, if only Piso himself lends his uplifting presence (*tu modo laetus ades*, 216) and drags him from total obscurity up to the sky heights (or at least earth's surface) of visibility:

> iuvat, optime, tecum
> degere cumque tuis virtutibus omne per aevum
> carminibus certare meis: sublimior ibo,

si famae mihi pandis iter, si detrahis umbram.
abdita quid prodest generosi vena metalli,
si cultore caret? (221–226)

> I would like to spend time with you, my outstanding Piso, and to try to
> match your merits in my songs forever and ever: I'll take a higher route,
> if you open out the path of fame for me—if you strip away the shadow.
> What use is a hidden vein of precious metal, if the miner is missing?

Although the simile looks a little ungainly (remember, poet is just starting
out?), we get the idea: more than sitting in the shade waiting for Piso to light
up the path for him, he is a seam of gold lying buried, crying out for a
miner to dig him into the daylight of full value.[45] Piso's job, like Maecenas'
in a few lines, is to bring to light (*patefecit*, 236); otherwise, poet could
remain *ignotus* forever, like a Virgil stuck in the shade (*umbram*) of the
grove or the groove of pastoral (234–235).[46]

Poet lays on thick this same metaphorical spread of darkness and light,
obscurity and fame, near closing time:[47]

tu nanti protende manum: tu, Piso, latentem
exsere. nos humilis domus et sincera parentum
sed tenuis fortuna sua caligine celat.
possumus impositis caput exonerare tenebris
et lucem spectare novam, si quid modo laetus
adnuis et nostris subscribis, candide, votis. (253–258)[48]

> Offer your hand to a swimmer: you, Piso, bring out someone stuck in
> hiding. My ancestral home is humble and honest, but its slim resources
> stow me away in its darkness. We can unburden my head from the dark
> that has settled on it, we can see some new light, if only you say the word,
> my gleaming gem, and sign off on my prayers.

The plea is for just a little of that reflected glory (*candide*), so that poet
can get himself out of the dark corner of drowning in water, being unknown (*latentem*), of obscure ancestry, head covered up: some Pisonian
brightness to penetrate the fog, pretty please. The imagery is obvious and
has already pricked up comment.[49] All I want to point out is how it seems
conveniently to *will*, to predicate the poem on, the very same conditions
of an unknown poet that we scholars so vehemently resent to have inherited. The poem works to parade itself as the product of an as-yet Anon, a

poet who has not quite made his name, *any* name, which aligns with its anonymous state. And so this is a fog we might want to work with, rather than against.

The moment that this dedicated obscurity seems to crack ever so slightly is the very end of the poem, where poet profiles himself with a partial sphragis:

> est mihi, crede, meis animus constantior annis,
> quamvis nunc iuvenile decus mihi pingere malas
> coeperit et nondum vicesima venerit aestas. (259–261)

> Listen to me: I have pluck much firmer than my years, even if youthful grace has just begun to dye my cheeks, and my twentieth summer is yet to come.

The faux exactitude of the self-dating (almost twenty) distracts a little from the more interesting vagueness of the signature. We showed earlier how good poet's Piso is at being many things at once, and here, I think, poet allows himself the same leeway: *meis animus constantior annis* doesn't just mean that he is advanced for his years, precociously scribbling praise hexameters in the under-twenties category, but an occupant of many biographical points at once, a multitemporal[50] poet for a multitasking patron. Indeed the connection between Piso and poet is so deep here that certain key terms that poet deploys are basically Pisonian through and through.[51] *Iuvenile decus* may look anodyne, but *iuvenis* and *decus* are pretty much the *LP*'s two most common reference terms for Piso.[52] We could say the same thing about *pingere,* used of Piso's oratorical flexi-gifts back in line 63.[53] These are favorite descriptors because they are generic, flexible. They mold to fit the context; they settle in to suit the body of the moment, nice and decorously.

I have more to say about *decus* in a second. For now, let's just float that *iuvenile decus* is a perfect way to describe a poet, and a poem, that is constantly cutting and recutting itself to fit different times and different contexts. As *pingere malas / coeperit* implies, his face is not yet formed, his mask still in the making.[54] Indeed this final sphragis seems to thrust the idea of contextlessness in our faces, by giving us a vague age keyed to no historical time. Imagine if we had got something *Res Gestae*–esque, like the end of Horace's *Epistles* 1:

forte meum siquis te percontabitur aeuum,
me quater undenos sciat impleuisse Decembris
collegam Lepidum quo duxit Lollius anno. (Hor. *Ep.* 1.20.26–28)

Should someone happen to ask my age, they should know I finished my forty-fourth December in the year Lollius got Lepidus for colleague.

That is the kind of age-sphragis that historicist scholarship would want to write for the *LP:* not only an exact date of birth but a date of birth rooted in historical time. Oh, the possibilities, if only we knew this poem was the work of 40 CE! How many, how confident the political readings! But alas, we have to face the fact that poet lurks in the dark, no confident made man looking back on his forty-four years but a to-be-confirmed neophyte trapped in the tunnel of infinite potential, the time of *nondum.* Poet's words actively hustle to make this darkness generative and *timeless,* in its own way. We should listen up.

Serving Times

We have seen how poet cuts himself to fit very Pisonian specifications at the end. But we have also seen how Pisonian "qualities" are versatility, adaptability, flexibility. *Decus* is the key attribute of nothing and everything here. It spans generously across the poem's key characters, from Piso twice (34, 212) to Maecenas (as Piso? 243) to poet (260). Poet draws himself and Maecenas to match his desired patron; but the patron is a restless space filler. *Decus* is the perfect way of capturing the hero of this poem and his singer—both of whom stand for a poetics of decorum aiming to spread the poem far and wide, over time and context.

Earlier I skipped quickly over the *LP*'s long middle section on the nature of change. Here poet roots Piso's variability in nature, which cycles through its seasonal costumes:[55]

ipsa vices natura subit **variataque** cursus
ordinat, inversis et frondibus explicat annum. (145–146)

Even nature herself experiences change, orders her courses **through variation,** and unrolls the year by swapping its leaves.

There follows a nice roundup of the seasons complete with meteorological symptoms. Poet sums this up with a neat epigram, sharpening the nub of the entire poem:[56]

> **temporibus servire decet:** qui tempora certis
> ponderibus pensavit, eum si bella vocabunt,
> miles erit; si pax, positis toga vestiet armis.
> hunc fora pacatum, bellantem castra **decebunt.** (155–158)

> **It's apt to serve the times:** the one who has weighed the times with clear measures will be a soldier, if war comes a-knocking; if peace, he'll lose the arms and don the toga. The courts **will suit** him at peace; the camps at war.

We could easily push *decere* as the overriding principle of Piso and of the poem. Its tandem double helping with *tempora* here makes it difficult to miss. Piso's grace under the pressures of decorum is more than a character trait. It is a way of fitting a poem to infinite contexts, serving times *plural*. Indeed the shimmering capabilities of this super-patron, so dutifully serving many times as and when, seem to be directly related to the survival of the poem for *all time:*

> felix illa dies totumque canenda per aevum,
> quae tibi, vitales cum primum traderet auras,
> contulit innumeras intra tua pectora dotes. (159–161)

> A beautiful day, song-worthy for all time, which brought you gifts beyond number within your breast, as soon as it handed you breath in your lungs.

There is a correlation between those *innumeras . . . dotes* (in his *pectora* plural)[57] and the happy day to be sung on repeat *totumque . . . per aevum* (cf. *omne per aevum,* 222; *in totum aevum,* 243). The expansiveness of Piso, and the mirroring caddy work of poet, not only makes the lead character run with the seasons but also makes the poem eternally intelligible, eternally valid. That commitment to variability may put us in the dark, looking from the historicist's corner, but it makes the poem that much more durable.

And yet "historically" speaking, the *LP* does flag one context it obviously no longer belongs in: the Roman republic. When poet shrugs off the pressure to praise the Pisonian ancestors back down the family tree, he makes history look like a simple case of men serving the times and poets serving them as they serve them:

nec si cuncta velim breviter decurrere possim;
et prius aethereae moles circumvaga flammae
annua bissenis revocabit mensibus astra,
quam mihi priscorum titulos operosaque bella
contigerit memorare. manus sed bellica patrum
armorumque labor veteres **decuere** Quirites,
atque illos cecinere sui per carmina vates. (18–24)[58]

I couldn't run over everything in brief, even if I wanted; the huge cycling mass of ethereal flame will recall its yearly stars in its twelve-month period, before I could recall the titles and laborious wars of the older guard. But the war-ready hand of their fathers and work of weapons suited those citizen elders, and they had their own bards to sing them in song.

The old citizens got involved in military endeavor because it suited them. The poets, in tune (*sui*) with them, followed suit. At this point, we understand serving the times to mean serving roughly *present* times: steering clear of sterile nostalgia trips back to outmoded republican channels of glory. The (de . . . or re?)-militarization of Piso is a crucial sticking point for *LP* scholarship:[59] could the heavy reliance on leisure activities cast in fightin' words[60] actually play to answer some of the rumors about this Piso's thin military résumé?[61] I would argue, instead, that borrowing heavily from the repertory of old-school Pisonian achievement actually pluralizes Piso still further and makes him stand as a legible figure of the republican past, as well as a many-headed hero of the Caesarean present. Indeed that continuity is written up in a very literal way a few lines down the track. The move from wartime to peacetime glory was already happening in Cicero's day (35–36). And anyway, the audience remains exactly *the same*:

sed quae Pisonum claros visura triumphos
olim turba vias impleverat agmine denso,
ardua nunc **eadem** stipat fora, cum tua maestos
defensura reos vocem facundia mittit. (37–40)

That crowd that had once packed the streets to catch a glimpse of those famous Pisonian triumphs—**the very same one** now crams the challenging law courts, when your oratory emits its voice to get the anxious defendants off their charge.

It might be standard historical self-conception among the Roman elite that the "transition" from republic to principate just means a kind of redrawing of the lines on the pitch, where the same mob simply changes venue.[62] But *eadem* is a strange and forceful word, something altogether more than that. It's almost as if the people of the past have been teleported into the present to admire this new Piso, who is cut from the same cloth as those old Pisones. This (any) Piso's arena may have changed, slightly. But everything else remains as was, as is. Piso can slip into and under any emperor you care to periodize him with (*Caesareum grato cecinisti pectore numen?* 71). But he is fit to serve republican times too. Completely future-proofed, *and* past-proofed—retrofitted, we might say.

One of the other bolts of the *LP* is *resonare*—to resound, reecho. The courts ring and buzz with Piso's praises, no matter the court: *laudibus ipsa tuis resonant fora* (44). Both hands rattle with all the pieces Piso has managed to steal in a big haul of *ludus latrunculorum: et tibi captiva resonat manus utraque turba* (208). Finally, Horatian lyric strums out far and wide: *carmina Romanis etiam resonantia chordis* (241). That notion of resonating, sounding again, chimes harmonically with the repeated promises of the poem to travel down the track of all time (see earlier, on verse 159).[63] But this is not just the usual ambitious Latin poet singing out his intimations of eternity. This is an attempt not merely to make the poem last but to make it suit, make it sensible, within a host of future contexts. When poet talks *resonare,* he means a poetry that will flex to fit anything the future has in store for it: a poem that will serve the times, all of them.

Some Praise of a Piso

The *LP* keeps failing at the first hurdles of historicist scholarship because it is built precisely to knock them over. I have tried to show not only that this poem deliberately ditches the load-bearing structures of addressee, poet, and date but that it also works up a kind of universality dependent on that very fact. The mobile wonder-patron that is Piso manages to stand for every patron, past and future. His poet writes him up as a nobody, assuming the outside position and the multifunctionality of obscurity. And both these axes of unknown help liberate the *LP* from any particular point in political history, allowing it to serve the times beyond itself. Instead of treating this drifter as a deficient poem—a poem *without* X or Y or Z—perhaps we should be a little more open to its poetics of decorum, which need all those variables to stay just that: variable. In a sense, we could think of the *LP* as a brilliant solution to Sabine MacCormack's concept of the "in-built obsolescence" of panegyric, a genre whose whole edifice seems built on specificity, on direct communication between known parties.[64] How do you make a praise poem last? You make it a work for everyone, by no one, and so on, and on, anon.

6

The Timeless Pastoral of
Calpurnius Siculus

The context of the poems of Calpurnius is as timeless as their
text, the ambitious young poet ever on the verge of poverty, the
aristocratic patron dabbling in poetry and politics, the young
princeps around whom revolves the life of the world.
Were it not for a handful of references, most of them quite
obscure in nature, there would be no means of deciding between
Nero and Alexander.

—Edward Champlin (1978: 109)

THE PREVIOUS TWO CHAPTERS have handled various answers to the
question, how do you write as a no-name? I read Phaedrus as a lengthy
and elaborate comedy of sketching a first-person author whom nobody
knows, no matter how much he confects the evidence of making a splash
in contemporary Rome. In a similar light, we saw the *Laus Pisonis* also
work through the implications of cold-calling a patron who is as unknown
to the poet as he is to us. But the *Laus Pisonis* also came out as a stunning
example of a poem cut to fit across as many temporal contexts as possible.
Our next contender—the pastoral suite of Calpurnius Siculus (CS)—at least
meets (if not raises) Phaedrus and the *Laus Pisonis* on all these points. It is
at once a searching trial of what it means to be an author unknown as well
as a stunning instance of writing across contexts.

Calpurnian pastoral is having a renaissance of late. It's a similar, familiar
old story of "silver Latin": once consigned to the dustbin as derivative and

wooden, the work of a poetaster incapable of shaking the shade of predecessor Virgil, the *Eclogues* of CS have recently seen an upswing in more
generous critical treatment. These contributions tend to fall into a couple of
camps (often overlapping): in the majority, intertextualists have won him
back as an innovator in the pastoral tradition, riffing on the genre in the best
spirit of belated poet-transformer; in the minority, (mainly Neronian) his-
toricists have shown how his poems chime sweetly with contemporary imperial politics. My approach will shirk excessive intertextual comparisons,
from the conviction that these sometimes suffocate CS more than they do
support him. And as for the older-historicist project of folding him into the
contemporary scene, you will predictably feel my skepticism soon enough.
If anything, the politics of this collection of shepherd tones does not serve
any particular emperor at any one point. Rather, it serves the system of
principate by minting a work that fits into all the repeated moments of succession, because it assumes that those moments will always be repeated.

"Calpurnius Siculus" deserves the quotation marks with which no one
bothers to surround him.[1] Despite increasingly confident scholarship thud-
ding down the mountain,[2] we still haven't the foggiest who this author
was or when these strange pastoral creations somehow bearing this name
were committed to the page.[3] As with many of our floating anonyms in this
book, CS scholarship has driven itself to distraction around the questions
of authorship, dating, and context. But these questions are especially divi-
sive, and elastic, when it comes to CS. Ever since Moriz Haupt sorted the
separation of this corpus from the poems of Nemesianus to give CS 1–7 its
own neat package,[4] main consensus has filed the poems under *N* for Nero
and, more specifically, early in the reign when the future was still looking
golden. But since Champlin, a growing chorus of influential voices has
plumped for a poet scribbling mid-third century CE, among the Severans.
The evidence for each case is weak enough to split scholars pretty much
purely along ideological preferences. Dating debates are par for the course
in this field. But a dispute over an imperial Latin author that generates bold
lunges of historicist pinning to several poets, patrons, and emperors in a
two-hundred-year diameter . . . now that is something else entirely.

So what's the deal? This chapter will have no time for rehearsing the arguments of old historicist scholarship or proposing a new home for this
especially tumble-dried text. Rather, I would like to work *with* (rather than
against) the *Eclogues'* radical timelessness. If years of scholarly effort have

done little more than spin us around in circles and tie us up in knots, the time may well be upon us to ask *why*. I shall propose that CS is a suite of poems set up to strain its own relationship with historical reality, especially insofar as that "outside" is in critics' hands and an object of their lust. This remarkable corpus actively silences its source and scuppers the sleuthing required to fix its temporal coordinates. As such, it is a strange creature designed to slip into every context under the sun and slide unfussily into the tradition of timeless pastoral, the pastoral of timeless tradition, without an author to get in its way.

Naming Thine Herdsman

Pastoral has always had a vexed relationship with the historicist scholarship deployed to make sense of it. In some ways, it seems to "be asking for" allegorical reading: Virgil surely wants to be read as his herdsman representative on the inside, Tityrus.[5] Likewise, CS *must* want the same for his supposed ambassador, Corydon.[6] And once we've broken the seal of pastoral pseudonymity with these examples of author substitutes, what should stop us having a field day prizing off the masks for any and every innocent shepherd name we come across?[7] Why not make this or that Meliboeus moonlight as the real Seneca, say? On the other hand, such a mode of curious reading—branching all the way from antiquity to now— seems simplistic, impoverishing, and not a little invasive. Why not let the herdsmen be herdsmen?

The big two of the pastoral tradition behind CS seem almost eerily sensitive to the biographizing critical habits of the people who would read them in subsequent years. They tease the allegorical urge by implanting "real" names among all the cows and willows. Theocritus' *Idylls* famously straddle town and country, offsetting the hard-core bucolic stuff with nods to the townie Ptolemies of his own courtly setup.[8] Virgil's *Eclogues* perhaps drill even bigger airholes in the green cabinet: alongside those timeless names, we also have identified Roman luminaries such as Varius and Pollio and Gallus and Caesar, all sharing the same lush breathing space.[9] The scaffolding of the "real" (i.e., urban, "Roman") furnished by these names, combined with the first-person tunneling that equates Virgil with his avatar Tityrus, has the effect of making us want to "penetrate" beneath the other names of the corpus, to dig out flesh-and-blood referents, men behind the masks. However difficult Virgil makes it to "place" these poems in historical time, and historical Rome, they seem to sue for *some* relationship . . . something, anything.

The most frustrating thing for historicist scholarship on CS is that we cannot even get that far, for we completely lack the infrastructure of names to help us there.[10] In imperial literature, we usually choose our contexts by the Caesar. But true to the fuzzy allegorical form of the triumviral Virgilian *Eclogues*—left blank with tags like the *iuvenis deus* of Virgil *Eclogues* (from now on VE) 1,[11] perhaps precisely because of the politically indeterminate times[12]—CS has no specific, individuated Caesar to set our watch by (more on this later in this chapter, particularly in the section "Close But Not Close Enough"). There are no real-world figures, whether patron or poet, to support us. These two stock roles are completely covered by the shade of the shepherd name (Meliboeus Patron; Corydon Poet). Moreover, there is no equivalent capital-R Real event to frame the backdrop. Virgil put the land confiscations right in there, rooting us in the chaos of *the* civil wars at the death knell of the republic. CS's equivalent (i.e., vague references to civil discord within "Faunus's" open prophecy of future goldenness [CS 1]) could work with a number of periods.[13] Space-wise, it is often said that pastoral occupies a no-man's-land. But when we compare Virgil's city-visit poem (VE 1) with CS's (7), we see that an increase in fog holds even for the geographical markers across these poets: VE 1 names Rome as the destination of Tityrus' fantastic visit, but CS 7 merely puts us in an *urbs* (not necessarily The *Urbs*), complete with unidentifiable wooden amphitheater.[14] All of this is to say that the *Eclogues* of CS are especially moveable feasts, in space as well as time.

This deep commitment to dislocation almost prospectively trolls the historicist scholarship that tries to resist it.[15] The dislocation also makes things particularly intractable when that scholarship performs the standard allegorical move of reading for the poet. Most scholars make the "natural," inferential step of taking Corydon—the corpus's most important name (if not character), which gets a leading speaking part in all three of the big hinge points (1, 4, 7)—as a stand-in for "Calpurnius" himself.[16] This is based on the analogy of Tityrus-Virgil and the assumption that CS, stunned imitator that he is, would do the same thing (over and over again). But Virgil seems to authorize the conflation by having his first-person self directly addressed as Tityrus (by none less than Apollo) in VE 6. And this is but one example in a collection chock-a-block with first-person voice. CS, on the other hand, never launches an explicit baptism as "Corydon"; no Apollo or equivalent dubs him that. What's more, he actively whittles down the *propria persona* content, such that there is actually no real first-person "poet" figure left to work with beyond two neutral introductions (to CS 2 and 5), both of which give absolutely no indication of authorial position. The leap leashing Corydon to CS might be one we desperately want to make. But the anti-I of the disappearing author, such as there is one in this primarily dialogic collection, seems to permit no such thing.

So there is less "CS" in CS than there is "Virgil" in Virgil, because Corydon is less obviously tied to CS than Tityrus is to Virgil. But we should also examine how the name Corydon causes problems with singular reference in general (not just to the supposed author figure offstage). Pastoral names, in general, have a strained rapport with referentiality. Because they form a limited corpus, they offer spiky stumbling blocks to modern readers invested in naming as a shorthand for specification, for identification. With pastoral names, we are never sure how much continuity there is between *that* Tityrus and *this* Tityrus or *this* Meliboeus and *that* Meliboeus.[17] But that is especially—even *more*—the case with CS's poet figure Corydon. The name already springs referential traps because of its commonness in Virgil[18] and the self-conscious ways a new Corydon must be set aside from the older one. In VE 2, the narrator Corydon seems almost to broker a schizoid relationship with the name, so dense is his reference to himself in the third person: *a, Corydon, Corydon, quae te dementia cepit!* (Virg. *Ecl.* 2.69). By VE 5, "Corydon" is italicized into a fictional character, furniture belonging to a song that Menalcas has learned:

> hac te nos fragili donabimus ante cicuta.
> haec nos "formosum Corydon ardebat Alexin,"
> haec eadem docuit "cuium pecus? an Meliboei?" (Virg. *Ecl.* 5.85–87)

> First, I'll gift you this brittle reed. It taught me "Corydon burned for lovely Alexis," as well as "Whose flock? Meliboeus'?"

Then, come VE 7, when (another?) Meliboeus decides the song contest between Corydon and Thyrsis in Corydon's favor, the geminated name seems built to flag that this is a *new* Corydon, the *true* Corydon, not to be confused with all the other Corydons that have come before:

Haec memini, et victum frustra contendere Thyrsin.
ex illo Corydon Corydon est tempore nobis. (Virg. *Ecl.* 7.69–70)

I remember as much, how Thyrsis struggled against defeat, all for nothing.
From then on, *this* here Corydon is our Corydon.

We could almost punctuate to clarify the relationship between specific Corydon and type "Corydon" here:[19] from now on, *this here* Corydon is *the* "Corydon" for us. That aside, my point here is that the name Corydon is already a particularly recalcitrant one,[20] throwing up more problems of identification than it solves.

That is why, I would bet, CS chooses him for the load-bearing name of the collection.[21] From Virgil, the question always dogging the name "Corydon" is "which Corydon?!" And that is precisely what we are plunged into asking every time we meet a new Corydon in CS. Many scholars read the march of Corydons in CS 1, 4, and 7 as a story of increasing poetic swagger (sound familiar? Cf. Phaedrus):[22] the small-fry Corydon of 1, skirting the margins of patronage, turns into the more confident and experimental Corydon of 4 (now securely in patron Meliboeus' sphere of concern), becomes the arrogant wannabe city slicker of 7, who now looks down on the tumbleweeds and the hicks in favor of urban chic. But the continuity of name masks the bald, uncomfortable truth that these Corydons are very different characters indeed.[23] They seem to have different statuses and family relations militating against our urge to coalesce them. The Corydon of CS 1, for example, is very much the junior partner to bigger (taller) brother Ornytus' tree-climbing[24] and reading initiative. But then in CS 4, Corydon seems to have *another* brother, Amyntas, who plays his age equal and poetic collaborator on the same level, except for the awkward fact that Meliboeus recalls him branding Amyntas as *puer* once upon a time (and Corydon seems to call the shots more here, at least much more than in CS 1).[25] But then the Corydon of 7 is all on his lonesome, with no attested family. So these Corydons do look a little similar. But there is also a clear effort to put them in different company, to separate them, and to retain—from Virgil—the substrate of *distinct* Corydons.

Apart from the desire to sandwich them together, pricked largely by the historicist disappointment that comes when the author has well and truly vanished, I see no pressing necessity to make nice that these are the same guys, merely because they have the same name. If the Calpurnian "Tityrus" can switch from the throwaway servant of CS 3 to the grand Virgil-hero of CS 4 within a few inches of verse,[26] then why not Corydon? The desperate search for an author in the text has led scholarship into a mirage of unity. I say, let's prize these Corydons apart.

Attributive Thinking

If these *Eclogues* wreak havoc with the referential power of their central pastoral name, flirting with a unitary bearer even as they tear him in very different directions, they also seem to distribute speech and/or subjectivity across two speakers where we might be expecting one. The amoebean exchanges of CS—such as they can be called that—are usually mild affairs, short on the sparky slanging matches of the tradition (such as VE 3), long on verse trading as a kind of collaboration between indistinguishable singers. Sometimes the voices are tough to slice apart, and this, I think, is precisely the point. Calpurnian pastoral tends to make herder singers work in concert, rather than competition (and when competition looms, as in 6, the whole enterprise actually breaks down before it can get going). In other words, two become one.[27]

This deep "equivalence" of speakers comes through particularly loud and clear in the first amoebean poem, CS 2. Two robust herdsmen lads make ready to have a sing-off over their common beloved, Crocale. Stakes are laid, until the judge Thyrsis steps in to cancel them. A finger game decides who goes first, and they're off trading verbal fours. In terms of this poem's intertextual stance vis-à-vis Virgil the Great, it is a case of one becoming two: the poem is heavily patterned on Corydon's monologue in VE 2, but now (that) Corydon speaks his remix through two new mouthpieces, Astacus and Idas.[28] The two contestants are profiled in anticipation of the match, but only to come across as complete clones:

> Intactam Crocalen puer Astacus et puer Idas,
> Idas lanigeri dominus gregis, Astacus horti,
> dilexere diu, formosus uterque nec impar
> voce sonans. hi cum terras gravis ureret aestas,
> ad gelidos fontes et easdem forte sub umbras
> conveniunt dulcique simul contendere cantu
> pignoribusque parant: placet, hic ne vellera septem,

ille sui victus ne messem vindicet horti;
et magnum certamen erat sub iudice Thyrsi. (CS *Ecl.* 2.1–9)[29]

The boy Astacus and the boy Idas had been in love with the virgin Crocale for a good while. Idas was master of a wooly flock, Astacus a garden.
Both were lovely and evenly matched at singing. Just as heavy high
summer was parching the earth, these two meet at a cool spring, by coincidence beneath the very same shade; they get ready to compete together
in honeyed song, for a stake. It's decided that Idas should give up seven
fleeces if he lost, and likewise Astacus should give up a whole garden har-
vest; it was a big contest, with Thyrsis serving as judge.

Both *pueri,* both in love with the same lucky lady (*Crocale*), both good-
looking, both sounding equally good,[30] they just happen to "converge"
(*conveniunt*) under the very same shady patch, and they prime themselves
to contend "together." The only thing that really sets them apart is their
occupations[31] and the stakes picked to match. This seems a pretty harmonious lead-up to a singing comp.[32] Indeed the harmony reverbs through the
audience, with beasts, gods, and men all lining up at once: the generalized
shepherd *quicumque* (12), like the two contestants, coming together (*con-
venit,* 12). After nature stops stock still, falling into a hush for the eagerly
awaited performance, the middleman Thyrsis even removes the only dif-
ferentiating feature from the equation.[33] Out go the stakes:

iamque sub annosa medius consederat umbra
Thyrsis et "o pueri me iudice pignora" dixit
"irrita sint moneo: satis hoc mercedis habeto,
si laudem victor, si fert opprobria victus.
et nunc alternos magis ut distinguere cantus
possitis, ter quisque manus iactate micantes."
nec mora: decernunt digitis, prior incipit Idas. (2.21–27)

Now, beneath the old shade, Thyrsis sat down in the middle and said:
"My boys, when I judge, I move that the stakes shouldn't count: you
should get enough reward if the victor takes the glory, and the loser the
shame. Now so you can mark off your exchanges better, both of you raise
and flash your hands three times." No fuss: the fingers decide, and Idas
goes first.

Thyrsis leans into his rocking chair and rules that the sport is its own reward.
This is a remarkably[34] relaxed beginning to verbal combat: no wrangling,

no insults. Indeed so blandly blended are these "contestants" that the only way to distinguish (*distinguere*) them is through the random scissor-paper-rock technique. There is no way to decide who goes first apart from the flipping of a coin.[35] *Distinguere* means to mark off, divide clearly, even punctuate; the sense is that without this fairly arbitrary finger trick, we would have a hard time telling who speaks when. The game gives CS the aleatory alibi he needs to mark Idas as the first speaker. And it's all decided with a strange immediacy and ease (*nec mora*).

The way the poem moves, in this initial scene-setting, from minimal distinction and conflict (boy lovers of Crocale, all equal but with stakes) to even less of the stuff (same but no stakes) is mirrored in its larger architecture. The trend seems to dip toward full-on convergence of "contestants," which is nicely mirrored in the verbs, pronouns, and possessives with which these herdsmen do their self-reference. At first, both boasting of their special treatment by different pastoral gods, the lads pitch themselves in the singular: *me* (28), *mea* (29), *mihi* (32), *me* (36). They do likewise when they start primping their agricultural achievements: *mea* (40, 42), *me* (44), *mihi* (48, 62), *ego* (51, 52). But when their binding tie of a lover is first paired across their traded fours, something funny happens. Astacus responds to Idas' *o si quis Crocalen deus afferat!* (52) with the first-person-plural *urimur in Crocalen* (56). This is no mere royal we, I'd wager, but a genuine attempt to seal this special homosocial bond. At first, Idas holds onto his vestiges of self-assertion via the singular, but it is a schizoid way of doing it, as if he has been split into two people:

> *Idas:* ne contemne casas et pastoralia tecta:
> rusticus est, fateor, sed non et barbarus Idas. (60–61)

> *Idas:* Don't look down on the house and the shepherd's hut: Idas is
> a bumpkin, sure, but he's no barbarian.

The Corydon of VE 2 had addressed himself—*rusticus es, Corydon* (56)—but not in the third person, as Idas does here. The first half of Idas' line here almost sounds like it could be his rival Astacus speaking in *praise* of Idas. And once Idas has split himself down the middle like so, cue Astacus' adoption of the first-person plural in earnest:

> *Astacus:* nos quoque pomiferi laribus consuevimus horti
> mittere primitias et fingere liba Priapo,

> rorantesque favos damus et liquentia mella;
> nec sunt grata minus, quam si caper imbuat aras. (64–67)[36]

Astacus: We too have got used to sending first fruits to the gods of the
apple garden and to making cakes for Priapus; we offer
oozing honeycombs and runny honey; nor are they less
welcome than if a goat stained the altar.

Nos and *damus* make it sound like Astacus is speaking on behalf of both
speakers, rather than his royal self. In the next trade, Idas starts to come
around by adopting these first-person-plural verbs, if not the pronouns. But
Astacus is slightly more on board with the unifying syntax, converging so
much that he even (almost) repeats a line:

Idas: mille sub uberibus balantes pascimus agnas,
totque Tarentinae praestant mihi vellera matres;
per totum niveus premitur mihi caseus annum:
si venias, Crocale, totus tibi serviet hornus.

Astacus: qui numerare velit quam multa sub arbore nostra
poma legam, tenues citius numerabit harenas.
semper holus metimus, nec bruma nec impedit aestas:
si venias, Crocale, totus tibi serviet hortus. (68–75)

Idas: We pasture a thousand bleating lambs at the teat, and just as
many Tarentine ewes furnish me with fleece; I press snowy
cheese the year round: if you come, Crocale, the whole year's
produce will be at your feet.

Astacus: Whoever would want to count the number of apples I collect
under our trees will sooner count grains of sand. We're always
cropping vegetables; neither winter nor summer stands in our
way: if you come, Crocale, the whole garden will be at your feet.

Although they are getting closer, there is still a little confusion over whether
these boys think of themselves as two or one. They are slipping fast and
furiously between singular and plural. Yet by the next pair of stanzas, the
singulars disappear completely. Idas says *dabimus* (78), and Astacus takes
him up on it (*nos, quos . . . dabimus*, 80–81). Then they suddenly switch
back to first-person-singular mode (*precor, videor*, 84; *decipior, tango*, 85;
sequor, 86; *conspicor*, 88; *admiror*, 89; *notavi*, 90). But interestingly we have
a slate of passive or deponent verbs in this group, and this chimes a charm
with the mirroring effect that Astacus is talking about in his next lines:

Astacus: fontibus in liquidis quotiens me conspicor, ipse
admiror totiens. etenim sic flore iuventae
induimur vultus, ut in arbore saepe notavi
cerea sub tenui lucere cydonia lana. (88–91)

Astacus: Whenever I catch myself in the clear stream, I'm awestruck.
For sure, my face is clothed with the flowers of youth such as
I've often seen on the tree where waxy quinces shimmer
beneath soft stubble.

Astacus, mimicking Idas, becomes a kind of split subject-object figure, a Narcissus admiring his own reflection in the stream. And that is what the plural *vultus* brings home: not only the doubled faces of Astacus, in and out of the water, but the two faces of Idas and Astacus, one the reflection of the other. Even when they return to the first person, Astacus manages to make them converge: *conveniunt* (6).

The poem thus moves to mix the "contestants" freely into each other, to make them dance quietly in and out of conceptualizing themselves as duet or as unit. So we are not exactly shocked when the moment of truth comes, the results of the "competition" are in, and the arbiter must arbitrate that there is to be no decision whatsoever:

vix ea finierant, senior cum talia Thyrsis:
"este pares et ob hoc concordes vivite; nam vos
et decor et cantus et amor sociavit et aetas." (98–100)

It was scarcely over when old Thyrsis said: "Be equals, and so live in harmony; your grace, song, love, and age have bonded you tight."

We have moved from an agreement that there would be distinguishing stakes up for grabs to an agreement that the stakes would no longer be necessary, for winner/loser would be enough, to an agreement that there will be neither winner nor loser, for both partners are created equal. The poem ends with the eerie harmony with which it began: contestants united (*pares, concordes*) in pretty much every respect (*decor, cantus, amor, aetas*). Umpire declares them indistinguishable.[37]

Most of these specifications, you might contend, are not exactly the flashiest updates in pastoral technology. They all have some kind of precedent in model-man Virgil. The initial equality of speakers grows from VE 7 (*ambo florentes aetatibus, Arcades ambo,/et cantare pares et respondere parati,* VE 7.4–5). The idea of quiet convergence blossoms out of a VE 5 bud (*boni quoniam convenimus ambo,* VE 5.1);[38] the umpire who can't decide replays Palaemon's fence-sitting at the end of VE 3 (108–110). But all of these Virgilian odd-number amoebeans contain a measure of concordance offset by competition, similarity by difference. VE 7 *does* distinguish Corydon as the triumphant doublet in the end, even if we can't figure out precisely why. VE 5 involves a situation where one speaker is definitely more senior than the other (Menalcas called *maior* by Mopsus, VE 5.4). And VE 3 stages a hostile wrangling between speakers throughout, which rift is perhaps what Palaemon's agnosticism is designed to heal. My point here is that, in the conversion and recombination process, CS completely drains the competitive/conflictual aspects from the "match" and ushers into the spotlight all the beautiful harmony and similarity. CS is interested in rinsing out the things that *tell the speakers apart.*

Of course, I am writing out the major occupational difference between Idas and Astacus, which inflects most of their verbal offerings. One is a goatherd, the other a gardener. And this arguably offers ground for playing out a conversation about genre (i.e., something like bucolic and georgic).[39] But this is emphatically not bucolic versus georgic, the one in opposition to the other. The "genres" of CS 2, like their representatives, are not so much in conflict but in harmony. They are not battling but working side by side, happily furnishing alternative ways of getting to the same place. This is perhaps why the didactic (georgic) mode slips in, later in the corpus, without any trouble whatsoever: CS 5[40] is a piece of instructive monologue, from the older generation to the younger generation, on sheep and goat farming. There are no teething problems in expressing pastoral care in a georgic key, because generic fissures and conflicts don't press with anywhere near the urgency of Virgil's *Eclogues.* There is no explosive and invasive Gallus figure (VE 10) imported to blow up pastoral with elegy. When hints of contrast come together in CS, they resolve into synthesis before they can even think about bickering.

The apparent outlier in this combinatorial ("*conven*tional"?) poetics is CS 6, which is, after all, nothing *but* bickering. The two would-be contenders, Astylus and Lycidas, spend nigh on the whole poem insulting each other in prelude to the match (i.e., VE 3's warm-up reheated into the main event). Not even the umpire, Mnasyllus, can be settled. Instead of giving a verdict on a nonexistent contest, he uses his end slot to throw up his hands and withdraw only a few lines after being appointed. But this exception, I think, underscores the very same rule set up by its second-from-the-beginning companion piece. For if CS 2 sets up harmony and convergence as the pre-conditions of amoebean trading, CS 6 shows us that song exchange can't even *happen* when there is radical conflict between contenders. When there is equivalence, things run fine. When there isn't, they break down. CS 6 doesn't show us the breakdown of pastoral song swaps so much as it does the felicity conditions for their performance: speakers who converge toward the same person.

The strange evenness of the "match" in CS 2 may make it impossible by definition to pick a winner. But when we come to the next great exchange of CS, we find ourselves in a pickle of attribution that is much more intractable. CS 4 is another poem that seems to make two from one. But in this case, the split consciousness is less predictable and even harder to track with regard to distinguishing which lines belong to which speakers. As in CS 2, so in CS 4, two evenly matched herdsmen do not quite compete but rather collaborate toward a common goal. Only this time, it is Caesar, not Crocale.

Unlike in CS 2, here we lack a narrator preamble. As a spin-off, the duet situation that evolves between Corydon and brother Amyntas actually takes us by surprise. Some seeds are planted early. At the beginning, patron Meliboeus chats to poet Corydon about his ambitions to rise. Corydon takes a bit of time out to name check his brother Amyntas, but it is unclear at this point exactly why:

> *Corydon:* quicquid id est, silvestre licet videatur acutis
> auribus et nostro tantum memorabile pago;
> nunc mea rusticitas, si non valet arte polita
> carminis, at certe valeat pietate probari.
> rupe sub hac eadem, quam proxima pinus obumbrat,
> haec eadem nobis frater meditatur Amyntas,
> quem vicina meis natalibus admovet aetas. (4.12–18)

> *Corydon:* No matter what my song is like, even if it reeks of the woods to discerning ears and is worth preserving only in my hometown—all the same, my country roughness—though it's not the best at polished, artsy song—should win some points for dedication. Under this same rock, which the next pine over shades, my brother Amyntas composes the very same things I do; his close age means we almost share a birthday.

As we saw earlier, this Amyntas is a different sort of brother from the Ornytus of CS 1: he is a kindred spirit, nearly an age equal, a performer of the *same* kind of poetry (*haec eadem*), under the *same* rock (*hac eadem*), by the *nearest* pine. The watchwords of this relationship are similarity and proximity—they are effectively *concordes* like the dear pals of 2. Even when Meliboeus picks Corydon up on this new attitude in the next section—how often he's heard Corydon discouraging his brother from poetry like a father (*fronte paterna,* 21) (i.e., not very brotherly!)—Corydon says he used to say that, but times have changed. The Caesar is different. So now the brothers are in harmony.

But as soon as Amyntas is brought up, he disappears from the equation for the moment, as long as Corydon needs to set out his poetic plans to his boss. *This* Corydon wants to be another Tityrus. He knows he can do it and asks Meliboeus to hear him try. At this point, we think that this poem will be all about Corydon performing for his patron in the singular, showcasing what he can do. But then Meliboeus effects a strange twist all of a sudden, which seems less deliberate, more a bolt of pure contingency:

> *Meliboeus:* incipe, nam faveo; sed prospice, ne tibi forte
> tinnula tam fragili respiret fistula buxo,
> quam resonare solet, si quando laudat Alexin.
> hos potius, magis hos calamos sectare: canales
> exprime qui dignas cecinerunt consule silvas.
> incipe, ne dubita. venit en et frater Amyntas:
> cantibus iste tuis alterno succinet ore.
> ducite, nec mora sit, vicibusque reducite carmen;
> tuque prior, Corydon, tu proximus ibis, Amynta. (73–81)

> *Meliboeus:* Start, I'm fully behind you. But watch out that your shrill pipe doesn't breathe from boxwood as brittle as usually comes out whenever it plays the praise of Alexis. Instead, these reeds, *these* you have to go after: press the water pipes that sang woods on a consular level. Start, don't dither. Right—here comes your brother Amyntas: let him sing along with your verses, amoebean style. Draw your song, don't put it off, and redraw it in turn; you go first, Corydon, and you next, Amyntas.

Okay, so a generic rise is afoot: not the lowland erotic stuff of VE 2 but the real Sunday best of VE 4, woods worthy of a consul![41] Even so, we still think we know that whatever comes next, it will be monologic in form—

as both VE 2 (all but short introduction) and VE 4 are. *Incipe, ne dubita: you* begin, don't *you* hesitate, Corydon. But then out of nowhere comes the smack of a curveball: look, it's your brother Amyntas! What we thought would be single speaker now instantly becomes an amoebean beast with two backs. The genius of this sudden turn is that the generic climb is marked not just with the new style, the new pipes, but with the number of speakers: woods so worthy of a consul that it takes two poets to sing them.

The drill laid out by Meliboeus is pretty clear and seems to follow the subtle pecking order: the brothers are pretty much the same age, but as the slightly senior partner, Corydon will go first, with Amyntas following in hot pursuit (*proximus*, 81). Corydon sets the pace. Amyntas keeps up in an accompanying role; *succinere* (79) connotes supplementation, singing *along with*. The problem is that the system seems to break down almost straightaway. Scholarship has run into a lot of difficulty attributing speech in this section, and that is because—if we maintain the alternation of Corydon/Amyntas—the brothers' roles seem to reverse soon after they are set.[42] Corydon begins with Jupiter and makes a roundabout prayer to an unspecified political divinity. But Amyntas comes right out and says Caesar, which seems to set the pace for Corydon rather than the other way round:

> *Amyntas:* me quoque facundo comitatus Apolline Caesar
> respiciat, montes neu dedignetur adire,
> quos et Phoebus amat, quos Iuppiter ipse tuetur:
> in quibus Augustos visuraque saepe triumphos
> laurus fructificat vicinaque nascitur arbos.
> *Corydon:* ipse polos etiam qui temperat igne geluque,
> Iuppiter ipse parens, cui tu iam proximus ipse,
> Caesar, abes, posito paulisper fulmine saepe
> Cresia rura petit viridique reclinis in antro
> carmina Dictaeis audit Curetica silvis. (87–96)

> *Amyntas:* I hope Caesar looks out for me too, with silver-tongued Apollo accompanying him, and I hope he doesn't think it beneath him to come to my hills, which Phoebus also loves and which Jupiter himself looks after: in those hills the laurel flourishes, set to see so many imperial triumphs, and the laurel's neighbor comes out there too.
> *Corydon:* He himself—the one who conditions the heavens with heat or chill, father Jupiter himself (whom you follow hard behind, Caesar), often puts down his thunderbolt for a while, makes

for the Cretan countryside, leans back in a green grotto, and
listens to Curetic songs in the woods of Dicte.

Amyntas almost corrects Corydon's first offering: Jupiter, yes, but Caesar
has to be right in there, right next door. Corydon, like a good brother, takes
Amyntas' cues of *Iuppiter ipse, Caesar,* and *saepe.* I would see Amyntas already starting to take the initiative here, but scholarship really runs into
problems in the next exchange,[43] where it is clear that Amyntas gets the
leader's prerogative of introducing a new topic, and brother Corydon
blandly follows suit:

Amyntas: adspicis, ut virides audito Caesare silvae
             conticeant? memini, quamvis urgente procella
             sic nemus immotis subito requiescere ramis,
             et dixi: "deus hinc, certe deus expulit euros."
             nec mora; Parrhasiae sonuerunt sibila cannae.
Corydon: adspicis, ut teneros subitus vigor excitet agnos?
             utque superfuso magis ubera lacte graventur
             et nuper tonsis exundent vellera fetis?
             hoc ego iam, memini, semel hac in valle notavi
             et venisse Palen pecoris dixisse magistros. (97–106)

Amyntas: Can you see how the green woods go silent at the mention of
             Caesar's name? I remember how, even with a storm pressing,
             the grove suddenly fell asleep, its branches dormant, and I
             said: "A god! Surely a god has chased the east winds out of
             here." Instantly, Parrhasian reeds slipped out their sounds.
Corydon: Can you see how a sudden excitement rouses the young
             lambs? How the teats hang heavier with teeming milk and
             the fleeces billow straight after shearing? I remember I
             marked that once in this valley, how the herdsmen said,
             "Pales has come."

Infecting Corydon with the same frame of *aspicis, ut . . .* , it's fairly clear
that Amyntas is now in the driver's seat. Amyntas sets the pace again with
the golden age imagery from 107 to 116. But then from 122, *Corydon* seems
to pick up the trendsetter role: his opener *ille dat* (122) is taken straight up
in Amyntas' "response" (*ille . . . dat,* 127). Amyntas seems only to start
talking about gods in his last speech (137–141) because Corydon had
broached the subject already in 132–136. But then Corydon's final effort
could also be read as a follow-up riff on Amyntas', in that they are both

prayers (*precor*) for Caesar's eternal life and rule. My point amid this thicket is that the simple structure proposed by Meliboeus—Corydon, you lead; Amyntas, you follow—is abandoned for something more complex and murky, where we can't quite make head or tail of who is head or tail. In the end, we even time out with an odd number of speeches (where we would definitely expect an even number rounding out the amoebean perfection). The upset symmetry confirms our suspicions that these brothers are not only alternating their nuggets of verse but also vacillating in their role-playing as follower and leader. They are a walking hysteron proteron, chicken and egg, arm in leg.

The strange effect of shifting "priorities" here is obviously something that classicizing scholars have a hard time abiding. There have been various attempts to reassign blocks of verse or transpose them or posit that chunks have dropped out here and there.[44] But the political point of the text as we have it must be that this Caesar praise, the common goal of this team of brothers, sounds the same no matter the mouth it comes from—the same, no matter who initiates and who follows up. Molding themselves to this "new" catch-all golden age perfectly, these brothers are in total harmony, their voices, positions, and sentiments all speaking as one. Caesar is getting multiple poets singing, and they're doing it from the same old mass-produced hymn sheet.

Out of Office

We have seen how these two amoebean poems of CS seem to visit a creative destruction on the very notion of singular poetic identity or individual authorship. They make two monologic Virgilian Eclogues (VE 2 and 4) into teams of two, and in both cases, we struggle—like the poor umpire Thyrsis—with the scholarly tasks of judgment, distinction, and attribution. The glue is so strong as to make the sticky combinations hard work to prize apart. But there is another context in CS where issues of attribution are even more directly at stake. True to its self-confessed status as "secondary" pastoral, CS features many moments when writing takes precedence over singing.[45] And these moments are littered with the kind of overdetermined acts of authorial signature we saw in Chapter 1. But the authors *themselves* are always out of office, making it hard for us yet again (in a different way) to verify the signature and answer the perennial "who speaks?" The first-person writers in CS seem keen to give their names to their scribbles, precisely because they are not there.

Before a quick run through CS 1 and 3, it might help some to spell out how Calpurnian textuality and authorship looks in the pull of its Virgilian roots. One of Virgil's main updates to pastoral, of course, is the very presence of writing as the tool of the herdsman-singer.[46] Two examples can distill both distance and proximity to what follows in CS. In VE 5, writing plays its classic double role as grounding and substitute, primary and secondary, presence and absence. On the one hand, we have Mopsus offering to read something he's prepared earlier:[47]

> *Mopsus:* Immo haec, in viridi nuper quae cortice fagi
>   carmina descripsi et modulans alterna notavi,
>   experiar: tu deinde iubeto certet Amyntas. (VE 5.13–15)

> *Mopsus:* No, I'll try these instead, verses I just carved on the green
>   bark of a beech and set to a tune, marking out words and
>   music: then tell Amyntas to come and compete!

Here we have author complementing text, owning it and activating it in a single recitatory bundle. On the other hand, writing features in that very recited song as epigraphic ersatz for its dead author:[48]

> *Mopsus:* et tumulum facite et tumulo superaddite carmen:
>   "Daphnis ego in silvis, hinc usque ad sidera notus,
>   formosi pecoris custos, formosior ipse." (42–44)

> *Mopsus:* And make a tomb, and add on it the verses: "I was Daphnis
>   of the woods, known from here to the sky. Shepherd of a fair
>   flock, I was even fairer."

The written world of CS is much more the latter than the former: mediating scripts that compensate for their absent authors by overwrought signatures of the type "Daphnis ego," tokens of a higher authority that evaporates as soon as you read.

At long last, this brings us back to where we never started: CS 1. This poem is one of the jewels in the CS propaganda crown. It is usually mined for clues about dating, and so the prophecy of Faunus, freshly carved on a beech tree, remains the focal point for most scholars.[49] But the preamble to it is deeply fascinating for our purposes. Two herdsmen—Corydon and Ornytus, again brothers (4, 8) as in CS 4—are sweltering in the late summer heat, so they decide to make a move to the shade of a grove. They make ready to while away the time with a song. Corydon asks Ornytus to bosh out something preprepared (*recondite*, 16), and so we expect a performance or a friendly trade. But again CS throws a spanner in the works. The song is already written, and it isn't what or where we might think:

> *Ornytus:* et iam captatae pariter successimus umbrae.
> sed quaenam sacra descripta est pagina fago,
> quam modo nescio quis properanti falce notavit?
> aspicis ut virides etiam nunc littera rimas
> servet et arenti nondum se laxet hiatu?
>
> *Corydon:* Ornyte, fer propius tua lumina: tu potes alto
> cortice descriptos citius percurrere versus;
> nam tibi longa satis pater internodia largus
> procerumque dedit mater non invida corpus.
>
> *Ornytus:* non pastor, non haec triviali more viator,
> sed deus ipse canit: nihil armentale resultat,
> nec montana sacros distinguunt iubila versus.
>
> *Corydon:* mira refers; sed rumpe moras oculoque sequaci
> quamprimum nobis divinum perlege carmen. (1.19–32)

> *Ornytus:* Now we've come under the shade we were looking for, together. But what's that sacred text transcribed onto the beech, which someone's marked out just now with hurried knife work? Do you see how even now the letters are keeping their green slashes and don't yet unfurl into a dry slit?
>
> *Corydon:* Ornytus, bring your eyes closer. You'd be quicker at running over the verses transcribed on the high bark; for a generous father gave you long limbs, and your mother didn't stint in giving you a big frame.
>
> *Ornytus:* It's no shepherd singing this, no traveler in run-of-the-mill style; it's really a god! No ring of the stables, and no mountain yodels mark the divine verses.
>
> *Corydon:* You're talking in marvels! But enough dawdling: focus your eyes and read the whole godly song for me as soon as you can.

In a sense, this is a dramatization of a scene of hick-style scholarship. Ornytus discovers a mystery text,[50] and the two start hashing out a detective-style exercise in attribution à la a poor man's Ted Champlin. Ornytus comments on the writing style: a rush job by anonymous (*nescioquis*—although *properanti falce* almost signs it as the Propertian Vertumnus),[51] and it's still green and so must have been done in the last five minutes.[52] Corydon's interest is piqued, so he tells his taller brother to get closer (*propius;* see later in this chapter). Ornytus strains with his green monocle to examine the object and decides it's the real deal: not the usual shepherd or traveler scribble but the work of a *god!* He can tell just by looking that no yodels mark off the verses (*distinguunt*)[53]—and by that he might simply mean that it is monologic rather than amoebean. In any case, this critic can tell a lot at first glance, before he has even got to the first line.

It turns out old Ornytus has an eye for talent. The very first verse tells us the same story, more specifically:

> *Ornytus:* "qui iuga, qui silvas tueor, satus aethere **Faunus,**
> haec populis ventura cano: iuvat arbore sacra
> laeta patefactis incidere carmina fatis." (33–35)

> *Ornytus:* "The god who looks after the ridges and forests, I, **Faunus,**
> born in heaven, I sing to the nations that this will happen:
> I chose to carve on this sacred tree these blessed songs,
> wherein fate is unveiled."

Faunus self-names and comprehensively identifies as god of ridge and forest, heaven-sent miracle, in the text's very first breath. This is an important moment: it turns Ornytus' mysterious *nescioquis,* whittled down to *deus,* into something specific, authoritative, accountable. All this business about a new golden age, the prophecy to come, needs this signature to be taken seriously, because it comes in written form. Any old Cesarean lackey could have written it up, if Faunus didn't stand tall and out himself in that first line and fool us into taking it as divine word.[54]

As I said earlier, that self-dropping name Faunus is a signature more in tune with the "Daphnis ego" of VE 5—the absent, remote master summoned up only through the epigraphic substitute but no less the powerful for that. Indeed, the bumpkin patter as usual (i.e., in CS as much as VE) contains a pretty shrewd understanding of how imperial power actually managed to flood out and operate in the vast majority of the Roman world that could never be under direct gaze: inscriptions looking impressive, doing the work of the absentee ruler for him. I'll have more to say about absent authority later, but for now I offer a quick point about the politics and poetics of that subtle word *descripta,* which actually revises that first Virgilian quote earlier. In Virgil, the act of transcription (*describere*) comes from Mopsus the herdsman himself (*descripsi,* VE 5.14): he orally composes, transcribes, then eventually (in the moment of the poem) reads out his Daphnis poem and stays there as author throughout the loop. What we get in CS 1, by contrast, is a transcription of an utterance made not by the herdsman but by the central authority. The two brothers Corydon and Ornytus don't have to compose anything—because it's all there ready to be read. These diktats of Faunus, direct from headquarters, perhaps codify the derivative world in which Calpurnian pastoral sings its tune. The hymn sheet is produced somewhere else, and all you have to do is roll with it.

The other place where writing comes up in CS[55] is closer to the Mopsus composition scene of VE 5, but there is much more of an attribution anxiety attached. This is born of the fact that writing is again the work of an absent author, which can undergo interference on the march from utterance to mediation to delivery. In CS 3, Lycidas' squeeze, Phyllis, has left him after a lover's tiff. Lycidas lopes along, moping in dire straits. So he crafts a love letter to try to get her back. His buddy Iollas acts as scribe and messenger. Lycidas is mindful that he's crafting a text and puts out a similar impatience to mark the letter's origin (and destination) with names:[56]

> *Lycidas:* "has tibi, Phylli, preces iam pallidus, hos tibi cantus
> dat Lycidas, quos nocte miser modulatur acerba,
> dum flet et excluso disperdit lumina somno.
> non sic destricta marcescit turdus oliva,
> non lepus, extremas legulus cum sustulit uvas,
> ut Lycidas domina sine Phyllide tabidus erro." (3.45–50)

> *Lycidas:* "Lycidas, pale from love, gives you these prayers, Phyllis; gives
> you these songs, which he plays miserably by bitter night, as
> he weeps and wrecks his eyes from lack of sleep. No thrush
> withers like this when the olive tree gets stripped, nor the
> hare, when the picker has taken the last grapes—not so much
> as I, Lycidas, wander, wasting away, without my lady Phyllis."

But when it comes to self-naming in this love letter, twice is not enough. He has to make absolutely *sure:*

> *Lycidas:* ille ego sum Lycidas, quo te cantante solebas
> dicere felicem, cui dulcia saepe dedisti

> oscula nec medios dubitasti rumpere cantus
> atque inter calamos errantia labra petisti. (55–59)

Lycidas: I am *that* Lycidas: the very one you used to say you were
happy to hear sing, to whom you often granted sweet little
kisses, and you didn't stint from interrupting the song to
snatch my lips as they wandered over the reeds.

I am *Lycidas*—that very Lycidas. *Ille ego sum Lycidas* sounds like a signature of Ovid's or the faux proem to the *Aeneid,*[57] a tag, in short, that seeks
to make the verse the genuine article. He even brings it home again at the
sign-off to the letter,[58] when he visualizes his own suicide note scrawled on
a tree (perhaps exactly the kind of graffiti that Ornytus could distinguish
from the Faunus prophecy in 1):

Lycidas: hi tamen ante mala figentur in arbore versus:
"credere, pastores, levibus nolite puellis;
Phyllida Mopsus habet, Lycidan habet ultima rerum." (89–91)

Lycidas: But first, have these verses posted on the wretched tree:
"Shepherds, don't trust fickle girls; Mopsus claims Phyllis, and
the ultimate end claims Lycidas."

Lycidas' letter is so autographic in principle, so oversaturated with nominal fingerprints, because it is *written.* As such, the lover is painfully aware
that the condition of writing is precisely authorial absence. For he tells us
where he will be right at the moment Iollas hands over the missive to Phyllis.
Not there:

Lycidas: nunc age, si quicquam miseris succurris, Iolla,
perfer et exora modulato Phyllida cantu.
ipse procul stabo vel acuta carice tectus
vel propius latitans vicina saepe sub horti. (92–95)

Lycidas: Come on, Iollas, if you want to be of any help in my sorry
state, take this to Phyllis and beg her with a tuneful melody.
I myself will stand distant, either stowed in nettling reed-grass
or hiding a little closer, beneath the garden hedge next door.

Standing far away or hiding a little closer—but invisible either way. This
superficially gratuitous account of what Lycidas will be up to at the handover
moment is actually quite important, because it articulates a feature of writing
that was latent in CS 1. There, the two brothers buy into the divine-author

claim fully. Those wondrous words must have been Faunus, and the words channel his presence directly. The brothers feel themselves getting *propius*. But in CS 3, the levels of mediation are spelled out: writing acts as substitute for an author who is not there, who is quite literally hiding. And as we shall see later in this chapter, this is exactly what all authority figures are doing in CS. They are standing *procul*. The further we get in chasing them, the further we have to go.

We have looked over two broad "attributive" modes thus far. The first crushes speakers into a collaborative song that makes them difficult to tell apart. This form of amoebean exchange is also, or at least stems from, a monologue—two from, and as, one. The second is explicitly *about* the attribution of writing and the overdetermination of authorship: how even (or especially) if the authorial seal is loud and proud, the author is still by definition gone. In the next section, we shall see how this enabling absence affects not just the internal authors but *all* the authorities of CS. Let's see if this can't wire some more key circuits regarding temporality, historicism, and names—a few of our favorite things.

Close But Not Close Enough:
The Antonomasia of Distance

Lycidas' spooky creep from *procul* to *propius* is a miniature diorama of the general pattern followed by authority figures in CS and the small fry obliged with the task of chasing them. The whole suite of these *Eclogues* seems to take the Corydons and us on a trek toward the horizon point of a nameless godhead, a mysterious Caesar hovering just over yonder in Rome. Even though this distance seems to shrink a little, the interesting point is that it never disappears entirely. In CS, the ultimate authority, Caesar, is always buffered and mediated. He shall always remain nameless. The best we can do is get closer, but not quite close enough to make out his identity. In this sense, CS locks its Corydons, and us, into an epistemological cloud that prevents full historicism from ever taking shape or gaining purchase. The *Eclogues* become a story of how we—not just Corydon—can never *quite* lock and load the specific Caesar at the end of the tunnel.

In CS 1, we, via Corydon, are perched at the furthest remove. The layers of mediation here are thick and impenetrable. Corydon can't read the prophetic verses himself. He needs his brother Ornytus to get closer (*propius*) to speak them aloud. And they are already a form of secondariness or Derridean trace, freshly carved but *descripta* (i.e., a kind of transcription of an originary oral event).[59] What's more, the details of the prophecy—in line with the genre—are studiously nonreferential. The brief description of the savior *iuvenis* (reprising the bumpkin-based vagueness of VE 1.42's *iuvenis*)[60] has been stumping scholars for years:

> *Ornytus:* "aurea secura cum pace renascitur aetas
> et redit ad terras tandem squalore situque
> alma Themis posito iuvenemque beata sequuntur
> saecula, maternis causam qui vicit Iulis." (1.42–45)

> *Ornytus:* "The golden age is reborn under peace and tranquility; at last
> our nurse Themis returns to earth, shaking off her dirt and
> decay; blessed ages follow the Young Man, who won the case
> for his mother's Julii."

That nightmare throwaway about the *iuvenis* pleading a case for the maternal Julii has been used by both early and late daters to hang their hats on a particular princeps or at least to narrow it down.[61] In addition, a touch of textual uncertainty plagues the line, messing especially with that last key word *Iulis*.[62] Even if we settle on it, the interpretative stretching and straining required to make it refer to something Neronian or Severan is not a pretty sight. Rather than take this as a cryptic riddle, containing the identity of the Caesar in question if only we could get it right, I would say it is designed precisely to throw us off the scent of *any* particular Caesar. In general, the praise content of this prophecy is run-of-the-mill, early accession hail-a-golden-age stuff. This nameless *deus* could be any new emperor taking the throne, sitting atop a predecessor figured and reviled as the ultimate elite evil of civil conflict:

> *Ornytus:* "dum populos deus ipse reget, dabit impia victas
> post tergum Bellona manus spoliataque telis
> in sua vesanos torquebit viscera morsus
> et, modo quae toto civilia distulit orbe,
> secum bella geret: nullos iam Roma Philippos
> deflebit, nullos ducet captiva triumphos." (46–51)

> *Ornytus:* "As long as he, this very god, rules over nations, the nasty
> Bellona will give up her hands, beaten and cuffed behind her

back; she'll be stripped of her weapons and will hack her
crazy teeth into her own insides and will wage the civil
wars—which she only now scattered across the globe—with
herself: now Rome won't have to weep for Philippi, nor will
she have to conduct triumphs as the captive of herself."

The point is not whether this fits Claudius or Elagabalus or a host of others
better or worse.[63] The point is that it fits them all pretty well. It heralds
any new dawn on the block (since Augustus, the original fit for the bill).
Even the comet—another historicist hook offered up later in the poem[64]—
doesn't exactly narrow it down. What is being written down here is the
public transcript of Caesarism—not *a* Caesar.[65]

That notion of the Big God in the Flesh (*deus ipse*) is all over the place
in CS (see later in this chapter). It recurs twice more in this very poem. The
vagueness of the allegorical mode is harnessed to jam the historicist witch
hunt in its tracks. The second time the phrase comes through, it seems to
nod to the same wonderful Caesar-savior (84). But the last time, it's given
to Faunus, the author of the script, with the sense that the two "gods" have
become one:

> *Corydon:* Ornyte, iam dudum velut ipso numine plenum
> me quatit et mixtus subit inter gaudia terror.
> sed bona facundi veneremur numina Fauni.
> *Ornytus:* carmina, quae nobis deus obtulit ipse canenda,
> dicamus teretique sonum modulemur avena:
> forsitan augustas feret haec Meliboeus ad aures. (89–94)

> *Corydon:* Ornytus, I've felt full of the god himself for a while now;
> fear shakes me, steals into me, though mingled with some
> joy. But let's pay our respects to the kind divine power of
> eloquent Faunus.
> *Ornytus:* Let's recite the verses that the god himself has given us to
> sing, and let's play the music on our smooth reed pipe:
> maybe Meliboeus will take them up to the emperor's ears.

These last lines of the poem are choked with various forms of distance and
mediation. *Deus . . . ipse* makes it seem almost as if the Caesar figure has
planted this message via Faunus. Then the brothers take up the song to sing
themselves. Then the less-than-reassuring *forsitan* whimpers out that it may,

it just *may* get back to these unnamed imperial ears via this man from the blue, Meliboeus. There is a lot standing between these herdsmen and the authority they can only *infer* exists. *Deus . . . ipse,* the nonspecific *augustas,* and the strange middleman Meliboeus[66] all step in to measure out the gulf.

When some other gents arrive on the praise scene in CS 4, another Corydon, and an actually materialized patron Meliboeus, the *deus ipse* is still basically inaccessible. Corydon says he wants to make some praise for this big divinity but keeps the specifics, as usual, under wraps. Meliboeus' coaching session as to how he should proceed is also broad brush:

> *Corydon:* carmina iam dudum, non quae nemorale resultent,
> volvimus, o Meliboee; sed haec, quibus aurea possint
> saecula cantari, quibus et deus ipse canatur,
> qui populos urbesque regit pacemque togatam.
> *Meliboeus:* dulce quidem resonas, nec te diversus Apollo
> despicit, o iuvenis, sed magnae numina Romae
> non ita cantari debent, ut ovile Menalcae. (4.5–11)

> *Corydon:* I've been rolling over these verses awhile, Meliboeus—not verses that smack of the woods but ones suited to singing the golden age, suited to singing the god himself, who governs peoples, cities, the peace of the toga.
> *Meliboeus:* You're making sweet sounds, and Apollo sure doesn't turn his back on you in disdain, young Corydon, but the gods of grand Rome shouldn't be sung in the register of Menalcas' sheepfold.

Corydon (the *iuvenis* this time) gives us another *deus ipse,* which Meliboeus multiplies into *numina* (cf. later in this chapter, on CS 7.78 and 80). The plural is no innocent glitch here[67] but an index of the general applicability of this little poetry workshop. The patron is giving tips on how to sing not just for one Caesar but for all of them. And it seems that Meliboeus *has* already got Corydon a little closer to that special something—at least the prospect, the whiff of some Caesarean contact. He thanks Meliboeus for saving him from the distance of exile. Had it not been for him, he wouldn't even be here, and the *deus ipse* wouldn't even be thinking about giving him an ear:

> *Corydon:* nec quisquam nostras inter dumeta Camenas
> respiceret; non ipse daret mihi forsitan aurem,

> ipse deus vacuam, longeque sonantia vota
> scilicet extremo non exaudiret in orbe. (46–49)

> *Corydon:* No one would take a second look at my muses among the
> thorns; maybe he himself, the god himself, would never give
> me an ear and truly wouldn't listen to my prayers ringing at
> the ends of the earth.

But yet again that *forsitan* intervenes: a Caesar reading still seems something remote, potential. In fact *forsitan* keeps intervening, twice more in quick succession (58, 71). Corydon's discourse is tentative, littered with the polite possibly-terribly-would-you-minds of an as-yet-unmade poet. And Caesar is not the only authority figure he admires from a vast distance. Tityrus (Virgil) too gets converted into an untouchable divinity:

> *Corydon:* est—fateor, Meliboee,—deus: sed nec mihi Phoebus
> forsitan abnuerit; tu tantum commodus audi:
> scimus enim, quam te non aspernetur Apollo. (70–72)

> *Corydon:* He's a god—there, I've said it, Meliboeus! But maybe
> Phoebus won't deny me; please, just hear me out, be recep-
> tive; we know how Apollo won't say no to you.

Tityrus is off in his own league, a true *deus* (i.e., the very thing that namesake Tityrus had asserted of the *iuvenis* in VE 1).[68] The most Corydon can hope for is Apollo "not saying no," because at least he's behind Meliboeus, and Meliboeus is on Corydon's side—again, layer upon layer of mediation, dimly reflected glory at best. The function of making these authority figures divine is to make them unattainably distant. Caesar *ipse* can then keep close company with Jupiter *ipse*:

> *Corydon:* ipse polos etiam qui temperat igne geluque,
> Iuppiter ipse parens, cui tu iam proximus ipse,
> Caesar, abes, posito paulisper fulmine saepe
> Cresia rura petit viridique reclinis in antro
> carmina Dictaeis audit Curetica silvis. (92–96)

> *Corydon:* He himself—the one who conditions the heavens with heat
> or chill, father Jupiter himself (whom you follow hard
> behind, Caesar)—often puts down his thunderbolt for a
> while, makes for the Cretan countryside, leans back in a
> green grotto, and listens to Curetic songs in the woods of
> Dicte.

But just as Caesar's proximity to Jupiter is an intimacy also defined by absence—*abes*[69]—so the herdsmen crowd can only catch emperor-god's presence obliquely, after the fact, at a distance. *Caesar* becomes a kind of magic word in the poem, at whose utterance the earth grows fat (*audito Caesare*, 97; *audito nomine*, 109).[70] But he is nothing *but* a god and nothing *but* a general name. Look how he becomes simply a collection of alternative formless forms, perhaps in disguise, perhaps in hiding:

> *Corydon:* tu quoque mutata seu Iuppiter ipse figura,
> Caesar, ades seu quis superum sub imagine falsa
> mortalique lates (es enim deus): (142–144)

> *Corydon:* You too, Caesar—whether you're here as Jupiter himself in a
> different form or whether you're hiding as one of the gods
> beneath a fake and mortal form (for you're a god yourself):

We can't reconstruct his human, political photograph, because the poetry does such a good job of putting him (and other authority figures) in another realm entirely. If our god is present (*ades*), it is only under the cloak of invisibility (*lates;* cf. Lycidas in the bushes earlier, 3.94–95). Again, this could be any Caesar/Caesar could be anyone.

What we are seeing, or not seeing here, is another version of the no-name posturing we have glimpsed ripening in Phaedrus and bearing full fruit in the *Laus Pisonis*. Indeed, CS is perhaps the summit of authorial distance here, because there is no real first person on offer to fail to recognize. The poetry writes its own disappointment as a historicist resource because its central characters are so far out of the loop that they have no idea how to paint the political structures they see in the far-off distance. To them, it is all a beautiful blur. This poetry of the unpatronized makes historicist and/or sociological reading so tough because its drama works precisely to stow it in a nook remote from history and "high" society. The mode of the no-name, the unintegrated outsider, is written into the subtle difference between what Corydon imagines happened with Virgil and Maecenas and what he asks from Meliboeus himself:

> *Corydon:* o mihi quae tereti decurrunt carmina versu
> tunc, Meliboee, sonent si quando montibus istis
> dicar habere Larem, si quando nostra videre
> pascua contingat! vellit nam saepius aurem
> invida paupertas et dicit: "ovilia cura!"

at tu, si qua tamen non aspernanda putabis,
fer, Meliboee, deo mea carmina: nam tibi fas est
sacra Palatini penetralia visere Phoebi.
tum mihi talis eris, qualis qui dulce sonantem
Tityron e silvis dominam deduxit in urbem
ostenditque deos et "spreto" dixit "ovili,
Tityre, rura prius, sed post cantabimus arma." (152–163)[71]

Corydon: These songs of mine that skate along on smooth verse—they
would truly sing out, if I were ever hailed a home owner in
these hills, if I ever got the chance to look on my own
pastures. But too often envious poverty plucks my ear and
says: "Get to the sheepfold!" But you, Meliboeus—if you
think any of my songs not half bad, take them to the god.
For you've got full visiting rights to the innermost sanctum
of Palatine Phoebus. Then you'll play the same role for me as
the man who brought Tityrus—the sweet singer—from the
woods to the Metropole, introduced him to the gods, and
said, "Forget the sheepfold, Tityrus; we'll sing the countryside first, then war."

This "aspiring" poet still has a long way to go. He languishes at the bottom
end, crunched beneath the grinding necessities of poverty. His request to
Meliboeus is similarly humble: take my poems if you think them worthy,
for you can actually get access to those *sacra penetralia.* A Meliboeus is yet
again entrusted as the mediator and messenger. But how different is the way
Corydon envisions the unnamed Maecenas taking Virgil under his wing:
whisking him directly into the city under his own steam, "showing him the
gods," brokering a face-to-face introduction. Indeed that *prop(i)er* eyewitness flight into the heavens actually enables Tityrus to climb the generic ladder too, accelerating from pastoral to epic in a few seconds. For
Corydon, the prospects are more limited. Stuck on the pauper's track, he
can only knock up some generic pastoral praise to "some God" and hope
that his patron can smuggle it into court. Virgil/Tityrus saw everything in
the flesh. Corydon can barely get his open letter posted.

By the time CS 7 rolls around—the supposed culmination of the
praise triad and the zenith of Corydon's independence[72]—the distance
doesn't seem to have narrowed much at all.[73] Granted, Corydon is now
reporting back on a trip to the (or an?) *urbs,* the big smoke, where he

got to sit in some amphitheater and see the show put on by the *iuvenis-deus* himself (6). The hick was *there*—even if it took him till the end of the collection to get to the same point that Tityrus had *already* reached early in VE 1 (a strong narrative flip that turns Virgil's poetry of the readily patronized into CS's poetry of the *never* patronized). But the account is so full of wonder that it paralyzes the description. Indeed we're not even sure how much he could actually see from his vantage point up in the worst stands:

> *Corydon:* quid tibi nunc referam, quae vix suffecimus ipsi
> per partes spectare suas? sic undique fulgor
> percussit. stabam defixus et ore patenti
> cunctaque mirabar necdum bona singula noram,
> cum mihi iam senior, lateri qui forte sinistro
> iunctus erat, "quid te stupefactum, rustice," dixit
> "ad tantas miraris opes, qui nescius auri
> sordida tecta, casas et sola mapalia nosti?
> en ego iam tremulus iam vertice canus et ista
> factus in urbe senex stupeo tamen omnia: certe
> vilia sunt nobis, quaecumque prioribus annis
> vidimus, et sordet quicquid spectavimus olim." (7.35–46)

> *Corydon:* Why should I now tell you things I myself could hardly make
> out in their details? The bright lights stunned me every
> which way. I stood there transfixed, mouth slung open,
> admiring everything, before I could even get every single
> feature, when suddenly an old man, who happened to be
> latched to me on my left, said: "Why are you so struck,
> country folk, that you're amazed by so much wealth, when
> you've never seen gold before, you only know your squalid
> huts, cottages, and cabins? Even I—trembling with age, my
> hair white, a resident of this city my whole life—can't believe
> it all: we sure now think what we saw in the past cheap, and
> whatever we watched then seems tacky."

Corydon struggles to drum up the language to describe all this in detail, because his vision isn't even able to make sense of it.[74] As his nameless next-door neighbor reminds him, he's a *rusticus*. And this kind of spectacle makes no sense within the terms of his knowledge and experience—another Corydon dumbstruck before the phenomena of distant divinity, just like in

CS 1. Corydon's epistemological frameworks are so limited that he fumbles around in vain even to *name* what he has seen:

> *Corydon:* ordine quid referam? vidi genus omne ferarum,
>   hic niveos lepores et non sine cornibus apros,
>   hic raram silvis etiam, quibus editur, alcen.
>   vidimus et tauros, quibus aut cervice levata
>   deformis scapulis torus eminet aut quibus hirtae
>   iactantur per colla iubae, quibus aspera mento
>   barba iacet tremulisque rigent palearia setis.
>   nec solum nobis silvestria cernere monstra
>   contigit: aequoreos ego cum certantibus ursis
>   spectavi vitulos et equorum nomine dictum,
>   sed deforme pecus, quod in illo nascitur amne
>   qui sata riparum vernantibus irrigat undis. (57–68)

> *Corydon:* Why tell you step by step? I saw every sort of beast: over
>   here snowy hares and boars with horns, over there some elk,
>   rare even in the forests where it exists. I saw bulls as well,
>   either those with a raised neck, an ugly lump rising from
>   their shoulder blades, or those with shagged manes falling
>   over their neck, a rough beard over their chin, their dewlaps
>   stiffening with bristling spikes. I didn't only get to see
>   woodland beasts either: I witnessed sea calves with fighting
>   bears, and those things called after the name of the horse, a
>   disgusting herd, which come from the river that irrigates the
>   crops on its banks with the new waters at spring.

Every kind of beast under the sun he may have seen, but look how language fails him.[75] He has to categorize the distinct buffalo and urus as two kinds of bull, via awkward periphrasis. Seals are glossed as "calves of the sea," for that's the closest he can get within his existing animal vocabulary. Hippopotami are swerved around via the generic *deforme pecus*, named after the horse,[76] from a river he can't name.[77] Even these mystery *ursi*—taken by some scholars as polar bears and hence recruited as another bonkers date marker[78]—might not really be *ursi*, given Corydon's impoverished frame of reference. What is happening with the animals here is another symptom of the same problem. As with the herdsman poet's inability to describe the amphitheater in general or his faltering attempts to name the vague superpower for which his verses are earmarked, the detail is the devil. Specificity is an ever-receding goal, because the rustic poet lacks the vision and the language to get there. He remains struck dumb, stuck fast in a different world.

And so it continues right up until the climactic scene of CS, the moment when we are pumped up for the big reveal, only to realize there is no one behind the curtain:

> *Lycotas:* o felix Corydon, quem non tremebunda senectus
> impedit! o felix, quod in haec tibi saecula primos
> indulgente deo demittere contigit annos!
> nunc, tibi si propius venerandum cernere numen
> fors dedit et praesens vultumque habitumque notasti,
> dic age dic, Corydon, quae sit mihi forma deorum.
> *Corydon:* o utinam nobis non rustica vestis inesset:
> vidissem propius mea numina! sed mihi sordes
> pullaque paupertas et adunco fibula morsu
> obfuerunt. utcumque tamen conspeximus ipsum
> longius; ac, nisi me visus decepit, in uno
> et Martis vultus et Apollinis esse putavi. (73–84)
> *Lycotas:* Corydon, you lucky man! The trembles of old age don't hold
> you back. Lucky man! You got to put down your early years
> in this age, thanks be to god! Now, if fortune gave you the
> chance to see our reverend divinity at closer quarters, and
> you've clocked his face and dress in the flesh, tell me—go on,
> Corydon!—what the gods look like.
> *Corydon:* I wish I hadn't been dressed shepherd style! I would have
> seen my gods at closer quarters! But my squalor, my filthy
> poverty, my brooch with a crooked clip got in the way. In
> any case, I saw him at a distance. And if my eyesight didn't
> deceive me, I thought he had the face of Mars and Apollo, all
> rolled into one.

Lycotas asks his happy wonderer for the full eyewitness report on this *deus*, presumably the one we have been too far off to see in the flesh. If you had the chance to get closer (*propius*), if you could actually see his face, describe it to us. Tell us what the form of the gods (plural) is. Historicist scholarship rubs its hands together, ready to see which Caesar it has been all along.[79] But it turns out that those ifs were big ones. Corydon never actually gets close enough (*propius*) to see his *numina* (again, plural; both *deorum* and *numina* capture the uncertainty and stretch).[80] Instead, poverty stood cold in the way, turning the indicative divini-vision of Tityrus in VE 1.42 (*hic illum vidi iuvenem*) into the remote subjunctive of an outside chance (*vidissem*).[81] All Corydon could do was catch a vague glimpse from afar (*longius*).[82] And that brief flash is hesitantly (*nisi me visus decepit*) converted into a pretty sorry-looking "description." He seemed to have the face of Mars and Apollo rolled into one. Big deal. Try finding any emperor to whom that sort of description wouldn't apply.[83] The Mars-and-Apollo comment cashes out the plural *deorum* and *numina* pretty neatly indeed. For to the poor Corydon squinting his heart out from the very top of the stands, this god is inevitably seen in double. But beyond that, he just cannot be narrowed down.[84]

This brilliant antirevelation is the furthest we get in the slow creep of *propius* that sees the no-name Corydon-poets of CS continue to rot on the margins, while the authority figures of whom they daydream float away into their far-off heaven. Like in the *Laus Pisonis,* the ultimate authority (there Piso, here some *iuvenis/deus/Caesar* type) is a deliberate puddle of vagary and multiplicity—and it is not just the failure of scholarship to solve the riddle. It is a narrative necessity, a mimetic must. These different Corydons are always so far from the goal that they can never find a proper name for it. They are poor young Tityri, outsider poets one stage shy of being swallowed into the folds of patronage and temporality. They have no place in imperial history. As such, they cannot be historicized under any emperor.

Timelessness of No-Name: Future-Proofing?

As I have busted a gut to show, CS is a poet who actively grates against referentiality and against attribution. His pastoral names seem to refer to the same but different people. His herder poets are indistinguishable or keep switching places without telling us. The names and references that would give us the silver bullet to politically "contextualize" the corpus are scrupulously withheld, because the country singers are too far from the action to scope beyond the generic praise heard on the grapevine. In a sense, CS is the most radical attempt at "pure pastoral" of anything we have from antiquity.[85] It is so timeless, or "time-full" in the Felskian sense,[86] that you can't fit it definitively anywhere within a space of hundreds of years.

The dynamics of the no-name that gloss this "timelessness" work similarly to the *Laus Pisonis* but perhaps go one better. In the *Laus Pisonis,* the poet wrote his story of obscurity into the first person. CS, on the other hand, palms off the tale of marginality to several internal characters, whom we cannot connect to any historical author, because the moment of biographizing authorization (I, Tityrus, Virgil) is missing in action. "CS" *ipse* is *procul,* or hiding somewhere *propius.* But like the fabulous *deus* in the impenetrable fortress of the big city, he is nowhere to be seen.[87]

Moreover, what these fascinating blanks and wipes of authority figures—the particular Caesar but also the author—do is make the text "timeless" in the sense of future-proofing. In an unpredictable climate of cut-and-thrust imperial politics, where emperors and dynasties were expiring all the time, perhaps the best solution to the longevity problem was to leave everything nameless. The way forward was to leave the field open to any Caesar who wished to fantasize himself into the referent position. The ideological corollary here is that the principate itself is also, in a sense, protected from the ravages of time, as a system eternally self-regenerating. For no matter where you stand, it is *always* an Augustan liberation from civil war, a foundation and rescue, a golden age permanently renewed. The absence of authority brings a reach far greater than it would have been, had specific names found their way in. Likewise with the author: the effect of vacancy, the fact that there seems to be no proper name or historical figure behind these poems, allows them to serve as templates for whatever praise-pastoral needs to be knocked up next. Minus defined author and Caesar, the *Eclogues* gain the ultimate pastoral prize of the timeless, well-gotten through the nameless. If only we could stop looking at the trees, take a step back, and start admiring that dark wood: the growth of many centuries at once.

III

WHENCE AND WHEN

In the misty past of Part II, we watched our authors (fully) unknown do the opposite of strutting their stuff, in texts fashioned for maximal contextual reach. Two interrogatives came up regularly, if only implicitly. The first was something like "whence?" or "from whom?": whence did those fables really come from, when the author dangles so cheekily the home truth that we cannot really know him? How does that *unde* at the beginning of the *Laus Pisonis* actually channel *the* scholarly question we are always asking of it? To whom should we attribute those words carved on the tree or those emerging from herdsman X's or Y's mouth? A second interrogative refrain was surely "when?" When is the moment of the *Laus Pisonis*—and what would it mean to write an occasional poem scripted for multiple possible occasions? When is the "when" of Calpurnius Siculus—Neronian, Severan, or much thicker than either alternative would suggest, context-richness neat?

Part III grabs these questions more directly by the horns. These chapters will jam together a twin double act of two prose works back-to-back. The first combination of *Apocolocyntosis* and *Satyrica* is dedicated to the first question: whence? Here I want to show how both texts—according to their vastly different programs—think hard about the reliability of source and context, the framing devices we critics tend to live by. The second team of Tacitus' *Dialogus* and [Longinus'] *On the Sublime* will run with the second question: when? Their answers will be slightly different, but their common solution will be about multiple temporalities and contexts. Both of them push a strong bid for their own transcendence and timefullness, which grates palpably against the trappings of material history weighing them down.

As for anonymity proper, all of these works, you might say, have authorship issues. But they range from the once-upon-a-time-entertained-but-nowadays-little-disputed authorship (*Apocolocyntosis* of Seneca; *Dialogus* of Tacitus) to raising fairly serious doubts over author and date (*Satyrica* of Petronius?) to giving us precious little certainty over who and when (hence *On the Sublime* of the bracketed [Longinus]). While I tentatively suggest ways in which we might resurrect the anonymous authorship hypotheses behind the *Apocolocyntosis* or the *Dialogus,* largely on the basis of the internal dynamics I try to scoop out, the role of "true" anonymity in those cases is a little more speculative. I go further with, and make more of, the prospect of convergence between internal and external in the two cases where there are more grounds for the unknown, namely, the *Satyrica* and *On the Sublime.* The latter in particular, I shall argue, makes anonymity strangely crucial to the transcendence at which it grasps. In any case—whether authors show up, partly show up, or play no-show altogether—these texts have a lot to tell us about these favorite questions, the whence and the when.

7

Whence

Sources, Frames, Contexts

WITH THE INSTANT EXCEPTION of Chapter 1, so far this book has tested its whack-job ideas exclusively through my native mode (sustained close readings of verse texts). This section will try to go out on a longer limb in its focus on prose and its attempt to charge up two texts with mutually flattering comparisons. Well, *almost* prose. The first two in the lineup—*Apocolocyntosis* (*Apocol.*) and *Satyrica*—are strictly *prosimetric,* and that form is crucial for tracking the pulses at work here. The chapter will busy itself with two problems germane to anonymity: the source and the frame. Both are interrupted regularly by the very fact of swinging prose and verse, which always begs, and almost as often scuppers, these key questions: from where?[1] And which frames which?

The twain of *Apocol.* and *Satyrica* can sometimes seem to gel more in theory than in practice.[2] Content-wise they are worlds apart: the *Apocol.* a quick and dirty satire on the failed apotheosis of the emperor Claudius and his subsequent kick back down into hell; the *Satyrica* a lengthy and hopelessly fragmented satiric "novel" charting the various misadventures of a homoerotic threesome (with the third character subbed halfway), all told through the eyes of the participant-observer, the try-hard intellectual Encolpius. This chapter will bid to connect these texts, in the sense of drawing parallel rather than intersecting lines. I shall posit that both effect some kind of symbiosis between their inner and outer lives (i.e., both texts flash a fascination with some form of anonymity or, in the *Satyrica*'s case, strictly, mistitling) that could ripple out into the very conditions of their making and reading. That argument should look nice and battle-worn by now. I shall claim that their common denominator lies in messing around with important (and slightly different) epistemic settings. By which, I mean that each in its own way tampers with some critical information for readers trying to make sense of text and/or world. The *Apocol.* stalks around in the engine room of source and origin. It turns Claudius into no usual pumpkin but renders him homeless and stateless, common property, which eerily mirrors the proverbs without provenance brandished to bring him down. Along the way, we move from *asking* whence to *knowing to where.* While the *Apocol.* manipulates source, the *Satyrica* does the same for *frame.* The bunk *tituli* of its pages seem to speak to how this "untitled" text reads in the world beyond them. If *Apocol.* jerks us around but convinces us, with text authorized precisely through *lack* of context, *Satyrica* shows how context (or paratext) can mislead. Either way—we might catch them saying—we can get along perfectly well without it.

Apocolocyntosis: Death by Proverb

An anonymous genius is a different matter.

—P. T. Eden (1984: 8)

The *Apocol.* is one of those works. It has fallen into our laps without giving us much to go on: what it's called, what it is (Menippean satire?[3] Something else?), whom it's by have all been, and in some cases are still, very much up for grabs.[4] The last question—authorship—has been as settled as is humanly possible for a good while.[5] The working assumption, that this is the *Apocol.* of Seneca, now surfs a reassuring orthodoxy. Interestingly, however, the possibility of *initial* anonymous circulation still wins an airing from time to time.[6] This section, by contrast, will aim to throw something more behind the idea that we were never meant to know to whom this whacky text belonged.

The very few tentative fans of the "initial anonymity" hypothesis tend to overestimate the danger rationale: the author would have an incentive to circulate the text in a murmuring, clandestine fashion because the political climate immediately after Claudius' death would have been unpredictable. Claiming a kneejerk outburst of anger against him would have been risky till the coast was certifiably clear.[7] Then, when all was golden and the denigration of predecessor firmly in place, out pops Seneca—it was me all along folks! But this fails to take into account the continuing utility of anonymity for the purposes of memory management. In Chapter 3, we saw how the political force of *Octavia* is not muted but *magnified* by the fact of its homelessness. Its anonymity turns the relief of the few into the outrage of the many. For the *Apocol.*, committed as it is to a parallel project of ensuring that the worst of the recently deceased emperor seeps into the dominant tradition,[8] the benefits of anonymity are similar. This is no petty cry from a singularly aggrieved figure in the upper echelons of the court. This is a yell of proper satiric *damnatio*, delivered by a chorus of possibilities. The *Apocol.* poses nicely as the emphatic sigh of collective relief, as well as the exacting of collective vengeance. And if we know it's just old Seneca digging the knife in, the voodoo curse is called right off.

Having said that, I should row back a little. While the analogy with the *Octavia* feels roughly right to me, the limits are fluorescently visible: the overwhelming likelihood that Seneca was behind this, because of the snug fit with his style and thematics elsewhere;[9] the fact that we might lose some buzz of irony or brinksmanship if we abandon a Senecan author effect; the reality that this very different genre of elite satiric squib has nowhere *near* the universalist purchase of a dramatic text. One way through this minefield—and I wouldn't claim to come out the other end without some heavy losses, whichever route we pick—is to stress that the *Apocol.* is no simple shared exhalation representing this two-bit scholar's vision of the symphony of "all society"[10] but an elite text that is *parasitic* on the Saturnalian energy of release and relief.[11] The author joins forces with the crowd singing Claudius' backhanded funeral dirge (cf. *omnes laeti, hilares; populus Romanus tanquam liber, Apocol.* 12). The framing as *collective* liberation gives the condemnation its force, and the same goes for the sunny praise of the new Neronian golden age (*Apocol.* 4). In other words, the pose of Saturnalian outburst is waved as an ideological butter knife to spread the sentiment all the way across the board. Anonymity *adds* something here. So before taking Seneca as the final culprit, why not keep it, not him, in mind?

As in the *Octavia*, there are a host of internal winks to the idea that the whole enterprise is aided by, even built on, the power of namelessness. The question of *unde* looms over this bizarre creation, a question pricked by many of its key markers of form and content: the mixed media of prosimetry, which disrupts the text in such a way that we are constantly wondering from where the shock of the new voice comes[12] and upsets our strictures on a unitary origin for literary discourse; then the role of the ubiquitous proverbs and anonymized quotations,[13] which bring up "from what? from whom?" only to make us realize that those aren't the right questions; finally, the status of the man-monster himself, Claudius, whom no one can really place, categorize, or domesticate. Forms of anonymity bring entertainment here, no doubt; but they also breed terror and chaos, and we readers are not immune. So let's ask the *Apocol.* its own question: *unde?*

Unde

Stories of emperor deaths all raise the problem of source and knowledge:[14] how did these words get from the deathbed or the hara-kiri scene to this, here, the thing we're reading? The *Apocol.* begins with a version of the crux. The author—who, we might note, gives absolutely no credentials and flashes no ID card to put us at ease—anticipates a few questions on how he came to know all this but reserves his right to remain silent or to make it up as he goes along:[15]

> Quid actum sit in caelo ante diem III idus Octobris anno novo, initio saeculi felicissimi, volo memoriae tradere. Nihil nec offensae nec gratiae dabitur. Haec ita vera. Si quis quaesiverit **unde** sciam, primum, si noluero, non respondebo. Quis coacturus est? Ego scio me liberum factum, ex quo suum diem obiit ille, qui verum proverbium fecerat, aut regem aut fatuum nasci oportere. Si libuerit respondere, dicam quod mihi in buccam venerit. Quis unquam ab historico iuratores exegit?[16] (*Apocol.* 1)

> I want to put on the record what went down in heaven last October 13 in this new year, hailing the start of a blessed age. There'll be nothing conceded to malice or sycophancy. These things are true. If anyone asks after the source from which I know that, above all, I don't have to reply if I don't want to. Who'll force the issue? What I certainly know is that I got my freedom on the very same day on which he met his end—the man who made the proverb true, that you have to be born either a king or a fool. If I feel like replying, I'll say whatever comes to my lips. Who ever demanded witnesses from a historian?

The author will probably get that thousand-dollar-question *unde?* But he fires back with a few of his own (*quis . . . quis*)—come on, step out, who is going to make me? The tease of withholding in *non respondebo* goes well with the reticent suppression of Claudius' name in this defensive opener. Instead, the author opts for a proverb as a periphrasis. Indeed the use of unidentified proverbs as a way of circulating a perverse kind of "authority,"[17] the verdict of the commons (recall that Quintilian passage in the Introduction),[18] will become a basic strategy of the *Apocol.* As well as the "pumpkinification" of Claudius, this text is also about his *proverbialization:* turning him into the cliché of the bad emperor, who will travel easily along the drooling mouths of Rome's gossip columns. As well as Claudius making proverbs true, the proverbs make him true. No one asks where proverbs come from. They are true, and that is that.

When the author does eventually fold to supply us with the real source (*auctorem producere*), he names no names, or at least not the crucial one:

> Tamen si necesse fuerit auctorem producere, quaerito ab eo qui Drusillam euntem in caelum vidit: idem Claudium vidisse se dicet iter facientem "non passibus aequis." Velit nolit, necesse est illi omnia videre, quae in caelo aguntur: Appiae viae curator est, qua scis et divum Augustum et Tiberium Caesarem ad deos isse. Hunc si interrogaveris, soli narrabit: coram pluribus nunquam verbum faciet. Nam ex quo in senatu iuravit se Drusillam vidisse caelum ascendentem et illi pro tam bono nuntio nemo credidit, quod viderit, verbis conceptis affirmavit se non indicaturum, etiam si in medio foro hominem occisum vidisset. Ab hoc ego quae tum audivi, certa clara affero, ita illum salvum et felicem habeam. (1)

> But if I have to produce an authoritative source, ask the man who saw Drusilla on her way up to heaven: the same man says he saw Claudius traipsing there "with uneven steps." Whether he wants to or not, everything that happens in heaven, he's forced to witness: he's the caretaker of the Appian way, by which you know both the deified Augustus and Tiberius Caesar joined the gods. If you ask him, he'll tell you and you alone: he'll never offer a peep in the presence of others. That's because he swore in the senate that he saw Drusilla rising to heaven, and in exchange for the good news, no one believed him, so he swore with religious words that he won't testify to what he has seen, even if he saw a man killed in the middle of the street. It was from him I heard this, and I hand it on plain and simple, so help him god.

This so-called *auctor* makes like our own author. He says that he saw Claudius, but only in private; and the way he says it, liberally peppering the statement with an unattributed quote *non passibus aequis,*[19] in fact makes it difficult to tell who (this *auctor* or our author) is doing the quoting.[20] The quote is recognizably Virgil, yes, but it is a Virgil so boringly familiar, so neutrally "famous,"[21] as to be essentially proverbial. The quotation encourages us to forget about context, as soon as we get the obvious joke that Virgil and others[22] are talking about differences in stature between two people, Aeneas and Ascanius, while Claudius is out of step with himself.[23] In this kind of quasi-historical source production scene,[24] we might expect a "serious" author to name his authority right from the off. But whoever our *ego* is, he does everything he can to write out his *auctor*'s identity through those time-honored techniques of periphrasis and substitution. In this opening section, we are jealously guarded from indulging any kind of tracing impulse. We enjoy authors without names, and quotations that need no attribution.

And just when we thought the orientation couldn't get any fuzzier, suddenly, out of the blue, comes the verse from nowhere:[25]

> Iam Phoebus breviore via contraxerat arcum
> lucis, et obscuri crescebant tempora somni,
> iamque suum victrix augebat Cynthia regnum,
> et deformis hiemps gratos carpebat honores
> divitis autumni, iussoque senescere Baccho
> carpebat raras serus vindemitor uvas. (2)

> Phoebus had already taken in the arc of his light with a shorter course, and the time for sleep was growing, and Cynthia the Conqueror was already expanding her dominion, and horrid winter was plucking the lovely honors of rich autumn, and Bacchus was commanded to age, and the lingering picker was gathering the last dregs of grape cluster.

The author seemed to have sorted—albeit in an inadequate, roundabout way—the question of where he got the information. But now we fall into another shock of *unde:* Whose verses are these? What relation do they have to the prose body?[26] Are they quotation, like the snippet of Virgil? Or live at the improv? We soon work out (?) that they are engineered for maximum anonymity, made to look like one of those long-winded temporal periphrases that make epic epic. But the point is that temporal periphrasis is *all* that the verses contain; they peter out before the main event can arrive (autumn was already here, when . . . ?). So not only are they the hack verses of *any* high poet doing the rounds in contemporary Rome;[27] they concoct paranoid atmospherics by getting us stuck in a temporal loop[28] and leaving out the crucial information of *what actually happened.*

Once we cut through the impenetrable thicket, what we take from the lines is a rough time of year. The prose voice comes back and spells out the date as October 13, estimates the hour as between midday and one, only then to admit absolute certainty is impossible.[29] It seems that the job of prose is to establish greater precision. But even the prose can't get us all the way to absolute certainty. The doubt only seems to open the floodgates for the next round of sound cloud:

> Iam medium curru Phoebus diviserat orbem
> et propior nocti fessas quatiebat habenas
> obliquo flexam deducens tramite lucem: (2)

> Phoebus in his chariot had already split the middle of his course and was shaking the reins closer to night, bringing the bent light down in an angled side path:

Which repeats, in ambient verse, what the prose timekeeping has already told us. And here too, we never get the payoff of an event, only the window dressing around it. When the prose supplements it, we are still left waiting for something definitive to happen: *Claudius animam agere coepit nec invenire exitum poterat* (2). The repeated nonevents across the prose and verse don't set up an opposition or a relationship of "prose certainty clarifying verse mess" *vel sim.* Rather, the two modes work in cahoots to capture a Claudian atmosphere of dithering in-betweenness, of getting no resolution, no relief. The author is broadcasting that exact knowledge of time, and the certainty of its provenance, is impossible in an epistemologically messy Rome.[30] So the verse actually works well toward this end: the blanker, the better. Its value lies precisely in the fact that it doesn't really tell us anything—and *not knowing* is what this early *Apocol.* is all about.

Just as the real source of this tale can't quite be divulged—and whoever it is will deny it if pressed anyway—so the exact time of death can't quite be ascertained for the postmortem. Knowledge, *and* lack thereof, is set up here as basic to the *Apocol.* The author can't say for certain the proper hour (*horam non possum certam tibi dicere,* 2), and nor can the astrologers—but that's because *no one* does (*Et tamen non est mirum si errant et horam eius nemo novit; nemo enim unquam illum natum putavit,* 3). Claudius struggles to die all by himself, so Mercury steps in to make the fate Clotho finally cut the cord. The swerve into verse then tells us how Nero gets a longer measure as compensation. But when the moment of truth arrives, we are still in the dark, at least in one respect:

> Claudium autem iubent omnes
> "χαίροντας, εὐφημοῦντας ἐκπέμπειν δόμων."

> Et ille quidem animam ebulliit, et ex eo desiit vivere videri. Expiravit autem dum comoedos audit, ut scias me non sine causa illos timere. Ultima vox eius haec inter homines audita est, cum maiorem sonitum emisisset illa parte, qua facilius loquebatur: "vae me, puto, concacavi me." Quod an fecerit, nescio: omnia certe concacavit. (4)

> But as for Claudius, they tell everyone
> "to send him from the house, rejoicing, crying out in triumph."

> And straightaway he gurgled out his ghost and from that point on stopped pretending he was alive. He was listening to some comic actors as he breathed his last, just so you know I'm not wary of them without good reason. His last words among the living were these. When he had let out a bigger sound from that part, by which he found it easier to talk: "Oh boy, I think I've shat myself." Whether it happened or not, I don't know; but I can certainly say he shat on everything else.

Again, the unmarked quotation—supposedly from the lost Cresphontes of Euripides but suspiciously obscure here[31]—comes in train with an epistemological shrug: we know his last words, but we *don't* know whether he actually did the deed.[32] And that state of unknowing pairs well with Claudius' own stuttered hedging—*puto!*[33] If the source himself isn't sure, then what chance do we have?

At this point, I should come out of the closet on a point of method. Would that quote look "suspiciously obscure" if Euripides' *Cresphontes* hadn't slipped through our perforated corpus of textual survivors? Perhaps not. My point, however, is that there is no real payoff to "interpreting" this kind of *unmarked* quotation in the *Apocol.,* even when we can source it confidently (the case is different for *marked* quotation—see the Homer moment in the next section). The "quote" here is so general as to lose its birthmark. The point is its transferability, rather than its origins. It is there to give the order for what *everyone* should feel: joy, relief, in unison, not finicky source scouring. That may sound shocking within the terms of our neurotic intertextualist fetish in Latin studies: What do you mean we shouldn't chase down the source text and make the allusion pout in sexy ways?! What do you mean we shouldn't rip up the quotes by the root and compare contexts?! It's a hard pill to swallow, but I would argue that many of these literary citations function in the *Apocol.* precisely as dead ends, which invite us to do the usual fiddly scholarly work only to leave us shrugging. Aporia might seem a tepid cop-out, and it sure doesn't come naturally to us—but it is also a critical pose we might want to try out on a text that starts off so aporetically.

Well, shrugging is one option. But it is an option predicated on us always asking, along with the gods in heaven, from where? And it is predicated, equally, on us never getting a good answer to it. The job of the *Apocol.*, I shall argue later concerning Augustus' intervention, is to train us out of asking that automated question and move us from a state of ignorance to a state of knowledge. As our author says right from the off, he doesn't have to reply to our source inquiries (though he does, and then he doesn't). The important thing is that he *knows* (*ego scio,* 1; cf. Augustus in the next section) Claudius' death day was a liberation for him. And shortly, we will be coerced into *knowing* that it was so for us too. In fact a lot of the *Apocol.*'s knowledge is packaged as asserted or assumed, and it is all the more ideologically powerful for that: cf. the collective *scitis* (5) telling us we *know* what happened on earth immediately after Claudius' death (of course we don't). In general, the *Apocol.* sorts out what it's impossible to know from what it's important to know *for sure*: as the narrator's joke puts it at Claudius' death-by-diarrhea, he can't say for certain whether Claudius shat himself on expiry; but he can definitely (*certe*)[34] assert that he shat on everything else. In other words, the momentum of the *Apocol.*'s smaller narrative units (as well as the whole arc of the story) takes us from Saturnalian chaos, with internal characters and us readers reveling in confusion, to a cold hard definition, the true knowledge that Claudius is monster over fool. We stop with the philological puzzles of categorization (but *from where?*) and go over the real knowledge (names and numbers of Claudius' victims, 11, 13–14). The *Apocol.* puts Claudius in his place, back into the ownership of everyone. As we shall see in the next section, the proverb is key to that project, because it is shared knowledge of which no one asks *from where?*

Nice (Not) to Know You

As we have seen, the *Apocol.* fires up in a fit of knowledge and ignorance, certainty and doubt. The cloudy side clusters mainly around Claudius. In fact, "not knowing" becomes one of Claudius' cardinal sins later in the work, over against the emphatic knowledges (*ego scio,* 1 and 10) of narrator and Augustus (and in some form, the reader: see later in this section on *qua scis,* 1). But early on, epistemological mess affects most things our uncategorizable subject touches.[35] After opting out of any detailed account of what happened on earth immediately after Claudius' death—on the grounds that "everyone knows" and *nemo felicitatis suae obliviscitur* (5; itself another cheeky move to make Claudius' death a cause for universal celebration)—our author moves us swiftly up to the sky. He carefully cites (and disclaims responsibility onto) his unnamed source yet again: *in caelo quae acta sint, audite: fides penes auctorem erit* (5). But that reassurance seems to crumble beneath the confusion reigning upstairs:

> Nuntiatur Iovi venisse quendam bonae staturae, bene canum; **nescio** quid illum minari, assidue enim caput movere; pedem dextrum trahere. Quaesisse se, cuius nationis esset: respondisse **nescio** quid perturbato sono et voce confusa; non intellegere se linguam eius, nec Graecum esse nec Romanum nec ullius gentis notae. (5)

> A report goes to Jupiter that someone of good stature and fairly gray hair has arrived; that he was threatening **something (not sure what)**, for he was shaking his head constantly; and that he was dragging his right foot. They asked him what nation he was from: he responded **something (not sure what)** in an agitated mumble and an upset voice; they didn't understand his language, and he was neither Greek nor Roman, nor of any known race for that matter.

Claudius' debut is an epistemological nightmare: suddenly the news comes to Jupiter (from nowhere—note the passive, anonymous *nuntiatur*)[36] that "someone" (*quendam*) has arrived. The *nescio* components of the "somethings" he says are hooks for the growing theme of not knowing. But whereas Claudius later stars as the one who doesn't know, here he becomes the unknown object itself. In Rumsfeldian parlance, he is a known unknown. No one can place him; no one knows what he is saying.[37] Jupiter sends Hercules—seasoned traveler as he is—to work out who the hell

they're dealing with here. At first he is completely stumped and takes him
for a monster, another labor. But when he gets closer and realizes this is
something approaching human (*quasi homo*),[38] he addresses Claudius with
the clarion call of civilization: τίς πόθεν εἰς ἀνδρῶν, πόθι τοι πόλις ἠδὲ τοκῆες;
(5). It is no coincidence that this Homeric line is the hexameter version of
unde (πόθεν, πόθι).[39] The goal is to work out *from where* this monster
hails. But this time it *is* important to work out the origin of the *verse*:

> Claudius gaudet esse illic philologos homines: sperat futurum aliquem his-
> toriis suis locum. Itaque et ipse Homerico versu Caesarem se esse signifi-
> cans ait:

> "Ἰλιόθεν με φέρων ἄνεμος Κικόνεσσι πέλασσεν."

> Erat autem sequens versus verior, aeque Homericus:

> "ἔνθα δ' ἐγὼ πόλιν ἔπραθον, ὤλεσα δ' αὐτούς." (5)

Claudius is excited to find fellow philologists there; he hopes there'll be
a place for his *Histories*. So he goes on to say he's Caesar, indicating as
much with a Homeric verse:

> "The wind brought me to the Cicones, taking me from Troy."

The next line would actually have been truer, also Homeric:

> "There I sacked the city and massacred the people."

The author supplements Claudius' "from where" response—"from Troy"—
with a corrective "there," which overwrites Claudius' pretentious lineage
with some hard evidence of character.[40] Hercules and the gods may not
know where this strange creature comes from. But it sure pays to know
from where those lines.[41] No one in the text thinks to make the supplement, but we on the outside *do*. Here, the philologizing narrator uses context to beat Claudius at his own game.

Slowly but surely, the text sets up a pattern whereby ignorance is traded
up for knowledge, lies cut through for truth. As earlier, narrator upgrades
Claudius' "incorrect" Homeric line with something much truer (*verior*).
Febris too, Claudius' best divine acquaintance, takes issue with his bunk
origin myth in the most brutally corrective way: of course he doesn't
hail from Troy but from Lyon (6). This is explicitly designed to correct
Hercules (as well as us) from being taken in by the nonentity show.

Claudius mutters a reply that no one can understand (*Quid diceret, nemo intellegebat,* 6). And again, to stop us getting lost in the dim lights, the narrator weighs in by decoding the Claudius speak for us: he's actually giving the nod to have Febris executed. But it seems no one is paying much attention anyway (*Putares omnes illius esse libertos: adeo illum **nemo** curabat,* 6).[42] So Hercules, fed up, decides to put the *unde* question another way—in verse:

> Tum Hercules "audi me" inquit "tu desine fatuari. Venisti huc, ubi mures ferrum rodunt. Citius mihi verum, ne tibi alogias excutiam." Et quo terribilior esset, tragicus fit et ait:
>
> > "exprome propere, sede qua genitus cluas,
> > hoc ne peremptus stipite ad terram accidas;
> > haec clava reges saepe mactavit feros.
> > quid nunc profatu vocis incerto sonas?
> > quae patria, quae gens mobile eduxit caput?
> > edissere. equidem regna tergemini petens
> > longinqua regis, unde ab Hesperio mari
> > Inachiam ad urbem nobile advexi pecus,
> > vidi duobus imminens fluviis iugum,
> > quod Phoebus ortu semper obverso videt,
> > ubi Rhodanus ingens amne praerapido fluit
> > Ararque, dubitans quo suos cursus agat,
> > tacitus quietis adluit ripas vadis.
> > estne illa tellus spiritus altrix tui?" (7)

Then Hercules said: "Listen to me: stop fooling around. You've come here, where the mice munch iron. Give me the truth quick, or I'll shake your follies out of you." To become more intimidating, he went full tragic, and said:

"Declare it right now, where you claim your place of birth, or take a blow from my stick and collapse to the ground; this club has often killed savage kings. Why do you now mutter out an unintelligible utterance? What country, what clan has raised your trembling head? Speak out. When I was looking for the distant kingdom of the triple kings, where I brought a noble herd of cattle from the Hesperian sea to the Inachian city, I saw a ridge looking out over two rivers, which Phoebus always sees opposite his rising, where the mighty Rhone flows in quick torrents, and the Arar, hesitating over which way to go, silently washes the banks with placid shallows. Was it this land that reared you?!"

Hercules' tragic set piece is pretty much one series of questions, and speculations, about Claudius' origins. He tries to narrow the remote suggestion down (*unde . . . ubi*), but the geography is against him: in this region, even the rivers don't really know which way they're going (*dubitans*). But the interesting point is that Hercules warms up to all this where-speak with a way of defining their current location in the timeless wonderworld of myth: *ubi mures ferrum rodunt*. Once again, the unprovenanced proverb for "nowhere" helps feed the aporia: no idea where he's from, nor where we're at (not to mention what this means . . .).[43] As with the "Euripides" earlier, perhaps this is just another by-product of loss—alas, if only we spoke the idiomatic Latin of the mid-first century, we might be able to make this proverb work. That may be. But eerily, conveniently, our own readerly puzzlement maps perfectly onto a Claudius who can't be understood and a Hercules failing to get through. Even with forces like Febris and narrator working overtime to fill us in, we are still lagging beneath the weight of not knowing.

Claudius pleads with Hercules through another unintelligible speech.[44] His words then fortuitously fritter away into the limit case of unintelligibility: a lacuna.[45] After the break, some god is delivering his or her two cents. And here almost three layers of problems with "who speaks" seem to coalesce beautifully. First, we have no idea (thanks lacuna) to which divine speaker the words belong; second, the topic again is Claudius' deeply uncategorizable form; third, the ante is well and truly upped with regard to quotations, some of which are tough to attribute:

> Non mirum quod in curiam impetum fecisti: nihil tibi clausi est. Modo dic nobis, qualem deum istum fieri velis. Ἐπικούρειος θεὸς non potest esse: οὔτε αὐτὸς πρᾶγμα ἔχει τι οὔτε ἄλλοις παρέχει. Stoicus? Quomodo potest "rotundus" esse, ut ait Varro, "sine capite, sine praeputio"? Est aliquid in illo Stoici dei, iam video: nec cor nec caput habet. (8)

> No wonder you broke and entered the senate house: nothing can keep you out. Only say what sort of god you'd like him to be. He can't be an Epicurean god: for that type "neither has any troubles nor causes them." Stoic? How can he be "spherical," as Varro says, "sans head, sans foreskin?" There is something of a Stoic god in him, now I see it: he's got neither heart nor head.

Claudius can't really be placed as a god—but nor can the Greek "quotations," which seem to belong to the Epicurean commons without precisely overlapping with any attested maxim.[46] Granted, Varro is name-checked. But off-the-record proverbs keep flowing in ever thicker and faster.[47] After the speaker has nodded to the bewildering Silanus "incest" story, the discourse starts springing leaks of nameless quotes all over the shop:

> "Quare" inquis "quaero enim, sororem suam?" Stulte, stude: Athenis dimidium licet, Alexandriae totum. Quia "Romae" inquis "mures molas lingunt." Hic nobis curva corrigit? quid in cubiculo suo faciat, **nescio**, et iam "caeli scrutatur plagas"? Deus fieri vult? parum est quod templum in Britannia habet, quod hunc barbari colunt et ut deum orant μωροῦ εὐιλάτου τνχεῖν? (8)

> "Why, I'm begging you, why his own sister?" Do some study, stupid: you can do it halfway in Athens, all the way in Alexandria. Because "at Rome," you say, "the mice lap up meal." Does this guy straighten out our kinks? What happens in his bedroom, **I have no idea**; now he's "scanning heaven's zones"? He wants to be a god? Isn't it enough to have a temple in Britain, that barbarians worship him, and pray to him as a god "to light on a fool in a good mood"?

It's anyone's guess what that second mice-based proverb means. But yet again, the point to note is the conjunction of explicit ignorance about Claudius on the part of both speaker (*quid in cubiculo suo faciat, **nescio***) and audience (*quare . . . quero*) with a quick-fire round of unattributed quotations.[48] The jolting, code-switching, mode-switching discourse bogs us down in attributive purgatory. As we read, we think the very same thing this perplexed audience thinks of Claudius: *from where?* The *Apocol.* at this point is running rings around the reader, even as it fills them in. And it does this not just by playing allusive games but by showing, at least initially and experientially, what it's like *not to know*.

The next gods to say their piece—Janus and Diespiter—are similarly heavy on the quotation and proverb, both Greek and Latin.[49] Diespiter's move in favor of Claudius' admission into heaven features a piece of verse whose origin is now lost (*ferventia rapa vorare*, 9). In general the *Apocol.*'s "quotation" of the commonest chunks of verse, the best-known in popular tradition, makes most of its "quotations" "proverbial" anyway. This is how it catches us with our pants down early on. At first, we cannot help ask *unde* of its monstrous "citations." But *unde* makes no sense addressed to a proverb, which has no origin by definition. Not only this: the proverbial logic tumbles over into the realm of "genuine" citation, such that not even these deauthored and oralized nuggets yield up any meaningful information on their context. The *Apocol.* threatens to crash out into a vain pursuit of the answer to a misplaced question. What happens in the end is that we learn not to ask.

And that is because, finally, we are *told*. The *Apocol.*'s knowledge becomes that which is asserted on *authority*, rather than proven with evidence. It relies on two whopping great authority figures to bring order to its proceedings in heaven. The first is Jupiter, who shuts up the confused babble of the anonymous god-senator and moves the debate to the real heavyweights (Janus, Diespiter, Augustus).[50] The head speaker puts a cork in question time:

> Tandem Iovi venit in mentem, privatis intra curiam morantibus <senatoribus non licere> sententiam dicere nec disputare. "Ego" inquit "p.c. interrogare vobis permiseram, vos mera mapalia fecistis. Volo ut servetis disciplinam curiae. Hic qualiscunque est, quid de nobis existimabit?" (9)

> At last it popped into Jupiter's head that with strangers hanging around inside the senate house the senators shouldn't give nor debate their motions. He said: "I allowed you some question time, conscript fathers, and you have made a proper barnyard farce. I'd like you to observe the rules of the senate house. This man, whatever he is, what will he think of us?!"

No more question time (*interrogare*): proper *sententiae* only from this point on, thank you. Questions are no longer welcome (cf. *Hunc si interrogaveris, soli narrabit*, 1). But Jupiter is still agnostic on whom we might be dealing with here. To clear that up, we'll need our second imported authority figure. And he doubles as one of the most interesting practitioners of quote-dropping in the *Apocol.* You guessed it: Augustus himself. When the ultimate authority[51] kicks into gear, he starts making use of a slightly different mode of quotation, based precisely on *acknowledgment of source:*

> Confugiendum est itaque ad Messalae Corvini, disertissimi viri, illam sententiam "pudet imperii." (10)

> So I have to fall back on that saying of Messala Corvinus, most eloquent of men: "I'm ashamed of this power."

Augustus' first quotation comes from high, and attributed, places—the *sententia* of Messala Corvinus no less. Ellen O'Gorman notes that the quote ends up saying more than Augustus bargained for.[52] I wonder also whether Augustus might not be pulling a fast one with Messala's name here, given that the quote is unattested elsewhere.[53] But the point to note is the energy expended on giving the quote a name (and an authority who had proposed Augustus' most treasured title *pater patriae*, no less).[54] Of course, the Big Man does go on to invoke a proverb in the familiar, slightly obscure way:[55]

> Non vacat deflere publicas clades intuenti domestica mala. Itaque illa omittam, haec referam; nam etiam si soror mea Graece **nescit, ego scio**: ἔγγιον γόνυ κνήμης. (10)

> There's no time to mourn public catastrophe for someone contemplating private disasters. So I'll leave the former and go through the latter; even if my sister **knows no** Greek, **I know it**: the knee is nearer than the shin.

But this is explicitly a proverb aimed not at the sensation of aporia, of *unde*, but of fixing knowledge: *ego scio* is one of the strongest assertions of certainty in all of the *Apocol.*—on par, that is, with the narrator's *ego scio* right at the beginning. In fact Augustus beamed this effect of certainty onto the reader back then too—remember?

> Velit nolit, necesse est illi omnia videre, quae in caelo aguntur: Appiae viae curator est, qua scis et divum Augustum et Tiberium Caesarem ad deos isse. (1)

> Whether he wants to or not, everything that happens in heaven, he's forced to witness: he's the caretaker of the Appian way, by which you *know* both the deified Augustus and Tiberius Caesar joined the gods.

The Augustan (and Tiberian) precedent is crucial to anchoring knowledge and belief, even when that knowledge is strictly "untrue" (Tiberius in heaven?!). This knowledge may have been about the process of apotheosis itself back in 1, but now Augustus moves to play guarantor of the party line on Claudius. His solar pull of authority, then, brings both narrator and reader into the orbit of true knowledge, just as it leaves the unknowing Claudius unmoved, on his own.

This project of fixing knowledge is the wider function of Augustus' speech here, which is precisely about cutting through all the retarding forces of Claudian indeterminacy we have suffered through so far. There is no

Menippean mess of "who is this?," "where is he from?," or "what has he done?"—just cold hard imperial definition, sticking the crimes to the man:

> Iste quem videtis, **per tot annos sub meo nomine latens**, hanc mihi gratiam rettulit, ut duas Iulias proneptes meas occideret, alteram ferro, alteram fame; unum abnepotem L. Silanum: videris, Iuppiter, an in causa mala, certe in tua, si aequus futurus es. (10)

> This man right here, **hiding under my name for so many years**, has done me the good grace of murdering the two Julias, my great granddaughters, one with the sword, another by starvation; one great-great-grandson, Lucius Silanus—you'll see if his case was flawed or not, Jupiter, but certainly it was the same as yours, if you're going to be fair about it.

This speech of Augustus in fact becomes a giant project of restoring true names to things: identifying Claudius, distancing himself from this monster so far using his name in vain like a grim imperial pseudepigraphist, and directly naming all the monster's victims. When Augustus darkly quips that Claudius restored Crassus' son's name—Magnus—while removing his head (*Gaius Crassi filium vetuit Magnum vocari: hic nomen illi reddidit, caput tulit*, 11), he is also mirroring his own project. From Messala Corvinus' *sententia* to all these dead aristocrats to Claudius' guilt, the idea is to *reddere nomina*.[56]

Augustus' last two quotations encapsulate his self-appointed mission of attributing responsibility and restoring names. First round, he gives Claudius his own telling speech, in the midst of giving him his victims:

> Tu Messalinam, cuius aeque avunculus maior eram quam tuus, occidisti. "**Nescio**" inquis? Di tibi male faciant: adeo istuc turpius est, quod nescisti, quam quod occidisti. (11)

> You killed Messalina, whose great-great-uncle I was just as much as yours. "**I don't know**," you say? God damn you: that you didn't know is so much more disgusting than the fact that you killed.

Claudius' ignorance is fired back at him as his own speech. *Nescio* becomes the negative to Augustus' emphatic *ego scio*. This is a brilliant piece of quotation, for it catches Claudius in the act of disavowal and makes him guiltily own it. Again, the speech has clear paternity.[57] But the second and final citation is even more important. As he delivers his clincher, here I think we see Augustus drawing on the authorial character we already know well from the *Res Gestae*[58] and Suetonius. The final authority, the end of the recursive proof, is *himself*:[59]

> "Ego pro sententia mea hoc censeo:" (atque ita ex tabella recitavit) "quando quidem divus Claudius occidit socerum suum Appium Silanum, generos duos Magnum Pompeium et L. Silanum, socerum filiae suae Crassum Frugi, hominem tam similem sibi quam ovo ovum, Scriboniam socrum filiae suae, uxorem suam Messalinam et ceteros quorum numerus iniri non potuit, placet mihi in eum severe animadverti, nec illi rerum iudicandarum vacationem dari, eumque quam primum exportari, et caelo intra triginta dies excedere, Olympo intra diem tertium." (11)

> "I put this forward as my motion": and he read it out from a tablet: "since the divine Claudius put his father-in-law Appius Silanus to death, his two sons-in-law Pompeius Magnus and Lucius Silanus, his daughter's father-in-law Crassus Frugi, as similar to him as two peas in a pod, Scribonia, his daughter's mother-in-law, his own wife Messalina, and all the others whose number is beyond calculation, I propose that serious action be taken against him, that he be given no suspension of legal process, that he be banished with immediate effect, and that he leave heaven within thirty days, Olympus within three."

Augustus may have warmed up by rattling off the *sententia* of Messala Corvinus, but now he gives us his own—and crucially, we have it in writing. It speaks volumes that he is *reading* something he prepared earlier (*atque ita ex tabella recitavit*).[60] This is the written and writing Augustus we know and love, the one who won't say anything that isn't written down[61] but also the one who lays claim to that writing, who stands up, reads it out, puts a name to it. This quotation—Augustus' *sententia*—is one of the few explicitly attributed quotations in the whole quotation-mad *Apocol.*; it is the centerpiece tailor-made to add maximum authority to the universal character assassination of Claudius. The weight of Augustus *in writing* is now added to the weight of the anonymous collective wending its way in recyclable snippets of *speech*. And so finally, we get an overwhelming answer to *unde,* no longer about Claudius' origin but about his destination:

> Pedibus in hanc sententiam itum est. Nec mora, Cyllenius illum collo
>   obtorto trahit ad inferos a caelo
> "**unde** negant redire quemquam." (11)

They take to their feet and vote through the motion. Immediately Mercury twists his neck and yanks him to the underworld, **"from where** they say no one returns."

Unde reformulated: no longer a question, that is, but an answer. A *sentence.* In some ways, this little hit of Catullus 3 perfectly embodies the jointing of proverb and citation that we have seen to date. It is something so famous that it wriggles out of context and origin, partly because what it "quotes" is a sentiment so general that you don't really need a quote for it—it is something said, something about anyone (*quemquam*) "they (don't) say" (*negant*).[62] Again, the reorientation from question to answer stems our philological impulse. We are learning, slowly, not to ask.

Everybody Knows: The Proverbs Made True

After Augustus has set the record straight, the force of anonymous speech and proverb starts tearing into Claudius without mercy. As Mercury whips the condemned man downward, we pause on earth briefly only to listen to his funeral dirge in anapests—a tour-de-force of backhanded praise, sung heartily (in unison) by a huge rejoicing crowd (*cantabatur,* 12). In the underworld, too, Claudius' litany of former victims erupts in collective joy: *Cum plausu procedunt cantantes:* εὑρήκαμεν, σνγχαίρωμεν (13). When Pedo Pompeius (one of Claudius' victims but otherwise unknown) brings Claudius to Aeacus for the final sentencing, he makes sure to supply his *name* once again—and the charge, boiled down, makes use of a proverbial Homeric expression for the numberless:

> Postulat, nomen eius recipiat; edit subscriptionem: occisos senatores XXXV, equites R. CCXXI, ceteros ὅσα ψάμαθός τε κόνις τε. (14)
>
> Pedo asks the judge to take down his name; he brings out an official writ: 35 senators killed; 221 Roman knights; the rest, "as many as sands and dust."

This is citation of formula rather than specific Homeric moment (we could compare the πόθεν "quote" earlier).[63] The infinity of the proverb matches the scale and frequency of the killings, which are now distended beyond the upper classes, to *everyone.*[64] The proverb here lends the charge the force of obvious knowledge, decks it out with common authority (impossible to counter), even as it pushes Claudius' damage well beyond his own social neighbors, out into the wilderness of "the masses." And behind the charge, the authority of writing (*subscriptionem*) comes through loud and clear. Underworld judge Aeacus is all over the power of the proverb when he makes the final pronouncement in good Claudian fashion, without hearing both sides of the argument:

> Incipit patronus velle respondere. Aeacus, homo iustissimus, vetat, et illum altera tantum parte audita condemnat et ait: αἴκε πάθοις τά ἔρεξες δίκη ἰθεῖα γένοιτο. Ingens silentium factum est. Stupebant omnes novitate rei attoniti, negabant hoc unquam factum. (14)

> The defense advocate starts trying to reply. Aeacus, justice personified, vetoes it. He condemns him with only half the case heard and says: "If you suffered what you inflicted, that'd be justice done right." Cue a huge silence. Everyone was floored by the novelty of it all; they said that this had never happened.

Aeacus pounds the gavel with a beautiful piece of common wisdom, and everyone shuts up.[65] The power of the proverb is the verdict of the collective. It is something with which there is simply no arguing. This other kind of *sentence* is kitted out to have the last word.

In a sense, the *Apocol.* is one big project of Claudius' "proverbialization," a claim for his restoration to collective ownership and passage into the form of a proverbial monster.[66] The plurality of the verdict becomes too convincing to resist. It shuts down the skeptical question "from where?" by pushing it into the realm of the insensible. What matters in the end is not where this man (or this knowledge) has come from but where it is going and that it is *true*.[67] Jokes rest on common / assumed knowledge. But they also *establish* the commonness of that knowledge in the process. The final scene of the *Apocol.* seals the deal on this grand restitution to the (elite) commons.[68] As soon as Aeacus determines his punishment—futile dice-shaking for eternity, à la Sisyphus et al.—we get one more outbreak of anonymous hexameters, writing Claudius into the mythological landscape of the underworld by describing his eternal woes fumbling the dice through a holey dice box (and repeat). But then the work trails off into a universal transfer, where Claudius quite literally becomes the property of everyone who can get hands on him:[69]

> Apparuit subito C. Caesar et petere illum in servitutem coepit. Producit testes, qui illum viderant ab illo flagris, ferulis, colaphis vapulantem. Adi-

udicatur C. Caesari; Caesar illum Aeaco donat. Is Menandro liberto suo tradidit, ut a cognitionibus esset. (15)[70]

Suddenly Caligula turned up and made to claim Claudius as a slave. He produces witnesses who had seen Claudius being beaten by him—with whips, rods, fists. Claudius is assigned to Caligula; Caligula passes him on to Aeacus. Aeacus gives him to his freedman Menander, to be his legal secretary.

Caligula snatches him up as personal slave but then suddenly pinballs him on to Aeacus, who in turn dropkicks him to his freedman Menander.[71] The man who belonged nowhere now belongs to everyone. What's more, he ends up in a (granted, basement) version of precisely the same role he was performing on the ground floor of life: looking after the judicial inquiries (*cognitiones*), which are also, ironically, forms of "knowledge" (*cognitio*), of getting to know something. The originally unknowable Claudius ends up profoundly known, put back in his place. And look at the way Caligula underwrites it: he *producit testes,* calls anonymous witnesses who can vouch for Claudius' rightful abjection / subjection, in the very same way that our author *producit* his nameless guarantor at the beginning (*producere,* 1). In this sense, the *Apocol.* reflects sharply on its own project of yanking Claudius monster into common ownership and collective knowledge *through* the authority of anonymous witnesses. It does this at the internal level (unnamed *auctor,* mystery *testes*) but perhaps at the external level too (the effacement of its actual author). The point is to absorb Claudius into the clutches of the proverbial, the boisterous assertions of "it just *is* that way," and make of him a pumpkin that no one can refuse—for it comes out of nowhere, from no one, and that is why it belongs to all.

The *Apocol.* begins with the question *unde* to suit its unplaceable satiric target, the nonentity Claudius himself. There, the deployment of unattributed proverb and quotation helps sculpt a sense of the monster without origin. But after Augustus intervenes to name the names and assign responsibility, we catch the proverb nudging Claudius in a slightly different direction. The anonymous quotation becomes a key pressure by which Claudius is boxed and squashed into the bad emperor forevermore. As soon as we give up on the question *unde,* which works with neither proverb nor Claudius, we snap out of the epistemological nightmare of senseless source-inquisition, to sit back and enjoy the "truth" washing over us. The power of that "truth" resides, like memory, primarily in the fact of repetition and retention, a quote that stays afloat and does the rounds. Like an act of *abolitio,* a piece of defacement striking through the names and busts of public identity, the *Apocol.* gains its spiteful, retributive power from the fact that it could have been written by any number of hands. With the stamp of authorship removed, the *Apocol.* becomes a proverb writ large. We're coerced to take its truth for granted, with no right of appeal: *unde negant redire quemquam.*

Adumbrata inscriptione derisi: *Satyrica*

With the *Apocol.,* we have seen another possible click between the "internal" and "external" dynamics of anonymity. The text has a field day with the question "from where?" even as it scrambles the signals of its authorial origin, to boost its project of the proverbial. In this section, I shall track similar twists in another text, which has always tempted (if not delivered) comparison due to (prosimetric, satir-*ish*) form and (putative) date:[72] Petronius' *Satyrica.*

While the *Satyrica* may seem one of the least controversial, most "fixed" points in this book of movable feasts, it's worth floating that the question of its date is very much still open season. Most scholars do now identify it as the work of Petronius Arbiter, the Neronian courtier.[73] But the recent dissenters are multiplying,[74] and the ease with which they prosecute the switch from Neronian to Trajanic and beyond pours cold water over too zealous a historicist enterprise. No evidence really provides a slam dunk, whether individually or collectively. The "lowlife" character set, with the faintly specified geographical locations, means we have very few historical reference points to set the watch by. Like other novel(ish)[75] works from antiquity, the *Satyrica* races through a suspended dreamworld, framed entirely by an unreliable first-person narrator—all of which makes tough work for daters and placers.

The work itself makes tough work of "attribution" at a local level as well. At one end, this could be chalked up to the quirks of manuscript tradition. The fragmentary form of the text often—especially outside the (more or less) intact *Cena Trimalchionis*—makes it difficult to work out, after coming out of the lacuna-coma and regaining consciousness, who speaks.[76] In this way, reading Petronius is always an exercise in attribution.[77] The Menippean form of mixed verse-prose has a similarly disruptive effect. Sometimes it is clear that internal characters are reciting or "improvising" verse in their own voice, but sometimes we become fuddled by whether the verse comes from *Encolpius auctor,* or *actor,*[78] or direct from the "hidden author" himself;[79] and sometimes we get lost on how the verse pitches, captions, contextualizes (or is contextualized by)[80] the prose action, that is, the relationship between the verse and prose.[81] But the *Satyrica* also gels with another branch of "attributive" worries. It is threaded throughout with scenes throwing into relief the fragility and superficiality of naming and inscription. The text's world makes hash of any reliable "titular" practice. It is up to us to apply it to the conditions of its own making.

If we pictured the *Apocol.* as a collaboration between the Augustan weltanschauung of secure naming and the satiric spirit of deauthorization—both, I have suggested, are wielded as weapons in the war on Claudius—the *Satyrica*'s balance sheet looks different. With no such grand political end in sight, its role is more to make hash of the soothing faith in written identification that the Augustus of the *Apocol.* (and of his own making; cf. Chapter 1) is inflated to embody. The *Satyrica* throws down a gauntlet to this imperial way of knowing and shaping the world; it repeatedly shows that the written supplements used—by us, by readers—as sense-making crutches often turn out rickety. What all these internal moments of inscriptional breakdown might point to is a text that itself lacks any prop of context to lean back on, just as those lacking props on the outside might point inward to the textual moments we can still inhabit. It would be another case of internal and external working overtime as one. And even if it didn't work like that *then,* perhaps we could allow it to do so now.

Untitled

The *Satyrica* goes heavy on writing. It is a world full of wannabe litterateurs who often scribble on the spot; but it also showcases an epigraphic landscape packed with ads and signs,[82] all of which tend to attract the eye of the literary-minded narrator filtering the data. The *titulus,* along with its close relative the *inscriptio,* makes for a key concept in the *Satyrica.* It is the written frame that often labels the visual reality, lassoes it into a particular context. But the label is usually straight-up deceptive. It becomes the tag we are trained not to trust.

A *titulus* isn't quite the same thing as a *nomen*,[83] but for a brief moment let's press the conceptual analogy between them. Both are forms of "label" that manage expectations and route our grasp of the contents into certain channels. They are paratextual forces punching well above their weight in words and wielding disproportionate cognitive effects. Just as our museums and galleries feature the tiny information plates that compose the object of looking in crucial ways, so the *titulus* helped Roman readers get in the right frame of mind: as well as meaning "inscription" in general, it was also the technical term for the ticket at the end of the scroll, the thing bearing the identifiers of name and title.[84] In this section, I am interested in what messing with *tituli* on the inside of the *Satyrica* might do for its outside. For if this text often ends up writing off names, titles, and contexts as worthless or misleading, is it more than a coincidence that it becomes hard for us to catalog?

The first aficionado of the inscriptional art is the great showman Trimalchio. The space of the *cena* is particularly epigraphic. When our heroes arrive at the door, they're greeted with a spate of signage:[85]

> Sequimur nos admiratione iam saturi et cum Agamemnone ad ianuam pervenimus, in cuius poste libellus erat cum hac inscriptione fixus: "Quisquis servus sine dominico iussu foras exierit, accipiet plagas centum." (28)

> We followed, full of awe, and came to the door with Agamemnon. On the doorpost was a note pinned up, with this inscription: "Any slave that leaves the premises without the express orders of his master will get a hundred strokes."

> Ad sinistram enim intrantibus non longe ab ostiarii cella canis ingens, catena vinctus, in pariete erat pictus superque quadrata littera scriptum "Cave canem." Et collegae quidem mei riserunt, ego autem collecto spiritu non destiti totum parietem persequi. Erat autem venalicium <cum> titulis pictum, et ipse Trimalchio capillatus caduceum tenebat . . . (29)

> For on the left as you entered, not far from the doorkeeper's quarters, was a huge dog, chained up, painted on the wall, and above him was written in capital letters: "BEWARE THE DOG." My friends sure laughed at me, but I gathered myself and managed to look over the whole wall. It had a slave market painted on it, with labels. Trimalchio was there, long-haired, brandishing Mercury's magic wand.

In the second passage especially, we see writing work as a kind of supplement to the visual, a caption grounding context. In the case of the slave-market picture, the written "name tags" (or price tags?)[86] give the slaves a measure of identification. The *titulus* then comes back at the entrance to the dining room:

> Et quod praecipue miratus sum, in postibus triclinii fasces erant cum securibus fixi, quorum imam partem quasi embolum navis aeneum finiebat, in quo erat scriptum: "C. Pompeio Trimalchioni, seviro Augustali, Cinnamus dispensator." Sub eodem titulo et lucerna bilychnis de camera pendebat. <Erant> et duae tabulae in utroque poste defixae, quarum altera, si bene memini, hoc habebat inscriptum: "III. et pridie kalendas Ianuarias C. noster foras cenat," altera lunae cursum stellarumque septem imagines pictas; et qui dies boni quique incommodi essent, distinguente bulla notabantur. (30)

> I was particularly shocked that rods and axes were hanging on the doorposts of the dining room; the bottom part of them ended in a sort of bronze ship beak, with the inscription: "From Cinnamus the household steward to Gaius Pompeius Trimalchio, priest of the Augustan college." Beneath the same inscription a double lamp hung from the ceiling; two tablets were hung on either doorpost, and one of them—if memory serves—had this inscription: "Our Gaius eats out on December 30 and 31." The other had painted on it the moon's course and representations of her seven stars; good days and inauspicious days were marked with distinguishing knobs.

At the outside edge (marginal notes) of Trimalchio-land, writing puts its best face forward: it projects a prestige to the rest of the world[87] and names the figures in the pretty pictures who are worth the time of day. But the *titulus'* role as value increaser also makes it suspect in certain cases of clear mistake or foul play. We may not know at this point who Cinnamus is or whether Trimalchio is really a *sevir,* but next time we spy a *titulus,* it is pretty clear that either the writing or the wine is off:

> Statim allatae sunt amphorae vitreae diligenter gypsatae, quarum in cervicibus pittacia erant affixa cum hoc titulo: "Falernum Opimianum annorum centum." Dum titulos perlegimus, complosit Trimalchio manus et "Eheu" inquit "ergo diutius vivit vinum quam homuncio. Quare tangomenas faciamus. Vinum vita est. Verum Opimianum praesto. Heri non tam bonum posui, et multo honestiores cenabant." (34)

Right that moment wine jars were brought in, glass ones sealed with gypsum, and they had labels attached to their necks with the message: "Opimian Falernian, a hundred years aged." While we were reading the inscriptions, Trimalchio clapped his hands and said, "Ah! So wine out-lives pitiful little man. Bottoms up then. Wine is life. I'm providing real Opimian. Yesterday I didn't serve such good stuff, and the guests dining were much posher."

These *tituli* have obviously been tailored to maximize the illusion of maturity: Opimian wine (consul 121 BC) would have been pretty disgusting by that point, so the labels are obviously fake.[88] Branding the jar a "Falernian Opimian" instantly ups the value. Trimalchio knows the art of creative titling[89] as well as Phaedrus, who (remember) dropped in the "Aesop" solely for the resale value.[90]

Trimalchio's obsession with titling and branding runs through the *cena*. It comes out in characteristically outrageous ways. At one point, he sets a clumsy slave free and marks the occasion with a bit of ad-libbed doggerel verse that Trimalchio generously brands an *inscriptio*:

Comprobamus nos factum et quam in praecipiti res humanae essent, vario sermone garrimus. "Ita" inquit Trimalchio "non oportet hunc casum sine inscriptione transire" statimque codicillos poposcit et non diu cogi-tatione distorta haec recitavit:

"Quod non expectes, ex transverso fit . . .
et supra nos Fortuna negotia curat.
quare da nobis vina Falerna, puer." (55)

We clapped the deed and jabbered in various ways about the precarity of the human condition. "So," said Trimalchio, "one shouldn't let this op-portunity slide without a written marker." He immediately demanded writing tablets and recited this, not exactly torturing himself with long consideration:

"What you don't expect happens from a twist of fortune . . . and Fortune looks after our business high above us. For that reason, give us Falernian wine, my boy."

Trimalchio instantly "marks" the occasion with a written showpiece, which aims to contextualize the seemingly random affair with the slave into some kind of highbrow poetic meditation on the mutability of fortune. Again,

"Falernian" is used in the *inscriptio* to jack up the price of the thought. This little "epigram" kicks the conversation onto the topic of literature, where again Trimalchio seems to be desperate to inflate the basic material by whacking on an expensive tag:

> Ab hoc epigrammate coepit poetarum esse mentio diuque summa carminis penes Mopsum Thracem memorata est donec Trimalchio "Rogo" inquit "magister, quid putas inter Ciceronem et Publilium interesse? Ego alterum puto disertiorem fuisse, alterum honestiorem. Quid enim his melius dici potest?

> "'Luxuriae rictu Martis marcent moenia.
> Tuo palato clausus pavo pascitur
> plumato amictus aureo Babylonico,
> gallina tibi Numidica, tibi gallus spado;
> ciconia etiam, grata peregrina hospita
> pietaticultrix gracilipes crotalistria,
> avis exul hiemis, **titulus** tepidi temporis,
> nequitiae nidum in caccabo fecit modo.'" (55)

> Out of this epigram came some talk about poets, and for a long time people were saying that the height of poetry was Mopsus of Thrace, till Trimalchio said: "I ask—and this is coming from a scholar—how do you think Cicero and Publilius stack up against each other? I'd say one is more eloquent, the other more sound. What words better than these?

> "'The walls of Mars shrivel under Luxury's bite. The peacock is caged and fed for your palate, wreathed in his golden feathers from Babylon, the Numidian hen is for you, also the castrated rooster; even the stork, that favorite foreign guest, lover of parental duty, thin-footed, a castanet-rattler, winter's exile of a bird, warning notice of warmer weather, she's now built a nest in your cook pot of sin.'"

Tossing up between the fairly incompatible Cicero and Publilius,[91] Trimalchio proceeds to "quote" a chunk of something at us to back up his claim. Note that he never explicitly assigns the words either way, and part of the joke might be to entertain the idea of these flat verses being attributed to Cicero.[92] But the poem is so entry-level and cumbersome[93] that I'd wager that the real "poet" here is the host himself.[94] That is, Trimalchio is moving to smuggle in some subpar material under the cover of Cicero's/Publilius' name. To fool this kind of audience, all you need is a convincing (this time verbal) *titulus* to go along with the product. The reliability of the stork as weathervane (*titulus tepidi temporis*)[95] perhaps distracts us from the notion that the authorial brand on this verbal *titulus* is bunk.

As a proud owner of a mammoth inventory, Trimalchio relishes the label as shortcut to adding value to things. He (and his freedmen buddies) are ever keen to write their own names on their stuff[96] and to provide interpretive guidelines to objects so they are never undervalued. Trimalchio is an expert dealer in paratext or (strictly) peritext, and his biggest artistic product is himself. His most blustering self-work is his tomb,[97] which he imagines for fellow freedman Habinnas in finer detail. The all-important inscription is left carefully for the end:[98]

> Horologium in medio, ut quisquis horas inspiciet, velit nolit, nomen meum legat. Inscriptio quoque vide diligenter si haec satis idonea tibi videtur: "C. Pompeius Trimalchio Maecenatianus hic requiescit. Huic seviratus absenti decretus est. Cum posset in omnibus decuriis Romae esse, tamen noluit. Pius, fortis, fidelis, ex parvo crevit, sestertium reliquit trecenties, nec unquam philosophum audivit. Vale: et tu." (71)

> And a clock in the middle, so that anyone who looks to tell the time will have to read my name, like it or lump it. Also, mull carefully over whether this inscription seems to work: "Gaius Pompeius Trimalchio Maecenatianus lies here. He was declared a priest of Augustus in absentia. Although he could have been on any and every magistrate at Rome, he chose not to. Dutiful, brave, reliable, he grew from nothing, left thirty million sesterces, never ever listened to a philosopher. Goodbye; and to you too."

Trimalchio's vision for the words to fix his character in the records of eternity is a brilliant exercise in hype as well as puncture. He wants his name out there, so he puts it in the middle of a clock. And when he gives it with the inscription, he goes to town on it, posting up all three names plus the posh title *Maecenatianus*.[99] But the caption also serves as a marker of emptiness, a placeholder for titles that might be expected in the elite genre of epitaph on which this inscription is based.[100] Trimalchio got his "sevirate" in absentia.[101] He *could have* served as a staffer to any magistrate at Rome but didn't want to anyway (*noluit*). The inscription here becomes a genre earmarked for puffing up things undone, for padding out the résumé.[102]

We might think Trimalchio a special case. But the *Satyrica* lays out the deceptiveness of the name, the mark, the title, the context-fixing label, well beyond the *cena*. Shortly after bumping into our narrator in the picture gallery, the attention-starved poet Eumolpus makes Encolpius (and us) suffer through his *Troiae halosis* poem (which is itself a kind of epigrammatic "supplement" to the visual representation in the *pinacoteca*).[103] Eumolpus sets the Trojan horse scene and tells us why the locals were so taken in:

"O patria, pulsas mille credidimus rates
solumque bello liberum: hoc titulus fero
incisus, hoc ad furta compositus Sinon
firmabat et mens semper in damnum potens." (89)

"My country! We thought the thousand ships beaten back and the land freed from war: the inscription carved on this animal, Sinon's plan for the trickery, and his mind (always ready for damage) were making us too confident."

Sinon does a good convincing job, but the first and foremost force in the deception is the *titulus,* the inscription—the gift note presumably framing the spirit in which this giant beast was delivered.[104] As with Trimalchio's bogus Opimian Falernian, so with the gift borne by the Greeks: the *titulus* is the all-important framing device that makes the object into something it is definitely not.

The most elaborate case of a deceptive inscription falls in the brilliant episode aboard Lichas' boat. Encolpius and Giton must go way back with Lichas and Tryphaena (something terrible obviously happened before the launch of our extant text),[105] because when Eumolpus tells them they've boarded Lichas' boat, they panic big time and start fumbling around for a plan to stay incognito. Eumolpus' suggestion wins the day. He proposes some face-painting, the unmistakable mark of the slave:[106]

Immo potius facite, quod iubeo. Mercennarius meus, ut ex novacula comperistis, tonsor est: hic continuo radat utriusque non solum capita, sed etiam supercilia. Sequar ego frontes notans inscriptione sollerti, ut videamini stigmate esse puniti. Ita eaedem litterae et suspicionem declinabunt quaerentium et vultus umbra supplicii tegent. (103)

No: better to do what I say. My slave, as you gathered from the razor, is a barber: let him shave both your heads straightaway, your eyebrows too. I'll follow up by marking your foreheads with a crafty inscription, so you seem like slaves punished by the brand. These same letters will deflect the suspicions of the curious and hide your faces under the eye shadow of punishment.

Tellingly, this "concealer" is writing itself: the marks aren't just marks but a full-on *inscriptio*.[107] We have seen how Trimalchio uses such inscriptions to claim ownership in some sense, even if that be the broad ownership of control, of fixing meaning. Here Eumolpus, the proper ink-ready poet, is doing something analogous with the tattoos: writing all over the faces of Encolpius and Giton, so that they become, quite literally, his personal effects.

The plan seems a good idea till word inevitably gets back to Lichas the captain that some heads were shaved on his ship—one of the worst acts of personal grooming you could perform at sea[108]—and presses Eumolpus on why. Ever the poet, Eumolpus claims that it was actually meant to enhance the reading process (i.e., to allow their slavery to be written on their foreheads for all to see):

> simul ut notae quoque litterarum non obumbratae comarum praesidio totae ad oculos legentium acciderent. (105)

> At the same time, I didn't want the letter marks screened by the barrier of their hair; I wanted them to be fully visible to the readers' eyes.

Eumolpus originally conceived of the facial inscription as a kind of *umbra* masking his companion's true identities. Here, he pretends the hair was the thing concealing their marked forms and claims to be avoiding any kind of dangerously *obumbratae* forehead tattoos. Tryphaena is taken in by the composition (hook, line, and sinker). But it doesn't take long for Lichas to cry foul and set her straight:

> concitatus iracundia prosiliit Lichas et "O te" inquit "feminam simplicem, tanquam vulnera ferro praeparata litteras biberint. Utinam quidem hac se inscriptione frontis maculassent; haberemus nos extremum solacium. Nunc mimicis artibus petiti sumus et adumbrata inscriptione derisi." (106)

> Lichas surged with anger, jumped out, and said, "You basic woman, as if these wounds were made by the iron, as if they branded the letters. If only they had stained their foreheads with this sort of inscription, we'd have some last-ditch consolation. As things stand, we've been attacked by mime techniques and made fun of by a mere sketch of an inscription.

Lichas cuts through the transparent trick with a sobering redefinition of *adumbrata:* no longer the marks concealed by something else but the inscription itself as empty, outlined, fake, a *figure* of deception. Some scholars have noted the double duty of *frons* here as both forehead and outer part of a book roll, the part that would have contained the title.[109] *Inscriptione frontis* thus seems to motion toward the scroll of the *Satyrica* itself. Like the *titulus* of the wine, or the horse, it makes us wiser to the idea of not judging a book by its cover.

This little allegory on the unreliability of the tag seems to affirm what we have been gathering so far anyway: the *Satyrica*'s arc of illusionism might be long sometimes, but it bends toward an unmasking, the process of making titles melt into the reality they try to disguise, like ink off a face. But there is one more flashpoint in the *Satyrica* where writing as deception seems to sprawl out into head-bending levels of complexity. At a crucial pivot in the extant text, Encolpius loses Giton to Ascyltus. He is devastated by the abandonment, but suddenly, strangely, we have two standards of cryptic verse that seem conscripted to process the event:

> Egreditur superbus cum praemio Ascyltos et paulo ante carissimum sibi commilitonem fortunaeque etiam similitudine parem in loco peregrino destituit abiectum.

> Nomen amicitiae sic, quatenus expedit, haeret;
> calculus in tabula mobile ducit opus.
> Cum fortuna manet, vultum servatis, amici;
> cum cecidit, turpi vertitis ora fuga.
> Grex agit in scaena mimum: pater ille vocatur,
> filius hic, nomen divitis ille tenet.
> Mox ubi ridendas inclusit pagina partes,
> vera redit facies, dum simulata perit. . . .

> Nec diu tamen lacrimis indulsi, . . . (80–81)

> Ascyltos went out all puffed up with his prize and left his fellow soldier—a little while ago his dearest pal and his equal in fortune—devastated, in a foreign environment.

> The name of friendship sticks as long as it's useful; the marker on the board adapts to the game. With a run of fortune, you maintain your happy face, my friends; when it leaves me, you turn away your faces and unceremoniously abandon me.

> The crew acts a mime onstage: this one's called the Dad, this one the Son,
> this one has the name of Rich Man. Soon enough, when the page has shut
> the book on the comic roles, the true faces return, while the mask drops . . .

> But I didn't waste much more time weeping.

These mysterious verses have enjoyed / suffered reams of comment, partly because they are so difficult to square with the context: are these both the work of Encolpius narrator? Or the author? Should the two poems even be one?[110] Niall Slater picks the *grex agit* stanza as a virtual epigraph of the *Satyrica,* and I find that framing instinct revealing.[111] For the verses themselves are about the *frame* and the relation between title (this time *nomen*) and reality. For the length and purposes of the mime, characters bear certain names, but these names are confined within the bounds of the page; from underneath, the "true face" returns. Text is the province of illusionism, and "outside" the text, the real—that tired old binary.

The confusing thing here is that the mixed metaphor relies on a sense of performance too: this is a mime, and once the mime is over, the truth comes flooding back. In a sense, this string of couplets reinforces what we have come to suspect so far: that names, like titles, are temporary things, flimsy tags that fake things till they make things. After the show is done, the actors come onstage as themselves: *vera redit facies, dum simulata perit.* But the problem with text (as opposed to performance) is that this ritual of return to the real never takes place. No reassuring author figure comes on to turn on the lights and turn off the illusion. And this is particularly the case with the *Satyrica.* The *pagina* never "shuts in"[112] the comic parts, because we never really begin, and we certainly never end. The true face never returns, the masks never slip, because this hidden author remains just that.[113] If the *Satyrica* plies us, internally, with stories about titles dropping off to leave the bare reality below, "externally," it will never give us the satisfaction.

At close, let's bring it back to the *titulus.* We saw how this disproportionately important form of frame never gives us the right idea in the whole of the *Satyrica.* More than that, writing itself becomes synonymous with the trumped up, the padded, the fibbed, the faked. How much of a coincidence is it, then, that we have lost a trustworthy *titulus* for the text itself? Like the *Apocol.,* debates still swirl around it, disputing title and author.[114]

Although the vision borders on hallucination, I can't help wondering whether our author ultimately opted to go one better than the bogus titling of his ultragraphic text, by appending to it no orienting *titulus* at all.[115] That would have been the greatest revenge on the Trimalchian frame builders of the *Satyrica*, all of whom try to mark reality in their own image, to make it mean what they want it to mean with a little help from the written stickers they slap on it. None of them manages to pull it off.

From Where the Frame?

The *Apocol.* and the *Satyrica*, as I said, are often plastered together for kinship in time and genre. This chapter has sandwiched them together using slightly different criteria. I have tried to show that both of these messy, lacunose, prosimetric "satires" evince complex inner lives that dwell on the problems of attribution and "contextualization," to match the confusion around their conditions of birth. The *Apocol.* thrust its protagonist and its quotations in our face to drag out of us the dogged question "from where?" But it ended up making use of the response "everywhere." Its project was to make a proverb of an emperor, to translate the monster's image into common parlance. The *Satyrica* also thought attributively but from a different angle. Its internal scenes of titling and inscription end up coming off as tendentious acts of steerage and deception. The peritext always lies. The real face never comes back.

The difference between the *Apocol.* and the *Satyrica* nestles in the way they read writing. For the *Apocol.*, writing is the imperial technology par excellence. It polishes off the Augustan work of attributing responsibility, in the best faith. It teams up with the certifying anonymity of proverbial speech, and both forces are working in tandem toward the same goal. On the flip side, the *Satyrica* brackets writing, and especially the paratextual writing used to press reality into certain geometries, as inherently suspect. It takes issue with the Augustan graphic habit by showing how hollow it looks when misapplied. In other words, it deauthorizes its own medium. That central paradox—absent from the *Apocol.*—helps to power the *Satyrica* and to re-create in its readers the experience of which it talks.

The prose-verse form shared by both texts arguably always pricks an intensified version of the question "who speaks?" for any curious reader.

The "author" of the prosimetric masterpiece is by definition bifurcated, plural, at odds with his or her other in a very different way from the split personalities we usually see in a Lucan (or even a Virgil).[116] But these texts also have their own specific, and different, reasons for acting out anonymous. For the *Apocol.*, anonymity helps rather than hinders the political goal. Like a comic version of the *Octavia,* but with Claudius down and Nero up, its unattributed versatility would seek to inject the denigratory juices straight into the mainstream tradition—to take the joke as read and make it a given. For the *Satyrica,* the resistance to providing a *titulus* could be the best (quietest) reproach to the ownership-mad internal authors, Trimalchio and Eumolpus, who simply can't get enough of making their marks all over the world. In both cases, there is much to be said for rubbing out ~~Seneca~~ and ~~Petronius~~ and leaving question marks to inflect eloquently in their stead.

8

Historical Transcendence

> The classical, then, is certainly "timeless," but this
> timelessness is a mode of historical being.
>
> —Hans Gadamer (1975: 257)

O NE OF THE THUNDERING repetitions of this book has been the
problem of literature without history, texts without contexts. Rather
than mindlessly pile driving square texts into round holes with our historicizing reflexes, I have advocated that we step aside for a second and test
the possibilities of anonymizing the cultural offcuts we are always so desperate to source, date, and frame into a condition of value, a place of inter-
pretability. Again and again, I have tried to draw out how these texts can
willfully blind themselves to history and context, for any number of good
reasons. In this chapter, I shall juxtapose two prose texts that confront head-
on the role of history in literary/rhetorical production: Tacitus' *Dialogus*
and [Longinus]' *On the Sublime*. I want to show how both texts have ways
of abstracting and disembedding themselves from history. In the *Dialogus'*
case, this process happens even as political history and the role of the present seem to loom ever larger over the course of the conversation. In *On
the Sublime,* the prospect of political history shaping literature is discarded,
as [Longinus] dramatizes his own absorption into the transcendental realm
of a "timeless" classic.

In some ways, these two deserve each other. The *Dialogus* is a Ciceronian-
style dialogue on the question of why Roman oratory has gone so off in
the contemporary world (dramatic date of 75 CE). But it is also so much

more than that, encompassing a range of live literary-critical issues, such as the place of poetry in the sociopolitical realm or the Roman habit of automatically praising the old stuff over the new stuff. *On the Sublime,* too, is a work in the tradition of ancient literary criticism but is much more directly didactic than the *Dialogus.* Written in who-knows' first person, it tells us readers (through its addressee, Terentianus) how we too can achieve sublime effects in our writing, through imitation of the great authors, dazzling rhetorical effects, and so on. The main synergy with regard to content is the strange fact that both works end with the bang of the *Dialogus'* founding question: what's behind the decline of rhetoric and/or literature? Is it political context, morality, something else? As we shall see, both works offer up different proposals. But both also work to shrink the notion of one-off and singular temporality, or present history, on which the political version of decline is based.

Of the two texts, only the handsomely bracketed [Longinus] is still considered strictly anonymous nowadays.[1] When we get there, we shall see how the condition of the brackets actually serves and complements the internal currents of the text. As for the *Dialogus,* it would be impossibly bold to bend the wind back to a denial of Tacitean authorship, or perhaps (more plausibly) a *non liquet.*[2] But I would like at least to drag attention back to the anonymity and context resistance[3] inherent in the text's careful evasions, which make it determinedly difficult to assign the *Dialogus* to an author, or a date,[4] solely on its own terms.[5] As we shall see, the *Dialogus* has excellent excuses to fiddle (as it does) with the ownership of speech, to experiment with silence and retraction, to sweep the contemporary rug out from under us—and so, in a nutshell, could well have lain down and played anonymous.[6] And yet we don't desperately need the *Dialogus'* historical/actual anonymity to argue for a reticent first-person persona and a stripped (or distributed) context. For whether Tacitus' or no, this text surely makes a habit of immanence. Instead of singularity, it builds a long-term sediment of repetition and custom, in answer to our insistent question, the one we often (*saepe*) ask in concert with Fabius Iustus: when?

Moving/Staying with the Times

One of the reasons readers have often emerged from the other end of the *Dialogus* a little flummoxed on the question "To Tacitus or not to Tacitus?"

is its structure and style, which make this text look like the spitting image of a Ciceronian dialogue on oratory.[7] The broad-brush overtones of the dramatic scenario are textbook Cicero: established (?) orator recounting a conversation he overheard in his youth, on the topic of oratory, between a bunch of off-duty oratorical luminaries of the day.[8] Style-wise, the Latin smells completely different from "trademark" Tacitus, opting for a clear Ciceronian idiom over the tortured language-bending compression of the later works.[9] The *Dialogus* has always felt a little like Tacitus not being himself,[10] under cover of a committed homage, an act of being Cicero.[11]

Yet, ironically, that wiping of the Tacitean self is one of the least Ciceronian things about the *Dialogus*. Many commentators have been struck by the key twist of authorial absence shrouding the text, which looks particularly pronounced when set against Cicero's lovable habit of including *himself* as a speaker in his own dialogues.[12] This wonderful, originary act of evasion is perhaps designed to ink up the limit case of (wannabe) Ciceronianism in the principate: now the supposed star orator figure, the framing first-person who introduces this dialogue of memories, does not allow himself to speak. The decline of oratory? QED.

The opening of the *Dialogus* seems to pit two alternative modes of authorship against each other in the clearest terms. These could square along various axes, but let's invoke a few: past versus present, republican versus imperial, original versus derivative, owning versus disowning, straightness versus evasion.[13] All of these structural frictions seem to come out in the parade piece at the beginning, which sets our author (in his brief, longest appearance *in propria persona*) against his evil twin, the outspoken playwright Maternus. Before the author nails the dramatic setting of the story, he gives us the setting of the *text*'s story: where the prompt to write came from, what it's all about,[14] and how none of it is really "by him":

> Saepe ex me requiris, Iuste Fabi, cur, cum priora saecula tot eminentium oratorum ingeniis gloriaque floruerint, nostra potissimum aetas deserta et laude eloquentiae orbata vix nomen ipsum oratoris retineat; neque enim ita appellamus nisi antiquos, horum autem temporum diserti causidici et advocati et patroni et quidvis potius quam oratores vocantur. Cui percontationi tuae respondere et tam magnae quaestionis pondus excipere, ut aut de ingeniis nostris male existimandum *sit,* si idem adsequi non possumus, aut de iudiciis, si nolumus, vix hercule auderem, si mihi mea sententia proferenda ac non disertissimorum, ut nostris temporibus,

hominum sermo repetendus esset, quos eandem hanc quaestionem per-
tractantes iuvenis admodum audivi. Ita non ingenio, sed memoria et re-
cordatione opus est, ut quae a praestantissimis viris et excogitata subti-
liter et dicta graviter accepi, cum singuli diversas [vel easdem] sed
probabilis causas adferrent, dum formam sui quisque et animi et ingenii
redderent, isdem nunc numeris isdemque rationibus persequar, servato ordine disputationis. Neque enim defuit qui diversam quoque partem susci-
peret, ac multum vexata et inrisa vetustate nostrorum temporum eloquen-
tiam antiquorum ingeniis anteferret. (*Dialogus* 1)[15]

My dear Justus Fabius: you often ask me why it is that—though previous
generations have blossomed with the talent and glory of great orators—our
own generation is especially empty in that regard, stripped of the dis-
tinctions of elegance, and hardly even holds onto the very name "orator."
We don't call anyone that unless ancient; by contrast, the skilled public
speakers of our own time are called "pleaders," "lawyers," "patrons"
(i.e., anything but "orators"). To respond to your inquiry is to take on a
burden of such a huge investigation, with the result that either we have
to conclude we have no outstanding talent, if we can't achieve this, or
we are lacking in judgment, if we can but don't want to. I would
scarcely make this attempt, if it were my opinion I had to put forward,
rather than repeating a conversation of extremely eloquent men (by the
standards of our own time too), whom I listened to probing this very
question, while I was still a young man. So I don't need original talent,
merely powers of memory and recollection, in order to transmit the subtle
thoughts and serious words I heard from these outstanding men, using
again the same structure and arguments, preserving intact the order of
speaking. Each man put forward different yet equally plausible reasons,
each projected the form of his mind and genius. For there was also
someone present to take up the opposite opinion: harassing and ridiculing
antiquity and putting our own eloquence above the outstanding talent
of the past.

The brilliant move of this opener is to bring the authorial pose perfectly
into line with the "decline of oratory" theme. The author turns himself into
a secondary, nonmotive force beneath the bigger players in the text. He is
a mere respondent to Fabius Iustus,[16] who is chronically (note *saepe*, the
first and perhaps one of the most important words of the *Dialogus*)[17] putting the question in question to him. In tune with the schema of decline, he
is also a mere recorder of the information he heard long ago,[18] a passive

transcriber[19] (intact) of the thoughts of the great men on whose conversation he once had the privilege of eavesdropping. This is a work that yields to the hectoring prompt of an external party and conserves the opinions of other people. This author is not authoring much at all. Orators nowadays scarcely have a name—and nor does our author.

Our cipher claims that all of his megastars are perfectly in harmony with their self-consistent opinions—indeed they express, in speech, a straightforward index of their inner thoughts: *dum formam sui quisque et animi et ingenii redderent. Forma* and friends is another absolutely crucial word-complex in the *Dialogus,* which will move a long way from here under the whisper-transmission distortions of subsequent speakers. But for now, it gives us the "form" of ideal authorship: speakers saying what they are thinking and *owning* that speech with an outstanding individuality/originality (*ingenium*). And this model of authorship is pretty much what we get as soon as the first great elder is introduced. The drama falls precisely in the hangover of (the "day after") Maternus' public recitation of his controversial tragedy *Cato*. Maternus invested in the Cato (or his *Cato*) so completely that he "forgot himself" (*sui oblitus*).[20] Rome is flooded with charged gossip about this act of offending "the minds of the powerful,"[21] but when the party stumbles into Maternus' house, they find the bold tragedian completely unrepentant:

> Igitur ut intravimus cubiculum Materni, sedentem ipsum*que* quem pridie recitaverat librum, inter manus habentem deprehendimus.
>
> Tum Secundus "Nihilne te" inquit, "Materne, fabulae malignorum terrent, quo minus offensas Catonis tui ames? an ideo librum istum adprehendisti, ut diligentius retractares, et sublatis si qua pravae interpretationi materiam dederunt, emitteres Catonem non quidem meliorem, sed tamen securiorem?"
>
> Tum ille "leges" inquit "tu quid Maternus sibi debuerit, et adgnosces quae audisti. Quod si qua omisit Cato, sequenti recitatione Thyestes dicet; hanc enim tragoediam disposui iam et intra me ipse formavi. Atque ideo maturare libri huius editionem festino, ut dimissa priore cura novae cogitationi toto pectore incumbam." (3)
>
> So, as we entered Maternus' bedroom, we sprung him sitting and holding *between his hands* the very book from which he had recited the day before. Secundus said at this point: "Does the chatter of your enemies not

turn you off loving your offensive *Cato*? Or have you picked that book of yours up precisely to revise it more carefully and remove whatever gives grounds for a negative interpretation, so you can put out another *Cato*—not exactly better, but safer?"

Maternus replied: "You will read what Maternus owed to himself, and you will recognize exactly what you've heard. But if my *Cato* has left something out, my *Thyestes* will say it at the next recitation; I've already constructed this tragedy and formed it myself, all by myself. That's why I'm rushing to bring this book to publication, so I can free myself of the last responsibility and set to the next project with my full attention."

Any implicit hope we might have had of Maternus' backpedaling for safety is shattered as soon as we peek inside the doors and spy him positively cuddling[22] the physical text from which he was reading the previous day. Secundus tries to turn this emphatic physical declaration of authorship into something a little more conciliatory—perhaps Maternus is holding the *Cato* to pare it back into something more innocuous? But no, definitely not. Maternus stands tall and names himself. He swears full consistency from performance to text and back again: *adgnosces quae audisti.* Anything omitted will be given in the forthcoming *Thyestes*—a work that Maternus also preemptively owns as the singular fruit of his imagination, a product of his mind and his only (note *intra me ipse formavi,* picking up *formam . . . et animi et ingenii* earlier). Maternus has a limitless supply of bolshy sentiment that needs expressing in theater[23]—and he is prepared to line up behind all of it with a big hug of an imprimatur.

At this point, the *Dialogus* seems a drama perched on the brink. It dives into a charged "historical" moment that could not seem more urgent, more pressing, more *present.* One could say that the job of this precise frame is to plant us firmly in the imperial contemporary,[24] a long way from the very different pressures of Ciceronian Rome—to make it seem, that is, a *point* in time, a one-off. The problem (if it is a problem) is that the singular moment immediately spins off into whirlwind of precedents. Aper pipes up that Maternus is *always* (*omne tempus,* 3) doing this sort of thing. If it's not the *Thyestes-to-be,* it was the *Medea* of not so long ago (*modo,* 3); and if it's not the *Cato,* it's the *Domitius.* Aper fires us off at least one more example of each category of Greek and Roman tragedies, in the style of those we just heard about. Maternus' self-consistency stretches beyond the bounds of present *Cato* and future *Thyestes* into the aggressive political plays of Christmases past. Maternus then picks up Aper's invitation to walk down memory lane hand in hand:

> et Maternus: "perturbarer hac tua severitate, nisi **frequens** et **assidua** nobis contentio iam prope in **consuetudinem** vertisset. Nam nec tu agitare et insequi poetas intermittis, et ego, cui desidiam advocationum obicis, **cotidianum** hoc patrocinium defendendae adversus te poeticae exerceo." (4)

> Maternus said: "I would be upset by your harshness, if **frequent, constant** debate had not basically become a **habit** for us by now. You for one never quit harrying and attacking the poets, and I—whom you target for defaulting on my obligations as an advocate—carry out my **daily** act of patronage, which is to defend poetry from you."

All of those words in bold become buzzwords of the *Dialogus,* which showcases a world of frequency, consistency, habit, everydayness—in other words, all forms of *repeated* action. What I want to point out here is the direction of travel from specificity to generality. We started at what seemed a very particular point: the day after an apocalyptically dangerous act of brinksmanship on the part of the rebellious poet Maternus. But in time, the urgency of the situation is neutralized into a dynamic that happens *all the time.*[25] Aper is always (nonstop) hassling poets; Maternus is forced to defend himself on a daily basis. These men are just acting out their characters, doing as they always do. Like good old Fabius Iustus pestering our author reliably and repeatedly (*saepe,* 1), they inhabit the space of the continuing rather than the one-off action, the tense of the present continuous/imperfect over the perfect. What we are witnessing is merely an exemplary cross-section of an endless compulsion to revert to type.

This turn to customary action, and the direction of travel from "one-off" to pattern, goes well beyond the opening—so much so that it forms a kind of catch-cry for the *Dialogus'* paradoxical poetics of the lasting point in time, the enduring occasion. The concept comes through especially clearly in the brief exchanges between the set-piece speeches. The first one, Aper's sweeping attack on Maternus' decision to withdraw from the practical world of oratory to the *nemora et luci* of poetry, seems a little too much, until the understated narrator reminds us,

> Quae cum dixisset Aper acrius, **ut solebat**, et intento ore, remissus et subridens Maternus. . . . inquit: (11)

When Aper had spoken a little too harshly, **as was his tendency,** and with a strained face, Maternus replied in a relaxed and ironic way:

This is simply business as usual (albeit with a small twist: Maternus' wry response acknowledges that Aper had taken the argument in a slightly unexpected direction). When Messalla enters to the audible jitters of most involved (paranoid as they are about Messalla rolling with a crowd of delators that might spill the beans on the more controversial topics of this relaxed "chat"),[26] the same act of "normalization" happens. Aper hears Messalla's subtle dig at him for being all contemporary in his leisure habits, and says he's heard it all before:

> Tum Aper: "**non desinis,** Messalla, vetera tantum et antiqua mirari, nostrorum autem temporum studia inridere atque contemnere. Nam hunc tuum sermonem **saepe** excepi, . . ." (15)

> Aper came in: "Messalla! **You never stop** fetishizing only the old and ancient, while you poke fun and scorn at the cultural scene of our own times. Indeed, I've **often** heard this speech from you, . . ."

Messalla's schtick is always the same, the *laudator temporis acti.* But Messalla's delatory genius is not only to own the opinion dispersed in time but to flood it across his audience too. According to him, everyone in earshot actually thinks the same thing:

> "Neque illius" inquit "sermonis mei paenitentiam ago, neque aut Secundum aut Maternum aut te ipsum, Aper, quamquam interdum in contrarium disputes, aliter sentire credo. Ac velim impetratum ab aliquo vestrum ut causas huius infinitae differentiae scrutetur ac reddat, quas mecum ipse **plerumque** conquiro." (15)

> Messalla said: "I have no regrets for the sort of talk you mean, nor do I believe that Secundus or Maternus or even you, Aper, think any differently—even if you argue the opposite case from time to time. I just wish I could prevail on one of you to examine and report the reasons for this huge gap—I often find myself wondering about them."

What's more, he "regularly" (*plerumque*) puts himself the very founding question of the *Dialogus* (i.e., becomes Fabius Iustus)[27] and our author all rolled into one. Messalla digs himself out with plural (we all think this) and duration (I've always asked this).

We are heating up toward the second topic of debate (the old versus the new), but with Messalla now in the mix, no one wants to go first. So Secundus invites the new arrival to get the ball rolling. Messalla agrees but on the condition that it won't be his speech alone:

> Et Messalla "aperiam" inquit "cogitationes meas, si illud a vobis ante impetravero, ut vos quoque sermonem hunc nostrum adiuvetis." (16)

> Messalla came back: "I'll let you know my opinion, if I can first get your guarantee that you'll help me with this speech of ours."

This is very different from the style of "inner thought" presentation we had from Maternus at the beginning (cf. *cogitationi,* 3): full disclosure, as long as everyone participates in making "our little speech" (*nostrum* better taken as literal plural here; cf. *cogitationes*). Maternus agrees that he and Secundus will play along with the assigned parts but also volunteers Aper to act antagonist—for that is his *style:*

> "Pro duobus" inquit Maternus "promitto: nam et ego et Secundus exsequemur eas partis, quas intellexerimus te non tam omisisse quam nobis reliquisse. **Aprum enim solere dissentire et tu paulo ante dixisti et ipse satis manifestus est iam dudum** in contrarium accingi nec aequo animo perferre hanc nostram pro antiquorum laude concordiam." (16)

> Maternus said: "I commit for the two of us: both Secundus and I will follow up those points that we understand you to have not so much passed over as purposely left for us. **On Aper: you said a little while ago he has a tendency to be contrarian, and he has pretty clearly** been girding up for the fight **for some time now**—and that our seeing eye to eye on this praise of the ancients is more than he can take.

In fact there are two strands of customary behavior in action here: Aper's "tendency" (*solere*) to play contrarian, which he has been chomping at the bit to perform for some time (*iam dudum*); but also Messalla's habit of observing this habit of Aper's (*tu paulo ante dixisti*; cf. Aper's *ut paulo ante dicebam,* 19). These men aren't so much speaking off the cuff in the privacy of Maternus' home as they are performing their behavioral tics and conversational standards, the kind of thing they always say.

As the *Dialogus* rolls on, we get an even stronger sense that these "characters" are not only reading from the scripts of themselves and expressing views that transcend the particular occasion but also borrowing lines from others. When Aper is done plugging his contemporary scene (a speech actually much shorter on current names and details than his opener—a knock-on of Messalla's entry?), Maternus butts in with praise but also a recognition that Aper has simply borrowed the devil's advocate technique[28] from the Roman philosophers:

> ac ne ipse quidem ita sentit, sed more vetere et a nostris philosophis **saepe** celebrato sumpsit sibi contra dicendi partis. (24)

> He doesn't even truly think that—instead he employs an old habit, one **often** made much of by Roman philosophers, and takes on himself the opponent's role.

The precedent for such a technique is deep. By this point it is almost a cultural habit (*more vetere*), enjoying a particular trend (*saepe,* that word again) among philosophers. As from the very start, so here: Aper the timely, the now-man, is reduced to a long paper trail before him—only that this time the precedents come from the wider "culture," rather than himself. But Maternus is generous with his precedents. He supplies them not only for Aper but for Messalla too. He gives the next speaker the lines of his next speech, and the speaker makes sure to follow the prompts:

> Tum Messalla: "sequar **praescriptam** a te, Materne, **formam**; neque enim diu contra dicendum est Apro, qui primum, ut opinor, nominis controversiam movit . . ." (25)

> At which point Messalla said: "I'll follow **the pattern you've prescribed,** Maternus; we don't need to spend too long refuting Aper, who elicits a declamation, it seems to me, about a mere name . . ."

This is no longer the pure transcript of individual opinion that our author promised at the beginning (*dum formam sui quisque et animi et ingenii redderent*). The *forma* is now scripted in advance, a kind of template or pattern going beyond the individual follower. By now, we realize there is no such thing as "speaking one's mind"—no version of Messalla's idealized Brutus: *sed simpliciter et **ingenue iudicium animi** sui detexisse.* (25; cf. 27). Indeed, it is no coincidence that this is precisely the point where Messalla reaches for a piece of anonymous gossip to authenticate his claim about the effeminate riffs of modern oratory:

Unde oritur illa foeda et **praepostera,** sed tamen **frequens** †sicut his cla . . . et exclamatio, ut oratores nostri tenere dicere, histriones diserte saltare dicantur. (26)[29]

This is where the expression comes from—ugly and **paradoxical, yet in common currency**—that "our orators speak smoothly, and our actors dance eloquently."

Just as Messalla had grounded his speech in the script of Maternus, so he roots his local point here in the everywhere and always (*frequens* again) of public opinion. This sentiment is also timeless in the sense that it is quite literally "out of time" (*praepostera*).

Although Messalla is just following the script, he does threaten to veer off into doing the thing that Aper, in his resolutely generic speech, had failed to do: name names. But Maternus stops him in his tracks and brings him back to the main road with another citation of Messalla's custom, what he was saying just a little before:

Neque enim hoc colligi desideramus, disertiores esse antiquos, quod apud me quidem in confesso est, sed causas exquirimus, **quas te solitum tractare paulo ante dixisti,** plane mitior et eloquentiae temporum nostrorum minus iratus, antequam te Aper offenderet maiores tuos lacessendo. (27)[30]

We don't want you to end up saying the ancients were more eloquent, which—at least for me—is already granted. We want the actual reasons, **which you said a little while ago you tend to think about repeatedly**; you were calmer then, not so outraged at contemporary eloquence, before Aper offended you by attacking your forefathers.

Maternus interestingly reroutes the conversation back to Messalla's *solitum,* again something like the founding question of the *Dialogus.* In other words, he puts Messalla back in the habit, back to what he was saying "a little while before." Messalla replies that he's not offended in the least. It's the "law" (*legem,* 25) of this kind of talk to wear one's innermost thoughts on one's sleeve (*iudicium animi citra damnum adfectus proferre,* 25).[31] But when Maternus invites Messalla to do just that, he retracts again into the shell of the shared and the common.[32] It's *obvious:*

Et Messalla "non reconditas, Materne, causas requiris, nec aut tibi ipsi aut huic Secundo vel huic Apro ignotas, etiam si mihi partes adsignatis

proferendi in medium quae omnes sentimus. Quis enim ignorat et eloquen-
tiam et ceteras artes descivisse ab illa vetere gloria non inopia hominum,
sed desidia iuventutis et neglegentia parentum et inscientia praecipien-
tium et oblivione moris antiqui?" (28)

Messalla came back: "Maternus, the reasons you ask for aren't exactly
inaccessible. You yourself, Secundus here, Aper here—you all know them
already, even if you assign me the role of bringing out into the open what
we're all thinking. Who doesn't know that eloquence and the other arts
have tumbled from their former glory not for want of men but from the
terrible work ethic of our youth, parental neglect, incompetent teachers,
and the loss of ancient customs?"

Messalla is a master prevaricator. He never owns any sentiment without
making it a collaboration among many or the common property of all. He
pathologically speaks outside himself.

Messalla goes on for a few chapters in this vein. He argues for an education of the orator based on mixing and matching scripts to suit the audience, perhaps the very method he has embodied as a speaker thus far.
To furnish a sufficient archive for his thoughts on philosophy being the
key to oratory, he names (*nominabo,* 32) both Demosthenes and Cicero.
As promised, he then leaves it to the other speakers to pick up whatever
slack there has been—but not before invoking the concept of "habit" to
do the usual:

> Sunt aliae causae, magnae et graves, quas a vobis aperiri aequum est, quo-
> niam quidem ego iam meum munus explevi, et **quod mihi in consuetu-**
> **dine est,** satis multos offendi, quos, si forte haec audierint, certum habeo
> dicturos me, dum iuris et philosophiae scientiam tamquam oratori ne-
> cessariam laudo, ineptiis meis plausisse. (32)

> There are some other reasons—important, serious ones too—which you
> should really unearth, since I've fulfilled my end of the bargain and have
> offended quite a lot of people (**as is my wont**), whom I'm sure will say—
> if they happen to hear all of this—that in praising knowledge of law and
> philosophy as something the orator needs, I've just been clapping my own
> hobbies.

Messalla's devotion to the script is so all-consuming that he can even pre-
dict the reaction he will get once his words get beyond the immediate

moment (and Messalla always assumes they will; cf. 14).[33] He has said this sort of thing so many times, that is, that he knows exactly what the fallout will be. The public conversation will play out in the customary way, like Aper and Maternus' routine brouhaha at the beginning. But the notable twist is that now, at this point in the *Dialogus*, "custom" is spreading from the habitual behavior of an Aper or a Messalla or a public to a *topic* of the dialogue itself. This section is dealing with the olde-style educational system of Roman oratory: what the *boni viri, periti dicendi* used to do, over and over again, to become what they became. Maternus flags this when he tries to make Messalla move yet again in a different direction:

> Nam quibus *artibus* instrui veteres oratores **soliti sint,** dixisti differen-
> tiamque nostrae desidiae et inscientiae adversus acerrima et fecundis-
> sima eorum studia demonstrasti: (33)[34]

> You've talked about the skills in which the old orators **tended** to be
> trained, and you've shown the distance between our laziness and igno-
> rance and their culture of drive and productivity:

So much for those habits. Now we want these:

> ita hoc quoque cognoscam, quibus exercitationibus iuvenes iam et forum
> ingressuri confirmare et alere ingenia sua **soliti sint.** (33)

> I also want to know the forms of training by which young men, on the
> point of making their entry into the forum, **tended** to reinforce and ex-
> pand their talents.

Messalla picks up the *soliti sint* at the beginning of his next speech, to truly make a habit of it. The key ingredient in his recollection of the ideal training days actually becomes the imperfect tense (from section 34, imperfect verbs are rife). The young apprentice orator gets in the swing of things via re-peated exposure:

> Hunc sectari, hunc prosequi, huius omnibus dictionibus interesse sive in
> iudiciis sive in contionibus **adsuescebat,** (34)

> The young man **was in the habit** of following his mentor, accompanying
> him, attending all his speaking engagements, whether in the courts or the
> assembly,

And so important is this process of customization that Messalla almost defines his subject as someone *formed* through habit, repetition, the enduring time of *saepe:*

> Atque hercule sub eius modi praeceptoribus iuvenis ille, de quo loquimur, oratorum discipulus, fori auditor, sectator iudiciorum, eruditus et **adsuefactus** alienis experimentis, cui **cotidie** audienti notae leges, non novi iudicum vultus, **frequens** in oculis **consuetudo** contionum, **saepe** cognitae populi aures, sive accusationem susceperat sive defensionem, solus statim et unus cuicumque causae par erat. (34)

> For sure, under this kind of teacher this young man under discussion, the student of orators proper, the one who listened in the forum, who **frequented** the law courts, trained and habituated by other people testing him, who knew the law by hearing it **every single day**, who recognized all the faces in court, who made watching the assembly into a **compulsive habit**, and **often** got familiar with the people's ear—whether he took up prosecution or defense, he was immediately up to every kind of case, and needed no help.

Messalla talks in terms of "used to"—both in the imperfect and the customary sense. Time stretches into the general continuous past. Of course Messalla's main point is that they don't make them like they *used to*. There is a historical rupture. But it is a rupture dividing a flat period of "then" from a flat period of "now." History is understood as large swathes of repeated action.

Messalla is just getting into the topic of "contemporary" training habits—the trite gymnastics of declamation, *quidquid in schola cotidie agitur* (35)—when the lacuna suddenly shuts him up.[35] Back on air, we're thrust into the middle of Maternus' famous clincher speech: the peroration exposing the very different, political causes of the decline of oratory.[36] But Maternus adopts exactly the same binary schema of past and present and speaks with exactly the same kind of continuous time. The bad old days were a *constant* drag of legislation and conflict:

> Hinc leges **assiduae** et populare nomen, hinc contiones magistratuum paene pernoctantium in rostris, hinc accusationes potentium reorum et adsignatae etiam domibus inimicitiae, hinc procerum factiones et **assidua** senatus adversus plebem certamina. (36)

> Here were the roots of the **constant** legislation, the name "popularis," the assemblies of the magistrates who were almost sleeping the night on the

speakers' platform, prosecutions against powerful criminals, hostile ac-
cusations even within families, aristocratic factions and the **unending**
struggles of senate versus people.

The adjective *assiduus* drags on throughout the sentence like the interminable legal wrangling on which it serves duty.[37] Now that the *sermo* is in
such general terms, and such extended time, Maternus talks the talk to
match:

> non quia tanti fuit rei publicae malos ferre cives, ut uberem ad dicendum
> materiam oratores haberent, sed, **ut subinde admoneo,** quaestionis me-
> minerimus sciamusque nos de ea re loqui, quae facilius turbidis et inqui-
> etis temporibus existit. (37)

> That's not because it was so worthwhile for the state to make bad citi-
> zens, just so our orators had rich pickings for their speeches, but—**as I'm
> often warning you**—we should remember the topic and should know
> that the thing we're talking about survives more easily in turbulent and
> chaotic times.

Maternus places his speech act in a kind of continuous present, *subinde.*
This gels with the message of the section, that the more "often" (*sae-
pius*) eloquence is used, the more it develops—repetition, in past and
present.

My point here is that Maternus (like Messalla) works in terms of the
habitual no matter what broad time period he is treating. In section 38, he
picks right up on Messalla's buzzword:

> Transeo ad **formam** et **consuetudinem** veterum iudiciorum. (38)

> I move on to **the form** and **usual procedure** of the old courts.

The close cohabiting of these two heavy lifters of the *Dialogus* is important here. The last time we see a *forma,* it is even further from the individual possession of the beginning—and more a synonym for "system," the
rules that set what everyone does. In days of yore, you could speak as long
as you wanted, without the judge interfering. Nowadays, the judge more
often than not just gets in the way:

> quia **saepe** interrogat iudex, quando incipias, et ex interrogatione eius in-
> cipiendum est. **Frequenter** probationibus et testibus silentium [patronus]
> indicit. (39)

Because **often** the judge asks you when you'll actually start—so you have to start when he asks. **Almost as often** he demands silence while you're in the middle of the proofs or the evidence.

Then from the habitual actions of the present, we ping back to those of the past, for instance, on the difference between modern and ancient audiences for oratory:

Oratori autem clamore plausuque opus est et velut quodam theatro; qualia **cotidie** antiquis oratoribus contingebant, cum tot pariter ac tam nobiles forum coartarent, (39)

But the orator has to have cheers and claps, just like a sort of theater; the orators of old got those things **every single day**, when the audience jammed into the forum was as huge as it was well bred.

Another instance of returning to the past centers on the nonstop *contiones:*[38]

Iam vero contiones **assiduae** et datum ius potentissimum quemque vexandi atque ipsa inimicitiarum gloria, (40)

All those **constant** public assemblies and the readily granted right of railing against the powerful and the real glory of doing it against one's enemies,

Although this last speech of Maternus may seem the most historically "rooted" of the whole *Dialogus,*[39] in practice, it studiously avoids talking about any historical particulars in any depth. Instead, it paints two long time periods with the broadest of brushes, using repeated actions as *longue durée* strokes.

Messalla had been working the whole way (only building on what he had been given, mind you) to present speech and thought as something both habitual (over time) and shared (among the audience), a kind of alibi strategy to the nth degree. In the Messallan scheme, there is no such thing as the thought of an individual on the spot, but there's a precedent, a consensus, for everything. This, too, is pretty much where Maternus ends up, with his famous thought experiment to close:[40]

si aut vos prioribus saeculis aut illi, quos miramur, his nati essent, ac deus aliquis vitas ac [vestra] tempora repente mutasset, nec vobis summa illa laus et gloria in eloquentia neque illis modus et temperamentum defuisset:

nunc, quoniam nemo eodem tempore adsequi potest magnam famam et magnam quietem, bono saeculi sui quisque citra obtrectationem alterius utatur. (41)

If you had been born in the olden times or those orators we admire had been born now—say some god had suddenly switched the times—the highest praise and glory of eloquence would be yours, as much as measure and moderation theirs: now, since no one can attain great fame and the great quiet life at the same time, let each man make use of the good his own age can provide, without slighting any other.

We started the *Dialogus* with the promise that each man would give the inner makeup of his individual mind (*formam **sui quisque** et animi et ingenii*, 1). We end with each making good of his own "age" (*bono saeculi **sui quisque***), all in a uniform way.[41] The *Dialogus* makes itself stand not for a point in time but a period, a duration—that is, a good while.

The time scheme in which we end up at close of play is roughly a two-track system, then and now, republic and principate. But these lumps of time only look relatively "historical" because they nuance what had been Aper's one-size-fits-all approach.[42] Back in his speech celebrating the contemporary over the antique, he claimed that there wasn't much separating the now from the then (way way back when), in the grander scheme of things:

Nam si, ut Cicero in Hortensio scribit, is est magnus et verus annus quo eadem positio caeli siderumque quae cum maxime est, rursum exsistet, isque annus horum quos nos vocamus annorum duodecim milia nongentos quinquaginta quattuor complectitur, incipit Demosthenes vester, quem vos veterem et antiquum fingitis, non solum eodem anno quo nos, sed etiam eodem mense exstitisse. (16)

If—as Cicero says in the *Hortensius*—the Great Year, or the True Year, is the moment at which the position of the heavens and the stars goes back to what it is at any given time, if this year contains 12,954 of those things we call "years," your Demosthenes, whom you make out to be old and ancient, emerges to have lived not only in the same year as us but even in the same month.

Just as Aper invokes the coming around again (*rursum*) of the great year, so he doubles back to Cicero to close the circle. The invocation of the big orator enacts the same message we shall see in the next section, where the point is the general proximity of the current age to Cicero's:

> Statue sex et quinquaginta annos, quibus mox divus Augustus rem publicam rexit; adice Tiberii tres et viginti, et prope quadriennium Gai, ac bis quaternos denos Claudii et Neronis annos, atque illum Galbae et Othonis et Vitelli longum et unum annum, ac sextam iam felicis huius principatus stationem quo Vespasianus rem publicam fovet: centum et viginti anni ab interitu Ciceronis in hunc diem colliguntur, unius hominis aetas. (17)

> Lay down the fifty-six years in which the to-be-deified Augustus governed the state; plus Tiberius' twenty-three, basically four for Caligula, fourteen a piece for Claudius and Nero, the single endless year for Galba, Otho, and Vitellius, and now the sixth post of this wonderful principate in which Vespasian fosters the state: that makes 120 years from the death of Cicero to our day, the life span of a single man.

That is, we're all just part of one big happy temporal family, from Cicero to now.[43] Many scholars have tried using this passage at least to pinpoint the dramatic (if not compositional) date of the *Dialogus;* the problem has always been deciphering the obscure *sextam . . . stationem.*[44] But why make it so hard?[45] The point, I think, is that for all Aper's talk of the contemporary, his understanding of the contemporary doesn't deem today, or yesterday, substantially different from 120 years prior.[46] *Statio* is something that stands still (cf. *statue*); it doesn't really matter if we're in the sixth or the forty-fourth unit of measurement. The principate brings stability (*statio*) of time. Aper moves—very much like the modern scholar, who intuitively reckons in terms of political periodization—by longer-term cycles, *reigns* or politically defined *eras* rather than *years,* and this is perhaps where the strange ordinal "sixth" comes from:[47] Augustus (1), Tiberius (2), Caligula (3), the Claudius-Nero bundle (4), the year of the four emperors (5), and now Vespasian, us, number 6;[48] or, counting down differently: Augustus (1), Tiberius (2), Caligula (3), Claudius (4), Nero (5), disqualified Year of Exceptions (0), Vespasian (6). That is, whichever way we do the arithmetic, we're situated, *stationed,* not in a particular year (74, 75, or 77 CE) but somewhere in the current cycle—and all those cycles together only sum to the mere life of a single man. The point isn't the point. It's the *period.*

The *Dialogus'* morbid fascination with repeated action, then, makes it hard to date by drama. But coincidentally, I think it also makes tough work

of dating its composition. The "dedication" to Fabius at the beginning gives
no hint of an "occasion" and amounts to little more than an *obiter dictus*.
As we have been saying all along, that opening *saepe* invalidates attempts
to uncover a point in time, when the period is at play. One of the only other
tools for nailing down the written date has been the supposed allusion of
Pliny (*Ep.* 9.10.2) to the *in nemora et lucos* of Aper's first speech.[49] But this
phrase is explicitly marked as a proverb—*utque ipsi dicunt*—the cliché that
poets say, over and over again.[50] As a rack on which to hang an argument
about dating, it is remarkably wobbly.[51] Rather than building castles in the
air, perhaps it's time we cleared it.

   David Levene has pointed out that there are two ways of placing literature in the *Dialogus,* which roughly square with what we do as scholars
now: either literature gets rooted in political history, or it gets placed in
relation to its predecessors, *intertextually.*[52] The *Dialogus* itself might lack
markers of time in the first sense. But in the second, it is pretty clearly a
work of its time, inhabiting the (post-)Quintilianic moment of debate on
the place of rhetoric in the contemporary world.[53] But just like *in nemora
et lucos* at the level of phraseology, so with the corruption of eloquence at
a thematic level: it is a question posed across time, no more of Cicero than
of Seneca the Elder, no more Quintilian than the *Dialogus* or [Longinus].
The way intertextuality places literature is very different from the way history dates it. In the *Dialogus,* it is a space where speakers can take up the
same moment as Cicero, where the mouthpiece for Quintilian can share a
platform with the mouthpiece of Virgil—in short, a force for collapsing
time, rather than marking it.[54]

   I have tried to show that the *Dialogus* is a text that *repeatedly* shuns the
one-off for the over-again. The reason it cannot be fixed to any particular
date (or, in my view, any particular author) is that it bends over backward
to replace occasion with duration. At one point, Messalla complains that
modern speakers have lost sight of the ideals of broad education that informed the golden age orators. Nowadays, they even let the filth of *cotid-
iani sermonis* (32) into their speeches. But the *Dialogus* admits *sermo cotidianus* in another sense of the term. In a way, it *is sermo cotidianus:* a
dialogue in the old style that happens every day, day in, day out, the personal and cultural *habit* of a period much bigger than itself. Similarly, it is
sermo frequens (2), the unattributable gossip[55] flying around in the wake
of (another) Maternan bombshell. It is *sermo* in the spaces of *saepe, solere,*

cotidie, assiduus, frequens, consuetudo, forma—the tenses of present and past continuous. The specificity, historicity, and contemporaneity are knocked clean out of it.

If the *Dialogus* has a context, it is not that of 101 or 102 CE. It belongs to the compulsively rerun traumas and public discourse of the imperial period, Augustus to Vespasian and (for an ill-defined time) beyond.[56] Again, its anonymity is help rather than hindrance. For all we know of our unnamed author, he is just responding to a habitual question from someone else and offering other people's answers in response. He disappears as soon as he arrives on the scene of the *sermo*. He leaves as soon as it is over (*cum adrisissent, discessimus*, 42).[57] He hands his *sermo* over to the other speakers, and they end up handing it to each other, or to previous and future versions of themselves, who palm it off into text[58] and on to us. It's no wonder we don't know *when*. I would like to see us unlearning *who*, while we're at it.

Between the Brackets: [On the Sublime], Any Time

> But it is extravagantly uneconomical
> to posit an unattested genius.
>
> —Malcolm Heath (2000: 69)

> Unanchored in time and place, *On the Sublime* lends itself all
> too easily to the timeless pretensions of its subject.
>
> —James Porter (2016: 59)

[Longinus] has always looked eerily good next to the *Dialogus*.[59] Both these imperial works on rhetoric plumb their respective traditions[60] of "criticism" to end up roughly the same length and roughly on the same ground of debate: the reasons for the decline of wordsmithery in the contemporary world.[61] The fact that these two texts seem to converge on this question (though with answers inverted) has always struck scholars, and when scholars are struck, they often date: many have argued that the *Dialogus* had to have been in the air when [Longinus] was writing up his sublime.[62] Could it be: a *terminus post quem?!*[63] But the overlap of these otherwise pretty disparate works on that particular topic is more probably testament to the truth of the *Dialogus' saepe:* that this topic was on the lips of all the *pepaideumenoi* of the long second sophistic period, "Greek" and/or "Roman." The topic is *sermo frequens:* undatable.

Keeping left of this done-to-death connection, this section will focus instead on another, less obvious piece of shared property. Earlier, I tried to show that the *Dialogus'* specificity melted away beneath its play with iterative time and its bold withdrawal of the nameless author. In *On the Sublime,* we tune into a nameless first-person author throughout, but there is no dramatic setting. The only "context" given is the frame of a conversation with an unknown addressee by the name of Postumius Terentianus.[64] In this section, I want to show how [Longinus] takes to a stronger conclusion some of the issues of author, time, and context we have spied in the *Dialogus* (but also littered everywhere, all over this book). I shall argue that [Longinus] sets himself the earthly frame of a treatise with a named destination purely to "transcend" the constraints of a conversation between two individual subjectivities and hence to boost his words into the timeless sublime beyond the moment of utterance.[65] In this project of self-sublimation, anonymous quotation (a focal point of this section) punches above its weight. While it is still in the minority next to [Longinus]' many named snippets, anonymous quotation functions as a load-bearing and underappreciated vehicle of the Longinian sublime. As we shall see, it is a special and radical manifestation of [Longinus]' citational tic of decontextualization: that is, quoting chunks of text without any information on which works they are cut from (even if we do usually have the author's name in the mix).[66] Anonymizing quotation also prepares the ground for the author's climactic debate with an anonymous philosopher, which works to write history out of the picture on many levels. But again, as we have seen over and over in this book, external and internal anonymities converge. It is also the unknown quality of the *author* between the brackets that helps the text do its thing. For [Longinus], those brackets serve the conservative literary agenda of transcendent classicism. They make *On the Sublime* a work of high "tradition," exportable and transportable over many times, escaping the lassos of history and politics that would seek to yank it back down to size and/or earth.[67]

On the Sublime begins by locking down some sort of addressee: Postumius Florus Terentianus, with some help of textual conjecture.[68] [Longinus] had been reading his predecessor Caecilius' work[69] on the same topic with Terentianus, and the shortcomings of this most recent crack at writing up the sublime had rubbed both author and addressee up the wrong way. Terentianus suggested [Longinus] throw together some of his own thoughts for his sake (εἰς σὴν ὑπομνηματίσασθαι χάριν, 1), and what we're reading is the fruit of, and response to, that request. But before we go mistaking this for a modest cobbling together of notes for Terentianus' eyes (and benefit) only, [Longinus] makes sure to drop hints of a much more elastic ambition:

ἐπεὶ δ᾽ ἐνεκελεύσω καὶ ἡμᾶς τι περὶ ὕψους πάντως εἰς σὴν ὑπομνηματίσασθαι χάριν, φέρε, εἴ τι δὴ δοκοῦμεν ἀνδράσι πολιτικοῖς τεθεωρηκέναι χρήσιμον ἐπισκεψώμεθα. αὐτὸς δ᾽ ἡμῖν, ἑταῖρε, τὰ ἐπὶ μέρους, ὡς πέφυκας καὶ καθήκει, συνεπικρινεῖς ἀληθέστατα· εὖ γὰρ δὴ ὁ ἀποφηνάμενος, τί θεοῖς ὅμοιον ἔχομεν, "εὐεργεσίαν" εἶπας "καὶ ἀλήθειαν." γράφων δὲ πρὸς σέ, φίλτατε, τὸν παιδείας ἐπιστήμονα, σχεδὸν ἀπήλλαγμαι καὶ τοῦ διὰ πλειόνων προϋποτίθεσθαι, ὡς ἀκρότης καὶ ἐξοχή τις λόγων ἐστὶ τὰ ὕψη, καὶ ποιητῶν τε οἱ μέγιστοι καὶ συγγραφέων οὐκ ἄλλοθεν ἢ ἐνθένδε ποθὲν ἐπρώτευσαν καὶ ταῖς ἑαυτῶν περιέβαλον εὐκλείαις τὸν αἰῶνα. οὐ γὰρ εἰς πειθὼ τοὺς ἀκροωμένους ἀλλ εἰς ἔκστασιν ἄγει τὰ ὑπερφυᾶ· (*On the Sublime* 1)[70]

But since you've asked me to sketch out, at any rate, some first notes for you on the sublime, come, let's see if our thoughts have any use whatsoever for politicians. But you, my friend, give me detailed criticism, truthful as possible, as your nature and ethics demand. For he put it well, whoever said that what we have in common with the gods is "selfless service and truth." Writing for someone like you, dearest friend, with such an education, I'm essentially freed from having to lay all the prefatory groundwork: how the sublime is a perfection and summit of language and that the greatest poets and writers made their first rank from no other source than this and dressed themselves in eternity. For lofty nature brings the audience not to persuasion but to a state of being genuinely beside themselves:

The audience of one immediately turns into many: Terentianus becomes the general "politicos" (ἀνδράσι πολιτικοῖς).[71] Rather than a constraint calling the shots of the treatise by gravitational weight, this addressee is a kind of liberating presence (ἀπήλλαγμαι), saving [Longinus] the hassle of having to start at the beginning, with the Sublime 101. In that sense, he is a sublime influence himself. He allows [Longinus] a form of *ekstasis:*[72] moving beyond the usual starting point of the sublime, as well as moving beyond the single addressee.[73] That "transcendence," moreover, is written into the anonymous quotation, which has been variously given to Pythagoras, Demosthenes, Aristotle, and others.[74] The public-domain, multiply-authored quote channels the "commonness" of which it speaks. In several ways, this first section sensitizes us to a major function of sublimity: to allow literary words to break the bounds of their original context and float beyond the frame of first utterance.

What is implicit in that first leap beyond Terentianus is theorized, I think, a few chapters later, when [Longinus] comes to define the sublime as a mass verdict of multiple audiences over time—the reliable consensus of past, present, and future combined. As Yun Lee Too has brilliantly documented,[75] the Longinian sublime is a deeply "intersubjective" experience, which makes author and reader/listener switch places:

φύσει γάρ πως ὑπὸ τἀληθοῦς ὕψους ἐπαίρεταί τε ἡμῶν ἡ ψυχὴ καὶ γαῦρόν τι ἀνάστημα λαμβάνουσα πληροῦται χαρᾶς καὶ μεγαλαυχίας, ὡς αὐτὴ γεννήσασα ὅπερ ἤκουσεν. (7)

For the true sublime effortlessly raises up our soul; bringing on a state of inspired majesty, it's filled with delight and pride, as if it had produced the very thing it had heard.

In the terms of dubious authorship surrounding the treatise, this is picture perfect. The brackets around our putative author capture the forces of the flexible and the substitutable,[76] all the better to give us the sense that *we* are producing[77] the very treatise we are reading. But the sublime is more than the one-off burst of readers thinking themselves into the role of author. It is about this happening again and again, over a long period of time:

ὅταν οὖν ὑπ᾽ ἀνδρὸς ἔμφρονος καὶ ἐμπείρου λόγων πολλάκις ἀκουόμενόν τι πρὸς μεγαλοφροσύνην τὴν ψυχὴν μὴ συνδιατιθῇ μηδ᾽ ἐγκαταλείπῃ τῇ διανοίᾳ πλεῖον τοῦ λεγομένου τὸ ἀναθεωρούμενον, πίπτῃ δ᾽, ἂν αὐτὸ συνεχὲς ἐπισκοπῇς, εἰς ἀπαύξησιν, οὐκ ἂν ἔτ᾽ ἀληθὲς ὕψος εἴη μέχρι μόνης τῆς ἀκοῆς σωζόμενον. τοῦτο γὰρ τῷ ὄντι μέγα, οὗ πολλὴ μὲν ἡ ἀναθεώρησις, δύσκολος δὲ μᾶλλον δ᾽ ἀδύνατος ἡ κατεξανάστασις, ἰσχυρὰ δὲ ἡ μνήμη καὶ δυσε ξάλειπτος. ὅλως δὲ καλὰ νόμιζε ὕψη καὶ ἀληθινὰ τὰ διὰ παντὸς ἀρέσκοντα καὶ πᾶσιν. ὅταν γὰρ τοῖς ἀπὸ διαφόρων ἐπιτηδευμάτων βίων ζήλων ἡλικιῶν λόγων ἕν τι καὶ ταὐτὸν ἅμα περὶ τῶν αὐτῶν ἅπασιν δοκῇ, τόθ᾽ ἡ ἐξ ἀσυμφώνων ὡς κρίσις καὶ συγκατάθεσις τὴν ἐπὶ τῷ θαυμαζομένῳ πίστιν ἰσχυρὰν λαμβάνει καὶ ἀναμφίλεκτον. (7)[78]

So whenever a sensible man, experienced in words, hears something several times, and it doesn't cause him to react with sublime sympathy and doesn't deposit in his mind more matter for repeated contemplation than what the surface meaning says but sinks into a kind of deflation on second thought, then it's not the true sublime—that is, if it only lasts as long as a single hearing. The truly great is that which sustains a lot of repeated contemplation; it is hard, if not impossible, to resist it; its memory stays strong and unforgettable. In general, think of the beautiful and true sublime as the things that are always pleasing, to everyone. For whenever people hold the same opinion about the same writing, all those who are diverse in their customs, lives, goals, ages, and languages, then the unanimous "judgment" of such different people makes our trust in the object of our admiration strong and beyond argument.

The test of the truly sublime is endurance beyond that "single hearing" (μόνης τῆς ἀκοῆς). For [Longinus], the canon is actually a collective product of the mass universal audience stretched across "all time" (διὰ παντὸς).[79] This common denominator punches above the historical particulars and differences of the individual judges stretched out in time—their habits, biographies, interests, ages, languages, what(ever) have you—and makes the judgment all the more final because of it. In a very literal sense, the sublime is a timeless phenomenon.[80] It is stamped by its ability to echo out beyond the first hearing and sealed by its repeated confirmation among the aggregate consensus of *always*.[81]

This wide temporal reach is something that puts the human producers of sublime literature on par with the immortals—and sometimes a certain form of anonymity slicks the path up to the sky. Many of the quotations in [Longinus] are attributed by name, but many of them also lack any more specific pins of context (usually no work title is given to narrow it down).[82] This is standard practice with quotation in ancient literary criticism. And we often assume it doesn't matter, for the ancients, with their phenomenal memories, supposedly never needed chapter or verse to orient them, right?[83] But in [Longinus], the minimization of context has a very targeted, and polemic, effect. The quoted words are completely abstracted from their "original" context and reabsorbed into a new one. They are rendered more exportable, more recyclable, by the rinsing off of any lingering sense of the "original." Take, for instance, [Longinus]' first self-quotation:

Οὐ μὴν ἀλλ᾽ ἐπεὶ τὴν κρατίστην μοῖραν ἐπέχει τῶν ἄλλων τὸ πρῶτον, λέγω δὲ τὸ μεγαλοφυές, χρὴ κἀνταῦθα, καὶ εἰ δωρητὸν τὸ πρᾶγμα μᾶλλον ἢ κτητόν, ὅμως καθ᾽ ὅσον οἷόν τε τὰς ψυχὰς ἀνατρέφειν πρὸς τὰ μεγέθη καὶ ὥσπερ ἐγκύμονας ἀεὶ ποιεῖν γενναίου παραστήματος. τίνα, φήσεις, τρόπον; γέγραφά που καὶ ἑτέρωθι τὸ τοιοῦτον· ὕψος μεγαλοφροσύνης ἀπήχημα. (9)

Since the first element, i.e., natural greatness, takes a greater share than all the others, even if it's a matter more of nature than nurture, at this point too we should do as much as we can to cultivate our minds for greatness and in a sense always make them pregnant with noble courage. In what way? you ask. I've written this sort of thing elsewhere: "Sublimity is the echo of a great soul."

[Longinus]' claim to have written the tag, this sort of thing, "somewhere else" (που καὶ ἑτέρωθι) helps it bounce around like the "echo" of which it speaks,[84] helps it enter that realm of the "always" (ἀεὶ), the constant cultivation of mental "pregnancy." The approximation (rather than exactitude) strips the quote of its baggage and lets it travel light to the new destination—in other words, leaves it mobile for repetition. Another example of slicing away context would be the famous quotation of the beginning of Genesis.[85] Here [Longinus] maximizes traffic between Moses and the God of which he writes by leaving the mortal source of the words out and opting for a periphrasis:

ταύτῃ καὶ ὁ τῶν Ἰουδαίων θεσμοθέτης, οὐχ ὁ τυχὼν ἀνήρ, ἐπειδὴ τὴν τοῦ θείου δύναμιν κατὰ τὴν ἀξίαν ἐχώρησε κἀξέφηνεν, εὐθὺς ἐν τῇ εἰσβολῇ γράψας τῶν νόμων "εἶπεν ὁ θεός," φησί· τί; "γενέσθω φῶς, καὶ ἐγένετο· γενέσθω γῆ, καὶ ἐγένετο." (9)

In just this way the lawgiver of the Jews, no average guy, when he had worked out a worthy idea of god's power and expressed it, wrote right at the beginning of his Laws: "God said," he said; but what? "Let there be light, and there was light: let there be earth, and there was earth."

θεσμοθέτης yokes an anonymized Moses to ὁ θεός by a sacred kenning. Both are framed as simple agents of speech acts (εἶπεν; φησί) that have an uncanny power to bring what they say into being, for strictly both parties "speak" the magic words at the same time.[86] [Longinus]' sublime authors tend to blend perfectly into the parts of the text at hand, and they often do so approaching the divine subject that the snippet treats or touches (where there is a divine subject at play, of course).[87]

An important theoretical bedrock for the evacuation of "context" we have seen thus far is the Longinian advice about mimesis. At one point, he advises the budding sublime-artist to conjure up the writers of the past like a Sibylline medium:

πολλοὶ γὰρ ἀλλοτρίῳ θεοφοροῦνται πνεύματι τὸν αὐτὸν τρόπον ὃν καὶ τὴν Πυθίαν λόγος ἔχει τρίποδι πλησιάζουσαν, ἔνθα ῥῆγμά ἐστι γῆς ἀναπνέον ὥς φασιν, ἀτμὸν ἔνθεον, αὐτόθεν ἐγκύμονα τῆς δαιμονίου καθισταμένην δυνάμεως παραυτίκα χρησμῳδεῖν κατ᾽ ἐπίπνοιαν· οὕτως ἀπὸ τῆς τῶν ἀρχαίων μεγαλοφυΐας εἰς τὰς τῶν ζηλούντων ἐκείνους ψυχὰς ὡς ἀπὸ ἱερῶν στομίων ἀπόρροιαί τινες φέρονται, ὑφ᾽ ὧν ἐπιπνεόμενοι καὶ οἱ μὴ λίαν φοιβαστικοὶ τῷ ἑτέρων συνενθουσιῶσι μεγέθει. (13)

For many are enthused with divine inspiration from outside themselves in the same way as the story goes, that the Pythian priestess, approaching the tripod where there is—so they say—a kind of cleft in the earth that exhales divine breath, becomes from that source pregnant with divine power, and immediately she feels inspired to give her oracles; so too from the natural greatness of our predecessors to the souls of those who emulate them, there flows a kind of stream, as if out of sacred mouths. Enthused with that, even people who aren't particularly given to inspiration still feel an inspired sympathy with these others' greatness.

This is the classic idea of authorship as radical self-emptying: making space for the other to inhabit your body and speaking *as* them.[88] The hosting is multitemporal, reflected in the way [Longinus] voices the capital-*T* "Tradition" here in ὥς φασιν.[89] Writing like the authors of the past is tantamount to prophesying the future. And again, this wide temporal communion comes back soon after, when [Longinus] recommends imagining the big names of the past plus the general eyes of posterity as your direct audience:

προσπίπτοντα γὰρ ἡμῖν κατὰ ζῆλον ἐκεῖνα τὰ πρόσωπα καὶ οἷον διαπρέποντα τὰς ψυχὰς ἀνοίσει πως πρὸς τὰ ἀνειδωλοποιούμενα μέτρα· ἔτι δὲ μᾶλλον, εἰ κἀκεῖνο τῇ διανοίᾳ προσυπογράφοιμεν, πῶς ἂν τόδε τι ὑπ᾽ ἐμοῦ λεγόμενον παρὼν Ὅμηρος ἤκουσεν ἢ Δημοσθένης, ἢ πῶς ἂν ἐπὶ τούτῳ διετέθησαν; τῷ γὰρ ὄντι μέγα τὸ ἀγώνισμα, τοιοῦτον ὑποτίθεσθαι τῶν ἰδίων λόγων δικαστήριον καὶ θέατρον, καὶ ἐν τηλικούτοις ἥρωσι κριταῖς τε καὶ μάρτυσιν ὑπέχειν τῶν γραφομένων εὐθύνας πεπλάσθαι. πλέον δὲ τούτων παρορμητικόν, εἰ προστιθείης, πῶς ἂν ἐμοῦ ταῦτα γράψαντος ὁ μετ᾽ ἐμὲ πᾶς ἀκούσειεν αἰών; εἰ δέ τις αὐτόθεν φοβοῖτο, μὴ τοῦ ἰδίου βίου καὶ χρόνου φθέγξαιτό τι ὑπερήμερον, ἀνάγκη καὶ τὰ συλλαμβανόμενα ὑπὸ τῆς τούτου ψυχῆς ἀτελῆ καὶ τυφλὰ ὥσπερ ἀμβλοῦσθαι, πρὸς τὸν τῆς ὑστεροφημίας ὅλως μὴ τελεσφορούμενα χρόνον. (14)

Those characters will come to us through imitation, and their conspicuousness will bring our souls to standards conceived in the mind: even more, if we imagine in our thoughts: How would Homer or Demosthenes listen to this passage of mine if they were here? How would they be affected by it? The contest is great, if we take this caliber of company as the courtroom and theater of our words and make out we're supplying our writing to such hero-critics and hero-witnesses for correction. Even more exciting than this is to add: "How would the whole of eternity receive what I've written?" If someone is turned off by the idea of saying something that will outlast his life and times, then all the content made by that man's soul must be incomplete and blind, like an aborted embryo, falling far short of reaching the term of posthumous fame.

So sublimity through imitation is not just about keeping eyes trained on the great predecessors. It is about thinking big in the other direction too, internalizing the ear of ὁ πᾶς αἰών,[90] bringing your creation beyond embryo,[91] to term, right into the world of future fame (τῆς ὑστεροφημίας—cf. later in this chapter, on section 44), making it outlast your own lifetime.[92] This form of writing for posterity is a notch more serious than the usual confident trumpeting of "I will be read"–style announcements to which Latin poetry inoculates us.[93] To push the text a little, I would venture that this is about actively incorporating the future's point of view into what you write now and emptying the text of its workaday specifics, its earthly weight, so it can be *intelligible* (as well as valuable) to the future. Put differently, it is about clearing the text of historical rootedness, so it is free to play universal.

I editorialize significantly here. [Longinus] doesn't *quite* say any of that. But this sense that the sublime is something attainable through repetition, through an explosion beyond the parameters of the individual and the present, seeps into so many nooks and crannies of the treatise that we have to take it for a watchword concept. Anonymous quotation actually aids that explosion, especially when it comes to repetition as a kind of plurality. Again, I don't want to give the skewed impression that Longinian quotation is *primarily* anonymous (statistically this is far from the case). I merely want to mark up these moments as pregnant with a special potential for the sublime and show how they come across as particularly capacious vessels of transcendence, if you will.

In section 23, [Longinus] walks us through various options for conveying multitude by changes in grammatical number. First, there is the plural-made-singular approach:

φημὶ δὲ τῶν κατὰ τοὺς ἀριθμοὺς οὐ μόνα ταῦτα κοσμεῖν ὁπόσα τοῖς τύποις ἑνικὰ ὄντα τῇ δυνάμει κατὰ τὴν ἀναθεώρησιν πληθυντικὰ εὑρίσκεται·

αὐτίκα (φησί) λαὸς ἀπείρων
θύννον ἐπ᾽ ἠιόνεσσι διιστάμενοι κελάδησαν· (23)

When it comes to number, not only are these things employed for deco-
ration, wherever the singular is found, on second thought, to have the
force of the plural:

Straightaway (he says) a people without measure scatter all over the
beaches and sound out "Tunny!"

The boundless crowd, which is both singular and plural (λαὸς ... διισ
τάμενοι), shouts "Tunny" singular to stand for a huge school of the fish;
and the fact that the quote is unattributed (and unattributable)[94] sharpens
the image of crowd speech. Note how [Longinus] also pluralizes the reading
itself in the offhand glance to ἀναθεώρησις, the "second reading" or "repeated contemplation" earlier (τὸ ἀναθεωρούμενον, ἡ ἀναθεώρησις, 7). Then
there is the plural-for-singular technique. [Longinus] adds to Oedipus' fig-
urative over-the-top "marriages" with another nameless snapshot:

καὶ ὡς ἐκεῖνα πεπλεόνασται,
ἐξῆλθον Ἕκτορές τε καὶ Σαρπηδόνες. (23)

There's a multiplication effect also in "There came Hectors and
Sarpedons."

The quote's "plurality" is cranked up a notch by the fact that this could
come from any number of places—Hectors, Sarpedons, but also *poets*
plural. Not only that, but [Longinus]' use of quotation is itself a form of
pluralizing, which the next snippet gets at nicely:

καὶ τὸ Πλατωνικόν, ὃ καὶ ἑτέρωθι παρετεθείμεθα, ἐπὶ τῶν Ἀθηναίων· "οὐ
γὰρ Πέλοπες οὐδὲ Κάδμοι οὐδ᾽ Αἴγυπτοί τε καὶ Δαναοὶ οὐδ᾽ ἄλλοι πολλοὶ
φύσει βάρβαροι συνοικοῦσιν ἡμῖν, ἀλλ᾽ αὐτοὶ Ἕλληνες, οὐ μιξοβάρβαροι
οἰκοῦμεν" καὶ τὰ ἑξῆς. φύσει γὰρ ἐξακούεται τὰ πράγματα κομπωδέστερα
ἀγεληδὸν οὕτως τῶν ὀνομάτων ἐπισυντιθεμένων. (23)

And in the Plato passage on the Athenians, which we quoted elsewhere:
"For no Pelopses, nor Cadmuses, nor Aegytpuses and Danauses, nor any
of the other many natural barbarians share our home; we are proper
Greeks, nor do we live as half-barbarians," and so forth. The matter naturally sounds more puffed up from the herding of the names added one
on top of the other.

[Longinus] sounds the alert that a passage about plurals is best heard *repeatedly*. Again, he drops the vague ἑτέρωθι to give us a reading of the echoes beyond the text at hand. Plato talks plural when he talks of the Athenians. [Longinus] does his bit, by doubling up on the quotation. Repetition over time, as well as plural for singular, has a way of shoring up τὰ πράγματα, making them more confident in numbers (ἀγεληδὸν): authority through *reproduction*. As we cast around for all the possible occupants between those brackets and think of all the replication-as-quotation involved in this strange text, we could almost take that last sentence as a principle [Longinus] lives by.

What I am trying to throw up for inspection here is a very subtle yet nonetheless blossoming relationship between timelessness, anonymity, reproduction, and the sublime. The committed reproduction that is the hit after hit of quotation, in a sense, renders *all* the passages invoked radically timeless and authorless.[95] Reproduction (and reproducibility) is almost the way they *become* sublime, for the accumulation of quotes is the means by which the text in question bursts out of its authorial prison. Anonymizing quotation can thus be framed as a particularly strong form of the Longinian penchant for *decontextualizing* quotation more generally. In at least one case, the anonymous quotation is plucked precisely because it illustrates transcendence—that is, the fading into irrelevance of author and context— perfectly. This comes in 35/36, where [Longinus] goes over the genius of writers who are so great that their faults make no dent in their brilliance. As we have seen over and over again, genius kits these chosen ones out with a divine perspective that allows them to "go beyond"—but this is something wired into human nature in general:

τί ποτ' οὖν εἶδον οἱ ἰσόθεοι ἐκεῖνοι καὶ τῶν μεγίστων ἐπορεξάμενοι τῆς συγγραφῆς, τῆς δ᾽ ἐν ἅπασιν ἀκριβείας ὑπερφρονήσαντες; πρὸς πολλοῖς ἄλλοις ἐκεῖνο, ὅτι ἡ φύσις οὐ ταπεινὸν ἡμᾶς ζῷον οὐδ᾽ ἀγεννὲς ἔκρινε τὸν ἄνθρωπον, ἀλλ᾽ ὡς εἰς μεγάλην τινὰ πανήγυριν εἰς τὸν βίον καὶ εἰς τὸν σύμπαντα κόσμον ἐπάγουσα, θεατάς τινας τῶν ἄθλων αὐτῆς ἐσομένους καὶ φιλοτιμοτάτους ἀγωνιστάς, εὐθὺς ἄμαχον ἔρωτα ἐνέφυσεν ἡμῶν ταῖς ψυχαῖς παντὸς ἀεὶ τοῦ μεγάλου καὶ ὡς πρὸς ἡμᾶς δαιμονιωτέρου. διόπερ τῇ θεωρίας καὶ διανοίας τῆς ἀνθρωπίνης ἐπιβολῇ οὐδ᾽ ὁ σύμπας κόσμος ἀρκεῖ, ἀλλὰ καὶ τοὺς τοῦ περιέχοντος πολλάκις ὅρους ἐκβαίνουσιν αἱ ἐπίνοιαι· (35)

So what did those demigods see, who stretched themselves to the best writing and thought beyond plodding accuracy? More than everything else, this: that nature has decided man is neither a base nor lowly creature, but, as if she were having us to some great assembly, she has brought us into life, into the entire universe, to be spectators of her games, and enthusiastic participants, and she implanted in our souls from the beginning an invincible zest for everything, always, which is great and more divine than ourselves. So the entire universe is not enough for the apprehension of the human mind and human thought. On the contrary, our ideas often transcend the limits of the universe.

As earlier, thoughts travel. Here they explicitly breach the "limits" hemming us in,[96] and this happens in repeated time, πολλάκις (i.e., *saepe*), in any number of philosophical frameworks.[97] The thoughts survive, again, through the collective guardianship of all time (ὁ πᾶς αἰών; cf. earlier), which thought is captured best in another anonymous quote:

> καὶ τὰ μὲν ἄλλα τοὺς χρωμένους ἀνθρώπους ἐλέγχει, τὸ δ᾽ ὕψος ἐγγὺς αἴρει μεγαλοφροσύνης θεοῦ. καὶ τὸ μὲν ἄπταιστον οὐ ψέγεται, τὸ μέγα δὲ καὶ θαυμάζεται. τί χρὴ πρὸς τούτοις ἔτι λέγειν ὡς ἐκείνων τῶν ἀνδρῶν ἕκαστος ἅπαντα τὰ σφάλματα ἑνὶ ἐξωνεῖται πολλάκις ὕψει καὶ κατορθώματι, καὶ τὸ κυριώτατον, ὡς, εἴ τις ἐκλέξας τὰ Ὁμήρου, τὰ Δημοσθένους, τὰ Πλάτωνος, τῶν ἄλλων ὅσοι δὴ μέγιστοι, παραπτώματα πάντα ὁμόσε συναθροίσειεν, ἐλάχιστον ἄν τι, μᾶλλον δ᾽ οὐδὲ πολλοστημόριον ἂν εὑρεθείη τῶν ἐκείνοις τοῖς ἥρωσι πάντη κατορθουμένων. διὰ ταῦθ᾽ ὁ πᾶς αὐτοῖς αἰὼν καὶ βίος, οὐ δυνάμενος ὑπὸ τοῦ φθόνου παρανοίας ἁλῶναι, φέρων ἀπέδωκεν τὰ νικητήρια καὶ ἄχρι νῦν ἀναφαίρετα φυλάττει καὶ ἔοικε τηρήσειν, ἔστ᾽ ἂν ὕδωρ τε ῥέῃ καὶ δένδρεα μακρὰ τεθήλῃ. (36)

Other attributes show that those who have them are men; but sublimity lifts them up near the great mind of god. Precision brings no criticism; greatness inspires wonder too. Is it still necessary to add to this that each of these men, over and over, redeems all his faults by sublimity and perfection, and the clincher is that, if someone were to locate the slips of Homer, Demosthenes, Plato, and all the other greats, and fit them all together, we would find them a small part, no more than the tiniest particle of the cases of perfection found all over these heroes? Hence the judgment of all time, which can't be condemned for the mental distortions of envy, has given them the prize of victory, protects it to this day as something that cannot be taken away, and seems likely to watch over it "so long as the stream flows and tall trees flourish."

This unmarked treat hails from the anonymous so-called epitaph for Midas, quoted by Socrates in the *Phaedrus* as an egregious example of a composition out of order.[98] It doesn't matter where you put each of the four lines in the mix, for there is no organic sequence. That makes the poem especially ripe for chopping up into bits and recontextualizing, as [Longinus] does here with the usual aplomb. The value of this snippet inheres precisely in its timelessness, its anonymity; it is a quotation of a quotation, whose origin and order are unimportant to the point at issue. Indeed the more the origin and order are scratched away, the more the point about replicability and transcendence stands. This is the settled verdict of the nameless mass of time—past, present, future combined—and the illustrative quote is itself a stellar example of a thought that has passed beyond the limits once confining it.

As I hinted earlier, Longinian quotation in general is an anonymizing (in the sense of decontextualizing) force. The moment of repetition, even if Homer or Herodotus is offered up as owner, almost proves the claim to sublimity as soon as it happens, for it is the sure sign of getting outside the individual subjectivity in which the quote germinated. But nowhere is this framed more neatly than at the very end of the treatise. Section 44 is at once the most extensive case of quotation in the whole of [Longinus], at the same time as it is a lengthy meditation on many of the issues that we have so far thrust under the spotlight and that have formed constant companions throughout this book: history, context, timelessness.

[Longinus]' swan song takes shape as a long dialogue between a nameless philosopher and himself, on that familiar topic of the *Dialogus:* whence and wherefore the drop-off in the quality of contemporary letters? Broadly, the possible reasons tabled are comparable to the *Dialogus*—ethical/educational context versus political—with the order crucially reversed: whereas the *Dialogus* moves from the moralizing Messalla to the politicizing Maternus, [Longinus] outsources the political rationale to his unnamed generic philosopher, dispenses with it in first position, and then moves onto the ethical argument (which is given the legitimizing stamp of the first person).[99] The budding new critic incarnation of Charles Segal,[100] perhaps on the unconscious lookout for his own legitimizing stamp to ignore political context in criticism, was right, I think, to read this last argumentative move as bolstering one of [Longinus]' pet points: the ability of literature to wriggle free of contextual chains.[101] In what follows, I want to examine this claim in a touch more detail.

In some sense, both of these arguments for decline are historicist.[102] They explain a present state of letters through reference to an "external" constraint, whether that be the fetters of political disenfranchisement[103] or the trappings of luxury weighing down the soul. But [Longinus] has his ways and means of generalizing *both* opinions, in other words, of making debates about bounds break their bounds. The philosopher's speech may seem to take the more radical political position, but it is rent by Messalla-style hedging that scales back ownership.[104] From the off, [Longinus] assigns the words to an unspecified source—τις τῶν φιλοσόφων (44)—which knowingly marks the fact that the hackneyed opinion that this typical τις effuses could belong to any number of first/second CE philosophical persuasions. What's more, the philosopher agrees:

> "θαῦμά μ' ἔχει," λέγων, "ὡς ἀμέλει καὶ ἑτέρους πολλούς, πῶς ποτε κατὰ τὸν ἡμέτερον αἰῶνα πιθαναὶ μὲν ἐπ' ἄκρον καὶ πολιτικαί, δριμεῖαί τε καὶ ἐντρεχεῖς καὶ μάλιστα πρὸς ἡδονὰς λόγων εὔφοροι, ὑψηλαὶ δὲ λίαν καὶ ὑπερμεγέθεις, πλὴν εἰ μή τι σπάνιον, οὐκέτι γεννῶνται φύσεις. τοσαύτη λόγων κοσμική τις ἐπέχει τὸν βίον ἀφορία." (44)

> He said: "I'm amazed, as many others doubtless are too, how in this age there are natures persuasive in the extreme and suited for politics, sharp and skillful and well endowed with rhetorical charm, but truly sublime and exceedingly great natures are no more or at least are scarce. Such are the worldwide proportions of this shortage of literary talent that has a hold on our lives."

The thauma is real—but it isn't unique. It's naturalized and exported as the reaction of "many others." This kind of rhetoric could be a little incendiary, but the philosopher does his best to pour cold water on it wherever possible. The speech is full of qualification and equivocation—here already, πλὴν εἰ μή τι σπάνιον, but also,

> "ἢ νὴ Δί'" ἔφη "**πιστευτέον** ἐκείνῳ τῷ θρυλουμένῳ, ὡς ἡ δημοκρατία τῶν μεγάλων ἀγαθὴ τιθηνός, **ἣ μόνη σχεδὸν** καὶ συνήκμασαν οἱ περὶ λόγους δεινοὶ καὶ συναπέθανον; θρέψαι τε γάρ, **φασίν**, ἱκανὴ τὰ φρονήματα τῶν μεγαλοφρόνων ἡ ἐλευθερία καὶ ἐπελπίσαι καὶ ἅμα διεγείρειν τὸ πρόθυμον τῆς πρὸς ἀλλήλους ἔριδος καὶ τῆς περὶ τὰ πρωτεῖα φιλοτιμίας. . . . οἱ δὲ νῦν **ἐοίκαμεν**" ἔφη "παιδομαθεῖς εἶναι δουλείας δικαίας, . . . ὥσπερ οὖν, **εἴ γε**"

φησί "τοῦτο πιστόν ἐστιν ἀκούω, τὰ γλωττόκομα, ἐν οἷς οἱ πυγμαῖοι, καλούμενοι δὲ νᾶνοι τρέφονται, οὐ μόνον κωλύει τῶν ἐγκεκλεσμένων τὰς αὐξήσεις, ἀλλὰ καὶ συναραιοῖ διὰ τὸν περικείμενον τοῖς σώμασι δεσμόν, οὕτως ἅπασαν δουλείαν, κἂν ᾖ δικαιοτάτη, ψυχῆς γλωττόκομον καὶ κοινὸν ἄν τις ἀποφήναιτο δεσμωτήριον." (44)

He said: "**Should we really believe** this well-worn proposition, that democracy is the best nurse of outstanding types and that, **more or less**, the prodigies in literature reached their apogee only with democracy and died along with it? For—**so they say**—freedom is able to nurture the thoughts of noble minds, and to give them ambition, and at the same time to stir up our spirit of rivalry with each other and burning desire for preeminence. . . . But as it is now," he said, "**we seem** schooled from kindergarten in a just slavery. . . . And so," he goes on, "**if it's true what I hear**, that just as the cages in which they rear pygmies and so-called 'dwarfs' not only stunt the growth of their inmates but weaken them by laying bonds on their bodies, so **one might term** all slavery, **however just it may be**, as a kind of cage or common cell for the soul.

This philosopher is painfully tentative in endorsing the proposition that *seems* to be coming out of his mouth: he puts it as a cliché (ἐκείνῳ τῷ θρυλουμένῳ)[105] and converts it into a question; whittles it down to "more or less" (σχεδὸν); foists the opinion onto an external "they" (φησίν) (as [Longinus] does with him: ἔφη); plays around with subjunctive mincing (κἂν ᾖ δικαιοτάτη . . . ἄν τις ἀποφήναιτο). This *tis* is well versed in the art of "one might say": anonymous speech through and through.

When [Longinus] bursts in to take the philosopher up on these halfhearted arguments, he diffuses the diagnosis across subject and time even more:

ἐγὼ μέντοι γε ὑπολαβὼν "ῥάδιον," ἔφην "ὦ βέλτιστε, καὶ ἴδιον ἀνθρώπου τὸ καταμέμφεσθαι τὰ ἀεὶ παρόντα· ὅρα δὲ μή ποτε οὐχ ἡ τῆς οἰκουμένης εἰρήνη διαφθείρει τὰς μεγάλας φύσεις, πολὺ δὲ μᾶλλον ὁ κατέχων ἡμῶν τὰς ἐπιθυμίας ἀπεριόριστος οὑτοσὶ πόλεμος, καὶ νὴ Δία πρὸς τούτῳ τὰ φρουροῦντα τὸν νῦν βίον καὶ κατ' ἄκρας ἄγοντα καὶ φέροντα ταυτὶ πάθη." (44)

But I took over at this point and said: "It's easy, good man, and it's typical human to blame contemporary conditions. Think on it: maybe it's not the world's peace destroying our great souls but much more this infinite war taking possession of our desires, indeed these passions that lock up our lives in the present, making them come crashing down."

So the philosopher's sentiments aren't specific to him—they are a conse-
quence of being human. The complaints might stem from contemporary
conditions, τὰ ἀεὶ παρόντα, but it is hardwired human nature to have a go
at them. And the external forces that *are* operative (i.e., the consumptive
war of passions) are *boundlessly* (timelessly?) so (ἀπεριόριστος οὑτοσὶ
πόλεμος). That is, both the complaints and the conditions transcend time
and place. As [Longinus] develops his killer moral argument, we recognize those complaints as a retangling of various Platonic thought
strands[106] but also as a synthesis of the commonplaces mentioned earlier
(Velleius Paterculus, Seneca the Elder, Petronius, Tacitus, Juvenal)[107]—and
this is marked in the discourse by hedging mechanisms similar to those
he puts in the philosopher's mouth.[108] The argument sticks to moral ab-
stractions but makes sure to lodge them in the safe middle of common
speech:

ἡ γὰρ φιλοχρηματία, πρὸς ἣν **ἅπαντες** ἀπλήστως ἤδη νοσοῦμεν, καὶ ἡ
φιληδονία δουλαγωγοῦσι, μᾶλλον δέ, **ὡς ἂν εἴποι τις**, καταβυθίζουσιν
αὐτάνδρους ἤδη τοὺς βίους, φιλαργυρία μὲν νόσημα μικροποιὸν <ὄν>,
φιληδονία δ᾽ ἀγεννέστατον. οὐ δὴ ἔχω λογιζόμενος εὑρεῖν, ὡς οἷόν τε πλοῦτον
ἀόριστον ἐκτιμήσαντας, **τὸ δ᾽ ἀληθέστερον εἰπεῖν**, ἐκθειάσαντας, τὰ συμφυῆ
τούτῳ κατὰ εἰς τὰς ψυχὰς ἡμῶν ἐπεισιόντα μὴ παραδέχεσθαι. ἀκολουθεῖ γὰρ
τῷ ἀμέτρῳ πλούτῳ καὶ ἀκολάστῳ συνημμένη καὶ ἴσα, **φασί**, βαίνουσα
πολυτέλεια, καὶ ἅμα ἀνοίγοντος ἐκείνου τῶν πόλεων καὶ οἴκων τὰς εἰσόδους
εὐθὺς ἐμβαίνει καὶ συνοικίζεται. (44)

Indeed money-love, the incurable disease from which we're **all of us** now
suffering, and pleasure-love—these are enslaving us, or better, **as one
might say**, sinking the ship of our lives with everyone on board: silver-
love is a sickness that shrinks us, pleasure-love is the basest of them all.
I can't even discover, as much as I think about it—how, valuing as we do
this boundless wealth, **or to put it more truly**, make it into a god, we can
keep these ingrowing horrors from creeping onto our souls. For side by
side with immeasurable and incontinent wealth there follows, "together
and as one," **as they say**, luxury, and as soon as wealth has opened the
floodgates of the cities and houses, luxury comes straight in and sets up
shop.

"As one might say," "as they say"—to speak the Longinian truth is to say
what everyone else says, about a universal truth. "Everyone" does indeed
seem to say the same sort of thing about opening up cities and houses.[109]

And that "everyone" might as well be these generic philosophers plural,[110] who are dropped in the next sentence:

χρονίσαντα δὲ ταῦτα ἐν τοῖς βίοις νεοττοποιεῖται, **κατὰ τοὺς σοφοὺς** καὶ ταχέως γενόμενα περὶ τεκνοποιΐαν ἀλαζόνειάν τε γεννῶσι καὶ τῦφον καὶ τρυφήν, οὐ νόθα ἑαυτῶν γεννήματα ἀλλὰ καὶ πάνυ γνήσια. (44)

After they've been in our lives for a while, they build a nest—**according to the philosophers**—and quickly make to reproduce themselves—the children are Boasting, Delusion, and Luxury, bastards none of them, but their wholly legitimate offspring.

Everything is palmed off into common parlance. What [Longinus] is trying here, I think, is to give us a "timeless" argument that resists the quagmire of contemporary materialism, his own attempt at absent ὑστεροφημία-style thinking:[111]

ταῦτα γὰρ οὕτως ἀνάγκη γίνεσθαι καὶ μηκέτι τοὺς ἀνθρώπους ἀναβλέπειν μηδ **ὑστεροφημίας** εἶναι τινα λόγον, ἀλλὰ τοιούτων ἐν κύκλῳ τελεσιουργεῖσθαι κατ' ὀλίγον τὴν τῶν βίων διαφθοράν, φθίνειν δὲ καὶ καταμαραίνεσθαι τὰ ψυχικὰ μεγέθη καὶ ἄζηλα γίνεσθαι, ἡνίκα τὰ θνητὰ ἑαυτῶν μέρη καὶ ἀνόητα ἐκθαυμάζοιεν, παρέντες αὔξειν τἀθάνατα. (44)[112]

It has to happen this way; men no longer look up nor pay any attention to **future fame**, and instead, ever so gradually, they complete the destruction of their lives in the cycle of these vices, their breadth of soul wanes and withers and becomes unworthy of imitation, since they are obsessed with the parts of themselves that are mortal and mindless and fail to cultivate their immortal parts.

Through this tapestry of time-free arguments that have leaped from philosopher to philosopher to the point of full absorption into the intellectual commons, [Longinus] is enacting, at sunset, his own transfer into transcendence. For he is no longer quoting the classics—your Homers, your Demostheneses, your Platos.[113] He is quoting *himself*.[114] This last stirring speech about moral decay bumps [Longinus] up into the big leagues of quotability.[115] The words will stand the test of time, because they already have. Their first quotation is also their inaugural canonization.

For [Longinus], sublimity and classicism are forms of transcendence depending on the loss of particular author and particular context—hence his very last quotation, another seemingly innocent, anonymous pocket rocket:

"κράτιστον εἰκῆ ταῦτ᾽ ἐᾶν," ἐπὶ δὲ τὰ συνεχῆ χωρεῖν· ἦν δὲ ταῦτα τὰ πάθη, ... (44)

"It's best to let this go," and move to the next topic: that is, the emotions, ...

The transitional formula that helps [Longinus] wrap up his moral mono-logue and move on to the next subject[116] is a sound bite from Euripides' *Electra*. But the transplantation brings with it at least two dangling roots of anonymity. The first is that it's spoken by a character who is himself anonymous at that point in the play (379)—Orestes has gone incognito as his messenger and perhaps tries to talk like a generic messenger would.[117] The second is that the line is itself tarnished with suspicions of spurious-ness because of a conflict over attribution. Diogenes Laertius (2.33) quotes it as a line from Euripides' *Auge*. Socrates supposedly walked out of the theater as he heard this line about letting virtue go (a good line, then, to make a philosopher leave, i.e., close a Platonic peroration in [Longinus]?).[118] The line is, then, multicontextual—a perfect ambassador for the end of a treatise that has advocated for precisely that, over and over again. Fittingly, [Longinus] uses his last quotation to speak through brackets.

On the Sublime is a treatise dedicated to the time-scape of always. It is interested in stretching words and ideas beyond the brains that originally conceived them and the contexts that produced them. Sublimity is the force pumping words outside the limits of self and history. It makes no differ-ence whether [Longinus] is replicating the words of "others" or launching "his own." In the end they break down and mingle into a cultural com-mons preserved by unanimous approval and repetition over many times. [Longinus] is not just shooting for the universality of immortality. He is attracted to examples that horizontally, *culturally* transcend as well. Martin West has shown that many of his picks from Homer have strong Near Eastern analogues, indeed derive from them.[119] [Longinus] also looks west, to Rome: he addresses an unknown Roman aristocrat, drops a reference to Cicero alongside Demosthenes, and plants an ending that could work equally well in both Greek and Roman contexts, to very different effects.[120] And then there's that Longinian *genesis*. Not many second sophistic Greek authors are quoting from the Septuagint.[121] We should take his project of cultural transcendence seriously[122] and put it alongside his bid for the al-ways. But we should also make note of how his brackets serve both these projects beautifully, I mean, *ideologically*.[123] [Longinus] reads and purveys texts "unanchored in time and place," but he aims to be one too.[124] The brackets make the author provisional, the context multiple, and fetishize "the words themselves." It is hard to picture a [Longinus] wanting it any other way.

Conclusion

Unknowing Literature

Anonymous works provoke fantasy, and excesses of fantasy
may provoke in other scholars an excess of caution.

—Michael Reeve (1984: 42)

THIS BOOK HAS TRIED, I have tried, and you might think it by now past trying, to resist some of the most stubborn and abiding habits of classical scholarship. The results may seem to some readers cynical, the epistemology hopelessly pessimistic, a shrug subbed in for scholarship. For what I really want to say is that *sometimes* (not always) the terrifying and sublime "gaps" in our knowledge should be treated as contouring forces sculpting the objects of antiquity into their own unique and beautiful shapes, not as suffocating vacuums coming between us and them.[1] They are central to antiquity. The anonymous should be so to the study of it.

I have used primarily privative terms throughout to describe these homeless (there's another one) texts: anonymous, authorless, unauthored, nameless, unnamed, unknown. The poverty of language itself leaves my hands tied. It positively bakes in an ideology normalizing "onymity," fame, knowing and being known, as the zero-grade practice. It sets the burden of existential justification on those unknown featherweights of Roman literature that simply aren't equipped to joust on such terms. If I could flip the script by magical fiat, I would. But what would I name it? Perhaps that's not the right question for a book trying to accommodate us to the absence of names. But if pressed, it would be something like "name-free" literature. At the least, and last, I want to leave you with a sense of the author's name as weight or straitjacket to be shaken off, rather than sine qua non. If I've done the job right, the condition of the name-free should leave us with lighter shoulders.

One of my happy refrains is worth singing one more time. I have argued that we should abandon or qualify our notions of context, *in certain contexts*. Latin literary studies, and certainly the subsection focused on the period of the principate, has sometimes worked with an oppressive understanding of context as "political" (i.e., has wanted to situate literature sociologically among the upper echelons, primarily as a response to the princeps of the moment).[2] It has often preoccupied itself with questions of how literary works square with "imperial" or "elite" ideology. The approach is hard to shake, because it is enshrined, again, in the very names we use to slice up imperial literary history. "Augustan," "Neronian," "Flavian," "Trajanic," "Antonine," and so on are all terms making an implicit claim: that the best ways of sorting and understanding works of imperial literature should be to treat them as period pieces, written in the shadow of a great name for an aegis.[3] Other versions of context might bring different relationships to the fore. The burgeoning industry of putting texts up against material culture, for example, is perhaps more egalitarian than the older-style political historicism: art and text each shedding light on the other, rather than the bigger (capital-*H* History) brother surrounding or explaining the little guy (lowercase text). But all these practices of contextualism depend on horizontal, time-bound relationships. They need us to *know* the rough dates of the objects of study to bring them into meaningful relationship. Any dominant paradigm that privileges this kind of context will inevitably leave certain objects for dust. So if the information isn't forthcoming, we have to change the method of interrogation. Better still, we should probably take a break from asking altogether.[4]

This is the method of abstinence and charity I have more or less tried to exercise in this book: to stop torturing texts with endless interrogations pitched at extracting information they can't yield and to start treating them as fully functioning works of literature whose anonymity is a deep-set, constitutive *part* of them. Some of them—particularly in the early chapters on Augustus' *Res Gestae*, Suetonius' *Augustus,* and Ovid's *Ibis*—have been concerned more with anonymity *in* than anonymity *of*. These chapters tracked patterns and effects of antonomasia (*Res Gestae, Ibis*), notions of authorship and ownership (*Res Gestae, Augustus*), and how the power of anonymous writing might work inside these systems (*Res Gestae, Augustus*). But from Chapter 3 onward, I attempted to build various relationships between internal *and* external forms of the anonymous. I suggested that in each case, the work's anonymity, which exists for us (*Octavia,* Phaedrus, *Laus Pisonis,* Calpurnius Siculus, [Longinus]) or should be slated again as a real possibility (*Apocolocyntosis, Satyrica, Dialogus*), does that work a strange kind of service. That service might be boosting a text's political goals, if it were trying to bring down an emperor and make the world think that was what everyone was thinking (*Octavia, Apocolocyntosis*) or that the principate is as timeless as the shepherd's shade under which it's piped (Calpurnius Siculus); making a satire or a drama dependent on us not knowing the author (Phaedrus, *Laus Pisonis*), on distance and mediation (Calpurnius Siculus); making poetry durable beyond a particular patronage context (*Laus Pisonis*) or political context (Calpurnius Siculus); anarchically questioning the worth of names and titles (*Satyrica*); forming a text that tries to transcend its own temporal boundaries, its moment of utterance, by bidding for the habitual (*Dialogus*) or leapfrogging earthly constraints and shooting for the stars of the literary firmament ([Longinus]). In all these cases, it helps not to know.

This state of unknowing is something special about the dynamics of art. But it is also something that literature is particularly good at, as Derek Attridge has shown.[5] In discussing the ways literature can be said to know or not know, or make us live these processes and misrecognize them in the ascription of knowledge or aporia beyond ourselves, to the literary texts *themselves,* Attridge sums up Derrida's comments on literature's "secret":[6] "The work of literature—and we can extend this observation to all works of art—retains its secret because it is a secret without hidden depths, without concealment. A work of art states what it states, presents what it presents, no more, no less; and it refuses to say anything further, no matter how hard we press it."[7] The point of this secret is that it is bottomless and, strictly, contentless. The open secret is that there is no secret. Attridge goes on:

> But no work of art reveals everything we might want to know, precisely
> because its secrets have no depth to which we could penetrate in pursuit

of that knowledge—much as we're tempted to speculate on characters' inner lives and motives. I return to my point about the work of art as event and act: though the work may stage the search for knowledge, and the reader or viewer may feel thoroughly involved in this staged search, there is no knowledge as such waiting to be uncovered. Every work is a knowing work, every work smiles enigmatically, because there is no way we, or it, can satisfy the thirst for knowledge that it generates.[8]

The author-free works treated in this book are a hyperactive case study in this same general power of art: the paradox of its withholding something even as it has nothing to withhold. What I have tried out in the previous pages is a kind of critical submission to, or perhaps collaboration with, that power. Not knowing is one of the most important affective, cognitive, even metaphysical states that anyone walking through the ancient world must face. Here, I moved to do it proper justice.

As Seneca had it back in the Introduction, the unknown provokes all kinds of fear, worry, and speculation. Either we shun the abyss altogether or we take it as something to fill up with scholarly heroism or virtuosic sleuth work. Like the poet of the *Laus Pisonis,* or the scholars *on* the *Laus Pisonis,* we instinctively seek to turn darkness into light. I hope this book has shown that we need not be afraid of the dark. If we stop thrashing and groping and let our eyes get used to it, we might just land on something else, unnamed, unknown.

Acknowledgments

Books take villages to write, none more so than this one, which ushered me into the darker corners of Latin (and sometimes Greek) literature, often without a map or a torch. Given the size of this local population, it may well have taken a city. Let me start with the academic neighbors next door.

First, the roll call of readers and commenters: I could not have done without all these resident experts, who buoyed me up when feeling particularly out of my depth. John Henderson, always my ideal inner audience, groomed almost everything. Elena Giusti lent her formidable powers to the Introduction and Chapters 1 and 2. Irene Peirano Garrison cast her keen eye over the Introduction and Chapter 5—I am incredibly grateful to her for a deep reading and a generous recommendation of references to mop up the mess I made. Yelena Baraz heroically plowed through Chapter 6 when it was in particularly embryonic form. She also coined a key formulation: "anonymity is a feature, not a bug." Victoria Rimell absolutely disemboweled Chapter 7 in the best possible way. Her comments were transformative. Lastly, Chapter 8, in especially dire need, was subjected to a crack team of surgeons: Stephen Halliwell, David Levene, and Chris Whitton—the patient lives only because of you. Most of these people were actively solicited as readers, rudely, without much will on their part. In some particularly egregious cases, I hadn't even met them yet. I still find their generosity staggering. It allows me to go on thinking that academia can be a beautiful and collaborative sanctuary from as well as a cruel world.

A little deeper in time, but no less critical, are the classicists whose ideas and mentorship made me want to become one of their number. Without their wake, this book wouldn't be. Shane Butler, William Fitzgerald, Kirk Freudenburg, Emma Gee, Emily Gowers, Edith Hall, John Henderson,

Emily Matters, Frances Muecke, Ellen O'Gorman, Victoria Rimell: the creativity, intelligence, and humanity that you cultivate will always be the raising bar in front of me.

Those at the latest end of the production line need a huge shout-out. Thanks to the two anonymous readers for Harvard University Press, whose praise, wariness, reservations, provocations, and downright solid bibliography gave the book a much-needed face-lift. For initial interest in the project, hard work shepherding it through its genesis, growth, and evaluation, and huge help ironing out my regularly crumpled prose, I have to thank my editor, Sharmila Sen, as well as her brilliant and supportive assistant, Heather Hughes. When it comes to writing books, tough love is the best love. Sharmila was also the one who coined the book's title, which also gave me a conceptual push out of nowhere—the power of names, indeed.

Two particularly formative events and their organizers need urgent deanonymizing. First, a panel at the 2017 Classical Association conference "Texts without Contexts," organized by Emma Greensmith and Talitha Kearey: this was an absolutely crucial moment for the book, both locally (in that it was the first time the *Laus Pisonis* material was forced to see the light of day) and globally (in that the brilliant conversations of this panel helped me articulate better what I didn't quite know I was trying to do). The second is an event-turned-project: in June 2017, Elena Giusti—my most trusted reader, best colleague, closest collaborator, and dear friend—and I organized a St Andrews conference by the name "Unspeaking Volumes: Absence in Latin Texts," now grown into our handsome edited volume *Unspoken Rome: Absence in Latin Literature and Its Reception.* Elena and I banded together once we realized we were tackling a very similar phenomenon from different angles—she with her much-awaited project *The Great Unmentioned,* a cutting-edge investigation of the major political absences in Augustan literature; I with *Author Unknown.* Her influence is palpable on every page, and I thank her truly for linking arms to form one of the most satisfying intellectual partnerships I've ever known. I also thank the contributors for their stellar gifts to the conference and the volume. Not only did they turn up to talk absence, but they changed the way I think whatever is not there—a big part of what this book is all about.

The usual suspects get all their dues and then some. My friends on three continents (four, post-Brexit?) have kept me sane as can be through trial after trial of these past few years. You are my foundation, frame, prop, and beam, and I would be a heap of rubble without you. Grouped regionally, big love to Team Australia: Giulietta Amato, Teddy Amato, Saul Bert, Andrew Brooks, Robert d'Apice, Ben Etherington, Jet Geaghan, Liam Grealy,

Duncan Hilder, Taichi Hoshino, Serin Kasif, Barney Lewer, Astrid Lorange, Shona Macleod, Sean Murphy, Ivan Muniz Reed, Miro Sandev, Georgia Sholl, Camilla Wagstaff, and Marty Wieczorek; Team UK/Europe: Sarah Arens, Louise Benson, Raph Cormack, Carlos Cueva, Barbara Del Giovane, Patrick Errington, Will Ferguson, Natalie Fullwood, Yuddi Gershon, Guido Giovanardi, Elena Giusti, Sam Goff, Lucy Jackson, Emma Jones, Aris Komporozos-Athanasiou, Lotte Kühlbrandt, Adam Lecznar, Sophie Mallett, Ric McLauchlan, Michał Murawski, Steph O'Rourke, Sam Rose, Miguel Santa Clara, Laura Rosella Schluderer, Volker Schlue, Henry Stead, Ellie Stedall, and Katrina Zaat; Team US: Daniel Behar, Anna Bonnell-Freidin, Kacey Carter, Massimo Cè, Marina Connelly, Erin Freedman, Sergio Jarillo, Harvey Lederman, Alex Schultz, and Alex Schwennicke. If I could see you all, all the time, it wouldn't be nearly enough.

Plus-size thanks to the research and teaching communities that were also instrumental in the making. The students in my debut "Floating Words" class were my model first audience for a raw dress rehearsal of the ideas aired herein. My colleagues at St Andrews have modeled interest and patience in equal measure, even when I had to live absence directly. In those tracts of being away, colleagues at the University of Sydney and Harvard University picked up the slack. The CCANESA library at Sydney and Widener at Harvard both kept letting me in for no apparent reason. I am deeply grateful to these places for approximating the abstract model of community I sometimes feel I left behind in those gardens of Eden, Sydney and Cambridge—the closest things I have known to home. At the same time, I also feel a huge degree of guilt and shame that the majority of this book was written on expropriated homes: stolen indigenous land, whether that be in "New South Wales" or "New England." I acknowledge the traditional owners of these lands: the Cadical peoples of the Eora nation in Sydney and the Massachusett in Cambridge, Massachusetts. Solidarity to First Nations struggle worldwide, in all the places blighted by the bloody history and buckled present of colonialism.

This book is for three people. First is my mother, who has suffered beyond measure in the last few years. I hope this redeems your pain just a little. Second is my father, who has also had a rough time of it. Both of you have always encouraged me to chase whatever phantoms and flog whatever dead horses trot my way. I continue as advised. And above all, the dedicatee, Francesca Bellei. You are no longer my tightest coauthor. But our past five years together marked this book in unimaginable ways. I hope we continue to write each other, in other unimagined ways, even from a greater distance, for the rest of our lives.

Notes

Introduction

1. Even in periods most invested in individual authorship and solitary genius—such as the romantic—authorial kenosis remains an active fantasy. Cf., for example, Keats' definition of the poet with "no identity" (Bennett 2004: 65).

2. Although this could paradoxically be understood as a return of the self too: see Bennett 2004: 65; cf. also 71, 127. The feel for anonymity was shared by many a modernist (see Ferry 2002: 198–199)—indeed one of Virginia Woolf's last pieces of work was plotted as a hymn to it (Silver 1979).

3. On the New Criticism as a reaction against the overbiographizing of the previous guard, see Bennett 2004: 74.

4. Bennett 2004: 73, 112. Authorship is also a key concept in Roman literary history: the beginnings of a literature in Latin was almost coterminous with the advent of nameable individual authors (cf. Goldberg 2005: 27; cf. Feeney 2016: 227 on Livius Andronicus). The move from "anonymity" to "authorship" is often how we tend to picture the emergence of literature: see Woolf in Silver 1979: 385; cf. Ferry 2002: 196.

5. See North 2017: 1 and *passim*.

6. Cf. Hinds 2010: 371; North 2017: 142 on the misplaced metaphor of the pendulum.

7. See Bennett 2004: 89–93.

8. For the bias of classical scholarship toward synchronic over diachronic historicist approaches, see Roller 2010: 244–245.

9. The founding question of Barthes 1968; on Barthes' answer, "we cannot know," see also Bennett 2004: 12.

10. Classics has a particular sensitivity to the problems of projecting contexts (see Roller 2010: 240). For comparable problems of an unarticulated concept of context in art history, see Tanner 2000: 22. For a critical account of the totem of context in literary studies, see Felski 2015: 151–185; cf. Attridge 2015: 180–203.

11. Sedgwick 2003: 123–151; Felski 2015; North 2017. For a brilliant new challenge to contextual reading visited on literary modernism, see now Bronstein 2018.

12. The language of context as a straitjacketing, confinement, or imprisonment shows up in both Felski (2015: 155–157, 182–184) and North (2017: 182).

13. Whitmarsh 2017.

14. Indeed the earliest times: cf. Goldberg 2005: 62–68, 84–85 on the earliest Roman attempts to fix Plautus as individual and corpus, assign him an author function, and discipline him into legibility within elite literary culture. We could take the enterprise back to Hellenistic scholarship even (see, e.g., Pfeiffer 1968: 128n6 and the note's addenda). On ancient Echtheitskritik, see Speyer 1971: 112–128.

15. This scholarly distaste for anonymity shines through most, perhaps, in the almost complete absence of treatments of it as a means of literary categorization in antiquity (bar Bardon 1952 and perhaps, at a stretch, the very focused application of the concept in my own Geue 2017).

16. E.g., *Beowulf, Sir Gawain and the Green Knight,* the *Chanson de Roland,* the *Nibelungenlied, Njal's Saga*—thanks to David Levene for getting me to think comparatively here.

17. Such ascription of agency to works of literature is all over criticism: see Attridge 2015: 242–243 (the move has a particular lineage in classics); and Zanker 2013: 844–849 and Zanker 2016 (chapter 6).

18. See Rose 2017: 161, 172–173.

19. See Richards (1924) 2001: 15–16; North 2017: 31. Cf. Felski 2015: 178, and Attridge's (2015) conception of the work of art as an "event" rather than an "object."

20. For a brief suite of examples of historical motives for anonymous publication, see Griffin 1999: 885.

21. Peirano 2012: 5–6, 38–39; cf. Higbie 2017: 140; cf. Speyer 1971: 40.

22. Talk of a social turn in recent scholarship on Latin literature often has this in mind: "social" meaning "social performance," "self-fashioning," "competition"; see the paradigmatic overview in Lowrie 2010, e.g., "The aesthetic creates symbolic capital for its creator in a world governed by elite competition" (289). It has become a bit of a scholarly habit to assume that all Latin authors do is strategize for self-glorification—if not overtly, then covertly. See for example Riggsby 1988: 88; R. Gibson 2003: 251–252. Note the related obsession with "self-fashioning" (e.g., Dugan 2005; Pagán 2010). Some authors attract this more than others: Tacitus has traditionally been the reticent antitype to Plinian self-magnification (see Syme 1958: 113).

23. Although Martial's brand is underwritten by a strong strand of materiality: see Roman 2001. On self-naming as part of a Roman poet's repertoire of immortalizing moves, see de la Durantaye 2007: 71–72.

24. Ubiquitously—but, in particular, see *Ep.* 9.23, on Pliny's wish for his name to be well known (see R. Gibson 2003: 249).

25. On "Homer" as a retrospective act of reception, see Graziosi 2002 (and on his name, see esp. 51–89); cf. Nagy 1996: 92 and Bennett 2004: 34. Bennett also points out (35) that named authorship is often a retrospective phenomenon.

26. Cf. Peirano 2013: 267–268 on Homeric anonymity as marking authenticity. Such modesty grates against the kleos-seeking of Homer's internal characters (bar Odysseus—on whose anonymity see Van Nortwick 2009: 45–64).

27. Lauwers (2011: 237) reads this as a superficial point—but it was a big part of the Homeric effect.

28. Mullan 2007: 41–75.

29. For the importance of Homer as blank slate to his busy reception history, see Porter 2002.

30. This proximity of author to god, making the critic into the exegete priest, is precisely what Barthes wanted to throw out in his work of 1968; see Bennett 2004: 14. Bennett (2004: 21) also glosses Foucault's comments (1979: 144) on Barthes' ironic preservation of authorial privilege in his attempt to kill it off.

31. See also Graziosi 2013: 26–33 for Homer's ability to shift and shuttle viewing position—also considered a divine quality.

32. We could also understand it as a kind of sublimity, akin to Burke's "judicious obscurity" (in Boulton 1987: 58–64; see Williams 2015: 184–185).

33. Clarke 1997: 94–95; Swain 2001: 56–57; Peirano 2013: 268. On the importance of self-naming in the construction of the author figure, and for a brief history, see Bennett 2004: 122–123.

34. Katherine Clarke (1997) argues that Strabo's partial anonymity redirects accent onto his geographical project. Her point about the capaciousness of Strabo's phrases for "in my time" (1997: 102) screams Pausanias (Habicht 1985: 177).

35. Especially given the "missing" preface, and the absence of self-naming, which bring Pausanias close to Arrian: Bowie 2001: 27–28; cf. Habicht 1985: 8–9, 12, 18, 141, 151, 156 on Pausanian self-sobriety. Pausanias' citations are also anonymized (Habicht 1985: 144–145; C. Jones 2001: 33)—another relationship of internal to external name suppression (cf. chapters 2 and 3)? On Pausanias'/[Longinus]' balance of self-effacement in/as self-construction, see Porter 2001: 64.

36. See Mullan 2007: 9–40 on the anonymity of "Mischief"; cf. Bennett 2004: 54.

37. *Ep.* 9.27.2. On this strategy of deferred gratification in Pliny himself, see Morello 2003.

38. See Whitmarsh and Bartsch 2008: 250–251 (citing Winkler 1985 and Henderson 2001a); see also Kahane 2001; Swain 2001; Slater 2001: 218–219; Too 2001.

39. See also Bennett 2004: 18–19.

40. The language of game, play, and amusement has perhaps stuck because so many pseudonymous texts seem to be exercises in creating juvenilia: see Syme 1983: 5; Peirano 2012: 74–116.

41. Encouraging readers to fill the gaps, supplement: see Peirano 2012: 8–24; Higbie 2017: 19, 147–148, 155.

42. Kim 2013: 34–35.

43. Antonomasia is the focus of some brilliant recent work, e.g., Shearin 2015: 98–140 (on Lucretius).

44. Cf. Mullan 2007: 297: "That is the way it has always been."

45. For political (and social) squeezes experienced by authors under empire, see Rutledge 2001: 23–61; Dominik, Garthwaite, and Roche 2009; Penwill 2015; Wilson 2015; Ziogas 2015.

46. For anonymity as resistance, see Scott 1990.

47. Even the unapologetic first-person writers of our period make something complex and "elusive" of themselves: cf. Edwards 1997: 34–35 on Seneca.

48. Emphatically, this doesn't extend to subelite: see MacMullen 1982 on the "epigraphic habit." The epigraphic habit was particularly habitual among ex-slaves (Woolf 1996: 35). Evidence for the decline of elite self-memorialization is gathered in Eck 1984. Equestrian statues were not as much of a problem (Eck 1984: 144). See also C. Smith 2009: 76–78 on the general vogue for self-presentation in late second/early first century BCE.

49. Suet. *Aug.* 66; Dio Cassius 53.23.

50. The ethical anxieties predate the principate: on the codes of modesty regulating self-praise, see Marincola 1997: 175–182; R. Gibson 2003; Hardie 2012: 296, 316; Pelling 2013: 67. But there does seem to be a break in elite *monumental* self-representation, from republic to principate (see Eck 1984: 138, 148).

51. Cf. Henderson 2002b: 169–171; and cf. Tanner 2000: 45 on the decline of honorific veristic portrait statues, circa Augustan period.

52. Zadorojnyi 2010: 115; cf. Zadorojnyi 2013: 373.

53. On the genre, see Misch 1951. On late republican autobiography, see Cornell 2009; Pelling 2009; C. Smith 2009; Flower 2014.

54. Although see S. Harrison 2013 on oblique self-revelation in *Sat.* 2. Cf. Propertius 4, with P. Miller 2002: 29.

55. On Juvenal's expunging of the first person, see Uden 2015 and Geue 2017.

56. *Locus classicus:* Bowie 1970; Whitmarsh 2001: 17–26 complicates this claim.

57. *De Dea Syria,* with Elsner 2001: 152; Porter 2001: 90. On Lucianic "autobiography," see Humble and Sidwell 2006.

58. On the importance of "writing for the future," cf. Bronstein 2018: 2.

59. Zadorojnyi (2010: 118) writes well of this moment as "hijacking authority over a monument."

60. Uden 2015 regularly cross-references Lucian in discussing Juvenal: 56, 108, 166, 201.

61. The anonymous then becomes a super-size kind of literariness: "the self-awareness of the possibility of transcending the initial moment of production or reception is itself constitutive of the category of the 'literary.'" Feeney 2016: 195. Cf. also Whitmarsh 2017: 40–41, 43.

62. Lowrie 2009: 59–60. Cf. also Felski 2015: 160.

63. We might compare Roller's recent work on timeless/future-oriented Roman exempla, whose "deracination" and decontextualization allows full assimilation into later reception moments (2019: 19).

64. On the particularly anonymous dynamics of graffiti, see Milnor 2014: 12–14, 153–159, 187–188.

65. Milnor 2014: 156–159.

66. See Milnor 2014: 23–24, 34–36, 159.

67. As Schmeling (2011: xxxiv) notes, "realistic" is one of scholarship's favorite terms for the *Sat.*, and it has long been scooped for evidence about first-century social life. For a recent attempt to disentangle actual data about economic life from the *Sat.*, see Verboven 2009.

68. On the problems scholarship has in dealing with these elastic texts, see, e.g., Thomas 1998. Najman 2017 (cf. 2012) has written brilliantly on the need for embracing the "ongoing vitality and transformation of textual traditions" (515) in biblical studies (and classical philology).

69. Hopkins (1993) 2004: 213; cf. Pervo 1998: 119.

70. See note 72 below.

71. Conte 1996.

72. Cf. Slater 1990: 149–150 on clichéd freedman speech in the *Satyrica*: "they are the values of the culture thinking out loud." Language has been where the *Sat.* has won most of its "realist" brownie points: see Auerbach (1946) 2013: 24–33; Bodel 1999: 41; Petersmann 1999. We might also compare Niebuhr's anonymous *Carmina Convivialia*, loaded with the burden of representing "the common property of the nation"—see Goldberg 2005: 4 (cf. Wiseman 2008: 239–240 on these songs representing a "world before authors")—or the *Commentariolum Petitionis*, made to "illustrat[e] the practices of political life at Rome" (Syme 1983: 7).

73. On the proximity of these to political graffiti, see Zadorojnyi 2010: 122–123.

74. Slater (2014: 305–306) also notes the political effectiveness of anonymity here. Cf. Tiberius' response to unknown author verses (*incertis auctoribus*) at Tac. *Ann.* 1.72. See Moles 1998: 144; Del Giovane forthcoming; and on the connection with rumor, see Hardie 2012: 306.

75. Or at least an oscillation between the particular and the universal: see Wimsatt 1954: 69; and Derrida 1995: 142–143; cited in Bennett 2004: 126.

76. See Ferry 2002.

77. See Liddell and Scott ἀνώνυμος II.

78. E.g., Priam's undignified *sine nomine corpus*, Aeneid 2.558; cf. *naufragum illum sine nomine* Cicero, *De Fato* 5.

79. Adespota meaning "anonymous works" only becomes naturalized into English toward the end of the nineteenth century (see OED *adespota*). On *adespoton*, see Peirano 2012: 5.

80. Cic. *Ad Fam.*15.17.3: "De Hispania novi nihil, sed exspectatio valde magna; rumores tristiores sed ἀδέσποτοι"; D. H. *AR* 11.50: ὑπόληψις ... φήμαις τ᾽ ἀδεσπότοις καὶ εἰκασμοῖς αὐξηθεῖσα οὐκ ὀλίγοις.

81. Plutarch *Cic.* 15: τῷ Κράσσῳ μετὰ δεῖπνον ἐπιστολὰς ἀποδίδωσιν ὁ θυρωρός, ὑπὸ δή τινος ἀνθρώπου κομισθείσας ἀγνώστου, ἄλλας ἄλλοις ἐπιγεγραμμένας, αὐτῷ δὲ Κράσσῳ μίαν ἀδέσποτον.

82. For *sine auctore* used to disqualify gossip, rumor, or hearsay in this sense, Cic. *Ad Fam.* 12.9, 12.10; Q. Curtius Rufus *HAM* 6.2.15.4; Livy, *AUC* 3.36.9, 34.16.9, 37.51.8, 39.43.1. For *nullus auctor*, Cic. *Pro Caelio* 30.19. For *auctor incertus*, Tac. *Hist.* 2.73.4; Suet. *Caligula* 6.

83. Pliny *Ep.* 10.96.5.

84. Suet. *Aug.* 31.

85. Suet. *Gaius* 8.

86. *Ann.* 4.11.1.

87. See Chapter 1.

88. Cf. Quintilian *IO* 7.2.49: *aliena quae sunt dubia numquam possunt nocere nisi aut incerto auctore aut mortuo.*

89. Cf. Chapter 7 in this volume.

90. In a sense, I want to mime the process of thinking that is "reading" rather than "a reading"—cf. Attridge 2015: 249.

91. Ancient fakes/forgeries/pseudepigrapha also have a much more substantial paper trail than the anonymous: Speyer 1971 is a classic of the old guard, but more recently, cf. Martinez 2011, 2012, 2014; Ni-Mheallaigh 2014; and Cueva and Martinez 2016. For the classic synthetic work on literary fakes in general, see Ruthven 2001.

I. The Power of the Name

1. Cf. Shearin 2015: 138–140.

2. Pliny *NH* 8.11.

3. See Sciarrino 2004: 325.

4. Cf. my discussion of Cicero, *Pro Archia* in the Introduction.

1. Name Power

1. On the outsize effects of the Augustan historical moment for authorship, constituting a "new author function," see Martelli 2013: 2.

2. For the critical Augustan role of *auctor* and property of *auctoritas*, see Ziogas 2015: 117–119. Todisco (2007: 452–454) bulks out the link between the name Augustus and *auctoritas*, although Rowe (2013) has recently thrown cold water over the marriage. On Augustan *auctoritas* as "performative power dependent on representation," see Lowrie 2009: 280. The very term *auctor* comes to be the favorite for describing the state of authorship in the first and second centuries CE (see Hauser 2016b: 154).

3. A tension nicely embodied in the textual mess of the three "copies"—Ancyra, Antioch, Apollonia—we have to use to reconstruct the monumental original. See Cooley 2009: 7; Martelli 2010: 135. Lowrie (2009: 306–307) is excellent on the recursive effects of the *RG* as copy.

4. Though Scheid (2007: xxvi–xxviii) notably dissents from the majority confidence in Augustus' authorship.

5. Martelli 2010: 135, 149; cf. Slater 2008: 269.

6. Slater (2008: 253–254) positions the *RG* as a kind of written-oral hybrid, making Augustus "speak" in the heart of Rome.

7. Text is from Cooley 2009, with editorial brackets removed; translations are my own, unless indicated otherwise.

8. Cf. Slater 2008: 264. *RG* 35.2 (cf. 8, 25) is even more precise; on the composition date, see Cooley 2009: 42–43.

9. Although precisely what *quo pro merito* denotes is thorny: see Cooley 2009 *ad loc.*

10. In more ways than one: the chronology of naming and other honors here is telescoped something fierce (Cooley 2009 *ad loc.*).

11. Although for the depersonalized signature of the title *pater patriae,* see Martelli 2010: 139.

12. For Augustus as more "inscribed" than "inscriber," see Slater 2008: 265–266.

13. We should remember that Augustus fancied himself both *conditor* and *conservator Romani nominis,* acting in the very name of Rome (Yavetz 1984: 15).

14. For *meum nomen* as the "catch-all" bringing Augustus' different name phases to heel, see Martelli 2010: 135; see also Lowrie 2009: 293–294.

15. This sets up interesting historical irony against Augustus' act to clamp down on lampoons circulated under someone else's name (*sub alieno nomine*) in Suetonius, *Augustus* 55; see later in this chapter.

16. Cf. similar self-effacing claims in Tacitus, of Tiberius; see Eck 1984: 136.

17. Cf. Augustus removing statues of himself at *RG* 24. For these dynamics of self-promotion through self-effacement, see Lowrie 2009: 304; Martelli 2010: 135. Suetonius picks up on this grand gesture of anonymity (*Augustus* 31), which is pitted against Domitian's name mania (*Domitian* 5); cf. *Nero* 55.

18. Cf. the anecdote about Augustus' execution of Virgil's literary will, in which he becomes the author of the *Aeneid* (*auctore Augusto—Life of Virgil,* 41).

19. E.g., Wallace-Hadrill (2016: 268) nicely cautions against this narrative regarding the naming of Augustus.

20. For a comparison of Augustan ubiquity to Hitler's ubiquity in Hannah Arendt, see Giusti 2016.

21. The denial of names to The Enemy is of course part of the *RG*'s ideological work of turning civil into foreign wars (a high *RG* priority; see Cooley 2009: 36). On the way this technique creates reader collusion and gap filling, see Lowrie 2009: 305–306.

22. Cooley 2009 *ad loc.* rightly calls this mode of enemy reference "typically roundabout" and "typically negative."

23. Note especially the contrast with the luminous consular names P. Sulpicius and C. Valgius.

24. On Augustus' self-staging as Censor here, see Cooley 2009 *ad loc.*

25. For the *Caesars'* approximate publication date (within ten-ish years of 117 CE), see Wallace-Hadrill 1983: 1. Suetonius makes for our last positively dateable author in this book. (I say positively hesitantly. It is perfectly possible that Calpurnius Siculus percolated from the third century, and the [Longinus] question is still open; see Chapters 6 and 8.)

26. Scholars tend to limit its value as source, e.g., Lewis 1991: 3633 (although a structural influence is admitted at 3666; cf. Goodyear 1982: 661). Power (2014: 6–7) acknowledges stylistic connections but also resorts to a "common source" explanation for similarity. Gunderson (2014: 134) sees the *RG*'s exemplarity as

standing right behind Suetonius, and Langlands (2014: 114) fingers it as a possible reason for Suetonius' interleaving of sexual morality with imperial exemplarity.

27. Cf. the use of stylistic analysis to write off certain Horatian works as spurious in the *Life of Horace* 12; see Damon 2014: 41–42. On Suetonius as scholar, see Wallace-Hadrill 1983.

28. See Millar 1977: 207; although Suetonius is silent on *ab epistulis* life (Wallace-Hadrill 1983: 77, 87—the *a studiis* being similarly mysterious, 83–84).

29. For Augustus' graphomania, see also Slater 2008: 254; and cf. Chapter 7.

30. Augustus' project of fixing authorship could also be a response to the mess of Caesar's writings; see Suetonius *Julius* 55–56.

31. See note 61 below on Augustus's letters. On Suetonius' tendency to quote emperors in their own words, see Damon 2014 (cf. Wallace-Hadrill 1983: 21). On Suetonian literary quotation, an offshoot of this *ipsissima verba* approach, see Mitchell 2015.

32. Text OCT; translations my own unless indicated otherwise.

33. On the *notavi* autopsy claim, see Wardle 2014 *ad loc.*

34. With the big omission of the dodgiest title, *Imperator* as a *praenomen* (from 40 BCE); see Carter 1982: 96; Wardle 2014 *ad loc.* Wallace-Hadrill 2016 brings the possible power dynamics behind the naming ceremony to life.

35. Wallace-Hadrill 2016: 266; although the original etymologizing belongs to the Augustan scholar Verrius Flaccus, not Suetonius (Todisco 2007: 446–448).

36. Cf. Ziogas 2015: 117; on the relationship of "Augustus" to *auctoritas,* see Lowrie 2009: 298.

37. Cf. Wallace-Hadrill 2016: 264.

38. On the importance of the seal for authentication, see Higbie 2017: 176–177.

39. The sphinx ring was notoriously distributive of Augustan presence, because he supposedly had two of them and sometimes outsourced the signature (Plin. *NH* 37.10).

40. Wardle 2014 *ad loc.* is agnostic on how far this was an Augustan innovation. If Cicero's correspondence is a guide to practice, time and date stamping was much patchier pre-Augustus.

41. Gunderson (2014: 135) notes Augustus' very Suetonian interest in textual criticism here. For a more sinister resonance to this act of book burning, see Ziogas 2015: 123. Augustus' editorial activities are already flourishing in the *Julius* (see *Julius* 56; Wallace-Hadrill 1983: 82).

42. An extension of republican practice (see Wardle 2014 *ad loc.*).

43. On the role of such anonymous criticism in the *Caesars,* see Slater 2014 (cf. Zadorojnyi 2010 on political graffiti under the principate); Del Giovane, forthcoming.

44. For speculation on what material form these *libelli* might take (perhaps papyrus slips), see Slater 2014: 295.

45. Although Wardle (2014 *ad loc.*) invokes Ulpian *Dig.* 47.10.5.9 to suggest that this senatorial decree was an extension of the *lex Cornelia de iniuriis,* covering both anonymous and pseudonymous libel.

46. Cf. Rutledge 2001: 43. Peirano (2012: 46–47) combines these kinds of *libelli* with the phenomenon of publishing poems in someone else's name.

47. As Eck (1984: 136) points out, this Augustan/Tiberian modesty differs from later imperial practice, e.g., Septimius Severus and Caracalla naming themselves as Pantheon rebuilders.

48. And perhaps a full-scale generalization based on those moments: see Wardle 2014 *ad loc.*

49. I wonder if the verses might even be hinted to come from Augustus' self-erased tragedy (see Ziogas 2015: 120).

50. Wardle (2014 *ad loc.*) thinks the "forced use of πυρούμενον" also throws him off the scent.

51. Cf. Langlands 2014: 127 on Augustus' ultimate loss of control over his own exemplum, as the vicissitudes of the future take over.

52. See Geue, forthcoming.

53. The thinning of the *Caesars'* quality as they go is a stubborn commonplace of Suetonian scholarship: Goodyear 1982: 662; Wallace-Hadrill 1983: 61–62.

54. For the staging of the problem of biographical knowledge in the story of the Domitian's assassination, see Ash 2016; the *Domitian* in general raises the issue of inaccessible knowledge (Hulls 2014: 192–193, 195–196). Indeed, the limits of knowing the true content of an emperor might be behind Suetonius' multiangle technique of arrangement by rubric (Edwards 2000: xxv); cf. Wallace-Hadrill's (1983: 17) remark about the opacity of political life under autocracy.

55. These are aspects now well on their way to being handled with care: see Slater 2014; Del Giovane, forthcoming; on the role of rumor and gossip in a near contemporary (Tacitus), see Hardie 2012: 285–299.

56. For a similar breakdown of the two forms of source material, see Wallace-Hadrill 1983: 61–65.

57. On which, see Langlands 2014.

58. See Slater 2014: 298. Where there's anonymity, there are attribution attempts: for a list, see Wardle 2014 *ad loc.* These attempts are bunk: their value as Suetonian evidence of contemporary gossip inheres in their anonymity.

59. On the burgeoning authority of handwritten documents under the principate—and the new potential for forgery—see Higbie 2017: 175.

60. Straight from deep in the imperial archives. For the likely existence of such letter collections and Suetonius' access, see Louis 2010: 459.

61. Suetonius favors the Augustan letter as source over other supposed first-person Augustan writing (Slater 2008: 257); Augustan letters are a striking form of primary evidence deployed all over the first three lives (Goodyear 1982: 662; cf. Wallace-Hadrill 1983: 91). Augustus may have been sui generis in the volume of private correspondence produced in his own hand (Millar 1977: 215).

62. At least in terms of his mixed posthumous reception; see Champlin 2003: 1–35.

63. Wallace-Hadrill, for example, calls the *Vespasian*'s detail "extraordinarily thin" (1983: 61) and the *Titus* "one of the weakest, marred by uncritical panegyric" (1983: 177).

64. Contra Tatum (2014: 176), who reads Titus' forgery as enabling him to copycat a good model of princeps.

65. Note the contrast with Nero's crackdown on forgery (*Nero* 17).

66. The majority of emperor quotation in the Flavian lives is in the form of the casual, oral remark; the only written material quoted is a short excerpt from Domitian's *On Haircare* (*Domitian* 18).

67. See Damon 2014: 40.

2. Tongue Ties

1. The *Ibis'* qualifications as Ovidian are no longer seriously in question, but for a counterposition, identifying the work as a later pastiche, see Herrmann 1965.

2. I note here only that one of the *Ibis'* only marks in its limited reception history is on Martial *Ep.* 7.12, a poem complaining that other poets have written aggressive iambics in Martial's name (for brilliant discussion of the connection, see Hawkins 2014: 82–86). Oblique hints toward the *Ibis* as an act of pseudepigraphy?

3. General attempts to find method in the catalogic madness of this poem have been flung far forward by the work of Krasne (2012, 2016). This chapter tries to build on her wonderful comments regarding the function of name suppression in particular (2012: 44–83) by documenting a broader relationship between names and power. As Krasne notes, the Ibidic "rhetoric of *nomina*" puts it somewhere between the *Tristia*'s full anonymity and the *Ex Ponto*'s greater "onomastic freedom" (2012: 48)—I shall try to say roughly *where*. For the generalizing effects of name suppression in *Tr.* 4.2, cf. Lowrie 2009: 267.

4. On the connection, see Zipfel 1910; Watson 1991. La Penna (1957: xxvii–xxix) links *Ibis* more to the practice of *devotio*. But see Schiesaro 2011: 129–131 on the problems with tying too tight a knot between ritual and poem here.

5. A named victim is also the norm in iambus (another major generic flirtation of the *Ibis*); see Hawkins 2014: 40.

6. See Watson 1991: 204–205; Williams 1996: 10, 44; Schiesaro 2011: 81; Krasne 2012: 45. In fact, the act of naming was crucial to many forms of religious, legal, and political document: see Meyer 2004: 64.

7. The cloud of antonomasia is a general condition of the *Ibis,* one of its most striking special effects—which has been its most prolific generator of scholarship (see Schiesaro 2011: 81–82; Krasne 2012: 1–2).

8. The decision to adopt a pseudonym has unleashed hellish forces of scholarly imagination: see Williams 1996: 17–23 for the identification debate. I prefer to read Ibis as "flexible catch-all" (see Hawkins 2014: 72n93), in the Housmanian tradition of "Ibis as Nobody" (see Housman 1920: 316; Williams 1996: 18–23). I also wonder whether the namelessness could be taken as a generalizing device to stall the possibility of spring-back, à la Ahl's (1984) "figured speech."

9. For example in Hermesianax *Leontion.* For this feature of learned catalog poetry, see also Heslin 2011; Ziogas 2013. Thanks to the anonymous reviewer for pointing this / these out.

10. For this "name economy" in the exile poetry, see Nagle 1980: 77–82; Oliensis 1997.

11. Cf. Oliensis 1997: 185–186 on the centrality of Ovid's name in *Tristia.*

12. Cf. the Introduction. Ironically, the *Met.* is one poem that forgoes Ovid's self-naming in favor of an extravagant naming of others (cf. Butler 2015: 70, 75).

13. Krasne (2012: 75–77) also notes the power of name deprivation as a way to strip fame; cf.; Oliensis 1997: 190; Schiesaro 2011: 138. This is why there are problems with Williams' (1997: e.g., 16–17, 22–23) gestures to built-in futility and/or ineffectiveness in the poem. We needn't think of it so much as a failed curse poem but as a poem whose major curse consists precisely in the stripping of the name.

14. The *Ibis'* poetics of iambic self-harm is everywhere in recent scholarship, trading on clues in the poem that Ovid is his own worst enemy (embodied conveniently in the cryptic self-smearing of the *Ibis-sibi* mirror effect). The approach is typified by Krasne (2012: 84–95; cf. Krasne 2016: 164, taking cues from Hinds 1999: 65 and Hinds 2007: 206). See also Rosen 1988: 295–296; Hawkins 2014: 75–76. Rimell (2015: 308) explores the wish of exile and dismemberment, i.e., Ovid's own fate transferred to Ibis, and lands on a similar conclusion about Ibis as Ovid's "ghost of himself" (312–313). Hawkins (2014: 77) adds an overdue twist: the *Ibis'* function (following its eponymous bird) is also self-healing.

15. On the contrast between Ovid's and Ibis' nominal conduct here, see Williams 1996: 20–21.

16. Text OCT; translation is my own.

17. The principle of *nomen tacebo* meshes with the identical phrase of an undisclosed enemy at *Tr.* 4.9.1 (see Gordon 1992 *ad loc.*); in this, the *Ibis* takes its cue from the *Tristia* strand more generally (on which, see Oliensis 1997). On *quisquis is est* as marker of Ibis' flexibility, see Williams 1996: 20, 63.

18. On Ovid's consistent gestures toward Ibis' true name, without ever letting it slip, see Gordon 1992 *ad loc.*

19. Schiesaro 2011: 84–85.

20. The name Ibis is designedly multireferential, folding out into an Egyptian bird as well as a Callimachean poem (Schiesaro 2011: 104).

21. In Krasne's (2012: n2) convenient division of scholarly camps into "identity-theorists" (Williams 1996: 20), i.e., those who seek to pin Ibis to a definite target, and Housmanians, who see Ibis as an empty vessel (a "Nobody"; Housman 1920: 316), I voluntarily enroll as a Housmanian. But that isn't to say I take *Ibis* as an idle exercise in hyperbole. It has a lot to tell us about the dynamics of poetry as an antireferential phenomenon.

22. The designator *de tribus . . . una soror* bridges vaguely between Furies and *Parcae*: see Gordon 1992 *ad loc.* The intra-Ovidian bolt brought out by Ellis and La Penna (*e tribus una soror, Met.* 10.313) might actually tip us more toward one of the Eumenides.

23. Although it could still be a Fury speaking and a hard adversative *at* only moving us on to Clotho at 243 (Gordon 1992 *ad loc.*).

24. Cf. the infamous *Aeneid* preproem (with Peirano 2013: 273–274); Ovid *Tristia* 4.10.1. On the role of *ille ego* in the Ovidian corpus, see Farrell 2004: 47–52; Volk 2005; and in Calpurnius Siculus, see Chapter 6. The formula is an Ovidian favorite (*Met.* 1.757, 4.226, 15.500; *Tr.* 4.5.12); see Gordon 1992 *ad loc.*

25. Housman 1920: 298, of Prometheus in line 291.

26. Cf. Chapter 3.

27. Cf. Gordon 1992 *ad loc.*

28. For the flexible traditions on their names, see Gordon 1992 *ad* 269–270. For another connection between these myths (some versions made Phineus the son of Phoenix), see Gordon 1992 *ad* 263–264.

29. The name choice also spotlights the particular version of the myth that Ovid is telescoping: only father-son relations here; no mention of a faulty stepmother (see Gordon 1992 *ad loc.*).

30. Again, as with the Phinides, the wicked stepmother is written out of the myth (see Gordon 1992 *ad loc.*).

31. Elena Giusti *per litteras* points out to me that the huge number here is also an "intertextual clue," part of the gigantic "exercise" in intertextuality that is *Ibis*. My primarily intratextual reading risks losing some of that force. I would only add that the intertextuality of the *Ibis* is often not of the "targeted" allusion kind; as with the target Ibis itself, the vague phrasing allows multiple reference to several versions of the myth at hand, rather than any one manifestation thereof.

32. Thrown even more into relief by the fact that other Latin poets tended not to name him (Gordon 1992 *ad loc.*).

33. Although the compression here could take us equally well to the myth of Hercules going mad and killing his children (see Gordon 1992 *ad loc.*). And we should keep in mind that Hercules' death was also his apotheosis.

34. Hercules as victor is unnamed here too of course. But while those who have the upper hand are often anonymized, they win a direct name more often than the poem's victims.

35. Manuscripts and scholia branch out on the variants here (for the list, see Gordon 1992 *ad loc.*). Erechthides is Ellis' (1881) conjecture (who also follows codex T in reading *victus* for *quintus*). Gordon (1992) and La Penna (1957) prefer to stick with *Echecratides* and *quintus*.

36. The name Antaeus has special charge insofar as Ovid is his only namer in Augustan poetry, apart from a one-off in Propertius (3.22.10); see Gordon 1992 *ad loc.*

37. For discussion of the nameless "wife" in the *Tristia*, cf. Henderson 1997.

38. Schiesaro (2011: 82–83) rightly notes how remarkable it is that Augustus goes unnamed here. For Ibis-as-Augustus readings, see Casali 1997; Schiesaro 2011; Hawkins 2014: 72.

39. E.g., *Am.* 1.15.13; *Tr.* 2.367, 5.38.

40. On homonymy as target-blurring tactic, see Krasne 2012: 50.

41. On the legal term *transcribere*, see Gordon 1992 *ad loc.*

42. Gordon (1992) notes that Sisyphus is the only sinner named here but leaves it at that.

43. Gordon 1992 *ad* 501–502.

44. See Gordon 1992 *ad loc.*

45. Cf. also Cinna at 539–540. Could this also put an iambic slant on the name Battus here?

46. Although the last two, Pterelas and Nisus, aren't involved in incest, they are still the "victims" of their own flesh and blood (betrayed by their daughters).

47. On the problems of identifying Hipponax here, see Hawkins 2014: 42. Krasne (2016: 169) thinks it likely due to the iambic thematics in this section.

48. Rosen (1988: 295) reads *Athenin* with La Penna (1957) and even thinks the obscure *frater Medusae* of 447 could be Athenis too (293).

49. The latter's name is kenned in *tutatus* (Hector = "keeper" in Greek); see Gordon 1992 *ad loc.*

50. Gordon 1992 *ad loc.*

51. Krasne (2012: 58–71) is excellent on the homonymous fuzz in all these cases. On the Pyrrhi, see also Williams 1996: 94.

52. And there are a lot of them in harm's way: see Schiesaro 2011: 124; Krasne 2012: 68–71; Rimell 2015: 311.

53. Housman (1920) restored the manuscript's *conditor* (and so understood Cinna) in favor of the scholiasts' *cognitor* (i.e., Cinyras, father of Myrrha)—and that fits the context a treat.

54. See Krasne 2012: 75. On Cinna's programmatic importance as poet-victim, see Hinds 2007: 206; Schiesaro 2011: 125; Krasne 2012: 82; Krasne 2016: 176.

55. For this asymmetry of named Remus to omitted Romulus (reversing the usual pattern of repressing the victim of the fratricide), see Krasne 2012: 95.

56. On the *Ibis'* messing with temporality, see Williams 1996: 101; Hinds 1999: 62; Rimell 2015: 315–317. On the hyperbolic tendency toward infinity, see Schiesaro 2011: 135–137.

57. See Geue and Giusti, forthcoming.

58. Taking up the *quicumque es* of line 5; see Schiesaro 2011: 97.

59. Cf. Rimell 2015: 313.

60. I print the manuscript G's *qua*, not *quod* here; and *ei* for *et*.

61. Various forms of indefinite are common to many examples collected in J. Miller 1980.

62. Williams (1996: 41–42) thinks the exhaustiveness undercuts the appeal by exposing Ovid's desperation and isolation. But it is also about fomenting scatter-shot warfare.

63. See Miller 1980.

64. *Quisquis ades* works "part of a traditional formula"; see Gordon 1992 *ad loc.* The phrase also takes up Tibullus' birthday prayer for Cornutus (Tibullus 2.2.2; see Williams 1996: 44).

65. The modulation between singular and plural is fairly common in poetic ritual management (see Miller 1980 on Callimachus and the *Fasti*) but is particularly jarring here.

66. Cf. also 26, 117, 130, 160, 180 (twice), 419, 423.

67. See Chapter 5.

68. On the *quisquis-quidquid* connection and the "multiplicity of Ovidian role-play," see Williams 1996: 64.

69. This move also sends Ovid and Ibis into a tailspin-lock of eternal enmity that pivots off Ovid's spiriting away into the pervasive ether, his transformation into a *nomen indelebile,* and general liberation from bodily constraint at the end of the *Met.* (thanks to Elena Giusti for reminding me).

70. This too parallels Ovid's rocket trip (*super alta perennis/astra ferar, Met.* 15.875–876) into the stratosphere at the end of the *Met.* (all Elena Giusti, again).

71. For the *Ibis* as a bid for recovery of power and voice in exile, see Hawkins 2014: 62.

72. See note 6 above.

73. Williams (1996: e.g., 87, 128–129) is generally brilliant on the *Ibis'* claims to endlessness and omnipotence. I would only dissent from him insofar as he imposes a limiting futility to the poem (e.g., 129), where I see a swollen assertion of poetic power.

3. A Play without Names

1. On the destructive effects of the play's anonymity, see Goldberg 2003: 26–27; cf. Taylor 2010: 207.

2. On Salutati's initial suspicions toward the play's Senecan authorship, see Goldberg 2003: 14–17. For a summary of historical and stylistic arguments against Senecan authorship, see Goldberg 2003: 18–19; Boyle 2008: xiv–xv. For the historical arguments at length, see Carbone 1977. It's worthwhile remembering that the positive evidence for Senecan authorship is extremely flimsy *even for the "secure" tragedies* (Kohn 2003). For the general similarities and differences between *Octavia* and Senecan tragedy, see Poe 1989; Ferri 2003: 31–53 (a helpful list of verbal overlaps at Ferri 2003: 91–95). Ginsberg (2017) is a welcome crack at moving the intertextual conversations beyond Seneca, toward Augustan literature (see 8–10).

3. Although scholars still struggle with the idea that an *ignotus* can write something good: e.g., G. Harrison 2003: 112.

4. Ferri (2003: 16) puts the *terminus post quem* to the middle Flavian period (after the histories of Pliny and Fabius were out and about), with special likelihood reserved for the Vespasianic period due to its Claudian turn (16); but he also tracks possible references to Statius' *Silvae,* shunting a likely date forward to the 90s (17–26). Boyle (2008: xiv–vi; cf. J. Smith 2003: 427–429) prefers the early Vespasianic years, an argument fully worked out at Ginsberg 2017: 190–194 (for a convenient summary of dating positions, see 182n6). Kragelund (1982: 53–54) thinks it chimes with Galban republicanism (cf. Barnes 1982). For a Trajanic suggestion, see Runchina 1977–1978. The proportion of scholarship devoted to this question is immense and is still miles from consensus. I am consciously trying to give the *Octavia* a breather from it.

5. Wilson 2003: 63. For the continuing health of the *praetexta* tradition (and the unhelpfulness of the category), see Wiseman 2008: 194–199.

6. Still the questions of the lion's share of recent scholarship on *Octavia*. The tide is turning, however (see Ginsberg 2017: 4–5).

7. For the play's moments of "timelessness," especially applied to civil war, cf. Ginsberg 2017: 176, 178.

8. The effects of collapsed time have been well covered in an intertextual sense by Ginsberg 2017; my focus will be more on intratextual patterning.

9. In which capacity Ginsberg 2017 has now put it to good use.

10. Another possible effect of the *Octavia*'s anonymity is its underscoring of the already considerable thematic of causative forces governing the universe, which are beyond human ken (on which, see Boyle 2008: lxxiii).

11. The act of self-naming is almost constitutive of the Senecan theatrical self: see Fitch and McElduff 2002: 24–25.

12. See Boyle 2008 *ad* 71.

13. Cf. J. Smith 2003: 397–398.

14. For the namelessness (and placelessness) of declamation, and its mythic effects, see Beard 1993: 61–62. Dickey (2002: 246) notes how strange these declamatory interactions are, featuring e.g. "fathers addressing nameless sons."

15. The speech also doubles up on Octavia's opening material (and prepares for the wider pattern of duplication to come)—see Boyle 2008 *ad loc.*

16. Text from Fitch 2004 (2018); translation is my own.

17. On the various substrates of the common "sister-wife" combination used for Octavia in the play (Egyptian queen; Juno; Caligula's incest), see Boyle 2008 *ad loc.*

18. If Fitch (2004 [2018]) is right to print Peiper's *ardent* and take *mariti* in the adjectival sense. Ferri (2003) adopts Gronovius' *ardet maritus, mutua flagrant face.* Boyle (2008) opts for the manuscripts' reading.

19. *Nefas/nefandus* comes up sixteen times in the play. On *nefas* in Senecan tragedy, see Schiesaro 2003: 36–45 and *passim;* Mowbray 2012; Hanford 2014: 166–232. For the specific civil war literature valence of the term, see Ginsberg 2017: 116–117. The local effect of *nefandum* here also makes the *scelus* into any number of possibilities (e.g., Nero's marriage to Poppaea; or worry for Octavia's prospective assassination of Nero); see Ferri 2003 *ad loc.* and Boyle 2008.

20. See J. Smith 2003: 393n10, 397–400. A related question is why major characters like Seneca aren't identified upon entering (see Ferri 2003: 57–58; Van Noorden 2014: 271).

21. For other female mythological paradigms boiling under Octavia, see Ginsberg 2017: 53–58 (especially Dido).

22. For a deep intertextual reading of Octavia's Pompeian identity here, see Ginsberg 2017: 26–30; on the *nomen* to which Octavia is nodding here (Claudia? Caesar?), see Ginsberg 2017: 30–31. See also Buckley 2012: 149–150. J. Smith (2003: 399) reads Octavia's meaning here as "last member of her family."

23. Cf. Boyle 2008 *ad loc.* on the pointedly non-Senecan resonance here.

24. It is also applied to Octavia herself six times. See Boyle 2008 *ad* 25. For the Didonic ring of *miseranda,* see Ginsberg 2017: 55.

25. Cf. 110, 250, 899, 959. The ghost of Agrippina agrees (610, 620).

26. Cf. *infandae necis,* 114.

27. The anonymized collocation *fratrem ademptum* allows for a powerful wormhole with Catullus' brother (*frater adempte mihi,* Cat. 68.20, 92; 101.6); see Ferri 2003 *ad loc.* and Boyle 2008.

28. For the play's anomalous treatment of Acte, see Goldberg 2003: 22–23.

29. For the redefinition here, cf. Wilson 2003: 80–81.

30. The direct naming also reeks of a curse; see Boyle 2008 *ad loc.*

31. For the chorus' attempt to make Octavia into father's daughter as a way of breaking her relation to Nero, see J. Smith 2003: 408 (cf. 425–426). For the ironic

use of the name Claudia, see Boyle 2008 *ad* 71. Boyle 2008 *ad loc.* also points to the political charge of *Claudia proles* in the context of illegitimacy (*Nero inisitivus*).

32. Boyle 2008 *ad loc.* notes that Caesar is pinned to Nero only twice more in the play—once by Nero himself (457), the other by Poppaea's nurse (694).

33. This is a more charitable way of reading the play's sparing and repetitious language, which Fitch (2004 [2018]: 520) writes off as mediocrity or monotony (cf. Ferri 2003: 26: "second-rate and undistinguished poet"; Boyle [2008: lxii] is only slightly more diplomatic). For the formulaic style, see Ferri 2003: 34–39. Most of the play's avowed admirers deplore its clichés and commonplaces to the point of critical commonplace (see, e.g., Poe 1989: 435; Goldberg 2003: 32–36; even the otherwise enthusiastic Boyle 2008, on lines 245–251, 321, 396, and 890); sometimes I wonder whether these judgments are informed primarily by the play's orphan status. For more appreciative collaboration with the repetitions, see Ginsberg 2011.

34. Wilson 2003: 72; cf. Ginsberg 2017: 86 on Seneca's tendency to "speak timelessly" here. The play veers in general to working with abstract personifications such as Roma and Fortuna (see Wilson 2003); so abstract agents are named alongside the nameless human agents.

35. See Ginsberg 2017: 82 (and her note 73, with bibliography).

36. Wilson 2003: 72.

37. The quick-fire exchange between Nero and Prefect is also meant to cut through Seneca's "meandering verbiage" immediately before this (Boyle 2008 *ad loc.*).

38. As Boyle 2008 *ad loc.* registers, the scene begins with Nero's naming, ends with Seneca's—with no such names in between.

39. On Nero's incredible entrance here, which "indexes to whom the world belongs," see Boyle 2008: lxviii (and on Plautus's and Sulla's heads served up as indices of tyranny, see Boyle 2008 *ad loc.*).

40. Nero's linguistic counterblows go hand in hand with his rewriting of the Senecan version of Augustan memory here: see Ginsberg 2017: 89–90. Nero also knows which Senecan sources to mine (i.e., the tragedies, not the philosophy; J. Smith 2003: 411; Buckley 2012: 135–136). Taylor (2010: 214–215) reads this scene as Nero beating Seneca at his own game (qua philosopher and tragedian).

41. Cf. Ferri 2003: 70–73; Goldberg 2003: 23; Taylor 2010: 215; Buckley 2012: 134, 140; Van Noorden 2014: 278.

42. See G. Harrison 2003: 121. As Poe (1989: 450) points out, the Warner figure is usually a nobody; Seneca playing this role is a little jarring. On the implications of the play's two-figure scenes (one superior, one subordinate) for its view of power, see J. Smith 2003: 416.

43. For Seneca's sanitized version of history culled from key Augustan texts such as the *Aeneid* and the *Res Gestae,* see Ginsberg 2017: 72.

44. Nero raises the terror that Augustan history suppressed: see Ginsberg 2017: 95.

45. For the other Sulla in the proscriptive background here, see Buckley 2012: 143.

46. Ginsberg 2017 (chapters 2 and 3) reads the Seneca-Nero contretemps as a battle for the memory of Augustus.

47. Add to that *patres* playing on senators as well as neutral "fathers"; see Boyle 2008 *ad loc.*

48. One way in which Nero tortures the *Res Gestae* script deployed by Seneca (on which, see Ginsberg 2017: 71–77).

49. Zwierlein 1986 (plugged by Fitch and Ferri) posited a two-line lacuna after 590, in which Poppaea and the future heir were named. But this completely misses the *Octavia*'s habits and patterns of name suppression.

50. On the referential overlap with Octavia's use of *tyrannus* (and particularly *ferus tyrannus*, 959), see Boyle 2008 *ad loc.*

51. See note 55 below on the connection with memory sanctions. None of these treatments point out that the suppression of names in texts makes for a kind of visual equivalent to the scratched-out names of *abolitio*, where the visibility of the removal, the absent-presence, is the point: see Meyer 2004: 34–35 and Flower 2006: xxii.

52. Boyle 2008 *ad 609–612.*

53. See Ginsberg 2017: 36 (and Boyle 2008 *ad loc.*).

54. *Parvulus* harks back to Dido's wish that Aeneas had left her a little live memento (*Aeneid* 4.328–329); on this connection, see Buckley 2012: 138; Ginsberg 2017: 57.

55. Flower (2006: 202) remarks on the *Octavia*'s rarity as an artifact that both discusses memory sanctions and is itself an example of one (full discussion of its function as a blackener of Nero-memory at 202–208; see also Kragelund 1982: 53). For the play's relationship to other memory sanctions performed on historical imperial women, see Ginsberg 2017: 168–175.

56. Some readers would identify the *coniugis* of 655 as Poppaea (see Ferri 2003 *ad loc.*)—so could *famulae* not be a scathing gloss on the new bride?

57. Cf. *Claudia proles, 278.* And see Boyle 2008 *ad 671–672* (he also points out that simple Octavia is her only name in the *Acta Fratrum Arvalium*, which throws the play's suppression of that name into higher intensity).

58. *Diri . . . Neronis* and *Poppaea* undo the indirection of *nostri . . . principis* (277) and *nova coniunx* (276) in the first choral ode (see Boyle 2008 *ad 671–672*).

59. On the ambiguity here, see Carbone 1977: 57–61. He argues that the throat is Nero's, and Ferri (2003 *ad loc.*) agrees. Kragelund (1982: 13, 35) reads the ambiguity as deliberate (Boyle 2008 *ad loc.* goes with him).

60. Boyle 2008 *ad loc.*

61. Ferri 2003 *ad loc.* and Boyle 2008 *ad loc.* think Britannicus; Fitch (2004 [2018]), Nero.

62. Boyle 2008 *ad loc.* rightly fingers the same collocation used of the elder Agrippina at 935 (*clarum nomen*).

63. For the dating implications of taking this as Nero's throat, see Carbone 1977: 59–63.

64. For the nurse's clever rewrite of *condere* according to a different reading of the *Aeneid* here, see Ginsberg 2017: 53.

65. I print manuscript A's *furore* over Grotius' conjecture *favore* (slipped in by most modern editors)—the responsion with 785 and 827 is too strong to resist (for more valiant defense, see Boyle 2008 *ad loc.*).

66. Cf. Boyle 2008 *ad loc.*

67. As Boyle 2008 *ad loc.* singles out, Nero never refers to Octavia by either of her two names in this play (Claudia or Octavia).

68. Boyle 2008 *ad loc.*

69. On the anonymity of the prefect, see Ginsberg 2017: 138n70. Flower (2006: 205, positing a date very soon after Nero's death) assumes that the prefect (i.e., Tigellinus) has to be redacted, because he's in the audience! Ferri 2003 *ad loc.* wants to read Faenius Rufus into the nameless prefect here. Kragelund (1988: 498–453) says Tigellinus. Manuwald (2003: 54) thinks the prefect's anonymity throws Seneca's importance more into relief.

70. Boyle 2008 *ad loc.*

71. Joining Plautus and Sulla at 469 (Boyle 2008 *ad loc.*).

72. Boyle 2008 *ad loc.* responds to the blanking by making sure we know that the referent of these three adjectives is Octavia.

73. On Octavia's primarily passive role in the play, see Harrison 2003: 118–119.

74. The absent name here makes this categorically different to Boyle's (2008 *ad loc.*) "monumental feel"—it is a monument with only relational titles and no individual to anchor them.

75. As to which chorus (cf. note 84 below) speaks these lines, see Harrison 2003: 120; J. Smith (2003: 419) takes the indeterminacy of which chorus as a kind of unifier confirming the success of Nero's fearmongering.

76. For repetition as the play's "essential rhythm," see J. Smith 2003: 404–405.

77. Cf. Ferri 2003 and Boyle 2008 *ad loc.*; Ginsberg 2017: 177.

78. See note 4 above.

79. On the play's politics, I side more or less with Fitch 2004 (2018): 517: "the play's sympathies are fully aligned with Octavia and the Roman people, and against the emperor whom it portrays as their oppressor." Ferri (2003: 70–75) devotes his section on the politics of the play solely to its revisionist position on Seneca. For a floundering attempt at reading a more positive Nero, and less positive Octavia, see Garson 1975.

80. For the continuing live importance of Nero's memory after his death, see Champlin 2003: 1–35; Flower 2006: 199–201.

81. For the negative reaction of the lower classes to Nero's death, see Tacitus *Hist.* 1.4.

82. On the question of the play's performability, Goldberg (2003: 30) pushes for private recitation; cf. Ferri 2003: 2–3, 55–61; Harrison 2003: 113. Boyle (2008: xli) plumps for performance, with strong arguments also in J. Smith 2003, Flower 2006: 202–208, and the classic Wiseman 2008: 200–209 (cf. 198). Kragelund (2015) also adds to the chorus pushing performance. Ginsberg (2017: 16–17) is agnostic, interested as she is in textual dynamics.

83. See Manuwald 2003: 55 (cf. 2001: 292–296, 323–331); Wilson 2003: 62; Boyle 2008: lxii–iii; Fitch 2004 (2018): 514. For the civil-war-magnitude strife between chorus and emperor, see Ginsberg 2017: 115–140.

84. For a brilliant reading of the play's bifurcated chorus as a dramaturgic sublimation of civil strife, see Ginsberg 2017: 141–179 (she collects dissenting voices who push for one chorus at 141n1). For discussion of dual-chorus precedents, see Harrison 2003: 117.

85. Cf. Flower (2006: 205–206), who acknowledges the choral voice's centrality: "a voice that is as significant as that of Seneca or Nero himself." For a less cheering assessment of the primary chorus, see Ginsberg 2017: 154.

86. Galimberti and Ramelli 2001.

87. Ginsberg's (2017) approach to the play.

88. Cf. Wilson 2003: 74–75: the Octavia "is about transhistorical values, about the immortal." On the timelessness of Roman exempla in general, and their resistance to "historicist" views of the past, see Roller 2019: 17–23.

89. The play's name suppression as generalizing force, its interest in speaking for and about a "people," may have had deep roots in the republican tradition, particularly Cato's anonymized Origines (see Shearin 2015: 138–140, and earlier, in the introduction to Part I).

4. Phaedrus by Name

1. E.g., on the different tones Horace's body assumes, depending on the generic context, see Farrell 2007.

2. I speak in terms of the continuing dominance of persona approaches; most literary scholars in Classics stick to the realm of the imagined and fictional, rather than the "real." For a brilliant recent critique of this model applied to the history of lyric, see Culler 2015.

3. Although even that last fixed point can be questioned: see Fitton Brown 1985.

4. Cf. the Introduction and Chapter 2.

5. His self-marginalization seems to have worked so well as to shut him out of literary and scholarly history with barely a register: see Henderson 2001b: 65; Jennings 2009: 248; Lefkowitz 2016: 506. Cf. Geue 2017 on Juvenal.

6. Although even this claim is suspected nowadays, in preference for Phaedrian virtuosity from day one: see note 20 below.

7. We have no idea who the patrons named in Phaedrus were (Henderson 2001b: 69–70), which is why I sense that they may not exist; for some conjectures, see Bloomer 1997: 102.

8. As Lefkowitz (2016: 491) says, Phaedrus' persona is now treated as a fiction, just like any other Latin poet's. I would rather he be bumped up into a category all his own—degree, perhaps, rather than kind. But degree matters. As Jennings (2009: 231) says, "We know nothing about Phaedrus that is not projected by his persona"—not without precedent in antiquity but a rare condition nonetheless.

9. On trying to be Hesiod, for example, see Higbie 2017: 142.

10. Peirano 2012 (on posing as famous names, see esp. 49–53). Peirano discusses Phaedrus' use of Aesop's name in this way at 51–52. For a nice categorization of the various types of ancient fake, and the motives behind them, see Speyer 1971:

131–149. On fakes and forgeries in general, see Grafton 1990; Ruthven 2001; Higbie 2017.

11. For Phaedrus' investment in remaining outsider, beyond the mainstream Latin literary history, see Lefkowitz 2016: 505.

12. As with all the *anonymi* of this book, Phaedrus has copped his share of identity speculation and date guesstimates. Champlin 2005 is the outstanding case of sleuth work, beaming his x-ray goggles through the mask of the Augustan freedman to find a legally minded member of the Roman elite below. Cf. now Sciarrino 2010, who brilliantly pushes the political implications of positing an elite Wizard of Oz behind Phaedrus. Many other scholars take the freedman of Augustus claim (given in the manuscript's *titulus,* not text) seriously: Bloomer 1997: 75. While my argument rests on Champlin's basic contention that there was probably no such historical being as Phaedrus, I leave the private investigator role to him. Regarding dates, Champlin plumps for a post-Tiberian date (102: between 43–70); Sciarrino (2010: 232–233) provisionally agrees. But Phaedrus works well in multiple periods (Polt 2014: 186). Henderson (2001b: 11–15) is up front about unknowability but also shows how we need to think with the particular pins of "historicality" (12) that Phaedrus chooses to give us (e.g., the fall of Sejanus).

13. Kurke 2011: 3–4.

14. The two are related in their anonymity and mobility, if not identical: see Goldhill 2009: 100–102.

15. See e.g. Kurke 2011: 8–10 on the *Life of Aesop* as "the accretion of multiple acts and agents." Cf. Holzberg 1993: 11.

16. Phaedrus follows suit in largely avoiding spatio-temporal coordinates for his fables, with the marked exception of the Roman anecdotes (Polt 2014: 166; cf. Henderson 2001b: 11–15).

17. Text from Perry 1965; translations are my own.

18. Cf. Geue 2018a.

19. Of course the whole thing is complicated by the ape's status as stand-in for imitation itself (see Connors 2004).

20. The claim is common in recent scholarship: see Henderson 2001b: 64; Libby 2010: 546, 550–551; Lefkowitz 2016: 499–500. Polt (2014: 163) reads the independent spirit as there from the beginning; cf. Cavarzere 2001: 206, Lefkowitz 2017: 418.

21. A prime example is Horace vis-à-vis Lucilius in Horace's *Satires:* see Cavarzere 2001: 207; Park 2017: 55–56.

22. Cf. Glauthier 2009: 255–256, and 255n26.

23. For the importance of Virgil as high-poet background noise against which Phaedrus pipes his tune of marginality, see Lefkowitz 2016.

24. For the Ovidian pattern here, see Jennings 2009: 239.

25. Henderson 2001b: 73–79.

26. Horace is in general a master presence behind Phaedrus: see Cavarzere 2001: 207; Champlin 2003: 109–110, 117–120; Glauthier 2009: 254–255; Lefkowitz 2016: 490; Park 2017: 148–231.

27. Or not so particular: as Henderson (2001b: 66–67) points out, this slave name was a dime a dozen: "is the very unplaceability of the *libertus* exactly the

trademark of his cultural significance?" For some sport with "identifying" him, including Caligula's charioteer and freedman, see Henderson 2001b: 70–71.

28. Cf. Henderson 2001b: 66.

29. We could picture this moment as an extended front-ending sphragis—the authorial equipment charged with the most authenticity (see de la Durantaye 2007: 38–39) and often a play zone for fakery (see Peirano 2013).

30. *Nasonis* at *Ex P.* 2.4.1, 4.16.1; *Naso* at 1.1.1, 1.3.1, 1.5.2, 1.10.1, 2.2.2, 2.5.1, 2.6.2, 2.11.2, 3.1.3, 3.4.2, 3.5.4, 3.6.1, 4.3.10, 4.9.2, 4.15.2; *Nasonem* 1.7.4, 2.10.2, 4.6.2; *Nasone* 1.8.1.

31. Cf. Hor. *Sat.* 2.1.19–20.

32. Henderson 2001b: 60.

33. Henderson 2001b: 61.

34. For the Ovidian tones of the autobiographical event here, cf. Bloomer 1997: 105.

35. Cf. Glauthier 2009: 268.

36. See particularly Henderson 2001b: 57–92.

37. For other Phaedrian epimythia with a similar charge, see Lefkowitz 2017: 425–426. Cf. also Oliensis 1997: 174–175 on antonomasia in Ovid *Tr.* 1.5 bearing out the same effect.

38. On the Ovidian decline pose, see Williams 1994: 50–99.

39. Hence, as Jennings (2009: 238) has it, "We have been excluded from understanding."

40. For that, and other, ways to construe Phaedrus' name, see Henderson 2001b: 69, 74.

41. On the rhetorical functions of plagiarism claims, see Seo 2009; McGill 2012.

42. Fable 1.15. Polt (2014: 184) identifies a Cynic-stoic ethics of quietism at play here. On Phaedrus' general push for resignation before power, see Champlin 2005: 123.

43. Cf. Henderson 2001b: 80–81.

44. The famous *terminus ante quem* peg of Seneca's *Consolatio ad Polybium* (c. 43 BCE) might actually be a sign of Phaedrus' absence from the literary radar: not that Seneca didn't mention Phaedrus' attempts at Latinizing fable because they weren't written yet (so Champlin 2005: 101–102) but because they made no beep (for this and other speculative possibilities, see Henderson 2001b: 206n10).

45. Cf. Pliny *Ep.* 9.23.

46. On Phaedrus' residual "insecurity" about Eutychus' interest, see Glauthier 2009: 267.

47. As such, Particulo becomes a speaking name: the patron who becomes a "co-heir" of Phaedrus' literary inheritance (see *OLD particulo*; cf. Champlin 2005: 111).

48. Arguments resting on fable order are hazardous in Phaedrus, particularly so in this region of book 4 (see Henderson 1999: 311)—some grains of salt are called for.

49. And also undoes Phaedrus' self-promotion to the Aesopic role of authorial "discoverer" in 4.11.15: *non explicabit alius quam qui repperit* (see Lefkowitz 2017: 428).

50. On the thematic resonances of the Simonides fables with 5.1 and beyond to Phaedrus' own poet-patron situation, see Henderson 2001b: 152.

51. Phaedrus' authorial subjectivity is all over his creative promythia and epimythia: see Sciarrino 2010, 234; Lefkowitz 2017. These interventions as interpretative keys are partly what make us care so much about Phaedrus' authoriality (Henderson 2001b: 14).

52. On Phaedrus' self-enrollment as high poet à la Simonides, see Bloomer 1997: 102. For other moments of high "tradition"-ing in book 4, see Henderson 2002a: 228.

53. Libby 2010: 550.

54. Cf. Henderson 2001b: 153 on Aesop as "designer label," and Glauthier 2009: 274 on Phaedrus as "Aesopic plagiarist."

55. On Phaedrus' "lowest common denominator" demystification of patron-client economic relations, see Glauthier 2009: 270–271.

56. Henderson 2001b: 154–157; Geue 2018a: 98–99.

57. Admittedly, this could be more of a hit at Demetrius' ignorance (Libby 2010: 552).

58. *Scriptor* as run-of-the-mill scribe/copyist/drafter (see esp. *OLD* 1 and 2) has a much more workaday valence than *auctor* as "authority" or "originator" (see, e.g., *OLD* 4 and 10).

59. Cf. Henderson 2001b: 71–72.

60. Content-wise, the fables are also full of cautionary tales against entities trying to rise above their station (see Bloomer 1997: 84; cf. Cavarzere 2001: 215). On Phaedrus' constant comic self-debasing and highlighted failures, see Glauthier 2009: 270–271.

61. Cf. Lefkowitz 2016: 506.

62. For the theme of plagiarism in Martial, see Seo 2009; McGill 2012: 74–114.

63. For a compelling reading of this retreat into the purely literary as a way of whittling out elite subjectivity under autocracy, see Sciarrino 2010: 246–248.

64. Peirano (2012: 166) brings a similar context of unsolicited patronage request to the *Laus Pisonis*.

5. Poet Seeks Patron

1. Various possibilities have been floated, which Di Brazzano (2004: 64–84) collects in impressively exhaustive Italian style (arguments both for and against): Virgil, Ovid, Lucan, Statius, Saleius Bassus, or a medieval fake.

2. Although Di Brazzano (2004) now identifies consensus on which Piso after Champlin (1989) (also the conclusion of Reeve 1984): written around 39/40 for Piso the eventual Neronian conspirator, whom he pins as the grandson of Piso Pontifex. But most of this is speculative detective work analogous to Champlin's Phaedrus reconstruction. As he admits (1989: 117), the *LP* is markedly silent on any concrete biographical details about its Piso (cf. Peirano 2012: 149–150, 169). Green (2010) posits a later incarnation of the same Piso as imperial rival, gagging for legitimacy because of an underdeveloped military résumé.

3. Champlin (1989) pushes for 39/40, just after a preexile, hypothetical consulship of Piso conspirator-to-be; Green (2010: 499–501) knocks this over and repositions the poem in c. 65, just before conspiracy D-day (Mader 2013: 622–623 agrees). I find Peirano's (2012: 157) suggestion that the *LP* poet was knocking up a fiction based on Piso's reputation among the Martial/Juvenal generation the most compelling (and least straitening) of all. I follow her lead on reading this poem more as abstract exercise than concrete historical intervention (see esp. 169). Rees (2012: 96) also stays helpfully agnostic regarding date.

4. As Peirano (2012: 164) notes, both the *LP* and the *Panegyricus Messallae* lack a specific patron-oriented occasion. "The occasion, if one there is, is the poet's request for patronage."

5. Champlin 1989: 101.

6. Green 2010: 497.

7. See Geue 2018b.

8. The trick seems to have worked somehow; as Rees (2012: 104) notes, this work of a no-name has shown "remarkable durability."

9. The "consensus" now only seems to have stuck from sheer inertia. It's better I think to treat this Piso as patron extraordinaire, byword, symbol fogged up by layers of mediation rather than historical figure (see Peirano 2012: 157).

10. See now Mader 2013 on the poetic *psychagogia* connecting *LP* and *Ars Poetica* (although he makes nothing of the Piso overlap). Green (2010: 514n65) also logs a connection in passing.

11. Geue 2014.

12. Champlin 1989; Green 2010; Mader 2013.

13. Champlin 1989: 122–123. On possibilities for the missing sons, see Syme 1980.

14. Champlin 1989: 103. Cf. Rees 2012: 101.

15. Champlin 1989: 124. He thinks that Piso's generic characteristics of standard *nobilitas* are an indictment of this Piso vis-à-vis glorious ancestors.

16. Martial 12.36, 4.40; Juvenal 5.109; on which see Champlin 1989: 104–105; Rees 2012: 98–99.

17. Peirano (2012: 157–159) is excellent on this proverbialization (or Maecenatization) of Piso, and it is grist for her mill in taking the *LP* as later fiction playing with Piso's reputation as patron, a while after the event.

18. E.g., for the *Ars Poetica,* see Syme 1986: 380; Rudd 1989: 21. For Tacitus' *Dialogus,* see Chapter 8 in this volume. The problem goes right back to the *iuvenis* of *Ecl.* 1. Champlin (1989: 116) acknowledges the word's technical coverage up to forty-five- to fifty-year-olds but thinks it was usually understood to refer to men in their twenties or thirties. Green (2010: 520–521) stretches it long into a man's fifties to reconcile it with his putative 65 CE date (and points to Octavian/Augustus' status as perpetual *iuvenis;* 522).

19. Especially the protest of a helpless baby poet compared to the abundant achievements of the *laudandus* (cf. *Panegyricus Messallae* 1–17). Di Brazzano (2004 *ad* 18–22) cites Menander Rhetor 368.23. On the conventions and functions of epideictic literature in general, see Burgess 1902; Pernot 2015.

20. Text from Duff's Loeb; translations are my own.

21. For Horace's *Ars Poetica* as backdrop here, see Mader 2013: 626. As Peirano (2012: 154–155) notes, these terms of praise are conventional and generic as you like.

22. As Green (2010: 508) notes, these three are picked for military as well as rhetorical flair; cf. Mader 2013: 628. As Di Brazzano (2004 *ad* 57–64) picks up, they represent the tripartite *genera dicendi* (cf. Cic. *Brut.* 40).

23. Di Brazzano (2004) glosses 63, "ornare le parole in modo non celato ma evidente, esibito"—luminous Piso outshining his black hole of a celebrator?

24. *Numerosus,* 9, 66, 137; *numerare,* 70, 131. Irene Peirano Garrison rightly points me (*per litteras*) that this could also mean "rhythmical" praise, i.e., a Sunday-best, purple prose evoking the concept of *numerosa oratio,* which is everywhere in Cicero's *Orator* (e.g., 166, 168, 180, 198, 205, 210). If the senate speaks in measures, imagine how good this here *metrical* praise! Di Brazzano (2004) nicely nuts out *numerosa laude senatus/excipit:* "lode colletiva, piena, frequente e molteplice"—couldn't have stacked them better myself.

25. This moment of *gratiarum actio* is "the closest the poet of the *Laus* comes to giving any tangible detail at all about Piso"—and it is still pretty "generic" (Peirano 2012: 155).

26. Cf. Di Brazzano 2004 *ad loc.*

27. On the *variatio,* cf. Di Brazzano 2004 *ad loc.*

28. Compliments on physique are a staple of *laudationes:* see Di Brazzano 2004 *ad* 97–105, quoting Quint. *Inst.* 3.7.12 and Men. Rh. 398.14.

29. Di Brazzano nicely cites the Piso of Tac. *Ann.* 15.48.3 here: *corpus procerum, decora facies.*

30. For the Horatian (both *Odes* and *Ars Poetica*) discourse of *kairos/tempestivitas* in the poem, see Mader 2013: 631n27 and 632.

31. Cf. Di Brazzano 2004 *ad loc.*

32. On the cultural meanings, acceptability and unacceptability depending on context, and just plain old rules, of this game, see Green 2010: 514–517.

33. As Green (2010: 517) notes, this *mille* is puzzling; none of our other evidence for the rules of *ludus latrunculorum* engagement mention such rich variation. On the poet's *versatilità* matching Piso's here, see Di Brazzano 2004 *ad* 197–204.

34. Mader (2013: 623–624) also picks up on this aspect of Piso's characterization: "a balanced and versatile personality who does the right thing at the right time." Cf. 629–630.

35. Mader (2013: 640) thinks Virgil the main *comparandus* here, with Horace and Varius tacked on "for good measure." But that neglects the role of *varius* in the poem.

36. I print the reading of the florilegia *euexit* for Siccardo's *erexit;* as Di Brazzano (2004) argues, *evexit* goes more snugly with *eruit, ostendit,* and *patefecit.*

37. On the interpretation of 239–240—up there with the most difficult in the poem—see Di Brazzano 2004 *ad loc.*

38. In addition to his famous *Thyestes,* Horace mentions Lucius Varius Rufus qua big-time epic poet (*Sat.* 1.10.3). He suggests him for the job of Agrippa panegyric in *Odes* 1.6 (cf. the scholion on Hor. *Ep.* 1.16.27, which

mentions a supposed *Panegyricus Augusti* by him)—the *LP* poet's ancestor in praise?

39. On the double reference here, see Di Brazzano 2004 *ad* 243–245.

40. "Whether . . . or" and "both . . . and" are structures baked hard into ancient praise, especially in Latin verse panegyric: cf. *Panegyricus Messallae* 45–48, 101–105. See also Pernot 2015: 60–62 on the plenitude of metaphor in ancient epideictic, which works to a "both . . . and" logic.

41. On the structural weight of *si forte* in the poem, cf. Di Brazzano 2004 *ad* 163–164.

42. Cf. the interrogative adjective and pronoun (*quis . . . quis*) used at 55–56, with Di Brazzano's note (2004 *ad loc.*).

43. Cf. Chapter 7 in this volume on the *Apocolocyntosis*.

44. Such inferiority protests are par for the rhetorical course: see Men. Rh. 391.10, and Di Brazzano 2004 *ad loc.* See now also Matzner and Harrison 2018.

45. I read Piso as miner here, poet as gold (not the reverse), somewhat against the grain—but responding to the context of light/dark imagery elsewhere in the poem.

46. Cf. Mader 2013: 640.

47. Cf. Mader 2013: 639 and 639n40.

48. Although lines 254–255 have been emended to the nth degree to straighten out perceived inconsistency, I retain the reading of the florilegia, with Di Brazzano (2004). The moral qualities of poet's house are served up as beyond reproach—only the funds are lacking.

49. Mader 2013: 639–640.

50. Although it would be stretching it, I'm on the way to thinking the reading of the florilegia and Siccardo (*aetas* for *aestas*) better for that last line, at least as it pertains to the poem's ambitious multicontextualism: "my twentieth generation has not yet come," as if the poet were thrusting forward to the many future incarnations of this paradigm praise.

51. For further responsions between poet and patron, see Mader 2013: 636.

52. *Iuvenis*: 32, 109; *decus*: 34, 212 (and Maecenas as *decus*, 243).

53. Cf. Di Brazzano 2004 *ad* 260–261.

54. Thanks to Irene Peirano Garrison (*per litteras*) for pointing out the fictive implications of *pingere malas*.

55. Di Brazzano (2004 *ad* 145–151) thinks the season analogy not fit for purpose: it usually contains a notion of cyclicity, which sits awkwardly with a point about Pisonian versatility. But poet is puffing and panting to capture Piso's *habitual* versatility here, which does involve repetition.

56. Cf. Di Brazzano (2004)'s comment on *temporibus servire decet*: "A mio parere, anzi, in queste tre parole è racchiusa l'essenza non solo dell'ultima sezione, ma dell'intero poemetto."

57. Di Brazzano (2004) construes as "plurale poetico," but I'm not so sure. It almost pluralizes Piso himself.

58. The key term *decuere* appears in only one manuscript (Π), but it is infinitely preferable to the alternative *docuere*; for a good thematic defense, see Di Brazzano 2004 *ad loc.*

59. On the poet getting around the problem of elite display of *virtus* in the absence of military opportunity, see Champlin 1989: 119. Green (2010) makes this redemption of unproven military skill by other means the main propaganda point of the poem. Peirano (2012: 151–152, 156) sees more irony and humor in the situation of a noble whose main claim to fame is a board game.

60. For the intensive military language flooding most of Piso's activities, see Green 2010.

61. Green 2010.

62. Not to mention the fact that the late republican Forum as public space effectively combines triumphal procession and legal oratory, as well as many other crowd-heavy activities (see Millar 1998: 44).

63. As such, the work very literally thematizes Dimock's concept of "resonance": "What Wai Chee Dimock calls 'resonance' is this potential to signify and change across time, to accrue new meanings and associations, to trigger unexpected echoes in unexpected places. Resonance, she declares in an important essay, puts the temporal axis at the center of literary studies" (Felski 2015: 160, using Dimock 1997).

64. MacCormack 1975: 159.

6. The Timeless Pastoral of Calpurnius Siculus

1. The name is a mess in the various manuscripts. Siculus may just be a play with Theocritus; Calpurnius may be all we have (Champlin 1978: 107; cf. Karakasis 2016: 2–3).

2. Cf., e.g., Mayer 2006: 454; although CS is demoted back to the status of mechanical fiddler with Virgil at 463. Newlands (1987: 231) is generous without condescension.

3. For a good recent summary of the dating debacle, see Mayer 2006: 454–455; Di Lorenzo and Pellegrino 2008: 5–7. Before Haupt's (1854) separation of Calpurnius and Nemesianus, both were commonly pegged as third century (Baldwin 1995: 158). Since Haupt, consensus was pretty much settled on a Neronian date, until Champlin (1978) swooped in and proposed the Severan period (although he acknowledges the timelessness of it all—and hence flimsiness of his own radical redating—in the epigraph to this chapter). Neronian defenders are still in the majority: Mayer (1980) based his Champlin-response on prosody, allusion, and diction, and Townend (1980) did the same along historical lines, with Wiseman (1982) throwing his hat in the ring shortly after and Verdière (1982 and 1985) remaining stalwart. The Neronian position is stuck by in Mayer (2006: 456), despite a devastating attack by Armstrong (1986) in the interim, which picks holes in Mayer (1980) to support a post-Lucan date without locking a specific period à la Champlin (cf. also Champlin 1986, which doubles down on his position in the wake of the early 80s Neronian challengers). The recent Italian commentaries of Di Lorenzo and Pellegrino (2008) and Vinchesi (2014) stand by their man Nero with conviction (cf. most recently Henderson 2013: 184; and Karakasis 2016: 5). Baldwin (1995) got behind Champlin (but also, quite honestly, pours cold water on the whole project of historicist "unmasking"; 166–167). Newlands (1987: 218n1) is uncon-

vinced by both proposals. Horsfall (1997) offered a kind of reconciliatory position: late date but with many Neronian features (and his caution is admirable; see, e.g., 192, 195). Many of the arguments involve weak assumptions about probability in directions of intertextuality (e.g., Horsfall 1997: 178; Courtney 1987 uses "imitation" of Statius and Martial as a way of establishing CS's post-Flavian credentials—not exactly ironclad). The point is that both early and late daters have some grounds, while also respectively leaving many puzzles unsolved; that is why the full implications of agnosticism should be explored.

4. Haupt 1854.

5. On the allegorical reading habits of ancient readers of ancient pastoral, see Starr 1995; names could shift referents from line to line such that whether Tityrus = Virgil has to be decided in the individual context, over and over again (135–137). See also Farrell 2016. On the displacement of the author onto a fictionalized internal character in Theocritus, see Payne 2007: 114–145; Farrell 2016: 404–405.

6. See Magnelli 2006: 469–472; Karakasis 2016: 9–10; Kearey 2018: 140. For dissent from that identification, see Leach 1973: 86; Davis 1987: 39; Newlands 1987: 227–229. Cf. Martin 2003: 89 on the Corydon of CS 7. The CS-Corydon axis is assumed as much as it is argued (e.g., Champlin 1978: 100; Horsfall 1997: 167; Mayer 2006: 458).

7. So, notoriously, Herrmann 1952. Conte (1994: 435–436) claims that CS is especially, simplistically, allegorical. For attempts to identify Meliboeus' real-life version (usually Seneca or Calpurnius Piso), see Mayer 1982: 315–316; Wiseman 1982: 66; Schröder 1991: 29–34; Mayer 2006: 459. Horsfall (1997: 167) takes him as Nero; Champlin (1978: 108) as Marius Maximus. I clap Vinchesi (2014: 26), who calls for some sobriety in abstaining from "ogni identificazione."

8. The Theocritean corpus is especially mixed and so resistant to bucolic pigeonholing: see, e.g., Hunter 1999: 4–5, 11–12. CS's engagement with Theocritus is limited (Mayer 2006: 462). Virgil is the heavy shadow.

9. Varius 6.10, 6.12; Pollio 4.12; Caesar 9.47; Gallus 10.10.

10. Mayer (2006: 459) notes this key difference from Virgil (and suggests that it stems from a generic choice to go for purer pastoral; 463); cf. Kearey 2018: 141. For other ways in which CS modifies the Virgilian tradition, see Damon 1961; Newlands 1987; Mayer 2006: 460–461, 463; Karakasis 2010; Baraz 2015; Kearey 2018: 138. On the use of contemporary names as in part a marker of the lower poetic genres, see F. Jones 2006: 29. Kennedy (1993: 83; cf. Shearin 2015: 104–105) is brilliant on the way proper nouns in literature magically migrate our attention to a "reality" behind the text.

11. Most scholars read a young Caesar here, but other names have been offered: Asinius Pollio (Cairns 2008); Epicurus (Bing 2016).

12. Cf. Geue 2013.

13. See note 63 below.

14. Problems of amphitheater identification: Horsfall 1997: 171. Champlin (1978: 107) unproblematically takes it as the Colosseum, recently renovated by Alexander in 223 (Baldwin 1995: 160 lists other possibilities). Townend (1980: 169–170) critiques and restores Nero's wooden amphitheater as referent.

15. Cf. Hinds (2010: 372) on the teasing timelessness and placelessness of Keats' "Ode on a Grecian Urn."

16. See note 6 above.

17. For a brilliant recent discussion of this issue of pastoral *nomina* and (in)consistent personhood, see Kearey 2018: 148–153.

18. Corydon is recycled as a main speaking character (VE 2 and 7), along with the select gang of Tityrus (VE 1 and—if it counts—6), Meliboeus (VE 1 and 7), and Menalcas (VE 3 and 5).

19. *Pace* Leach (1973: 85), who reads them as the same character. On the contradictions in Virgil's Corydons, see Kearey 2018: 149–150.

20. On the multiple Virgilian Corydon's behind CS's Corydon, cf. Magnelli 2006: 471.

21. Cf. Kearey 2018: 148–149.

22. See Leach 1973: 54 (though 7 answers 4's hope with disappointment; 77); Newlands 1987: 227–228, although she also notes how far the Corydon of CS 7 is on the outside compared to the Tityrus of VE 1 (230).

23. Although Kearey 2018: 150 nicely reads CS's Corydon as a way of reconciling the contradictory Corydons of Virgil.

24. This tall Ornytus might channel the eponymous figure in *Aeneid* 11: Karakasis 2011: 17–18.

25. For the biographizing head-scratching caused by these brother sets (literal? metaphorical?), see Vinchesi 2014: 25.

26. On these two Tityri see Kearey 2018: 151–152.

27. This could be thought a twist and intensification of the tendency of Theocritean herdsmen to imitate each other (see Payne 2007: 92–113).

28. The adjective *formosus* splits the difference: applied to the object of desire Alexis in VE 2, now it moves to the singers themselves (*formosus uterque,* 3).

29. Text from Duff Loeb; translation is my own.

30. As Vinchesi 2014 *ad loc.* comments, the "both" motif has precedent (Ps. Theocr. 8.3–4, VE 7.4–5); on the latter, see later in this chapter.

31. On the novelty of the prominence of gardening as a pastoral job here, see Vinchesi 2014: 165–166; and Karakasis 2016: 196n12, with extensive bibliography.

32. And a fairly harmonious love-triangle situation in general (on the elegiac tones of which, see Karakasis 2016: 196–198).

33. Thyrsis is also himself a reformed figure of neutrality: now a judge, once the losing participant (in VE 7—see Hubbard 1996: 68).

34. On the exceptionally weird move of immediately canceling the stakes, see Vinchesi 2014 *ad* 22.

35. Taking cues from the decision by lot in Ps. Theocr. 8.30 (see Vinchesi 2014 *ad loc.*).

36. I print the *sunt* of manuscripts *NGP* (retained by Vinchesi 2014 and Fey-Wickert 2002) rather than the *fore* of manuscript *V* (Keene's [1996] choice).

37. As Mayer (2006: 461; cf. Vinchesi 2014 *ad* 98) points out, this is reminiscent of the undecided end of VE 3—but with much more concord. On the arbitrariness of the refusal to decide here, see Gibson 2004: 11. For other cases of poet parity, see CS 4.149, Theocr. 6.46 (see Vinchesi 2014 *ad* 98).

38. Cf. Vinchesi 2014 *ad* CS 2.5.

39. On Astacus' georgic qualifications (with qualifications), see Karakasis 2016: 203–204 and 203n42.

40. See Esposito 2012; Karakasis 2016: 157–191.

41. VE 4.3; Baraz 2015: 107–108.

42. Gibson (2004: 7) sees Amyntas' status as gradually improving over the course of the poem.

43. Leach (1973: 72) thinks this new theme should be given to Corydon. Vinchesi (2014) agrees (after Haupt 1854 and Herrmann 1952), positing a lacuna in place of Amyntas' putative reply to Corydon after 96 and so assigning Corydon the trailblazing role again from 97. For the history of various solutions to the problem, see Vinchesi 2014: 290. I prefer to read charitably and see this as an experiment in swapping amoebean initiative.

44. See note 43 above.

45. On Calpurnian writing, see Hubbard 1996: 69.

46. See in general Breed 2006 (e.g., 14–15).

47. See Breed 2006: 15, 57–58.

48. On Mopsus' effective impersonation of the Daphnis *ego* here, see Breed 2006: 62–63; cf. 71.

49. On the relationship of the Faunus prophecy to VE 4, see Gibson 2004: 2; Magnelli 2006: 468. Stöckinger (2017) nicely puts it in conversation with the beginning of *Aeneid* 6, and 3.441–462, on the question of prophetic medium (written / spoken).

50. On the general effect of mystery and inscrutability in graffiti ancient and modern, feeding this passage, see Milnor 2014: 277. As Vinchesi 2014 *ad loc.* notes, the indeterminacy feathers the anticipation.

51. Propertius 4.2.59; cf. Ovid *Her.* 5.22. See Mayer 2006: 462–463; Karakasis 2016: 22; Vinchesi 2014 *ad loc.*

52. Vinchesi 2014 *ad loc.* nicely compares *nuper* of the inscription in VE 5.13.

53. Milnor (2014: 276) thinks this feature marks writing itself as ill at ease in the pastoral world, more "a breath of the city."

54. It's also a hallmark of the prophetic *Ich-Stil;* see Vinchesi 2014 *ad loc.*

55. Stöckinger (2017: 294) calls CS graphocentric, as opposed to the phonologocentric *Aeneid.*

56. The nomination of sender and recipient right at the beginning is unmistakable epistolary style (see Vinchesi 2014 *ad loc.*).

57. Cf. Chapter 2 on the *Ibis.* For a good collection of other *ille ego* moments in Tibullus, Ovid, and Martial, see Vinchesi 2014 *ad loc.* (and on the development of the signature in general, see La Penna 1985).

58. As Vinchesi 2014 *ad loc.* documents, whacking both sender and receiver names into the conclusion is another move of epistolary song (cf. Ovid *Her.* 2.147).

59. Cf. VE 5.14, *carmina descripsi,* with Breed 2006: 58.

60. Henderson 2013: 177. Cf. Chapter 5 in this volume.

61. Neronians have taken it as a nod to Nero's speech *pro Iliensibus* in 53 CE. For the problems, see Champlin 1978: 98–100; Wiseman 1982: 57–58; Baldwin 1995: 159–160; Horsfall 1997: 168–169. Vinchesi 2014 *ad loc.* gives a concise history of the endless vexation.

62. Manuscript *A* has *in ulnis* instead of *iulis* (*NGPV*).

63. Champlin (1978: 98) thinks the Claudian reign unthinkable as civil war. Wiseman (1982: 59) disagrees. Baldwin (1995: 164) disagrees with the disagreement. Vinchesi 2014 *ad loc.* is excellent on how we can be talking both recent past and long historical view, Caesarism born of civil war (cf. Küppers 1985: 354; Martin 1996: 25–26; Narducci 2002: 32).

64. Champlin 1978: 97–98, 103; response in Townend 1980: 168; cf. Horsfall 1997: 167. As Baldwin (1995: 163–164) notes, comets were pretty thick on the ground.

65. As Horsfall (1997: 166; cf. 193) makes clear, CS's panegyrics go with any young emperor on the rise (cf. Leach 1973: 61; Champlin 1978: 96; Townend 1980: 167). Contrast the golden age bulletin in the *Apocolocyntosis,* which makes it abundantly clear that Nero is in the driver's seat (see later in this chapter).

66. On Meliboeus as intermediary, see Stöckinger 2017: 295; cf. Vinchesi 2014 *ad loc.* on distance and Meliboean mediation.

67. *Numina* has also been taken as genuine plural, to refer to Carinus and Numerianus; see Keene 1996 *ad loc.* for takedown. Of course it can also connect Apollo and Caesar here (see Vinchesi 2014 *ad loc.*).

68. Vinchesi 2014 *ad loc.* also compares the classic divine predecessors, Epicurus at *DRN* 5.8 and Daphnis at VE 5.64.

69. See Vinchesi 2014 *ad loc.* on the use of *abesse* "in unione con termine indicante prossimità."

70. Cf. Champlin 1978: 105–106.

71. Textual problems are rife in 152; I run with Keene's (1996) patchwork of manuscript readings to bleed sense, but Vinchesi 2014 prints *olim quam tereti decurrent carmina versu,* posits a lacuna after 152, then picks up with *NG*'s *nunc.*

72. At least the poem where Corydon seems to want to leave pastoral well and truly behind (7.4–6, 13–18).

73. Indeed, it may have increased: this poem lacks a Meliboeus go-between (cf. Champlin 1978: 107).

74. Of course the bumpkin characterization focalizes the description too: Newlands 1987: 222.

75. Cf. Leach 1973: 81; Vinchesi 2010: 156; and Vinchesi 2014 *ad loc.*

76. As Vinchesi 2014 *ad loc.* registers, hippopotamus is inadmissible in the hexameter—but the periphrasis has a point, showing the upending of the natural order.

77. The Nile; see Vinchesi 2014 *ad loc.*

78. See Baldwin 1995: 162.

79. Townend (1980: 173) reads the lack of visibility as itself a sign of Nero!

80. Cf. earlier on 4.11; not just the "plurale enfatico" (Vinchesi 2014 *ad loc.*).

81. Cf. Vinchesi 2014 *ad loc.*

82. See Newlands 1987: 230 on the distance of Corydon's *vidissem* from Tityrus' *vidi* in VE 1.42 (cf. Leach 1973: 84).

83. Indeed, the duo goes back to the paradigm case (Octavian/Augustus): Vinchesi 2014 *ad loc.*, citing Friedrich 1976: 249.

84. As polar opposite, cf. the panegyric of Nero at *Apocol.* 4: Phoebus himself spots Nero in his vanity mirror, with a face like his own (*mihi similis vultu similisque decore/nec cantu nec voce minor*); and precisely *which* Caesar is never left to the imagination (*talis Caesar adest, talem iam Roma Neronem /aspiciet.*).

85. I mean this in the sense that the Calpurnian corpus knocks up a particularly strong fortress of a green cabinet, isolated from the particulars of History and Politics, not that it fails to mess with and expand on bucolic as a genre (undeniable since Karakasis 2016).

86. Felski 2015: 161.

87. Cf. Kearey 2018: 142 on CS as "puppeteer" to Corydon vs. Virgil's Tityrus "mask."

7. Whence

1. On the literary history of the prosimetric form in Europe, see Dronke 1994; on the polyphonic effects of the form in Petronius, see esp. 11.

2. See Bonandini 2010: 23–28, which balances the contact and distance well. The two are often compared only to contrast (e.g., Laird 1999: 230) on their different deployments of verse.

3. See Motto and Clark 1983: 31; Relihan 1993: 75–90; Bonandini 2010: 29–31.

4. On the title problem, plus Dio's confusing gloss, see Bonandini 2010: 211–233; Freudenburg 2015: 93. Freudenburg also makes a suggestive connection between the unpronounceability of the title *Apocol.* and Claudius' stammer (95). According to Roncali (1974), the author's name was only added in the sixteenth century (though this is controversial: see Reeve 1984). Dio is the only one from antiquity to hand a work on the deification of Claudius to Seneca (Eden 1984: 6). The text was probably first doing the rounds soon after Claudius' death in October 54, perhaps for the December Saturnalia (Freudenburg 2015: 96; original hypothesis in Furneaux 1896: 23n11, 45n10, 171n1; cf. Eden 1984: 5).

5. Most literary readers take Senecan authorship as read. Dissent in Baldwin 1964: 45–48 and Roncali 1974, both discussed in Bringmann 1985: 885–889.

6. First suggested by Münscher (1922: 49–50 and 49n1). Eden (1984: 7) notes how easy anonymity could have been in practical terms, and thinks initial anonymity likely (13), but moves that the *Apocol.* is too good to be the work of a no-name and that Seneca has to be the ultimate author (8). On the reception end, could the fact that Erasmus left his *Julius Exclusus* (positing the *Apocol.* as ancestor) to go anonymous (see Grafton 1990: 45) tell us something?

7. Cf. Baldwin 1964: 47–48. For this Ahlean/Bartschean (Ahl 1984; Bartsch 1994), "figured speech" context of the *Apocol.*, see Robinson 2005: 225; on the context of uncertain imperial succession, Robinson 2005: 250.

8. For the serious political work of the *Apocol.*, cf. Freudenburg 2015: 97.

9. At least no obvious stylistic gulfs between *Apocol.* and non-*Apocol.* Senecas (Eden 1984: 7); with moments of special convergence (e.g., the *Hercules tragicus* of *Apocol.* 7 approaching the *Hercules Furens;* Eden 1984: 7).

10. In any case, the relief wasn't universal—for some, the party was over (e.g., the *iurisconsulti* of 12).

11. On the *Apocol.* as "Saturnalian" literature, see Nauta 1987; as he cautions (94), we shouldn't mistake the *Apocol.* for out-and-out, Bakhtin-esque, "popular laughter." The carnival spirit is certainly there (Motto and Clark 1983: 36); but we should be careful with the "purgation and release" (Motto and Clark 1983: 39)—in my view, the point at which the *Apocol.* gets ideological on us.

12. The polyphony of prosimetric/Menippean form is a commonplace: e.g., Osgood 2007: 330; cf. Rimell 2009 on the *Satyrica* as symphony/cacophony. Though Menippean form is prosimetric, that doesn't mean prosimetric = Menippean: see Conte 1996: 140–170; Schmeling 1999: 30.

13. This section owes a lot to O'Gorman (2005) on citationality in the *Apocol.*: "As well as employing a range of quotation and allusion, the *Apocol.* is also about quotation, what it means to quote, and what relationship with the past is configured by, within, the act of quotation" (96). Bonandini 2010 is impressively comprehensive on the *Apocol.*'s citations. For proverbs in the *Apocol.* (used as a means to distinguish it from the *Satyrica*), see Conte 1996: 155–156; on the favor for proverbs in Mennipean satire in general, and the *Apocol.* in particular, see Bonandini 2010 (cf. Eden 1984 *ad* 1.1). For a brilliant discussion of proverbs and *gnomai* as offcuts of a "textual collective" in the Greek context, see Leven 2013.

14. Cf. Chapter 1 in this volume on Suetonius.

15. Cf. Leach 1989: 205.

16. Text of *Apocol.* from Eden 1984; *Satyrica* from Schmeling 2011; translations are my own.

17. Slightly different to the named authorities O'Gorman (2005) tracks.

18. *IO* 5.11.36–41.

19. Virgil *Aeneid* 2.723–724; see Eden 1984 *ad loc.* As Star (2012: 154–155) nicely points out, Claudius is defined not by his own quotations but by those of others (citational vengeance!).

20. Cf. Damon 2010: 52.

21. Cf. Tarrant (2012 *ad Aen.* 12.218), who calls *non passibus aequis* "a famous phrase."

22. Bonandini (2010: 147) points out that this is already "un'immagine convenzionale" by the Flavian period.

23. See Bonandini 2010: 146–149.

24. This kind of historical form is a sitting duck for parodic targets, e.g., Lucian's *True History* (Schmeling 1998: 22–23 connects it with the *Apocol.*).

25. On the suddenness, see Bonandini 2010: 269. On the deformation of both historiography and poetry here, see Damon 2010: 49.

26. For the jostling between prose and verse—clambering over each other "to say the same thing"—see Damon 2010: 58–60.

27. Cf. Eden 1984 *ad loc.*: "the author satirizes . . . the bombastic circumlocutions of times of year and day beloved by poetasters." See Robinson 2005: 252–254 on the deliberately bland verse panegyric of Nero (*Apocol.* 4); *contra* Whitton 2013: 163–165.

28. Cf. Bonandini 2010: 270.

29. As Damon (2010: 65) notes, the overdetermination of time is a "smoke-screen" for the actual circumstances of Claudius' death; cf. Robinson 2005: 230.

30. Cf. O'Gorman (2005: 101) on the atmospheric point of the verse's circumlocution here.

31. Eur. *Cresphontes* fr. 449.4 Nauck. See Eden 1984 *ad loc.* for the contextual irony, and Bonandini 2010: 98–102.

32. For these last words as revealing of Claudius' true nature, see Star 2012: 143.

33. *Puto* could well just be an idiomatic unmarked "I suppose" here—but surely the sputtering form of the sentence is a punch line of sorts, hinting how unassertive Claudius is even at the end. And then there's the irony of *puto*'s original meaning, to cleanse.

34. Cf. *certa*, 1, or an equivalent of *certe, plane* (12, 13).

35. Cf. Robinson's (2005: 236) suggestion that the *Apocol.*'s unbalanced form apes Claudius' deformed speech.

36. Cf. Eden 1984 *ad loc.*

37. On the animalistic tones of *vox confusa*, see Osgood 2007: 344.

38. See Braund and James 1998 on Claudius' subhuman status.

39. I print πόθι τοι for the manuscripts' ποίη, to bring it into line with Homer *Od.* 1.171; but the possibility that Claudius is making a tiny howler remains (see Eden 1984 *ad loc.*).

40. Cf. Star 2012: 152.

41. Cf. O'Gorman 2005: 97–98. For all the prose and verse variants of the question "where are you from?" in the *Apocol.*, see Damon 2010: 62.

42. *Nemo* bounces through the *Apocol.* like nobody's business: at 1, 3 (twice), 5, 6 (twice), 11.

43. On the meaning of *ubi mures ferrum rodunt*, see Eden 1984 *ad loc.*: it both designates the off-grid realm of myth and also came to be associated with a particular place, the isle of Gyara.

44. For Claudius' incomprehensible speech, see Star 2012: 152–153; Osgood 2007: 330–331. Osgood (2007) in general shows how serious a flaw Claudius' defective speech was in a culture prizing rhetoric so highly.

45. Lacunae in general wreak havoc with attribution and contextualization; cf. Petronius later in this chapter. On the possible length and content of the lacuna here, see Eden 1984 *ad* 8.1.

46. See Eden 1984 *ad loc.* on comparable Epicurean testimony (esp. a nearby maxim of Epicurus, rattled off at Diogenes Laertius 10.139).

47. Some proverbs might be quasi-proverbs or difficult to detect as proverbs: cf. Eden on *stulte, stude* and *hic nobis curva corriget?* (1984 *ad* 8).

48. I stick with the manuscripts' *quid . . . nescio et iam;* Eden (1984) emends to *quid . . . nesciet: iam . . . ,* shoving the "not knowing" back onto Claudius (tempting given his penchant for not knowing elsewhere in the *Apocol.*, but the point here is to spread Claudian shrugs to the supposedly "omniscient" too).

49. Janus' code-switching brilliance is fittingly hinted in Greek: *qui semper videt* ἄμα πρόσσω καὶ ὀπίσσω (9); he uses the stuff in proverbs too: ἀρούρης καρπὸν ἔδουσιν and ζείδωρος ἄρουρα (9). Hercules' comeback at the end of 9 also features two proverbs,

one in the author's mouth (*videbat ferrum suum in igne esse*), one in his own (*manus manum lavat*).

50. Cf. Eden 1984 *ad* 8–11: "The decisive part of the debate follows Jupiter's intervention to impose orderly procedure."

51. Cf. O'Gorman 2005: 103; cf. Eden 1984 *ad* 10.1.

52. O'Gorman 2005: 105.

53. Eden 1984 *ad loc.* hooks it to the moment Messala resigns from *praefectus urbi* in 25 BCE, which would add an irony by positioning Augustus as a fiercely republican refusenik of his own imperial overreach.

54. Syme 1986: ch. 15.

55. Augustus' speech is in fact proverbial to a T here, as Eden 1984 *ad loc.* notes—kicking off with the phrase *muscam excitari*. For a serious crack at glossing the Greek in various ways here, see Bonandini 2010: 233–243.

56. For Augustus' role as censor here, cf. Freudenburg 2015: 100–101 (the satire turns on restoring real censorship after Claudius' faux censorship; 101–105).

57. Star (2012: 153) compares Augustus' scripting of Claudius here to Seneca's scripting of Nero.

58. For links with the *Res Gestae* here, see O'Gorman 2005: 104; Green 2016; and with Suetonius' *Augustus,* see Eden 1984 *ad loc.*

59. Cf. O'Gorman 2005: 106; although she thinks that this act of self-quotation actually deauthorizes Augustus, because it stows the authority elsewhere.

60. Common practice for the Roman senate (see Eden 1984 *ad loc.*); but no coincidence that Augustus is the one assigned the written part here.

61. Cf. O'Gorman 2005: 103; although this act of reading from a tablet keys in to a wider Roman practice of authoritative recitation (see Meyer 2004: 88–89).

62. There is also fog over whether the *unde* refers to hell or heaven. Eden (1984 *ad loc.*) follows Heinze's (1926: 72) suggestion and takes it with the latter, i.e., treats it as a citation inverting its original referent.

63. Although the actual formulation is quite singular, marking the climactic moment in the *Iliad* when Achilles digs in his infinite implacability and vows to remain unresponsive to Agamemnon's overtures no matter how many gifts he brings (9.385). Hainsworth 1993 *ad loc.* is surprised sand isn't used more often as a Homeric figure for the numberless, given its obviousness; φύλλα is the more common vehicle.

64. Cf. Motto and Clark 1983: 38–39.

65. The quote first pops up in Hesiod (*Megala Erga* fr. 286 M-W) but, as Eden 1984 *ad loc.* has it, soon migrates "into the realm of *proverbia adespota*" (see Aristotle *NE* 1132b).

66. Although it drags against my putative support for the *Apocol.*'s anonymity, it would be remiss to leave out that Seneca was understood as a particularly proverb/maxim/sententia–rich author—hence the long-standing attribution to him of that multiauthored work *incerti auctoris:* the *Proverbia Senecae.*

67. In the sense that it twists our arm to take it as true—I am not claiming (how could I?) that the *Apocol.* does perfect and impartial justice to the historical Claudius.

68. As a piece knocked up for closed circles, the *Apocol.* undoubtedly has less street-cred access to a popular audience; but the popular tradition of proverbial speech is at least harnessed to generalize the act of *damnatio* (see the introduction to this chapter).

69. Cf. Motto and Clark's (1983: 36) comparison of Claudius to the *pila:* "bouncing ball."

70. Eden limits the amount of pinging around by emending to *adiudicatur. C. Caesari illum Aeacus donat. is Menandro liberto suo tradidit* . . . I retain the manuscripts' reading to preserve the chaotic and cyclical pattern to the Claudian transactions (and to keep the pointed placement of Claudius as assistant to (the freedman of) *Aeacus,* the judge of judges, not Caligula).

71. On the masterful narrative acceleration here, see Motto and Clark 1983: 37-38.

72. For a list of parallels between the two, see Bagnani 1954: 80-82. Sometimes a vague perception of the two authors as "sworn enemies" gets in the way of comparison (Star 2012: 2). For a recent attempt to read the *Apocol.* alongside the *Satyrica* through the theme of soul-revealing speech, see Star 2012: 141-170. O'Gorman (2005: 95) thinks the sui generis *Apocol.* is difficult to link even to Petronius. But they at least overlap through the prosimetric form (Connors 1998: 15).

73. Most scholars identify the author of the *Satyrica* with the Petronius of Tacitus' *Annals* 16.18. See, e.g., Prag and Repath 2009: 6-8: "likely," "not certain" according to them. Most of the dateable references only give a *post quem* rather than a secure Neronian context (8); although now the functionality and fittingness of Neronian contextual readings have themselves become an argument for dating (9). Schmeling (2011: xiii-xv) identifies the faith in Tacitus' Petronius with Anglophone scholarship. In France, a "vocal minority" pipes up to push for a Flavian author or a much broader possible time scale; cf. Vout 2009: 111, invested in a Neronian date but pointing out the generic quality of the parallels to Nero/any emperor. But Anglophone scholars occasionally dissent too: Roth (2016) redates to the Trajanic period on the basis of the manumission scenes in the *Cena;* cf. Laird's (2007) challenge to the orthodoxy (difficulties of dating at 156-160; questioning of the Petronius Arbiter connection at 160-162; for a disambiguation of the various confused Petronii, see Völker and Rohmann 2011). On the "timelessness" of the *Satyrica,* see Slater 1990: 207.

74. See note 72 above.

75. The extent of the *Satyrica*'s soul-mating with Greek novels has been a sticky issue for scholarship since Heinze (1899) named it a parody of a conventional Greek romance (a literary lineage traced still by many today: Conte 1996: 32; Schmeling 2011: xxxi). Morgan (2009: 40-47) thinks the relationship limited (cf. Schmeling 1999: 28-29). S. Harrison (1999: xix) is more upbeat about the prospect. Laird (2007) uses the connection to nudge us more toward a possible late (second century) date for the *Satyrica.* Like the *Apocol.,* the *Satyrica*'s generic "unlabel-ability" and uniqueness is a staple of scholarship (cf. Sullivan 1968: 261; Zeitlin 1971: 634-635; Conte 1996: 141; Connors 1998: 6, 11; Panayotakis 2009: 60; Schmeling 2011: xxxiii-xxxiv).

76. A good example of this is the start of the extant text—seventeen chapters before we find out the name of who's speaking (Slater 2009: 17).

77. As a text buzzing with intertextual energy (for which see Conte 1996; Rimell 2002; Panayotakis 2009; Schmeling 2011: xxix–xxxv), the *Satyrica* also sends us in search of sources in that sense too.

78. For the complexities of first-person voice here, see most recently S. Harrison 1999: xxiv; Bartsch's section in Whitmarsh and Bartsch 2008; Schmeling 2011: xxvii. R. Beck 1973 is still a classic on the two Encolpii, early and late, *actor* in narrative and *auctor* retelling it retrospectively; cf. Conte 1996: 10. Perutelli 1990 is excellent on the distinction between Encolpius and other internal narrators (e.g., Eumolpus, 24–25).

79. Some think the poem at 80 is actually an authorial intrusion (see Sullivan 1968: 98; Slater 2009: 28; see also R. Beck 1973: 50 for list of other authorial assigners), some an Encolpian speech (R. Beck 1973: 50–54; Conte 1996: 81–83, cf. 187–188 on 132.15; Star 2012: 98). Cf. the virtual authorial intrusion in *exclamat* at 108.14 and Slater's brilliant commentary (1990: 171–173).

80. For the importance of reading the verse in context, see Connors 1998 (esp. 50–83).

81. Connors 1998 is the classic attempt to read the poems not as interruptive forces (e.g., Sullivan 1968: 97) adding to the general "cacophony" but as deeply integrated in the narrative (Connors 1998: 4; see also Schmeling 2011: xxxviii–xlviii; Setaioli 2014: 371–372). Cf. Slater 2009: 22–23 on the corrupted justice poem in the stolen cloak episode. Slater (1990: 160) is particularly suggestive on the role of the "unmarked" poems. R. Beck (1973) explains the Encolpian verses as either comments from the narrating present or reflections of the actor in the moment (e.g., 59). Cf. also Laird 1999: 229–230, which divides the *Satyrica*'s verses into two kinds and distinguishes them from the use of verse in the *Apocol.*

82. For a comprehensive look at writing in the *Satyrica*, see Nelis-Clément and Nelis 2005; and in the *cena*, see Tremoli 1960.

83. They are linked in Roman thought on fame and commemoration though: cf. Verginius Rufus' disgracefully bare tomb *sine titulo sine nomine* (Pliny *Ep.* 6.10.3). For Trimalchio's feel for name change and play, see Perkins 2005.

84. Lewis and Short *titulus* I, IIE.

85. Cf. Nelis-Clément and Nelis 2005: 6; Rimell 2007: 66. Roth (2014: 424) points out that this initial string of inscriptions is engineered to invoke epitaph, making Trimalchio already a marked man. Slater (1990: 219) shows how Encolpius' interpretation of the visual content here rests on the inscriptions. On the official context behind Trimalchio's inscription-happy habits, see Rosati 1999: 102. Text of the *Satyrica* is from Müller's Teubner (1995); translations are my own.

86. On these *tituli* as "sale tickets," see Schmeling 2011 *ad loc.*

87. Cf. Nelis-Clément and Nelis 2005: 12–15. On Trimalchio as writer, cf. Rimell 2007. Conte (1996: 70) tantalizingly suggests that Petronius qua hidden author is an aristocratic response to the excesses of Neronian display culture.

88. The glass bottles are already a dead giveaway (not used for wine storage till the early empire; Schmeling 2011 *ad loc.*).

89. Cf. Rimell 2007: 67.

90. See Chapter 4 in this volume.

91. The comparison form is tried and true ancient literary criticism—it's only the content that's off (Schmeling 2011 *ad loc.*).

92. As Slater (1990: 185–186) notes, it is hard to square these verses with known Publilian output; a Ciceronian "attribution" might help here.

93. For a nice reading of the verses in context, showing how "poetry's conventions tell only partial truths," see Connors 1998: 56–62.

94. Cf. Sullivan 1968: 192; Baldwin (1984) sees the verses as Trimalchio versifying Maecenas-style. Courtney (1991: 19–20) thinks Seneca the real target behind these "Publilian" verses (cf. Star 2012: 10); on this "misattribution," see Panayotakis 2009: 61.

95. As Smith 1975 spots *ad loc.*, this is a strained use of *titulus* and pushes the verse well beyond republican Latin.

96. On the sociological backdrop of this "epigraphic habit," see Woolf 1996, Nelis-Clément and Nelis 2005: 2–3, Rimell 2007: 75.

97. Nelis-Clément and Nelis 2005: 20–22. On Trimalchio's tomb's fit with contemporary art, see Whitehead 1993.

98. On the stock motifs of this inscription, see Whitehead 1993: 315–317. On its dual identity as both verisimilar and parodic, see Bodel 1999: 43.

99. For the pointed links with Maecenas here, see Star 2012: 171–172. As Schmeling (2011) has it *ad loc.*, the very adoption of an *agnomen* was a marker of a particularly pretentious freedman.

100. Trimalchio is definitely punching up here, toward the status and epitaphic pose of a genuine *eques Romanus:* see Schmeling 2011 *ad loc.*

101. The decree in absence would have evoked other big office announcements, like Marius' consulship (Whitehead 1993: 316). Whitehead (1993: 310) points out that this is also an attempt to fix Trimalchio's temporary sevirate into a permanent job.

102. While the inscription distorts old republican modes of elite self-representation, it also—like Trimalchio's tomb in general—marks itself out from the contemporary elite mythologizing and allegorizing themes by its *autobiographical* nature: see Whitehead 1993: 319.

103. Although it isn't marked as such within the poem (Slater 1990: 96, 223). As Slater (2011: 248; cf. 2009: 25) notes, this poem is framed as *extempore,* but it looks more like a set piece.

104. Rimell (2007: 73) nicely binds this moment to the riddling tags in the *Cena.* The inscription gets airtime in other accounts (Apollodorus *Bibliotheca* Epitome 5.15, Hyginus *Fab.* 108) but not in the *Aeneid* (see Schmeling 2011 *ad loc.*).

105. Schmeling (2011: xxiii) provisionally locates the episode in books 11–12, i.e., near the opening of our extant text in 14.

106. This scene might mirror Eumolpus' first appearance as a poet "marked" as such (*nota;* see Connors 1998: 63–64; Rimell 2007: 77).

107. Cf. Slater 2011: 251. They are also a kind of temporary scar: see Star 2012: 159.

108. See Schmeling 2011 *ad loc.*

109. See Rimell 2002: 114–115; Slater 2011: 251n10. Note also *frontes notans* earlier (103).

110. For a history of the debate, see Schmeling 2011 *ad loc.*

111. Slater 1990: 89; cf. Slater 2009: 30. The passage carries disproportionate weight as key to the *Satyrica,* e.g., as marker of self-conscious fictionality (Connors 1998: 13), or as a flag of oral-written hybridity (Rimell 2007: 61–62), or as a way of marking the *Satyrica*'s relationship to mime (Connors 1998: 13), or as a statement about realism (Sullivan 1968: 98; Conte 1996: 187–188).

112. On the strange claustrophobia of *inclusit,* see Rimell 2007: 72. On the various ways in which *pagina* has been glossed (written text of play, prompter's script, painted illustrations), see Schmeling 2011 *ad loc.*

113. Conte (1996: e.g., viii, 35–36) is not so interested in the fact of the author's disappearance as he is in the absence as a way of restoring a strong intentionality to the text, i.e., the author laughing at *scholastici* and coaxing us to join.

114. For author, see note 72 above; for title, see Schmeling 2011: xvii.

115. Slater (1990: e.g., 240, 249) draws attention to the process of reading the *Satyrica* as one of chasing an "absent presence," an elusive grounds for meaning, a definitive frame for interpretation (248); though he doesn't "frame" it as such, I wonder how much his reading is powered by the absent author.

116. At least the Lucan of Masters 1992, and the Virgil of Lyne 1987.

8. Historical Transcendence

1. See note 63 below.

2. For a recent snapshot of the debate (no longer much of a debate), see Mayer 2001: 19–22; Luce 2006 (1993): 380. No ancient author says anything about Tacitus' minor writings, so authenticity claims lack external testimony. Lange's (1832 [1928]: 5–8) detection of the *in nemora et lucos* allusion (see later in this chapter) turned the tide in the nineteenth century. Since then, there have been only a few recent-ish dissenters (e.g., Crook 1995: e.g., 10, 184, though he never justifies his decision at length) and none very recently (Van den Berg 2014: 31; Keeline 2018: 233). Differences in style aren't arguments against authorship (cf. Mayer 2001: 19–22), but nor are small overlaps in phraseology between Tacitean works positively *positive* evidence (*contra* Mayer 2001: 20–21).

3. Levene's (2004: 160–161) rough typology of texts that are more, or less, resistant to historical contextualization is helpful here. Levene 2004 is generally brilliant on how the *Dialogus* relates to itself as "literary history" that "situates itself in literary history" (161).

4. As Mayer (2001: 22) points out, chronological references to fix date of composition are thin on the ground. "Publication" is also hard to determine, with arguments usually resting on shaky props of allusion (Mayer [2001: 25] thinks sometime early in 100s the best we can do). Murgia (1980; via tracked "influences" on *Agricola* and *Germania,* 104–116; cf. also Murgia 1985) and Barnes (1986; resifting Murgia and citing more historical reasons) push to make the *Dialogus* Tacitus' first work, in 97; some push for 102, the date of Fabius Iustus' consulship; others go five-ish years later (see in general Luce 2006 (1993): 381). Brink (1993: 276) comes to a conclusion of 99–103 and shows how tenuous Murgia's arguments are (264, 276–

277), but he acknowledges the intractability of the problem above all (251, 275). For a brilliant analysis of this central paradox of historical unplaceability in a work that seems to pitch the importance of historical placement, see Levene 2004: 193–195. Cf. Van den Berg 2014: 33 on the (not quite) timeless atmosphere.

5. Whitton (2019: 459–468) restates and deepens the case for Plinian allusion (*Ep.* 9.10) to the *in nemora et lucos* of *Dialogus* 9 (see later in this chapter, in the conclusion to the "Moving / Staying with the Times" section), which (if accepted) has the obvious knock-on of sealing Tacitean authorship. Of course the case isn't watertight. But it is tight enough to make me cautious of disavowing Tacitean authorship outright.

6. Along with the other texts I have suggested are "served" by anonymity: particularly *Octavia, Laus Pisonis,* and *Apocolocyntosis.*

7. *Brutus* is a go-to model: see Mayer 2001: 12–13; Gowing 2005: 110–112, 117–118; but also *De Oratore* (Levene 2004: 188; Luce 2006 [1993]: 382; and Van den Berg 2014: 208–240, which is the most comprehensive comparison).

8. Approximating, in that form, more to the model of *De Oratore* than *Brutus:* set in the distant but not-too-distant past (91 BCE), involving the great speakers of the day (Scaevola, Antonius, Cotta, Rufus)—although Cicero gets the dialogue report secondhand from Cotta, rather than through direct autopsy.

9. See Mayer 2001: 26–28 (Ciceronian yes, but slavishly so, no); cf. Levene 2004: 188 and, on the depth of the characters' understanding of their Ciceronian models, 191–192; Gowing 2005: 110–112; Van den Berg 2014: 39–40.

10. Although that view implies a teleology or essence to the Tacitean self rooted in the later works, which David Levene (*per litteras*) rightly points out we should reject.

11. Cf. Murgia 1980: 111. The search for the author also manifests itself in the classic debate over which character subs in for Tacitus: for distribution of the Tacitean self across the characters, see Murgia 1980: 111; Brink 1993: 337–340; Luce 2006 (1993): 396, Goldberg 2009: 75, 82; for pro-Maternus and anti other speakers, see Barnes 1986: 236–243; for elements of all speakers in his future career but ultimate role model in Maternus, see Penwill 2003: 137–138; for revisionist recuperation of Aper, see Goldberg 1999; Van den Berg 2014: 216.

12. High-level deployment of authorial presence is an original Ciceronian addition to philosophical dialogue, both as preface-ego and speaker (see Schofield 2008: 64, 74–75, 83); the presence seems to be upped toward the end of his writing life (Stroup 2014: 131). Ironically, Mayer (2001: 19) thinks the lack of self-identification an argument for Tacitean authorship: the author isn't fussing overmuch about posing as Tacitus, unlike say the Pseudo-sallustian invective against Cicero. But the reticent self is also thematized in the *Dialogus* (cf. Levene 2004: 192–195), as it is in the *Agricola* (cf. Tacitus 2014: 10–11). Many scholars note the Tacitean retraction: Luce 2006 (1993): 382, 410; Too 1999: 181–182; Strunk 2010: 264.

13. Although Dressler (2013: 6–7) sees a hermeneutics of suspicion being encouraged by every single speaker in the *Dialogus,* including Tacitus himself; and the "denial of voice" that Tacitus himself practices comes out in the complicating strategies of the other speakers (29).

14. Although this précis is a fairly doctored version of what is to come, perhaps for diplomatic / self-censoring reasons: see Bartsch 1994: 98–101; Penwill 2015: 195.

15. Text is *OCT*; translations are my own.

16. And this "request" move is as formulaic a topos as they come, which adds to the point about unplaceability: see Janson 1964: 117–120; Murgia 1980: 124–125; Luce 2006 (1993): 383; Van den Berg 2014: 17.

17. *Saepe* is also common stock in these kinds of prefaces (cf. Cic. *Orat.* 1–3; see Mayer 2001 *ad loc.*), but the word takes on special power in the *Dialogus* (rearing up seven times: 15, 19, 20, 24, 34, 39; but similar concepts of the habitual and the regular come up even more).

18. For the vagaries and contradictions of the temporality here, see Levene 2004: 195; Van den Berg 2014: 33–34 (and on the *Dialogus'* obsession with temporalities, 236).

19. Although the pointed precision of the recollection grates against Messalla's later accusation of universal forgetfulness: Dressler 2013: 13.

20. This act of Catonian ventriloquism reeks of Cicero's claim to actually become Cato in his *Cato* (see Stroup 2014: 148). On *sui oblitus* as "playing the Stoic opposition," see Penwill 2003: 133; Gallia (2009: 171) sees it as a sign of a Catonian fate to come (cf. Cameron 1967: 259; Strunk 2010: 263). For the full identification between Cato and Maternus, we might also note Aper's point later that Maternus picked a character who would speak *cum auctoritate* (10)—authority but also authorial perspective? Van den Berg (2014: 44) makes this a cue to the *reader*'s performance of the speakers in the dialogue.

21. For a gloss on who these powerful might be (i.e., the delators), see Gallia 2009. Offense becomes a big part of the *Dialogus*: see Van den Berg 2014: 23.

22. As Mayer 2001 *ad loc.* notes, *inter manus* steps in for the much more run-of-the-mill *in manibus*—perhaps to bring home the staunch declaration of ownership?

23. For a dimmed view of Maternus' project of resistance here, see Gowing 2005: 117.

24. Although the lag between conversation and composition seems to pointedly reject the extreme presentness of Cicero's *Brutus* (presented as a conversation in the very recent past), to head more toward the long-term, distant memory of the *De Oratore* (see Stroup 2014: 138).

25. As David Levene rightly reminds me *per litteras,* this move from specific to general is a habit of Platonic dialogue (see, e.g., Nussbaum 1986: 134).

26. On Messalla's links with the delators (especially his half brother Regulus), see Murgia 1980: 124; Barnes 1986: 238; Mayer 2001: 37; Strunk 2010: 252; for Aper's affinities with them, see Strunk 2010: 249; on the delator cloud (under code of the *potentes*) in the *Dialogus*, see Gallia 2009. For Penwill (2003: 130–132), Messalla's presence changes the conversational tack and explains the disparity between Maternus versions 1.0 and 2.0. For Messalla's entrance as one interruption among a series, see Dressler 2013: 24–25.

27. Later punned on with *iustius* (16).

28. Aper's supposed role as devil's advocate has caused no end of discomfort. Mayer (2001: 46) explains it away; see also Luce 2006 (1993): 387–389. Dressler (2013: 20–23) points to markers indicating that other speakers could be acting out in the same way.

29. No editors have managed to bleed sense from *sicut his cla . . .* ; see Mayer 2001 *ad loc.*

30. I follow Mayer 2001 in printing Lipsius' supplement *dixisti.*

31. Cf. Messalla's praise of Brutus' straight talking at 25: *sed simpliciter et ingenue iudicium animi sui detexisse.*

32. Cf. Penwill 2003: 132 on Messalla's stubborn confinement to general sentiments here.

33. See Dressler 2013: 11–14.

34. I print (along with Mayer [2001] and most other editors) Schopen's supplement *artibus.*

35. On the lacuna debate, see Barnes 1986: 227–228; for the scholarly consensus, see Mayer 2001: 49–50 (lacuna is probably short, covers only a bit more of Messalla's speech, a brief exchange between speakers, and the beginning of Maternus' final speech).

36. On the problem of this last speech, the bibliography mushrooms: for the doublespeak qualities, see Murgia 1980: 123; Bartsch 1994: 98–125; Penwill 2003: 139; Strunk 2010; Reitz 2014: 5. Gallia (2009: 194) rejects the doublespeak reading by isolating Maternus' attack on the *potentes* from the emperor himself, leaving the principate well alone. Gordon Williams (1978: 26–51) famously split the two Maternus speeches along different temporal lines (the first reflecting dramatic setting, the second compositional): cf. Penwill 2003: 129. Luce (2006 [1993]: 397–405) resolves this sort of inconsistency with recourse to the permissible self-contradictions of declamatory argumentation. Brink (1993: 345) sees substantial continuity between the speeches.

37. I disagree big time with Mayer (2001 *ad loc.*), who thinks the repetition unintentional.

38. I retain *contiones* (as opposed to Richter's *contentiones*), even if it seems strange in this forensic context.

39. As Levene (2004: 186–187) says, the role of history in Maternus' speech is really an extension of (rather than alternative to) Messalla's discourse on the rupture in educational practice.

40. If this is about the power of historical context (see Luce 2006 [1993]: 386), context becomes, crucially, a depersonalizing force. For Horace-on-Lucilius as a literary-historicizing precedent here, see Van den Berg 2014: 287–290.

41. This is not just about focusing on the present (Gowing 2005: 120); it's about universalizing it.

42. As Mayer (2001: 41) points out, Aper's time scheme actually prepares the ground for Maternus' historical argument here (and on overlap between the two speeches, see Van den Berg 2014: 15). In fact the whole arc of the speeches gradually bends toward this increased role of history (Levene 2004). Strunk (2010: 256) reads Aper's and Maternus' periodizations in conflict (the first imperial ideology, the second anti-), but ultimately they are both incredibly broad brush. On the general "rapprochement" of imperial present and republican past in the *Dialogus,* see Gowing 2005: 109.

43. See Levene 2004: 173–174; as he notes (163), Aper already points to this with his claim at 8.2 that oratory manages to flourish in every age.

44. *Pace* Levene (2004: 173), who reads this moment as giving a pointedly identifiable dramatic date. As Van den Berg (2014: 31) says, even if we read this to mean "sixth year," it would clash with Aper's count of 120 years since 43 BCE (the first gives 74/75 CE; the second 77/78). On the oddness of the expression (and an attempt to force it into some sort of normalcy), see Mayer 2001 *ad loc.*

45. As Chris Whitton communicates *per litteras,* none of the issues with Aper's arithmetic would bother us if we knew more about Maternus' Cato—but Tacitus has happened (?) to pick three protagonists (Maternus, Aper, Messalla) about whom we know very little.

46. This may also account for the manuscripts' *novem* (emended to *sex* by Lipsius) in the reckoning of Augustus' reign: for Aper, near enough is good enough.

47. Mayer (2001 *ad loc.*) notes that *statio* becomes "almost a technical term" for the princeps' role (see Woodman 1977 on Vell. Pat. 2.124.2) but here anomalously comes to mean an individual year of a reign. I would prefer not to stretch it.

48. M. Beck (2001, reprising Koestermann 1932; and Norden 1898: 325n2) has recently taken a strong line in favor of this position—although, as Levene (2004: 173n46) points out, the *iam* throws a spanner in the works.

49. *Dial.* 9 (cf. Maternus' pickup of the phrase in 12). The first to spot it was Lange 1832 (1928): 5–8; for a nice intertextual treatment building on the connection, see Edwards 2008. The phrase is still held up as the silver bullet/golden ticket, proving Tacitean authorship beyond reasonable doubt (a view reasserted just now in Keeline 2018: 233). I can't help but call this out as little more than faith and desire dolled up in the positivist costume of "evidence."

50. And the phrase is of course repeated at close quarters in the *Dialogus* itself, by Maternus: *nemora vero et luci* (12). For a wonderfully delicate intertextual reading of Pliny 9.10 and 1.6 as response to both this moment and Quintilian *IO* 10.3.22, see Whitton 2019: 459–468.

51. As Whitton (2019: 467) has it, the allusion of Pliny *Ep.* 1.6 can only really help with relative chronology, rather than the "absolute dating" of the *Dialogus.*

52. For the *Dialogus'* use of intertext as an alternative form of context, see Levene 2004: e.g., 165–166.

53. On the rich intertextual tissue connecting Quintilian's *Institutio Oratoria* and the *Dialogus,* see recently Whitton 2018: 38–49.

54. While David Levene wouldn't want his approach abused to extend beyond the more "derivative" cases of historical text he discusses in Levene 2011, I can't help but be inspired by his sensitivity to texts that, because of their tralatitious nature, must needs partake of multiple times at once: "If—as we should—we want to think in terms of the ideology that the text generates, we have to treat it not as the ideology of one time when the text was produced, but a dynamic ideological system across centuries of Roman history" (Levene 2011: 16). What if we understood the Tacitus-Cicero relationship in these terms for the *Dialogus?*

55. On this kind of beyond-authorship *sermo* in 2, see Dressler 2013: 14.

56. That's not to say that there aren't hard markers, as David Levene (*per litteras*) stresses: between 69 and the death of someone who was a youth around then; and also by the life span of Fabius Iustus. In my view, that is still a pretty broad church.

57. Cf. Luce 2006 (1993): 410. Although Tacitus' failure to laugh here also singles him out, a form of "conspicuously absent *sphragis*": Dressler 2013: 3, 10. For a collective sigh of relief read into the laugh, see Reitz 2014: 118–120.

58. Textuality itself may be another Tacitean answer to what Mayer (2001: 6) calls "the ephemeral quality of contemporary oratorical effort." Cf. his point about the leitmotif of the book and Maternus' interest in the physical book as the hook of fame (36).

59. Indeed, the overlap between the two on the *corrupta eloquentia* theme has been a choice rivet used to bolt [Longinus] to the first century: cf. Russell 1964: xxv; Barnes 1986: 233.

60. As Porter (2016: 140) points out, [Longinus] almost claims to be a figure for tradition or "for the way the critical tradition recycles itself."

61. See the introduction to this chapter (prior to "Moving / Staying with the Times").

62. Barnes (1986: 233) backs Heldmann's (1982: 286–293) argument that [Longinus] is directly criticizing Tacitus but lifts the text into the second century (wherein the quote from Genesis makes more sense). Dating solely on the *corrupta eloquentia* theme is pretty flimsy but nevertheless often done, as Heath (2000: 52) points out.

63. *On the Sublime* has had early and late proponents roughly parallel to Calpurnius Siculus and a similar history of belief in each. Until the nineteenth century, *On the Sublime* was generally granted to the third-century senator and philosopher Cassius Longinus. Weiske (1809) gainsaid it, and most scholars have pushed for an early date since, although signs of late fever have recently stirred. (Early daters tend to assume an anonymous author; late daters tend to identify the author with Cassius Longinus). Early: Russell 1964: 146–147 (around 100 CE); Innes 2002: 259. Late: Heldmann 1982: 286–293; Barnes 1986: 233; Heath 2000 (third century).

64. Cf. Porter 2016: 57–58.

65. My approach in this section will work in the critical tradition of reading [Longinus] as an embodiment of the principles he logs—Pope's quotable mot that [Longinus] is "himself the great sublime he draws." See Russell 1964: 148; Hertz 1983: 579; Walsh 1988: 252; Innes 2006: 311, Porter 2016: 63. Cf. Lamb 1993: 546, 552–553. Whitmarsh (2001: 61–62) shows how [Longinus] mimes the sublime even in his flaws.

66. For the Longinian tendency to privilege the local, the passage, the bit over the whole, see Halliwell 2011: 352.

67. Some scholars have already hinted at the effect of [Longinus]' contextlessness (e.g., Too 1999: 188) but usually to disregard it as accidental or illusory (e.g., Porter 2016: 59).

68. The manuscript P reads Φλωρεντιανὲ rather than Τερεντιανὲ; Mazzucchi 2010 *ad* 1 adopts Vossius' (or probably Vossius') conjecture to settle on Postumius Florus Terentianus. For a couple of tentative suggestions as to Terentianus' identity, see Russell 1964: 147. For an analysis of the relationship (teacher-student) and a study in how Terentianus is verbally represented, see Allen 1941.

69. For Caecilius' putative place in the Longinian "response" and [Longinus] possible departures from Caecilius, see Innes 2002.

70. Text from Russell 1964, with the exceptions of συναραιοῖ for †συνάροι (44), τὰς εἰσόδους εὐθὺς ἐμβαίνει for τὰς εἰσόδους †εἰς ἅς ἐμβαίνει (44), ἀλαζόνειάν for πλεοναξίαν. Translations are my own.

71. On Terentianus representing the wider politicians, see Too 1999: 189.

72. 1.4; on Longinian ekstasis, see Doran 2015: 40–44. On the importance of ekstasis within ancient understandings of supra-individualized authorship, see de la Durantaye 2007: 69.

73. For the move beyond Terentianus, cf. also Porter's (2016: 107) point about the rhetorical questions dogging the treatise, addressed to "no one in particular."

74. Innes (2006: 303) thinks it likely [Longinus] took it as Demosthenes'; see also Russell 1964 ad loc.

75. See Too 1999: 190–191; the idea is rooted in this quotation. See also Halliwell 2011: 333–334.

76. Perhaps another example of Too's (1999: 195) "taxonomy of linguistic dislocations which in turn shifts the reading subject, enabling a series of alternative identifications of the reader."

77. For this vocabulary of creativity across the treatise, see Innes 2006: 308.

78. The reading λόγων has caused its fair share of trouble. I retain and understand it as "languages," with Dacier (see Russell 1964 ad loc.); it squares well with [Longinus]' attempt to spread out multilingually (see the last paragraph of this chapter).

79. Although, as Stephen Halliwell points out to me per litteras, the irony of "universal agreement" is pretty sour in a treatise built on fundamental disagreement with a rival critic, Caecilius.

80. See Segal 1959: 123–124. For the many places where [Longinus] emphasizes eternal over ephemeral, see Innes 2006: 307–308. This is all pace Porter (2016: e.g., 66, 69–70, 84, 138), whose revisionist account decommissions the transcendentalist and idealist wings of the Longinian sublime in favor of its didactic, rhetorical, practical, and materialist qualities (although cf. 400, 402, 611–612, where he situates the Longinian sublime in between the material and the immaterial; uncontroversial moments of transcendental sublime are picked apart as closet materialist, e.g., 35, 44.8; 615–617).

81. For the "surplus of meaning" here, and the Longinian sublime as a "quality of writing with extensive cognitive repercussions," see Halliwell 2011: 341–342.

82. Mazzucchi (1988: 223) recognizes [Longinus]' anonymizing citations. For the implications of [Longinus]' citation process, see Hertz 1983 (the famous "thickening of texture" at 586); Too 1999: 195. On the strange composite quotations from Homer, see Usher 2007. For the general importance of quotation to the Longinian sublime, see Porter 2016: 100–102, 143; cf. Porter 2001: 80: "the sublime exists only in a chain of citations."

83. A founding assumption of intertextuality but one challenged in Small 1997 (e.g., 4).

84. Cf. Porter 2016: 98–100. Heath 2000: 67 takes the terminology here as grist for a late date, connecting [Longinus] to Cassius Longinus and the later Neoplatonists.

85. This passage is a star of the Longinian firmament (see Russell 1964 ad loc. on the controversy over its authenticity, which he defends); on the interruption of

[Longinus]' voice through the subtle interrogative τί, see Porter 2016: 107–115, 169–170.

86. Cf. Porter 2016: 109–110.

87. For Longinian authors as heroes, see Segal 1987.

88. See Whitmarsh 2001: 58–60 (cf. Walsh 1988: 266) on the move from passive to active forms of imitation here. On the link with the collapse between author and reader, see Too 1999: 210–211; Innes 2002: 268. Hunter (2012: 43–44) highlights the Platonic contours of this passage (also in a reactive sense), although Porter (2016: 534) fingers other sources at play.

89. Cf. Porter 2016: 535.

90. See Segal 1959: 124.

91. For the pregnancy/abortion images threading this part of the treatise, see Innes 2006: 308; as Hauser (2016b: 166; cf. 2016a) shows, the metaphor of motherhood for authorship cuts across Greco-Roman literature.

92. For this future, fame-focused ethos as essentially a heroic one, see Segal 1987: 209–211; on the self-transcendence here, see Segal 1959: 137. The exclusion of fear here is heroic through and through: see Innes 1995: 330–331, 333.

93. E.g., *ore legar populi* (Ovid *Met.* 15.878); although Russell (1981: 85) compares the instruction to write for posterity to—Horace!

94. See Russell 1964 *ad loc.* For detailed interpretation, see Mazzucchi 1988: 223–226.

95. Cf. Porter 2001: 67, 83 on the fragmenting effects of Longinian quotation.

96. See Segal 1959: 135; for Halliwell 2011 (esp. 342–344, 359–360, 363), this metaphysical reach of the human mind is crucial to the Longinian sublime. For an antitranscendental, against-the-grain reading of this passage, see Porter 2016: 175–177.

97. As Russell 1964 *ad loc.* points out, the sentiment here is commonplace with mixed origins—Stoicism, Platonism, Pythagoreanism all poke their heads in: "The common spiritual fare of the educated in the first two centuries or so of the empire."

98. See *Phaedrus* 264C; another version at *Anth. Pal.* 7.153 (and see Russell 1964 *ad loc.*).

99. This ethical argument is prepared already in section 43: see Innes 2006: 302.

100. Segal had a long career and many scholarly incarnations. But the New Criticism would have been exerting a lot of pressure on him at time of writing this particular article (1959).

101. Segal 1959: esp. 140. Donini 1969 also pinned the relationship between the sublime and history as *the* key theme of the work, capped in section 44.

102. For an interesting early attempt to smooth over the differences between these two positions, see Rostagni 1947: xxxiii: "l'Autore affaccia ancora da parte sua un'altra soluzione, con la quale in certo modo corregge, tempera, svia le precedenti affermazioni, ma non le annulla."

103. On the imagery of slavery and bondage throughout the treatise in general, see Segal 1987: 215–216; Innes 2006: 308.

104. On the hints of the philosopher's distancing from his own argument, cf. Porter 2001: 76.

105. Cf. Mazzucchi 2010: 300.

106. From the *Laws* and the *Republic* in particular: see Segal 1959: 137; Lamb 1993: 561; Innes 2002: 268–269.

107. See Mayer 2001: 14; Luce 2006 (1993): 382–383; Van den Berg 2014: 47–49; cf. Brink 1993: 346 on the cliché.

108. In this sense, [Longinus]' stirring swan song is an extension of the prevaricating techniques of the philosopher, rather than an argumentative antidote to him or a depoliticization of his position (for a brilliant reading of which, showing the Longinian take as ambivalent, see Whitmarsh 2001: 67–71). Segal (1959: 122) also sees some overlap between philosopher and [Longinus], despite his general view that [Longinus]' argument rules the roost. Too (1999: 211–213) understands the political sphere not as something ruled out in this last section but merely as displaced from external to internal conditions.

109. Russell 1964 *ad loc.* donnishly terms it "something of a commonplace."

110. Stephen Halliwell points out to me *per litteras* that this is an oblique allusion to Plato, from whom [Longinus] gets the idea of fluffy nest-building (*Republic* 548a). But the fact that it is disguised under a generic plural ("the philosophers") adds to the overall fudging of the section.

111. For the ὑστεροφημία link with 14.3, see Russell 1981: 79; Innes 2006: 309.

112. I print μηδ᾿ ὑστεροφημίας, with Russell (1964); Reiske's conjecture for μηδ᾿ ἔτερα φήμης.

113. Although the last is particularly present here, especially in the notion of "looking upward," redoing the *Republic* passage quoted at 13.1: see Segal 1959: 137; Segal 1987: 211. For [Longinus]' restrictive canon, cf. Too 1999: 217.

114. We could see this as the ultimate case of [Longinus]' embodying/converging with his subject matter; indeed, the end of the treatise (esp. 39–42) sees a reduction in quotation of other authors to exemplify the point at hand, with a corresponding increase in self-illustration (i.e., [Longinus]' words *are* the point, they suffice in themselves—see Innes 1994: 48–53).

115. Russell (1964: 154) sees this as a Longinian performance for Terentianus in particular: look at how sound this teacher really is!

116. Probably a second work Περὶ πάθους; see Mazzucchi 1990 (esp. 159).

117. The "anonymized" sentiments in this part of the play perhaps also fed the allegations of spuriousness (on which see Cropp 2013 *ad* 367–400).

118. I owe these references to Mazzucchi 2010 *ad loc.*, much as he leaves them underdeveloped. For problems with Diogenes' attribution to the *Auge*, see Cropp 2013 *ad Electra* 379.

119. West 1995.

120. The political argument has usually been taken to refer to free republic versus unfree principate but can at least also work in the sense of Greece before/after Roman occupation (see Heath 2000: 54). Whitmarsh (2001: 66–67) thinks this refers to the Macedonian, then Roman, domination of Greece.

121. For the attempt to forge a universal Hellenism with this repertoire, see Whitmarsh 2001: 66.

122. Problems with cultural (and authorial) positionality are of course everywhere in second sophistic texts. Porter (2001: 89–90) nicely compares [Longinus] to Dio Chrysostom and Lucian on this front.

123. [Longinus]' reach for the "anytime" helps him form, and partake in, a politically conservative tradition of most any age: "egli ha il tipico volto, e il linguaggio, del conservatore di ogni tempo" (Donini 1969: 202).

124. Porter (2016: 59) gestures toward this link (see the epigraph to this section) but refuses to make anything of it. Cf. Porter 2001: 77.

Conclusion

1. Cf. Tamás, forthcoming.

2. I include some of my own previous work among this group but have tried to understand "the political" differently of late (see Geue 2018b).

3. E.g., Gowers 1994: 131: "Neronian literature demands to be read in the shadow, or rather, glare of its ruler."

4. As such, I follow Felski's (2015: 173) first recommendation for what a "postcritical reading" will refuse: "subject a text to interrogation."

5. See Attridge 2015: 239–258.

6. Attridge 2015: 256, using Derrida 1995: 20–24, 33–35n14; and Derrida 2008: 156–157.

7. Attridge 2015: 256.

8. Attridge 2015: 257.

References

Ahl, Frederick. 1984. "The Art of Safe Criticism in Greece and Rome." *American Journal of Philology* 105(2): 174–208.

Allen, Walter, Jr. 1941. "The Terentianus of the 'Peri Hypsous.'" *American Journal of Philology* 62(1): 51–64.

Armstrong, David. 1986. "Stylistics and the Date of Calpurnius Siculus." *Philologus* 130(1–2): 113–136.

Ash, Rhiannon. 2016. "Never Say Die! Assassinating Emperors in Suetonius' 'Lives of the Caesars.'" In *Writing Biography in Greece and Rome: Narrative Technique and Fictionalization,* edited by Koen de Temmerman and Kristoffel Demoen, 200–216. Cambridge: Cambridge University Press.

Attridge, Derek. 2015. *The Work of Literature.* Oxford: Oxford University Press.

Auerbach, Erich. (1946) 2013. *Mimesis: The Representation of Reality in Western Literature.* Princeton, NJ: Princeton University Press.

Bagnani, Gilbert. 1954. *Arbiter of Elegance: A Study of the Life and Works of C. Petronius.* Toronto: University of Toronto Press.

Baldwin, Barry. 1964. "Executions under Claudius: Seneca's 'Ludus de morte Claudii.'" *Phoenix* 18(1): 39–48.

———. 1984. "Trimalchio and Maecenas." *Latomus* 43: 402–403.

———. 1995. "Better Late than Early: Reflections on the Date of Calpurnius Siculus." *Illinois Classical Studies* 20: 157–167.

Baraz, Yelena. 2015. "Sound and Silence in Calpurnius Siculus." *American Journal of Philology* 136(1): 91–120.

Bardon, Henri. 1952. *La littérature latine inconnue.* Paris: Klincksieck.

Barnes, Timothy D. 1982. "The Date of 'Octavia.'" *Museum Helveticum* 39: 215–217.

———. 1986. "The Significance of Tacitus' 'Dialogus de Oratoribus.'" *Harvard Studies in Classical Philology* 90: 225–244.

Barthes, Roland. 1968. "La mort de l'auteur." *Manteia* 5: 12–17.

Bartsch, Shadi. 1994. *Actors in the Audience: Theatricality and Doublespeak from Nero to Hadrian.* Cambridge, MA: Harvard University Press.

Beard, Mary. 1993. "Looking (Harder) for Roman Myth: Dumézil, Declamation and the Problems of Definition." In *Mythos in mythenloser Gesellschaft: Das Paradigma Roms,* edited by Fritz Graf, 44–64. Stuttgart: Teubner.

Beck, Marcus. 2001. "Das dramatische Datum des 'Dialogus de Oratoribus': Überlegungen zu einer in Vergessenheit geratenen Streitfrage." *Rheinisches Museum für Philologie* 144(2): 159–171.

Beck, Roger Lyne. 1973. "Some Observations on the Narrative Technique of Petronius." *Phoenix* 27(1): 42–61.

Bennett, Andrew. 2004. *The Author.* London: Routledge.

Bing, Peter. 2016. "Epicurus and the 'Iuuenis' at Virgil's Eclogue 1.42." *Classical Quarterly* 66(1): 172–179.

Bloomer, W. Martin. 1997. *Latinity and Literary Society at Rome.* Philadelphia: University of Pennsylvania Press.

Bodel, John. 1999. "The 'Cena Trimalchionis.'" In *Latin Fiction: The Latin Novel in Context,* edited by Heinz Hofmann, 38–51. London: Routledge.

Bonandini, Alice. 2010. *Il contrasto menippeo: Prosimetro, citazioni e commutazione di codice nell'Apocolocyntosis di Seneca: Con un commento alle parti poetiche.* Trento: Università degli studi di Trento.

Bowie, Ewen L. 1970. "Greeks and Their Past in the Second Sophistic." *Past and Present:* 46: 3–41.

———. 2001. "Inspiration and Aspiration: Date, Genre, and Readership." In *Pausanias: Travel and Memory in Roman Greece,* edited by Susan E. Alcock, John F. Cherry, and Jas Elsner, 21–32. Oxford: Oxford University Press.

Boyle, Anthony James. 2008. *"Octavia": Attributed to Seneca.* Oxford: Oxford University Press.

Braund, Susanna Morton, and Paula James. 1998. "Quasi Homo: Distortion and Contortion in Seneca's 'Apocolocyntosis.'" *Arethusa* 31(3): 285–311.

Breed, Brian W. 2006. *Pastoral Inscriptions: Reading and Writing Virgil's "Eclogues."* London: Duckworth.

Bringmann, Klaus. 1985. "Senecas 'Apocolocyntosis': Ein Forschungsbericht 1959–1982." *Aufstieg und Niedergang der Römischen Welt II* 32(2): 885–914.

Brink, Charles Oscar. 1993. "History in the 'Dialogus de Oratoribus' and Tacitus the Historian: A New Approach to an Old Source." *Hermes* 121(3): 335–349.

Bronstein, Michaela. 2018. *Out of Context: The Uses of Modernist Fiction.* Oxford: Oxford University Press.

Buckley, Emma. 2012. "'Nero Insitiuus': Constructing Neronian Identity in the Pseudo-Senecan 'Octavia.'" In *The Julio-Claudian Succession: Reality and Perception of the "Augustan Model,"* edited by A. G. G. Gibson, 133–154. Leiden: Brill.

Burgess, Theodore C. 1902. *Epideictic Literature.* Chicago: University of Chicago Press.

Burke, Edmund. 1987. *A Philosophical Enquiry into the Origin of Our Ideas of the Sublime and Beautiful.* Oxford: Blackwell.

Butler, Shane. 2015. *The Ancient Phonograph.* New York: Zone Books.

Cairns, Francis. 2008. "C. Asinius Pollio and the 'Eclogues.'" *Cambridge Classical Journal* 54: 49–79.

Cameron, Alan. 1967. "Tacitus and the Date of Curiatius Maternus' Death."
Classical Review 17: 258–261.

Carbone, M. E. 1977. "The 'Octavia': Structure, Date and Authenticity." *Phoenix*
31: 48–67.

Carter, John Marshall. 1982. *Suetonius: "Divus Augustus."* Bristol: Bristol
Classical Press.

Casali, Sergio. 1997. "Quaerenti plura legendum: On the Necessity of 'Reading
More' in Ovid's Exile Poetry." *Ramus: Critical Studies in Greek and Latin
Literature* 26(1): 80–112.

Cavarzere, Alberto. 2001. "*Ego Polivi Versibus Senariis:* Phaedrus and
Iambic Poetry." In *Iambic Ideas: Essays on a Poetic Tradition from Archaic
Greece to the Late Roman Empire,* edited by Alberto Cavarzere, Antonio
Aloni, and Alessandro Barchiesi, 205–217. Lanham, MD: Rowman and
Littlefield.

Champlin, Edward J. 1978. "The Life and Times of Calpurnius Siculus." *Journal
of Roman Studies* 68: 95–110.

———. 1986. "History and the Date of Calpurnius Siculus." *Philologus* 130:
104–112.

———. 1989. "The Life and Times of Calpurnius Piso." *Museum Helveticum* 46:
101–124.

———. 2003. *Nero.* Cambridge, MA: Harvard University Press.

———. 2005. "Phaedrus the Fabulous." *Journal of Roman Studies* 95: 97–123.

Clarke, Katherine. 1997. "In Search of the Author of Strabo's Geography."
Journal of Roman Studies 87: 92–110.

Connors, Catherine. 1998. *Petronius the Poet: Verse and Literary Tradition in the
Satyricon.* Cambridge: Cambridge University Press.

———. 2004. "Monkey Business: Imitation, Authenticity, and Identity from
Pithekoussai to Plautus." *Classical Antiquity* 23(2): 179–207.

Conte, Gian Biagio. 1994. *Latin Literature: A History.* Edited by Don P. Fowler
and G. W. Most. Translated by Joseph B. Solodow. Baltimore: Johns Hopkins
University Press.

———. 1996. *The Hidden Author: An Interpretation of Petronius' Satyricon.*
Berkeley: University of California Press.

Cooley, Alison E. 2009. *Res Gestae Divi Augusti: Text, Translation, and Commentary.* Cambridge: Cambridge University Press.

Cornell, Tim J. 2009. "Cato the Elder and the Origins of Roman Autobiography."
In *The Lost Memoirs of Augustus and the Development of Roman Autobiog-
raphy,* edited by Christopher J. Smith, Anton Powell, and Tim J. Cornell, 15–40.
Swansea: Classical Press of Wales.

Courtney, Edward. 1987. "Imitation, chronologie littéraire et Calpurnius Siculus."
Revue des Études Latines 65: 148–157.

———. 1991. *The Poems of Petronius.* Atlanta: Scholars Press.

Crook, John Anthony. 1995. *Legal Advocacy in the Roman World.* Ithaca, NY:
Cornell University Press.

Cropp, Martin J. 2013. *Euripides: "Electra."* Liverpool: Liverpool University
Press.

Cueva, Edmund P., and Javier Martínez, eds. 2016. *"Splendide Mendax": Rethinking Fakes and Forgeries in Classical, Late Antique, and Early Christian Literature.* Groningen: Barkhuis.

Culler, Jonathan D. 2015. *Theory of the Lyric.* Cambridge, MA: Harvard University Press.

Damon, Cynthia. 2010. "Too Close? Historian and Poet in the 'Apocolocyntosis.'" In *Latin Historiography and Poetry in the Early Empire: Generic Interactions,* edited by John F. Miller and Anthony John Woodman, 49–70. Leiden: Brill.

———. 2014. "Suetonius the Ventriloquist." In *Suetonius, the Biographer: Studies in Roman Lives,* edited by Tristan Power and Roy K. Gibson, 38–57. Oxford: Oxford University Press.

Damon, Phillip. 1961. *Modes of Analogy in Ancient and Medieval Verse.* Berkeley: University of California Press.

Davis, Peter J. 1987. "Structure and Meaning in the 'Eclogues' of Calpurnius Siculus." *Ramus* 16: 32–54.

de la Durantaye, Katharina. 2007. "The Origins of the Protection of Literary Authorship in Ancient Rome." *Boston University International Law Journal* 25(1): 37–111.

Del Giovane, Barbara. Forthcoming. "Et Sine Auctore Notissimi Versus: Unauthored Poetry and Rome's Authoritative Turn." In *Unspoken Rome: Absence in Latin Literature and Its Reception,* edited by Tom Geue and Elena Giusti. Cambridge: Cambridge University Press.

Derrida, Jacques. 1995. *On the Name.* Edited by T. Dutoit. Translated by D. Wood, John P. Leavey Jr., and I. McLeod. Stanford, CA: Stanford University Press.

———. 2008. *The Gift of Death and Literature in Secret.* 2nd ed. Chicago: University of Chicago Press.

Di Brazzano, Stefano. 2004. *Laus Pisonis: Introduzione, edizione critica, traduzione e commento.* Pisa: Pubblicazioni della Classe di Lettere e Filosofia, Scuola Normale Superiore Pisa.

Dickey, Eleanor. 2002. *Latin Forms of Address: From Plautus to Apuleius.* Oxford: Oxford University Press.

Di Lorenzo, Enrico, and Bruno Pellegrino. 2008. *Eclogae: Calpurnio Siculo; Introduzione, testo critico, traduzione e commento.* Naples: Cuzzolin.

Dimock, Wai Chee. 1997. "A Theory of Resonance." *Publications of the Modern Language Association* 112(5): 1060–1071.

Dominik, William J., John Garthwaite, and Paul Roche. 2009. "Writing Imperial Politics: The Context." In *Writing Politics in Imperial Rome,* edited by William J. Dominik, John Garthwaite, and Paul Roche, 1–21. Leiden: Brill.

Donini, Pierluigi. 1969. "Il Sublime contro la storia nell'ultimo capitolo del Περί Ὕψους." *La Parola del Passato: Rivista di Studi Antichi* 24: 190–202.

Doran, Robert. 2015. *The Theory of the Sublime from Longinus to Kant.* Cambridge: Cambridge University Press.

Dressler, Alex. 2013. "Poetics of Conspiracy and Hermeneutics of Suspicion in Tacitus's 'Dialogus de Oratoribus.'" *Classical Antiquity* 32(1): 1–34.

Dronke, Peter. 1994. *Verse with Prose from Petronius to Dante: The Art and Scope of the Mixed Form.* Cambridge, MA: Harvard University Press.

Dugan, John. 2005. *Making a New Man: Ciceronian Self-Fashioning in the Rhetorical Works.* New York: Oxford University Press.

Eck, Werner. 1984. "Senatorial Self-Representation: Developments in the Augustan Period." In *Caesar Augustus: Seven Aspects,* edited by Fergus Millar and Erich Segal, 129–167. Oxford: Clarendon Press.

Eden, P. T. 1984. *Seneca: "Apocolocyntosis."* Cambridge: Cambridge University Press.

Edwards, Catharine. 1997. "Self-Scrutiny and Self-Transformation in Seneca's Letters." *Greece and Rome* 44(1): 23–28.

———. 2000. *Suetonius: "Lives of the Caesars."* Oxford: Oxford University Press.

Edwards, Rebecca. 2008. "Hunting for Boars with Pliny and Tacitus." *Classical Antiquity* 27(1): 35–58.

Ellis, Robinson. 1881. *P. Ovidii Nasonis Ibis.* Oxford: Oxford University Press.

Elsner, Jas. 2001. "Describing Self in the Language of Other: Pseudo (?) Lucian at the Temple of Hierapolis." In *Being Greek under Rome: Cultural Identity, the Second Sophistic and the Development of Empire,* edited by Simon Goldhill, 123–153. Cambridge: Cambridge University Press.

Esposito, Paolo. 2012. "Interaction between 'Bucolics' and 'Georgics': The Fifth Eclogue of Calpurnius Siculus." *Trends in Classics* 4(1): 48–72.

Farrell, Joseph A. 2004. "Ovid's Virgilian Career." *Materiali e Discussioni per l'Analisi dei Testi Classici* 52: 41–55.

———. 2007. "Horace's Body, Horace's Books." In *Classical Constructions: Papers in Memory of Don Fowler, Classicist and Epicurean,* edited by Stephen J. Harrison, Peta G. Fowler, and Stephen J. Heyworth, 174–193. Oxford: Oxford University Press.

———. 2016. "Ancient Commentaries on Theocritus' 'Idylls' and Virgil's 'Eclogues.'" In *Classical Commentaries: Explorations in a Scholarly Genre,* edited by Christina Kraus and Christopher Stray, 397–418. Oxford: Oxford University Press.

Feeney, Denis C. 2016. *Beyond Greek: The Beginnings of Latin Literature.* Cambridge, MA: Harvard University Press.

Felski, Rita. 2015. *The Limits of Critique.* Chicago: University of Chicago Press.

Ferri, Rolando. 2003. *"Octavia:" A Play Attributed to Seneca.* Cambridge: Cambridge University Press.

Ferry, Anne. 2002. "Anonymity: The Literary History of a Word." *New Literary History* 33(2): 193–214.

Fey-Wickert, Beate. 2002. *Calpurnius Siculus: Kommentar zur 2. und 3. Ekloge.* Trier, Germany: Wissenschaftlicher Verlag Trier.

Fitch, John G. 2004 (2018). *Seneca: "Oedipus," "Agamemnon," "Thyestes," "Hercules on Oeta," "Octavia."* Cambridge, MA: Harvard University Press.

Fitch, John G., and Siobhan McElduff. 2002. "Construction of the Self in Senecan Drama." *Mnemosyne: Bibliotheca Classica Batava* 55(1): 18–40.

Fitton Brown, A. D. 1985. "The Unreality of Ovid's Tomitan Exile." *Liverpool Classical Monthly* 10: 19–22.

Flower, Harriet I. 2006. *The Art of Forgetting: Disgrace and Oblivion in Roman Political Culture.* Chapel Hill: University of North Carolina Press.

———. 2014. "Memory and Memoirs in Republican Rome." In *Memoria Romana: Memory in Rome and Rome in Memory,* edited by G. Karl Galinsky, 27–40. Ann Arbor: University of Michigan Press.

Foucault, Michel. 1979. "What Is an Author?" In *Textual Strategies: Perspectives in Post-Structuralist Criticism,* edited and translated by Josué V Harari, 141–160. Ithaca NY: Cornell University Press.

Freudenburg, Kirk. 2015. "Seneca's 'Apocolocyntosis': Censors in the Afterworld." In *The Cambridge Companion to Seneca,* edited by Shadi Bartsch and Alessandro Schiesaro, 93–105. Cambridge: Cambridge University Press.

Friedrich, Werner. 1976. *Nachahmung und eigene Gestaltung in der bukolischen Dichtung des Titus Calpurnius Siculus.* Frankfurt: Stadt. U. Universitäts Frankfurt A.M.

Furneaux, Henry. 1896. *Annalium ab excessu divi Augusti libri = The Annals of Tacitus: Volume II.* Oxford: Clarendon Press.

Gadamer, Hans Georg. 2004. *Truth and Method.* Translated by Joel Weinsheimer and Donald G. Marshall. 2nd rev. ed. London: Continuum.

Galimberti, Alessandro, and Ilaria Ramelli. 2001. "L''Octavia' e il suo autore: P. Pomponio Secondo; 2: Publio Pomponio Secondo 'consularis' e poeta autore dell' 'Octavia'?" *Aevum* 75(1): 93–99.

Gallia, Andrew B. 2009. "'Potentes' and 'Potentia' in Tacitus's 'Dialogus de Oratoribus.'" *Transactions of the American Philological Association* 139(1): 169–206.

Garson, R. W. 1975. "The Pseudo-Senecan 'Octavia': A Plea for Nero." *Latomus* 34: 754–756.

Geue, Tom. 2013. "Princeps avant la lettre: The Foundations of Augustus in Pre-Augustan Poetry." In *La costruzione del mito augusteo,* edited by M. Labate and Gianpiero Rosati, 49–68. Heidelberg: Winter.

———. 2014. "Editing the Opposition: Horace's 'Ars Politica.'" *Materiali e Discussioni per l'Analisi dei Testi Classici* 72: 143–172.

———. 2017. *Juvenal and the Poetics of Anonymity.* Cambridge: Cambridge University Press.

———. 2018a. "Drawing Blanks: The Pale Shades of 'Phaedrus' and 'Juvenal.'" In *Complex Inferiorities: The Poetics of the Weaker Voice in Latin Literature,* edited by Sebastian Matzner and Stephen Harrison, 89–106. Oxford: Oxford University Press.

———. 2018b. "Soft Hands, Hard Power: Sponging Off the Empire of Leisure (Virgil, 'Georgics' 4)." *Journal of Roman Studies* 108: 115–240.

———. Forthcoming. "Keeping/Losing Records, Keeping/Losing Faith: Suetonius and Justin Do the Document." In *Literature and Culture in the Roman Empire, 96–235: Cross-Cultural Interactions,* edited by Alice Koenig, Rebecca Langlands, and James Uden. Cambridge: Cambridge University Press.

Geue, Tom, and Elena Giusti, eds. Forthcoming. *Unspoken Rome: Absence in Latin Literature and Its Reception.* Cambridge: Cambridge University Press.

Gibson, Bruce. 2004. "Song Contests in Calpurnius Siculus." *Proceedings of the Virgil Society* 25: 1–14.

Gibson, Roy K. 2003. "Pliny and the Art of (In)offensive Self-Praise." *Arethusa* 36(2): 235–254.

Ginsberg, Lauren Donovan. 2011. "'Ingens' as an Etymological Pun in the 'Octavia.'" *Classical Philology* 106(4): 357–360.

———. 2017 *Staging Memory, Staging Strife: Empire and Civil War in the "Octavia."* Oxford: Oxford University Press.

Giusti, Elena. 2016. "Did Somebody Say Augustan Totalitarianism? Duncan Kennedy's 'Reflections,' Hannah Arendt's Origins, and the Continental Divide over Virgil's *Aeneid.*" *Dictynna* 13. https://journals.openedition.org/dictynna/1282.

Glauthier, Patrick. 2009. "Phaedrus, Callimachus and the 'Recusatio' to Success." *Classical Antiquity* 28(2): 248–278.

Goldberg, Sander M. 1999. "Appreciating Aper: The Defence of Modernity in Tacitus' 'Dialogus de Oratoribus.'" *Classical Quarterly* 49(1): 224–237.

———. 2003. "Authorizing 'Octavia.'" *Prudentia* 35(1): 13–36.

———. 2005. *Constructing Literature in the Roman Republic: Poetry and Its Reception.* Cambridge: Cambridge University Press.

———. 2009. "The Faces of Eloquence: The 'Dialogus de Oratoribus.'" In *The Cambridge Companion to Tacitus,* edited by Anthony John Woodman, 73–84. Cambridge: Cambridge University Press.

Goldhill, Simon. 2009. "The Anecdote: Exploring the Boundaries between Oral and Literate Performance in the Second Sophistic." In *Ancient Literacies: The Culture of Reading in Greece and Rome,* edited by William A. Johnson and Holt N. Parker, 96–113. Oxford: Oxford University Press.

Goodyear, F. R. D. 1982. "Suetonius." In *The Cambridge History of Classical Literature,* vol. 2, *Latin Literature,* edited by E. J. Kenney, 661–664. Cambridge: Cambridge University Press.

Gordon, Carol Jean. 1992. "Poetry of Maledictions: A Commentary on the 'Ibis' of Ovid." PhD diss., McMaster University.

Gowers, Emily. 1994. "Persius and the Decoction of Nero." In *Reflections of Nero: Culture, History, and Representation,* edited by Jas Elsner and Jamie Masters, 131–150. Chapel Hill: University of North Carolina Press.

Gowing, Alain M. 2005. *Empire and Memory: The Representation of the Roman Republic in Imperial Culture.* Cambridge: Cambridge University Press.

Grafton, Anthony. 1990. *Forgers and Critics: Creativity and Duplicity in Western Scholarship.* Princeton, NJ: Princeton University Press.

Graziosi, Barbara. 2002. *Inventing Homer: The Early Reception of Epic.* Cambridge: Cambridge University Press.

———. 2013. "The Poet in the 'Iliad.'" In *The Author's Voice in Classical and Late Antiquity,* edited by Anna Marmodoro and Jonathan Hill, 9–38. Oxford: Oxford University Press.

Green, Steven J. 2010. "'(No) Arms and a Man': The Imperial Pretender, the Opportunistic Poet and the 'Laus Pisonis.'" *Classical Quarterly* 60(2): 497–523.

————. 2016. "Recollections of a Heavenly Augustus: Memory and the 'Res Gestae' in Seneca, 'Apocolocyntosis' 10.1–2." *Mnemosyne* 69(4): 685–690.

Griffin, Robert J. 1999. "Anonymity and Authorship." *New Literary History* 30(4): 877–895.

Gunderson, Erik. 2014. "E.g. Augustus: 'Exemplum' in the 'Augustus' and 'Tiberius.'" In *Suetonius, the Biographer: Studies in Roman Lives,* edited by Tristan Power and Roy K. Gibson, 130–145. Oxford: Oxford University Press.

Habicht, Christian. 1985. *Pausanias' Guide to Ancient Greece.* Berkeley: University of California Press.

Hainsworth, John Bryan. 1993. *The "Iliad:" A Commentary: Books 9–12.* Cambridge: Cambridge University Press.

Halliwell, F. Stephen. 2011. *Between Ecstasy and Truth: Interpretations of Greek Poetics from Homer to Longinus.* Oxford: Oxford University Press.

Hanford, Timothy. 2014. "Senecan Tragedy and Virgil's 'Aeneid': Repetition and Reversal." PhD diss., City University of New York.

Hardie, Philip R. 2012. *Rumour and Renown: Representations of Fama in Western Literature.* Cambridge: Cambridge University Press.

Harrison, George William Mallory. 2003. "Forms of Intertextuality in the 'Octavia.'" *Prudentia* 35(1): 112–125.

Harrison, Stephen J. 1999. "Introduction: Twentieth-Century Scholarship on the Roman Novel." In *Oxford Readings in the Roman Novel,* edited by Stephen J. Harrison, xi–xxxix. Oxford: Oxford University Press.

————. 2013. "Author and Speaker(s) in Horace's 'Satires' 2." In *The Author's Voice in Classical and Late Antiquity,* edited by Anna Marmodoro and Jonathan Hill, 153–171. Oxford: Oxford University Press.

Haupt, Moriz. 1854. *De carminibus bucolicis Calpurnii et Nemesiani.* Berlin: Typis Academicis.

Hauser, Emily. 2016a. "In Her Own Words: The Semantics of Female Authorship in Ancient Greece, from Sappho to Nossis." *Ramus: Critical Studies in Greek and Latin Literature* 45(2): 133–164.

————. 2016b. "'Optima tu proprii nominis auctor': The Semantics of Female Authorship in Ancient Rome, from Sulpicia to Proba." *Eugesta* 6: 151–186.

Hawkins, Tom. 2014. *Iambic Poetics in the Roman Empire.* Cambridge: Cambridge University Press.

Heath, Malcolm. 2000. "Longinus, 'On Sublimity.'" *Proceedings of the Cambridge Philological Society* 45: 43–73.

Heldmann, Konrad. 1982. *Antike Theorien über Entwicklung und Verfall der Redekunst.* Munich: Beck.

Heinze, Richard. 1899. "Petron und der Griechische Roman." *Hermes* 34: 494–519.

————. 1926. "Zu Senecas Apocolocyntosis." *Hermes* 61: 49–79.

Henderson, John. 1997. "Not Wavering but Frowning: Ovid as Isopleth (Tristia 1 through 10)." *Ramus: Critical Studies in Greek and Latin Literature* 26(2): 138–171.

————. 1999. "Phaedrus' 'Fables': The Original Corpus." *Mnemosyne* 52(3): 308–329.

———. 2001a. "In Ya (Pre)face." In *A Companion to the Prologue of Apuleius' "Metamorphoses*," edited by Ahuvia Kahane and Andrew Laird, 188–197. Oxford: Oxford University Press.

———. 2001b. *Telling Tales on Caesar: Roman Stories from Phaedrus*. Oxford: Oxford University Press.

———. 2002a. "The Law Is Not Mocked: Straightening Out a Crooked Will (Phaedrus 4.5)." In *Thinking Like a Lawyer: Essays on Legal History and General History for John Crook on His Eightieth Birthday*, edited by Paul McKechnie, 213–230. Leiden: Brill.

———. 2002b. *Pliny's Statue: The Letters, Self-Portraiture and Classical Art*. Exeter: Exeter University Press.

———. 2013. "The 'Carmina Einsidlensia' and Calpurnius Siculus' 'Eclogues.'" In *A Companion to the Neronian Age*, edited by Emma Buckley and Martin T. Dinter, 170–187. Oxford: Blackwell.

Herrmann, Ludwig. 1952. "Les pseudonymes dans les bucoliques de Calpurnius Siculus." *Latomus* 11: 27–44.

———. 1965. "La date et l'auteur du Contre Ibis." *Latomus* 24: 274–295.

Hertz, Neil. 1983. "A Reading of Longinus." *Critical Inquiry* 9(3): 579–596.

Heslin, Peter J. 2011. "Metapoetic Pseudonyms in Horace, Propertius and Ovid." *Journal of Roman Studies* 101: 51–72.

Higbie, Carolyn. 2017. *Collectors, Scholars, and Forgers in the Ancient World*. Oxford: Oxford University Press.

Hinds, Stephen. 1999. "After Exile: Time and Teleology from 'Metamorphoses' to 'Ibis.'" In *Ovidian Transformations: Essays on the "Metamorphoses" and Its Reception*, edited by Philip R. Hardie, Alessandro Barchiesi, and Stephen Hinds, 48–67. Cambridge: Cambridge Philological Society.

———. 2007. "Ovid among the Conspiracy Theorists." In *Classical Constructions: Papers in Memory of Don Fowler, Classicist and Epicurean*, edited by Stephen J. Harrison, Peta G. Fowler, and Stephen J. Heyworth, 194–220. Oxford: Oxford University Press.

———. 2010. "Historicism and Formalism." In *The Oxford Handbook of Roman Studies*, edited by Alessandro Barchiesi and Walter Scheidel, 369–385. Oxford: Oxford University Press.

Holzberg, Niklas. 1993. *Die antike Fabel: Eine Einführung*. Darmstadt, Germany: Wissenschaftliche Buchgesellschaft.

Hopkins, Keith. (1993) 2004. "Novel Evidence for Roman Slavery." In *Studies in Ancient Greek and Roman Society*, edited by Robin Osborne, 206–225. Cambridge: Cambridge University Press.

Horsfall, Nicholas. 1997. "Criteria for the Dating of Calpurnius Siculus." *Rivista di Filologia e di Istruzione Classica* 125(2): 166–196.

Housman, A. E. 1920. "The 'Ibis' of Ovid." *Journal of Philology* 35: 287–318.

Hubbard, Thomas K. 1996. "Calpurnius Siculus and the Unbearable Weight of Tradition." *Helios* 23(1): 67–89.

Hulls, Jean-Michel. 2014. "The Mirror in the Text: Privacy, Performance, and the Power of Suetonius' 'Domitian.'" In *Suetonius, the Biographer: Studies in Roman Lives*, edited by Tristan Power and Roy K. Gibson, 178–196. Oxford: Oxford University Press.

Humble, Noreen M., and Keith Sidwell. 2006. "Dreams of Glory: Lucian as Autobiographer." In *The Limits of Ancient Biography,* edited by Brian C. McGing, Judith M. Mossman, and Ewen L. Bowie, 213–225. Swansea: Classical Press of Wales.

Hunter, Richard L. 1999. *Theocritus: A Selection.* Edited by Richard L. Hunter. Cambridge: Cambridge University Press.

———. 2012. *Plato and the Traditions of Ancient Literature: The Silent Stream.* Cambridge: Cambridge University Press.

Innes, Doreen C. 1994. "Period and Colon: Theory and Example in Demetrius and Longinus." In *Peripatetic Rhetoric after Aristotle,* edited by William W. Fortenbaugh and David Cyrus Mirhady, 36–53. New Brunswick, NJ: Transaction Publishers.

———. 1995. "Longinus, Sublimity, and the Low Emotions." In *Ethics and Rhetoric: Classical Essays for Donald Russell on His Seventy-Fifth Birthday,* edited by Doreen C. Innes, Harry M. Hine, and Christopher B. R. Pelling, 323–333. Oxford: Oxford University Press.

———. 2002. "Longinus and Caecilius: Models of the Sublime." *Mnemosyne* 55(3): 259–284.

———. 2006. "Longinus: Structure and Unity." In *Oxford Readings in Ancient Literary Criticism,* edited by Andrew Laird, 300–312. Oxford: Oxford University Press.

Janson, Tore. 1964. *Latin Prose Prefaces: Studies in Literary Conventions.* Stockholm: Almqvist & Wiksell.

Jennings, Victoria. 2009. "Borrowed Plumes: Phaedrus' 'Fables,' Phaedrus' Failures." In *Writing Politics in Imperial Rome,* edited by William J. Dominik, John Garthwaite, and Paul A. Roche, 225–248. Leiden: Brill.

Jones, Christopher P. 2001. "Pausanias and His Guides." In *Pausanias: Travel and Memory in Roman Greece,* edited by Susan E. Alcock, John F. Cherry, and Jas Elsner, 33–39. Oxford: Oxford University Press.

Jones, Frederick M. A. 2006. "Names and Naming in 'Soft' Poetry." In *Studies in Latin Literature and Roman History,* vol. 13, edited by Carl Deroux, 5–31. Brussels: Latomus.

Kahane, Ahuvia. 2001. "Antiquity's Future: Writing, Speech, and Representation in the Prologue to Apuleius' 'Metamorphoses.'" In *A Companion to the Prologue of Apuleius' "Metamorphoses,"* edited by Ahuvia Kahane and Andrew Laird, 231–241. Oxford: Oxford University Press.

Karakasis, Evangelos. 2010. "'The (Singing) Game Is Not Afoot': Calpurnius Siculus' Sixth Eclogue." *Trends in Classics* 2(1): 175–206.

———. 2011. *Song Exchange in Roman Pastoral.* Berlin: De Gruyter.

———. 2016. *T. Calpurnius Siculus: A Pastoral Poet in Neronian Rome.* Berlin: De Gruyter.

Kearey, Talitha. 2018. "The Poet at Work: Concepts of Authorship in the Ancient Reception of Virgil." PhD diss., University of Cambridge.

Keeline, Thomas J. 2018. *The Reception of Cicero in the Early Roman Empire: The Rhetorical Schoolroom and the Creation of a Cultural Legend.* Cambridge: Cambridge University Press.

Keene, Charles Haines. 1996. *Calpurnius Siculus: The "Eclogues."* London: Bristol Classical Press.

Kennedy, Duncan F. 1993. *The Arts of Love: Five Studies in the Discourse of Roman Love Elegy.* Cambridge: Cambridge University Press.

Kim, Lawrence Young. 2013. "Figures of Silence in Dio Chrysostom's 'First Tarsian Oration' (Or. 33): Aposiopesis, 'Paraleipsis,' and 'Huposiôpêsis.'" *Greece and Rome* 60(1): 32–49.

Knowles, James. 1893. "'Remarks of Tennyson' in 'A Personal Reminiscence.'" *The Nineteenth Century* 33.

Koestermann, Erich. 1932. "Statio Principis." *Philologus* 87(3): 358–368, 430–444.

Kohn, Thomas D. 2003. "Who Wrote Seneca's Plays?" *Classical World* 96(3): 271–280.

Kragelund, Patrick. 1982. *Prophecy, Populism and Propaganda in the "Octavia."* Copenhagen: MT Forl.

———. 1988. "The Prefect's Dilemma and the Date of the 'Octavia.'" *Classical Quarterly* 38: 492–508.

———. 2015. *Roman Historical Drama: The "Octavia" in Antiquity and Beyond.* Oxford: Oxford University Press.

Krasne, Darcy. 2012. "The Pedant's Curse: Obscurity and Identity in Ovid's 'Ibis.'" *Dictynna* 9. https://journals.openedition.org/dictynna/912.

———. 2016. "Crippling Nostalgia: 'Nostos,' Poetics, and the Structure of the 'Ibis.'" *Transactions of the American Philological Association* 146(1): 149–189.

Küppers, Jochem. 1985. "Die Faunus-Prophezeiung in der 1. Ekloge des Calpurnius Siculus." *Hermes* 113: 340–361.

Kurke, Leslie. 2011. *Aesopic Conversations: Popular Tradition, Cultural Dialogue, and the Invention of Greek Prose.* Princeton, NJ: Princeton University Press.

Laird, Andrew. 1999. *Powers of Expression, Expressions of Power: Speech Presentation in Latin Literature.* Oxford: Oxford University Press.

———. 2007. "The True Nature of the '*Satyricon?*'" In *The Greek and Roman Novel: Parallel Readings,* edited by Michael Paschalis, Stavros A. Frangoulidis, Stephen J. Harrison, and Maaike Zimmerman, 151–168. Groningen, Netherlands: Barkhuis.

Lamb, Jonathan. 1993. "Longinus, the Dialectic, and the Practice of Mastery." *ELH: A Journal of English Literary History* 60: 545–567.

Lange, A. G. 1832 (1928). *Vermischte Schriften und Reden.* Leipzig: Teubner.

Langlands, Rebecca. 2014. "Exemplary Influences and Augustus' Pernicious Moral Legacy." In *Suetonius, the Biographer: Studies in Roman Lives,* edited by Tristan Power and Roy K. Gibson, 111–129. Oxford: Oxford University Press.

La Penna, Antonio. 1957. *Ibis: Prolegomeni, testo, app. crit. e commento.* Florence: La Nuova Italia.

———. 1985. "Ille ego qui quondam e i raccordati editoriali nell'antichità." *Studi Italiani di Filologia Classica* 3: 76–91.

Lauwers, Jeroen. 2011. "Reading Books, Talking Culture: The Performance of 'Paideia' in Imperial Greek Literature." In *Orality, Literacy and Performance in the Ancient World,* edited by Elizabeth Minchin, 227–244. Leiden: Brill.

Leach, Eleanor Winsor. 1973. "Corydon Revisited: An Interpretation of the Political Eclogues of Calpurnius Siculus." *Ramus: Critical Studies in Greek and Latin Literature* 2: 53–97.

———. 1989. "The Implied Reader and the Political Argument in Seneca's 'Apocolocyntosis' and 'De Clementia.'" *Arethusa* 22: 197–230.

Lefkowitz, Jeremy B. 2016. "Grand Allusions: Vergil in Phaedrus." *American Journal of Philology* 137(3): 487–509.

———. 2017. "Innovation and Artistry in Phaedrus' Morals." *Mnemosyne* 70(3): 417–435.

Leven, Pauline. 2013. "Reading the Octopus: Authorship, Intertexts, and a Hellenistic Anecdote (Machon Fr. 9 Gow)." *American Journal of Philology* 134(1): 23–35.

Levene, David S. 2004. "Tacitus' 'Dialogus' as Literary History." *Transactions of the American Philological Association* 134(1): 157–200.

———. 2011. "Historical Allusion and the Nature of the Historical Text." *Histos* 5: 1–17.

Lewis, R. G. 1991. "Suetonius' 'Caesares' and Their Literary Antecedents." *Aufstieg und Niedergang der Römischen Welt II* 33(5): 3623–3674.

Libby, Brigitte B. 2010. "The Intersection of Poetic and Imperial Authority in Phaedrus' 'Fables.'" *Classical Quarterly* 60(2): 545–558.

Louis, Nathalie. 2010. *Commentaire historique et traduction du "Diuus Augustus" de Suétone.* Edited by Nathalie Louis. Brussels: Éditions Latomus.

Lowrie, Michèle. 2009. *Writing, Performance, and Authority in Augustan Rome.* Oxford: Oxford University Press.

———. 2010. "Performance." In *The Oxford Handbook of Roman Studies,* edited by Alessandro Barchiesi and Walter Scheidel, 281–294. Oxford: Oxford University Press.

Luce, T. James. 2006 (1993). "Reading and Response in the 'Dialogus.'" In *Oxford Readings in Ancient Literary Criticism,* edited by Andrew Laird, 380–413. Oxford: Oxford University Press.

Lyne, Richard Oliver A. M. 1987. *Further Voices in Vergil's "Aeneid."* Oxford: Clarendon Press.

MacCormack, Sabine. 1975. "Latin Prose Panegyrics." In *Empire and Aftermath: Silver Latin II,* edited by Thomas Dorey, 143–205. London: Routledge.

MacMullen, Ramsay. 1982. "The Epigraphic Habit in the Roman Empire." *American Journal of Philology* 103: 233–246.

Mader, Gottfried Johannes. 2013. "Re-presenting Piso: Poetic and Political Agenda in the 'Laus Pisonis.'" *Classical World* 106(4): 621–643.

Magnelli, Enrico. 2006. "Bucolic Tradition and Poetic Programme in Calpurnius Siculus." In *Brill's Companion to Greek and Latin Pastoral,* edited by Marco Fantuzzi and Theodore Papanghelis, 467–477. Leiden: Brill.

Manuwald, Gesine. 2001. *Fabulae Praetextae: Spuren Einer Literarischen Gattung der Römer.* München: Beck.

———. 2003. "The Concepts of Tyranny in Seneca's 'Thyestes' and in 'Octavia.'" *Prudentia* 35(1): 37–59.

Marincola, John. 1997. *Authority and Tradition in Ancient Historiography.* Cambridge: Cambridge University Press.

Martelli, Francesca. 2010. "Signatures Events Contexts: Copyright at the End of the First Principate." *Ramus: Critical Studies in Greek and Latin Literature* 39(2): 130–159.

———. 2013. *Ovid's Revisions: The Editor as Author.* Cambridge: Cambridge University Press.

Martin, Beatrice. 1996. "Calpurnius Siculus' 'New' Aurea Aetas." *Acta Classica* 39: 17–38.

———. 2003. "Calpurnius Siculus: The Ultimate Imperial 'Toady.'" In *Literature, Art, History: Studies on Classical Antiquity and Tradition in Honour of W. J. Henderson,* edited by André F. Basson and William J. Dominik, 73–90. Frankfurt am Main: Peter Lang.

Martínez, Javier. 2011. *Fakes and Forgers of Classical Literature = Falsificaciones y falsarios de la literatura clásica.* Madrid: Ed. Clásicas.

———. 2012. *"Mundus Vult Decipi": Estudios interdisciplinares sobre falsificación textual y literaria.* Madrid: Ed. Clásicas.

———, ed. 2014. *Fakes and Forgers of Classical Literature: Ergo Decipiatur!* Leiden: Brill.

Masters, Jamie. 1992. *Poetry and Civil War in Lucan's "Bellum Civile."* Cambridge: Cambridge University Press.

Matzner, Sebastian, and Stephen Harrison, eds. 2018. *Complex Inferiorities: The Poetics of the Weaker Voice in Latin Literature.* Oxford: Oxford University Press.

Mayer, Roland G. 1980. "Calpurnius Siculus: Technique and Date." *Journal of Roman Studies* 70: 175–176.

———. 1982. "Neronian Classicism." *American Journal of Philology* 103: 305–318.

———. 2001. *Tacitus: "Dialogus de Oratoribus."* Cambridge: Cambridge University Press.

———. 2006. "Latin Pastoral after Virgil." In *Brill's Companion to Greek and Latin Pastoral,* edited by Marco Fantuzzi and Theodore Papanghelis, 451–466. Leiden: Brill.

Mazzucchi, Carlo Maria. 1988. "Tre citazioni adespote nel Sublime." *Aevum Antiquum* 1: 223–232.

———. 1990. "Come finiva il Περὶ ὕψους?" *Aevum Antiquum* 3: 143–162.

———. 2010. *Dionisio Longino: Del Sublime; Introduzione, testo critico, traduzione e commentario a cura di Carlo Maria Mazzucchi.* Milan: Vita e Pensiero.

McGill, Scott C. 2012. *Plagiarism in Latin Literature.* Cambridge: Cambridge University Press.

Meyer, Elizabeth A. 2004. *Legitimacy and Law in the Roman World: "Tabulae" in Roman Belief and Practice.* Cambridge: Cambridge University Press.

Millar, Fergus. 1977. *The Emperor in the Roman World, 31 B.C.–A.D. 337.* London: Duckworth.

———. 1998. *The Crowd in Rome in the Late Republic.* Ann Arbor: University of Michigan Press.

Miller, John F. 1980. "Ritual Directions in Ovid's 'Fasti': Dramatic Hymns and Didactic Poetry." *Classical Journal* 75: 204–214.

Miller, Paul Allen. 2002. *Latin Erotic Elegy: An Anthology and Reader*. London: Routledge.

Milnor, Kristina Lynn. 2014. *Graffiti and the Literary Landscape in Roman Pompeii*. Oxford: Oxford University Press.

Misch, Georg. 1951. *A History of Autobiography in Antiquity*. Cambridge, MA: Harvard University Press.

Mitchell, Jack. 2015. "Literary Quotation as Literary Performance in Suetonius." *Classical Journal* 110(3): 333–355.

Moles, John L. 1998. "Cry Freedom: Tacitus 'Annals' 4.32–35." *Histos* 2: 95–104.

Morello, Ruth. 2003. "Pliny and the Art of Saying Nothing." *Arethusa* 36(2): 187–209.

Morgan, J. 2009. "Petronius and Greek Literature." In *Petronius: A Handbook*, edited by Jonathan R. W. Prag and Ian D. Repath, 32–47. Chichester, UK: Wiley-Blackwell.

Motto, Anna Lydia, and John R. Clark. 1983. "Satiric Plotting in Seneca's 'Apocolocyntosis.'" *Emerita* 51: 29–40.

Mowbray, Carrie. 2012. "Captive Audience? The Aesthetics of 'Nefas' in Senecan Drama." In *Aesthetic Value in Classical Antiquity*, edited by Ineke Sluiter and Ralph M. Rosen, 393–420. Leiden: Brill.

Mullan, John. 2007. *Anonymity: A Secret History of English Literature*. Princeton, NJ: Princeton University Press.

Münscher, Karl. 1922. *Senecas Werke, Untersuchungen zur Abfassungszeit und Echtheit*. Leipzig: Teubner.

Murgia, Charles E. 1980. "The Date of Tacitus' 'Dialogus.'" *Harvard Studies in Classical Philology* 84: 99–125.

———. 1985. "Pliny's 'Letters' and the 'Dialogus.'" *Harvard Studies in Classical Philology* 89: 171–206.

Nagle, Betty Rose. 1980. *The Poetics of Exile: Program and Polemic in the "Tristia" and "Epistulae ex Ponto" of Ovid*. Brussels: Latomus.

Nagy, Gregory. 1996. *Homeric Questions*. Austin: University of Texas Press.

Najman, Hindy. 2012. "The Vitality of Scripture within and beyond the 'Canon.'" *Journal for the Study of Judaism in the Persian, Hellenistic and Roman Period* 43(4–5): 497–518.

———. 2017. "Ethical Reading: The Transformation of the Text and the Self." *Journal of Theological Studies* 68(2): 507–529.

Narducci, Emanuele. 2002. *Lucano: Un'epica contro l'impero: Interpretazione della "Pharsalia."* Rome: Laterza.

Nauta, Ruurd R. 1987. "Seneca's 'Apocolocyntosis' as Saturnalian Literature." *Mnemosyne* 40: 69–96.

Nelis-Clément, Jocelyne, and Damien P. Nelis. 2005. "Petronius' Epigraphic Habit." *Dictynna* 2. https://journals.openedition.org/dictynna/137.

Newlands, Carole Elizabeth. 1987. "Urban Pastoral: The Seventh Eclogue of Calpurnius Siculus." *Classical Antiquity* 6: 218–231.

Ní Mheallaigh, Karen. 2014. *Reading Fiction with Lucian: Fakes, Freaks and Hyperreality*. Cambridge: Cambridge University Press.

Norden, Eduard. 1898. *Die antike Kunstprosa vom VI. Jahrhundert v. Chr. bis in die Zeit der Renaissance*. Berlin: Teubner.

North, Joseph. 2017. *Literary Criticism: A Concise Political History*. Cambridge, MA: Harvard University Press.

Nussbaum, Martha Craven. 1986. *The Fragility of Goodness: Luck and Ethics in Greek Tragedy and Philosophy*. Cambridge: Cambridge University Press.

O'Gorman, Ellen. 2005. "Citation and Authority in Seneca's 'Apocolocyntosis.'" In *The Cambridge Companion to Roman Satire*, edited by Kirk Freudenburg, 95–108. Cambridge: Cambridge University Press.

Oliensis, Ellen. 1997. "Return to Sender: The Rhetoric of Nomina in Ovid's 'Tristia.'" *Ramus: Critical Studies in Greek and Latin Literature* 26(2): 172–193.

Osgood, Josiah Warren. 2007. "The Vox and Verba of an Emperor: Claudius, Seneca and 'Le Prince idéal.'" *Classical Journal* 102(4): 329–353.

Pagán, Victoria E. 2010. "The Power of the Epistolary Preface from Statius to Pliny." *Classical Quarterly* 60(1): 194–201.

Panayotakis, Costas. 2009. "Petronius and the Roman Literary Tradition." In *Petronius: A Handbook*, edited by Jonathan R. W. Prag and Ian D. Repath, 48–64. Chichester, UK: Wiley-Blackwell.

Park, Johannes. 2017. *Interfiguralität bei Phaedrus: Ein fabelhafter Fall von Selbstinszenierung*. Berlin: De Gruyter.

Payne, Mark. 2007. *Theocritus and the Invention of Fiction*. Cambridge: Cambridge University Press.

Peirano, Irene. 2012. *The Rhetoric of the Roman Fake: Latin Pseudepigrapha in Context*. Cambridge: Cambridge University Press.

———. 2013. "Ille ego qui quondam: On Authorial (An)onymity." In *The Author's Voice in Classical and Late Antiquity*, edited by Anna Marmodoro and Jonathan Hill, 251–285. Oxford: Oxford University Press.

Pelling, Christopher B. R. 2009. "Was There an Ancient Genre of 'Autobiography'? Or Did Augustus Know What He Was Doing?" In *The Lost Memoirs of Augustus and the Development of Roman Autobiography*, edited by Christopher J. Smith, Anton Powell, and Tim J. Cornell, 41–64. Swansea: Classical Press of Wales.

———. 2013. "Xenophon's and Caesar's Third-Person Narratives: Or Are They?" In *The Author's Voice in Classical and Late Antiquity*, edited by Anna Marmodoro and Jonathan Hill, 39–73. Oxford: Oxford University Press.

Penwill, John L. 2003. "What's Hecuba to Him . . . ? Reflections on Poetry and Politics in Tacitus' 'Dialogue on Orators.'" *Ramus: Critical Studies in Greek and Latin Literature* 32(2): 122–147.

———. 2015. "Compulsory Freedom: Literature in Trajan's Rome." In *The Art of Veiled Speech: Self-Censorship from Aristophanes to Hobbes*, edited by Han Baltussen and Peter J. Davis, 176–208. Philadelphia: University of Pennsylvania Press.

Perkins, Judith. 2005. "Trimalchio: Naming Power." In *Metaphor and the Ancient Novel*, edited by Stephen J. Harrison, Michael Pachalis, and Stavros A. Frangoulidis, 139–162. Eelde, Netherlands: Barkhuis.

Pernot, Laurent. 2015. *Epideictic Rhetoric: Questioning the Stakes of Ancient Praise.* Austin: University of Texas Press.

Perry, B. E. 1965. *Babrius and Phaedrus.* Cambridge, MA: Harvard University Press.

Perutelli, Alessandro. 1990. "Il narratore nel Satyricon." *Materiali e Discussioni per l'Analisi dei Testi Classici* 25: 9–25.

Pervo, Richard. 1998. "A Nihilist Fabula: Introducing the *Life of Aesop.*" In *Ancient Fiction and Early Christian Narrative,* edited by Ronald F. Hock, J. Bradley Chance, and Judith Perkins, 77–120. Atlanta: Scholars Press.

Petersmann, Hubert. 1999. "Environment, Linguistic Situation, and Levels of Style in Petronius' 'Satyrica.'" In *Oxford Readings in the Roman Novel,* edited by Stephen J. Harrison, 105–123. Oxford: Oxford University Press.

Pfeiffer, Rudolf. 1968. *History of Classical Scholarship from the Beginnings to the End of the Hellenistic Age.* Oxford: Oxford University Press.

Poe, Joe Park. 1989. "Octavia Praetexta and Its Senecan Model." *American Journal of Philology* 110: 434–459.

Polt, Christopher B. 2014. "Polity across the Pond: Democracy, Republic and Empire in Phaedrus 'Fables' 1.2." *Classical Journal* 110(2): 161–190.

Porter, James I. 2001. "Ideals and Ruins: Pausanias, Longinus, and the Second Sophistic." In *Pausanias: Travel and Memory in Roman Greece,* edited by Susan E. Alcock, John F. Cherry, and Jas Elsner, 63–92. Oxford: Oxford University Press.

———. 2002. "Homer: The Very Idea." *Arion* 10(2): 57–86.

———. 2016. *The Sublime in Antiquity.* Cambridge: Cambridge University Press.

Power, Tristan. 2014. "The Originality of Suetonius." In *Suetonius, the Biographer: Studies in Roman Lives,* edited by Tristan Power and Roy K. Gibson, 1–18. Oxford: Oxford University Press.

Prag, Jonathan R. W., and Ian D. Repath. 2009. Introduction to *Petronius: A Handbook,* edited by Jonathan R. W. Prag and Ian D. Repath, 1–14 Chichester, UK: Wiley-Blackwell.

Rees, Roger. 2012. "The Lousy Reputation of Piso." In *The Julio-Claudian Succession: Reality and Perception of the "Augustan Model,"* edited by A. G. G. Gibson, 95–106. Leiden: Brill.

Reeve, Michael D. 1984. "The Addressee of the 'Laus Pisonis.'" *Illinois Classical Studies* 9: 42–48.

Reitz, Bettina. 2014. "Denouncing One's Friends: The Ending of Tacitus' 'Dialogus.'" *Mnemosyne* 67(1): 115–121.

Relihan, Joel C. 1993. *Ancient Menippean Satire.* Baltimore: Johns Hopkins University Press.

Richards, I. A. (1924) 2001. *Principles of Literary Criticism.* London: Routledge.

Riggsby, Andrew M. 1998. "Self and Community in the Younger Pliny." *Arethusa* 31(1): 75–97.

Rimell, Victoria. 2002. *Petronius and the Anatomy of Fiction.* Cambridge: Cambridge University Press.

————. 2007. "The Inward Turn: Writing, Voice and the Imperial Author in Petronius." In *Seeing Tongues, Hearing Scripts: Orality and Representation in the Ancient Novel,* 61–85. Eelde, Netherlands: Barkhuis.

————. 2009. *Letting the Page Run On: Poetics, Rhetoric and Noise in the "Satyrica."* Edited by Jonathan R. W. Prag and Victoria Rimell. Chichester, UK: Wiley-Blackwell.

————. 2015. *The Closure of Space in Roman Poetics: Empire's Inward Turn.* Cambridge: Cambridge University Press.

Robinson, Timothy Jesse. 2005. "In the Court of Time: The Reckoning of a Monster in the 'Apocolocyntosis.'" *Arethusa* 38(2): 223–257.

Roller, Matthew. 2010. "Culture-Based Approaches." In *Oxford Handbook of Roman Studies,* edited by Alessandro Barchiesi and Walter Scheidel, 234–249. Oxford: Oxford University Press.

————. 2018. *Models from the Past in Roman Culture: A World of Exempla.* Cambridge: Cambridge University Press.

Roman, Luke. 2001. "The Representation of Literary Materiality in Martial's 'Epigrams.'" *Journal of Roman Studies* 91: 113–145.

Roncali, Renata. 1974. "L'anonima 'Apoteosi del Divo Claudio.'" *Belfagor* 29: 571–573.

Rosati, Gianpiero. 1999. "Trimalchio on Stage." In *Oxford Readings in the Roman Novel,* edited by Stephen J. Harrison, 85–144. Oxford: Oxford University Press.

Rose, Sam. 2017. "Close Looking and Conviction." *Art History* 40(1): 156–177.

Rosen, Ralph M. 1988. "Hipponax and His Enemies in Ovid's 'Ibis.'" *Classical Quarterly* 38: 291–296.

Rostagni, Augusto. 1947. *Anonimo, Del Sublime: Testo, traduzione e note.* Edited by Augusto Rostagni. Milan: Istituto editoriale Italiano.

Roth, Ulrike. 2014. "An(Other) Epitaph for Trimalchio: Sat. 30.2." *Classical Quarterly* 64 (1): 422–425.

————. 2016. "Liberating the 'Cena.'" *Classical Quarterly* 66(2): 614–634.

Rowe, Gregory. 2013. "Reconsidering the 'Auctoritas' of Augustus." *Journal of Roman Studies* 103: 1–15.

Rudd, Niall. 1989. *Epistles, Book II and Epistle to the Pisones (Ars Poetica).* Cambridge: Cambridge University Press.

Runchina, Giovanni. 1977–1978. "Il prologo della pretesta 'Octavia': Funzione scenica e motivi tematici." *Annali della Facoltà di Magistero dell'Università di Cagliari* 2: 65–86.

Russell, Donald Andrew. 1964. *On the Sublime.* Oxford: Clarendon Press.

————. 1981. "Longinus Revisited." *Mnemosyne* 34: 72–86.

Ruthven, K. K. 2001. *Faking Literature.* Cambridge: Cambridge University Press.

Rutledge, S. H. 2001. *Imperial Inquisitions: Prosecutors and Informants from Tiberius to Domitian.* London: Routledge.

Scheid, John. 2007. *Res Gestae Diui Augusti = Hauts faits du divin Auguste.* Paris: Les Belles Lettres.

Schiesaro, Alessandro. 2011. "Ibis Redibis." *Materiali e Discussioni per l'Analisi dei Testi Classici* 67: 79–150.

Schmeling, Gareth L. 1998. "The Spectrum of Narrative: Authority of the Author." In *Ancient Fiction and Early Christian and Jewish Narrative*, edited by Ronald F. Hock and Judith Perkins, 18–30. Atlanta: Scholars Press.

———. 1999. "Petronius and the 'Satyrica.'" In *Latin Fiction: The Latin Novel in Context*, edited by Heinz Hofmann, 23–37. London: Routledge.

———. 2011. *A Commentary on the "Satyrica" of Petronius with the Collaboration of Aldo Setaioli*. Oxford: Oxford University Press.

Schofield, Malcolm. 2008. "Ciceronian Dialogue." In *The End of Dialogue in Antiquity*, edited by Simon Goldhill, 63–84. Cambridge: Cambridge University Press.

Schröder, Burghard. 1991. *Carmina non quae nemorale resultent: Ein Kommentar zur 4. Ekloge des Calpurnius Siculus*. Frankfurt am Main: Lang.

Sciarrino, Enrica. 2004. "Putting Cato the Censor's 'Origines' in Its Place." *Classical Antiquity* 23(2): 323–357.

———. 2010. "What 'Lies' behind Phaedrus' 'Fables.'" In *Private and Public Lies: The Discourse of Despotism and Deceit in the Graeco-Roman World*, edited by J. Turner, James Kim On Chong-Gossard, and Frederik Vervaet, 231–248. Leiden: Brill.

Scott, James C. 1990. *Domination and the Arts of Resistance: Hidden Transcripts*. New Haven, CT: Yale University Press.

Sedgwick, Eve Kosofsky. 2003. *Touching Feeling: Affect, Pedagogy, Performativity*. Durham, NC: Duke University Press.

Segal, Charles. 1959. "Ὕψος and the Problem of Cultural Decline in the 'De Sublimitate.'" *Harvard Studies in Classical Philology* 44: 121–146.

———. 1987. "Writer as Hero: The Heroic Ethos in Longinus, 'On the Sublime.'" In *Stemmata: Mélanges de philologie, d'histoire et d'archéologie grecques offerts à Jules Labarbe*, edited by Jean Servais, Tony Hackens, and Brigitte Servais Soyez, 207–217. Liège: L'Antiquité classique.

Seo, Joanne Mira. 2009. "Plagiarism and Poetic Identity in Martial." *American Journal of Philology* 130(4): 567–593.

Setaioli, Aldo. 2014. "Poems in Petronius' 'Satyrica.'" In *A Companion to the Ancient Novel*, edited by Edmund Cueva and Shannon Byrne, 371–383. Chichester, UK: Wiley-Blackwell.

Shearin, W. H. 2015. *The Language of Atoms: Performativity and Politics in Lucretius' "De Rerum Natura."* Oxford: Oxford University Press.

Silver, Brenda R. 1979. "'Anon' and 'The Reader': Virginia Woolf's Last Essays." *Twentieth Century Literature* 25(3–4): 356–441.

Slater, Niall W. 1990. *Reading Petronius*. Baltimore: Johns Hopkins University Press.

———. 2001. "The Horizons of Reading." In *A Companion to the Prologue of Apuleius' "Metamorphoses,"* edited by Ahuvia Kahane and Andrew Laird, 213–221. Oxford: Oxford University Press.

———. 2008. "Orality and Autobiography: The Case of the 'Res Gestae.'" In *Orality, Literacy, Memory in the Ancient Greek and Roman World*, edited by Elizabeth Anne Mackay, 253–273. Leiden: Brill.

————. 2009. "Reading the 'Satyrica.'" In *Petronius: A Handbook*, edited by Jonathan R. W. Prag and Ian D. Repath, 16–31. Chichester, UK: Wiley-Blackwell.

————. 2011. "Eumolpus 'Poeta' at Work: Rehearsed Spontaneity in the 'Satyricon.'" In *Orality, Literacy and Performance in the Ancient World*, edited by Elizabeth Minchin, 245–264. Leiden: Brill.

————. 2014. "Speaking Verse to Power: Circulation of Oral and Written Critique in the 'Lives of the Caesars.'" In *Between Orality and Literacy: Communication and Adaptation in Antiquity*, edited by Ruth Scodel, 289–308. Leiden: Brill.

Small, Jocelyn Penny. 1997. *Wax Tablets of the Mind: Cognitive Studies of Memory and Literacy in Classical Antiquity*. London: Routledge.

Smith, Christopher J. 2009. "Sulla's 'Memoirs.'" In *The Lost Memoirs of Augustus and the Development of Roman Autobiography*, edited by Christopher J. Smith, Anton Powell, and Tim J. Cornell, 65–85. Swansea: Classical Press of Wales.

Smith, Joseph Andrew. 2003. "Flavian Drama: Looking Back with 'Octavia.'" In *Flavian Rome: Culture, Image, Text*, edited by Anthony James Boyle and William J. Dominik, 391–430. Leiden: Brill.

Smith, Martin S. 1975. *Cena Trimalchionis*. Oxford: Oxford University Press.

Speyer, Wolfgang. 1971. *Handbuch der Altertumswissenschaft. I. Abt., 2. Teil, die literarische Fälschung im heidnischen und christlichen Altertum. Ein Versuch ihrer Deutung*. München: Beck.

Star, Christopher. 2012. *The Empire of the Self: Self-Command and Political Speech in Seneca and Petronius*. Baltimore: Johns Hopkins University Press.

Starr, Raymond J. 1995. "Vergil's Seventh Eclogue and Its Readers: Biographical Allegory as an Interpretative Strategy in Antiquity and Late Antiquity." *Classical Philology* 90(2): 129–138.

Stöckinger, Martin. 2017. "Geschriebene und gesungene Prophezeiungen: Die 1. Ekloge des Calpurnius und ihre Intertexte." *Hermes* 145(3): 288–302.

Stroup, Sarah Culpepper. 2013. "'When I Read My Cato, It Is as If Cato Speaks': The Birth and Evolution of Cicero's Dialogic Voice." In *The Author's Voice in Classical and Late Antiquity*, edited by Anna Marmodoro and Jonathan Hill, 123–151. Oxford: Oxford University Press.

Strunk, Thomas E. 2010. "Offending the Powerful: Tacitus' 'Dialogus de Oratoribus' and Safe Criticism." *Mnemosyne* 63(2): 241–267.

Sullivan, John Patrick. 1968. *The "Satyricon" of Petronius: A Literary Study*. Bloomington: Indiana University Press.

Swain, Simon C. R. 2001. "The Hiding Author: Context and Implication." In *A Companion to the Prologue of Apuleius' "Metamorphoses,"* edited by Ahuvia Kahane and Andrew Laird, 55–63. Oxford: Oxford University Press.

Syme, Ronald. 1958. *Tacitus*. Oxford: Clarendon Press.

————. 1980. "The Sons of Piso the Pontifex." *American Journal of Philology* 101: 333–341.

————. 1983. *Historia Augusta Papers*. Oxford: Clarendon Press.

————. 1986. *The Augustan Aristocracy*. Oxford: Clarendon Press.

Tamás, Ábel. Forthcoming. "Catullus' Sapphic Lacuna: A Palimpsest of Absences and Presences." In *Unspoken Rome: Absence in Latin Literature and Its Reception,* edited by Tom Geue and Elena Giusti. Cambridge: Cambridge University Press.

Tanner, Jeremy. 2000. "Portraits, Power, and Patronage in the Late Roman Republic." *Journal of Roman Studies* 90: 18–50.

Tarrant, Richard John. 2012. *Virgil: "Aeneid:" Book 12.* Cambridge: Cambridge University Press.

Tatum, William Jeffrey. 2014. "Another Look at Suetonius' 'Titus.'" In *Suetonius, the Biographer: Studies in Roman Lives,* edited by Tristan Power and Roy K. Gibson, 159–177. Oxford: Oxford University Press.

Taylor, Matthew. 2010. "The Figure of Seneca in Tacitus and the 'Octavia.'" In *Latin Historiography and Poetry in the Early Empire: Generic Interactions,* edited by John F. Miller and Anthony John Woodman, 205–222. Leiden: Brill.

Thomas, Christine. 1998. "Stories without Texts and without Authors: The Problem of Fluidity in Ancient Novelistic Texts and Early Christian Literature." In *Ancient Fiction and Early Christian Narrative,* edited by Ronald F. Hock, J. Bradley Chance, and Judith Perkins, 273–291. Atlanta: Scholars Press.

Tremoli, Paolo. 1960. *Le Iscrizioni di Trimalchione.* Trieste: Università degli Studi.

Todisco, Elisabetta. 2007. "Il nome 'Augustus' e la 'fondazione' ideologica del principato." In *"Antidoron": Studi in onore di Barbara Scardigli Forster,* edited by Paolo Desideri, 441–462. Pisa: ETS.

Too, Yun Lee. 1999. *The Idea of Ancient Literary Criticism.* Oxford: Oxford University Press.

———. 2001. "Losing the Author's Voice: Cultural and Personal Identities in the 'Metamorphoses' Prologue." In *A Companion to the Prologue of Apuleius' "Metamorphoses,"* edited by Ahuvia Kahane and Andrew Laird, 177–187. Oxford: Oxford University Press.

Townend, Gavin. 1980. "Calpurnius Siculus and the Munus Neronis." *Journal of Roman Studies* 70: 166–174.

Uden, James. 2015. *The Invisible Satirist: Juvenal and Second Century Rome.* Oxford: Oxford University Press.

Usher, Mark David. 2007. "Theomachy, Creation, and the Poetics of Quotation in Longinus Chapter 9." *Classical Philology* 102(3): 292–303.

Van den Berg, Christopher S. 2014. *The World of Tacitus' "Dialogus de Oratoribus": Aesthetics and Empire in Ancient Rome.* Cambridge: Cambridge University Press.

Van Noorden, Helen. 2014. *Playing Hesiod: The "Myth of the Races" in Classical Antiquity.* Cambridge: Cambridge University Press.

Van Nortwick, Thomas. 2009. *The Unknown Odysseus: Alternate Worlds in Homer's "Odyssey."* Ann Arbor: University of Michigan Press.

Verboven, Koenraad. 2009. "A Funny Thing Happened on My Way to the Market: Reading Petronius to Write Economic History." In *Petronius: A Handbook,* edited by Jonathan Prag and Ian Repath, 125–139. Oxford: Wiley-Blackwell.

Verdière, Raoul. 1982. "A quelle époque vécut T. Calpurnius Siculus?" *Atti del Centro Ricerche e Documentazione sull'Antichittà Classica* 12: 125–138.

———. 1985. "Le genre bucolique à l'époque de Néron: Les 'Bucolica' de T. Calpurnius Siculus et les 'Carmina Einsidlensia'; État de la question et prospectives." *Aufstieg und Niedergang der römischen Welt II* 32(3): 1845–1924.

Vinchesi, Maria Assunta. 2010. "Aspetti della poesia bucolica di età neroniana: Per una lettura della VII ecloga di Calpurnio Siculo." In *"Documenta Antiquitatis": Atti dei Seminari di Dipartimento 2009,* edited by Giuseppe Zanetto and Massimiliano Ornaghi, 137–159. Milan: Cisalpino.

———. 2014. *Calpurnii Siculi Eclogae.* Florence: Felice Le Monnier.

Volk, Katharina. 2005. "'Ille ego': (Mis)reading Ovid's Elegiac Persona." *Antike und Abendland* 51: 83–96.

Völker, Thomas, and Dirk Rohmann. 2011. "'Praenomen Petronii': The Date and Author of the 'Satyricon' Reconsidered." *Classical Quarterly* 61(2): 660–676.

Vout, Caroline. 2009. "The 'Satyrica' and Neronian Culture." In *Petronius: A Handbook,* edited by Jonathan R. W. Prag and Ian D. Repath, 101–113. Chichester, UK: Wiley-Blackwell.

Wallace-Hadrill, Andrew. 1983. *Suetonius: The Scholar and His Caesars.* New Haven, CT: Yale University Press.

———. 2016. "The Naming of Augustus." *Maia* 68(2): 264–271.

Walsh, George B. 1988. "Sublime Method: Longinus on Language and Imitation." *Classical Antiquity* 7(2): 252–269.

Wardle, David. 2014. *Suetonius: "Life of Augustus."* Oxford: Oxford University Press.

Watson, Lindsay C. 1991. *Arae: The Curse Poetry of Antiquity.* Leeds, UK: Cairns.

Weiske, Benjamin. 1809. *Dionysii Longini de Sublimitate: Graece et Latine.* Leipzig: Teubner.

West, Martin L. 1995. "'Longinus' and the Grandeur of God." In *Ethics and Rhetoric: Classical Essays for Donald Russell on His Seventy-Fifth Birthday,* edited by Doreen C. Innes, Harry M. Hine, and Christopher B. R. Pelling, 335–342. New York: Oxford University Press.

Whitehead, Jane K. 1993. "The 'Cena Trimalchionis' and Biographical Narration in Roman Middle-Class Art." In *Narrative and Event in Ancient Art,* edited by Peter J. Holliday, 299–325. Cambridge: Cambridge University Press.

Whitmarsh, Tim. 2001. *Greek Literature and the Roman Empire: The Politics of Imitation.* Oxford: Oxford University Press.

———. 2017. "Quantum Classics: Literature, Historicism, Untimeliness, Uncertainty." In *Griechische Literaturgeschichtsschreibung: Traditionen, Probleme und Konzepte,* edited by Jonas Grethlein and Antonios Rengakos, 30–45. Berlin: De Gruyter.

Whitmarsh, Tim, and Shadi Bartsch. 2008. "Narrative." In *The Cambridge Companion to the Greek and Roman Novel,* edited by Tim Whitmarsh, 237–257. Cambridge: Cambridge University Press.

Whitton, Christopher L. 2013. "Seneca, 'Apocolocyntosis.'" In *A Companion to the Neronian Age,* edited by Emma Buckley and Martin T. Dinter, 149–169. Chichester, UK: Wiley-Blackwell.

———. 2018. "Quintilian, Pliny, Tacitus." In *Roman Literature under Nerva, Trajan and Hadrian: Literary Interactions, AD 96–138,* edited by Alice König and Christopher L. Whitton, 37–62. Cambridge: Cambridge University Press.

———. 2019. *The Arts of Imitation in Latin Prose: Pliny's Epistles/Quintilian in Brief.* Cambridge: Cambridge University Press.

Williams, Gareth D. 1994. *Banished Voices: Readings in Ovid's Exile Poetry.* Cambridge: Cambridge University Press.

———. 1996. *The Curse of Exile: A Study of Ovid's "Ibis."* Cambridge: Cambridge Philological Society.

———. 2015. "Minding the Gap: Seneca, the Self, and the Sublime." In *Roman Reflections: Studies in Latin Philosophy,* edited by Katharina Volk and Gareth D. Williams, 172–191. Oxford: Oxford University Press.

Williams, Gordon W. 1978. *Change and Decline: Roman Literature in the Early Empire.* Berkeley: University of California Press.

Wilson, Marcus. 2003. "Allegory and Apotheosis in the 'Octavia.'" *Prudentia* 35(1): 60–88.

———. 2015. "'Quae Quis Fugit Damnat': Outspoken Silence in Seneca's 'Epistles.'" In *The Art of Veiled Speech Self-Censorship from Aristophanes to Hobbes,* edited by Han Baltussen and Peter J. Davis, 137–156. Philadelphia: University of Pennsylvania Press.

Wimsatt, W. K., Jr. 1954. *The Verbal Icon: Studies in the Meaning of Poetry.* Lexington: University of Kentucky Press.

Winkler, John J. 1985. *Auctor et Actor: A Narratological Reading of Apuleius' "Golden Ass."* Berkeley: University of California Press.

Wiseman, Timothy Peter. 1982. "Calpurnius Siculus and the Claudian Civil War." *Journal of Roman Studies* 72: 57–67.

———. 2008. *Unwritten Rome.* Exeter: University of Exeter Press.

Woodman, Anthony J. 1977. *Velleius Paterculus: The Tiberian Narrative (2.94–131).* Cambridge: Cambridge University Press.

Woodman, Anthony J., and Christina S. Kraus. 2014. *Tacitus: "Agricola."* Cambridge: Cambridge University Press.

Woolf, Greg. 1996. "Monumental Writing and the Expansion of Roman Society in the Early Empire." *Journal of Roman Studies* 86: 22–39.

Yavetz, Zvi. 1984. "The 'Res Gestae' and Augustus' Public Image." In *Caesar Augustus: Seven Aspects,* edited by Fergus Millar and Erich Segal, 1–36. Oxford: Clarendon Press.

Zadorojnyi, Alexei V. 2011. "Transcripts of Dissent: Political Graffiti and Elite Ideology under the Principate." In *Ancient Graffiti in Context,* edited by J. A. Baird and Claire Taylor, 110–133. New York: Routledge.

———. 2013. "Shuffling Surfaces: Epigraphy, Power, and Integrity in the Graeco-Roman Narratives." In *Inscriptions and Their Uses in Greek and Latin Literature,* edited by Peter Liddel and Polly Low, 365–386. Oxford: Oxford University Press.

Zanker, Andreas Thomas. 2013. "Expressions of Meaning and the Intention of the Text." *Classical Quarterly* 63(2): 835–853.
———. 2016. *Greek and Latin Expressions of Meaning: The Classical Origins of a Modern Metaphor.* Munich: Beck.
Zeitlin, Froma I. 1971. "Petronius as Paradox: Anarchy and Artistic Integrity." *Transactions of the American Philological Association* 102: 631–684.
Ziogas, Ioannis V. 2013. *Ovid and Hesiod: The Metamorphosis of "The Catalogue of Women."* Cambridge: Cambridge University Press.
———. 2015. "The Poet as Prince: Author and Authority under Augustus." In *The Art of Veiled Speech: Self-Censorship from Aristophanes to Hobbes,* edited by Han Baltussen and Peter J. Davis, 115–136. Philadelphia: University of Pennsylvania Press.
Zipfel, K. 1910. "Quatenus Ovidius in Ibide Callimachum aliosque fontes inprimis defixiones secutus sit." PhD diss., Universität Leipzig.
Zwierlein, Otto, ed. 1986. *L. Annaei Senecae Tragoediae; Incertorum Auctorum Hercules [Oetaeus], Octavia.* Oxford: Clarendon Press.

General Index

Index Locorum